Shojo

Beauty is the Beast ™

2

Story & Art by Tomo Matsumoto

Table of Contents

BEAUTY
IS THE
BEAST

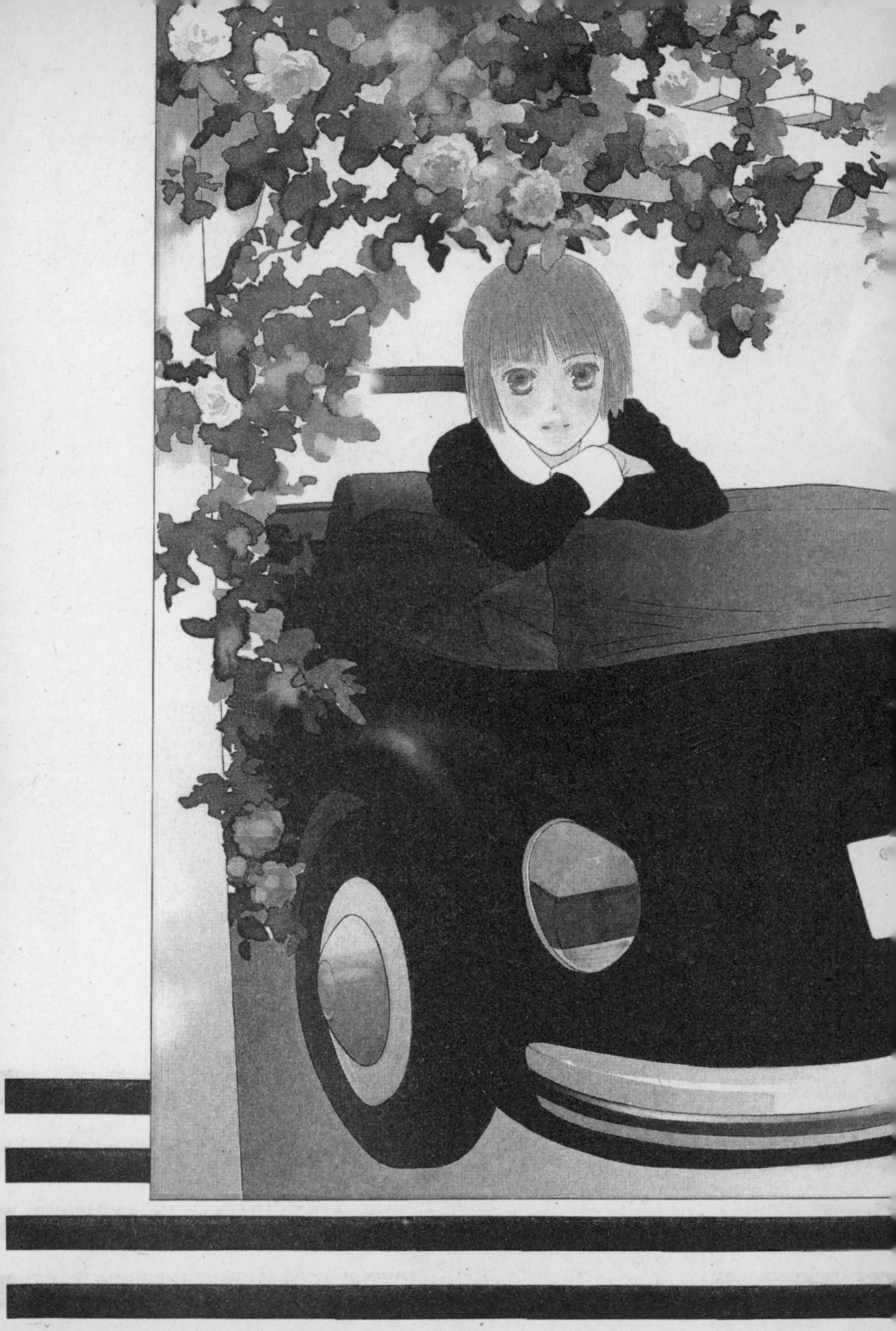

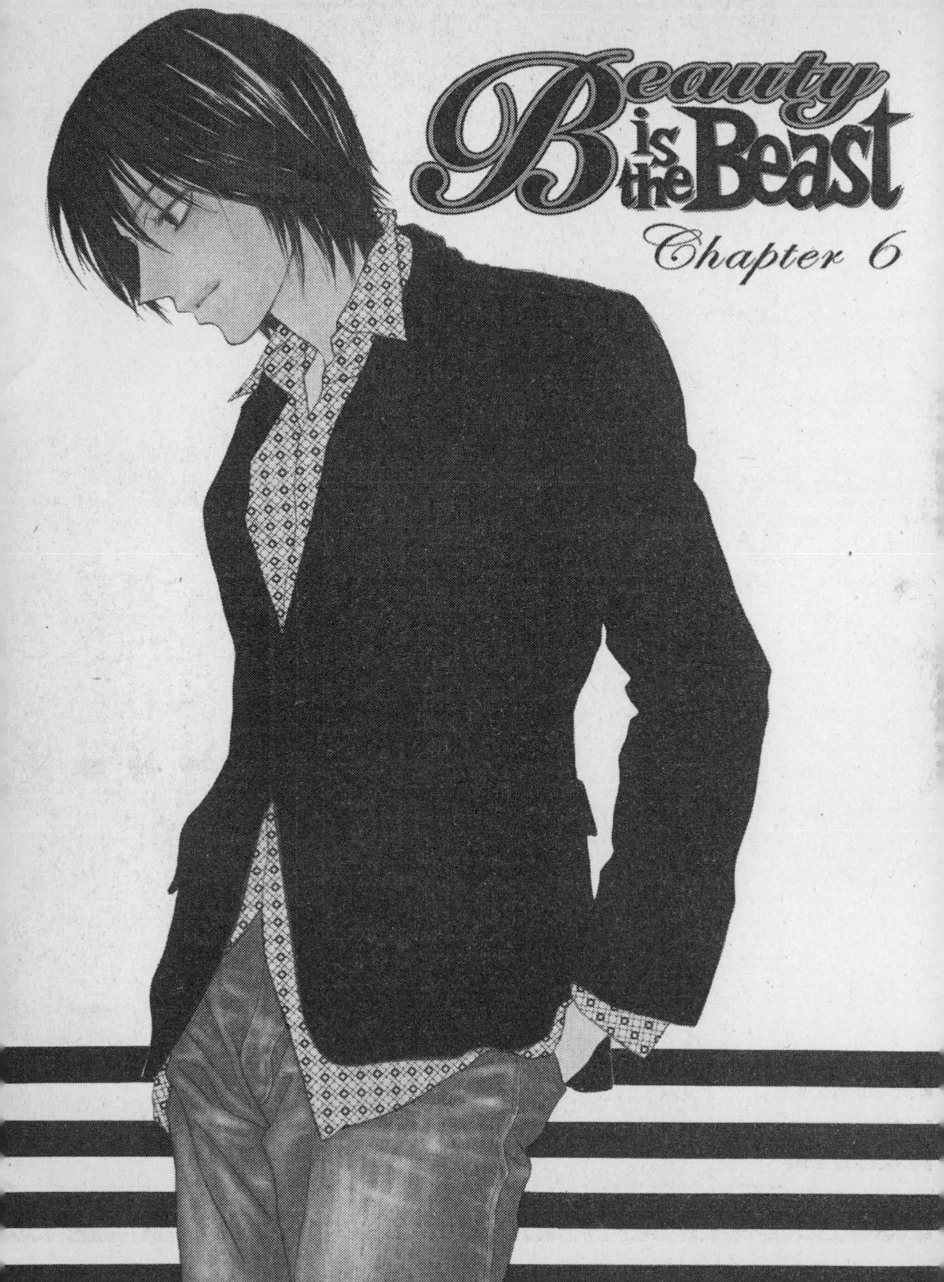
Beauty is the Beast
Chapter 6

BEAUTY
IS THE
BEAST

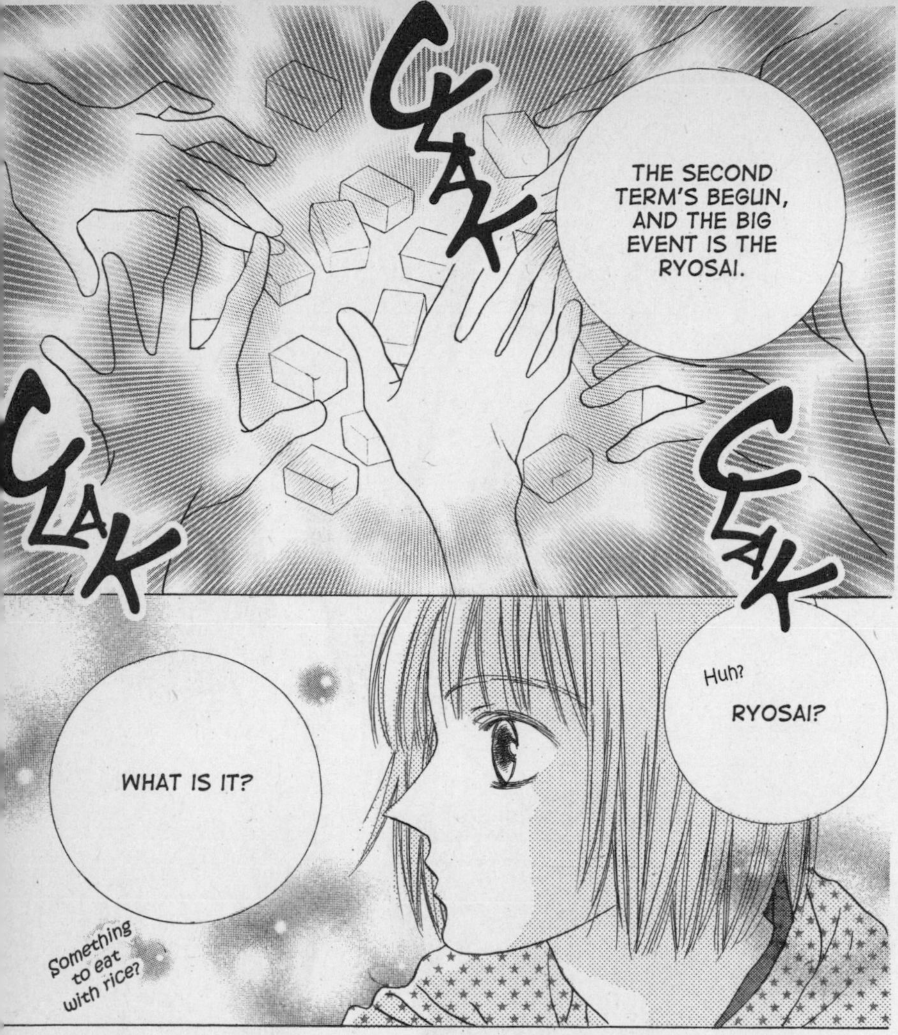
CLAK
THE SECOND TERM'S BEGUN, AND THE BIG EVENT IS THE RYOSAI.
CLAK
CLAK
Huh? RYOSAI?
WHAT IS IT?
Something to eat with rice?

I will put the dorm stories that I received from readers here.

Dorm Story 1
"My dorm is old, about as old as Eimi's dorm. The dorm rules are really strict, and when roll is called, we have to stand in the corridor and answer!! If you're not there, you'll be in real trouble!!"

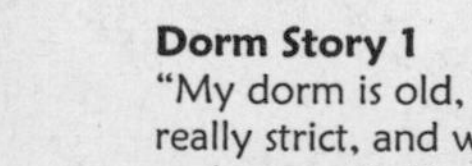

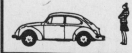

⇨ She's in college. (!)
But she is having fun. She's tough!

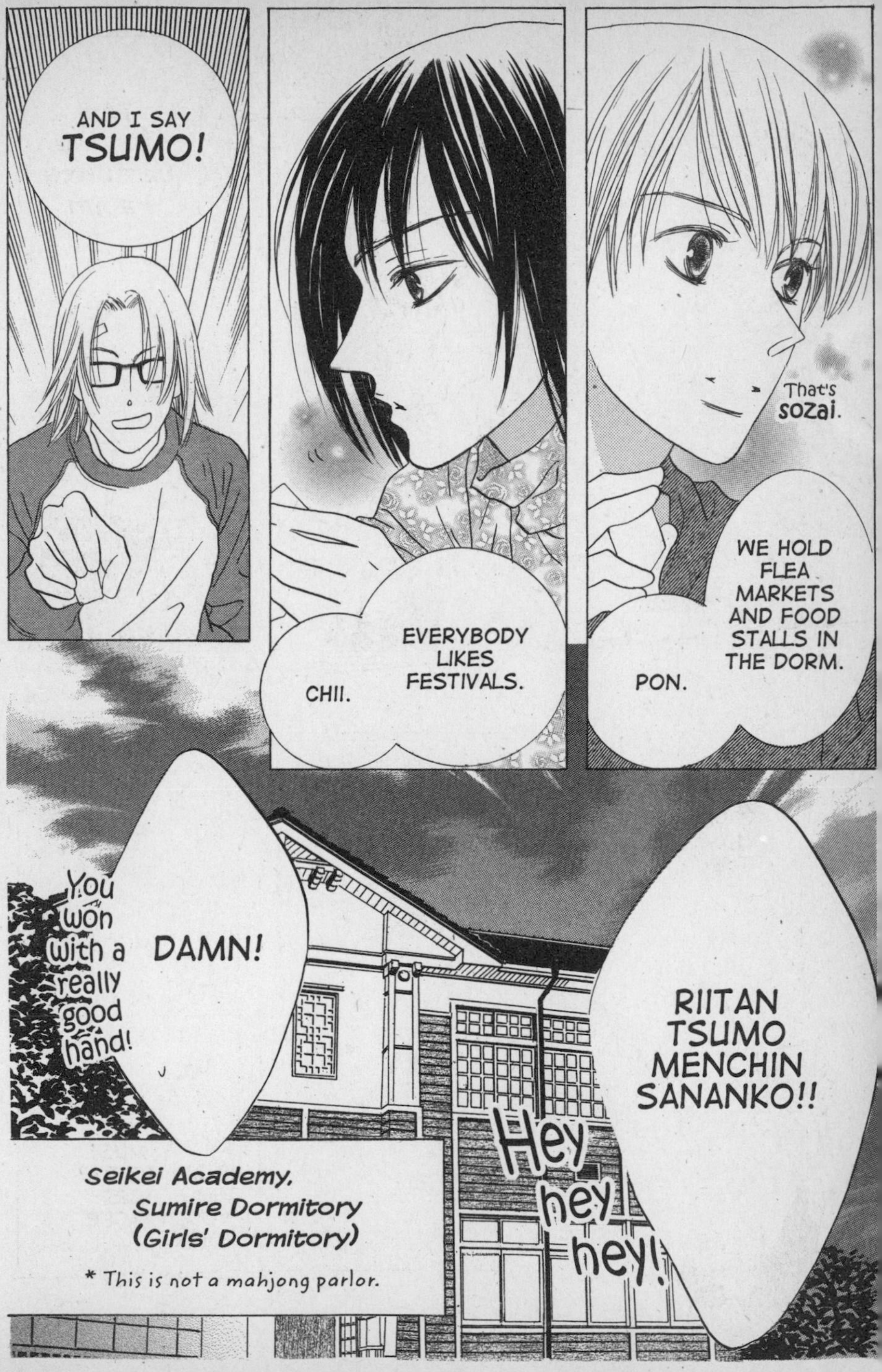

That's sozai.
WE HOLD FLEA MARKETS AND FOOD STALLS IN THE DORM.
PON.
EVERYBODY LIKES FESTIVALS.
CHII.
AND I SAY TSUMO!
RIITAN TSUMO MENCHIN SANANKO!!
Hey hey hey!
DAMN!
You won with a really good hand!
Seikei Academy, Sumire Dormitory (Girls' Dormitory)
* This is not a mahjong parlor.

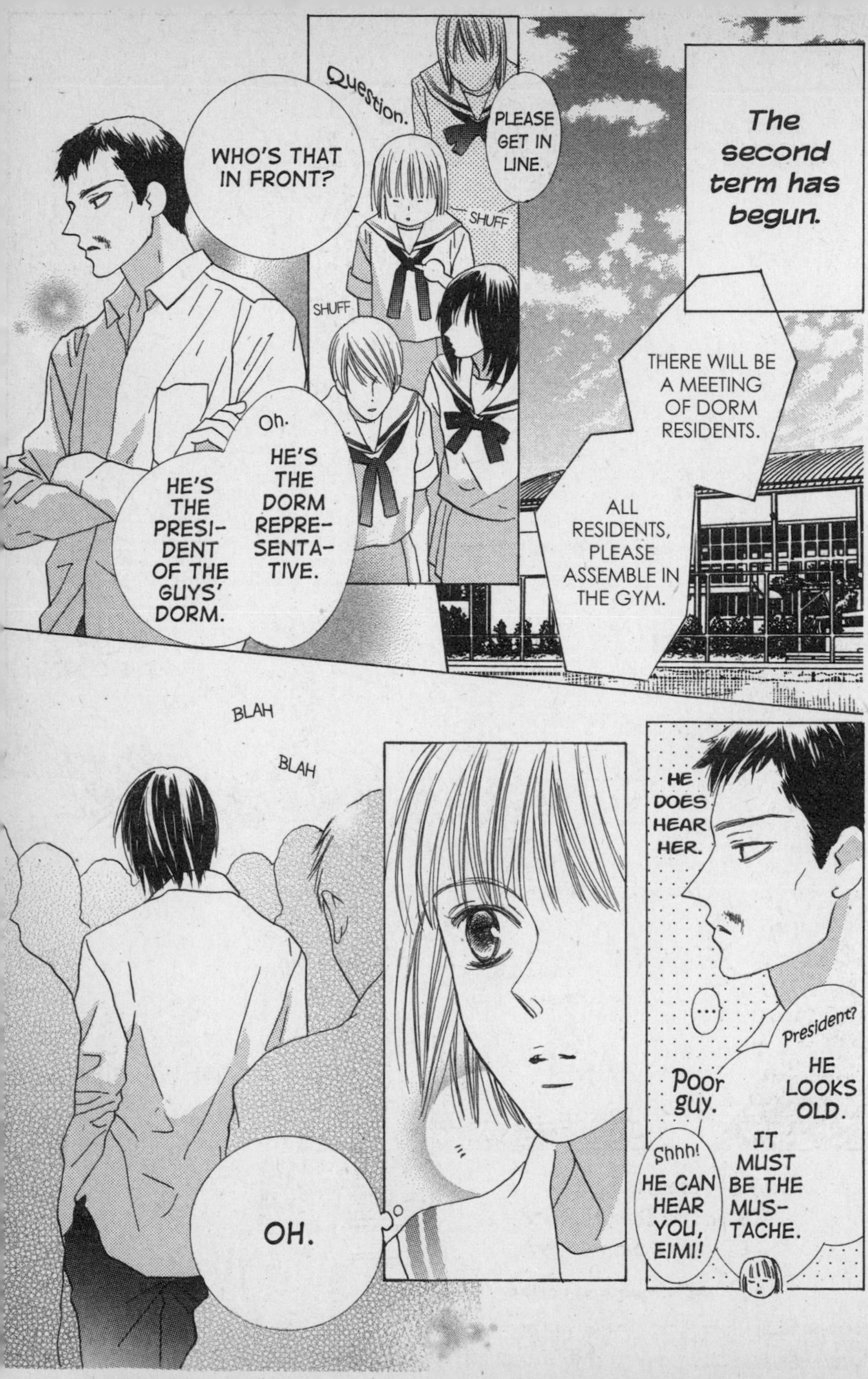
The second term has begun.
THERE WILL BE A MEETING OF DORM RESIDENTS.
ALL RESIDENTS, PLEASE ASSEMBLE IN THE GYM.
Question.
PLEASE GET IN LINE.
SHUFF
SHUFF
WHO'S THAT IN FRONT?
Oh.
HE'S THE DORM REPRESENTATIVE.
HE'S THE PRESIDENT OF THE GUYS' DORM.
HE DOES HEAR HER.
...
President?
HE LOOKS OLD.
Poor guy.
IT MUST BE THE MUSTACHE.
Shhh!
HE CAN HEAR YOU, EIMI!
OH.
BLAH
BLAH

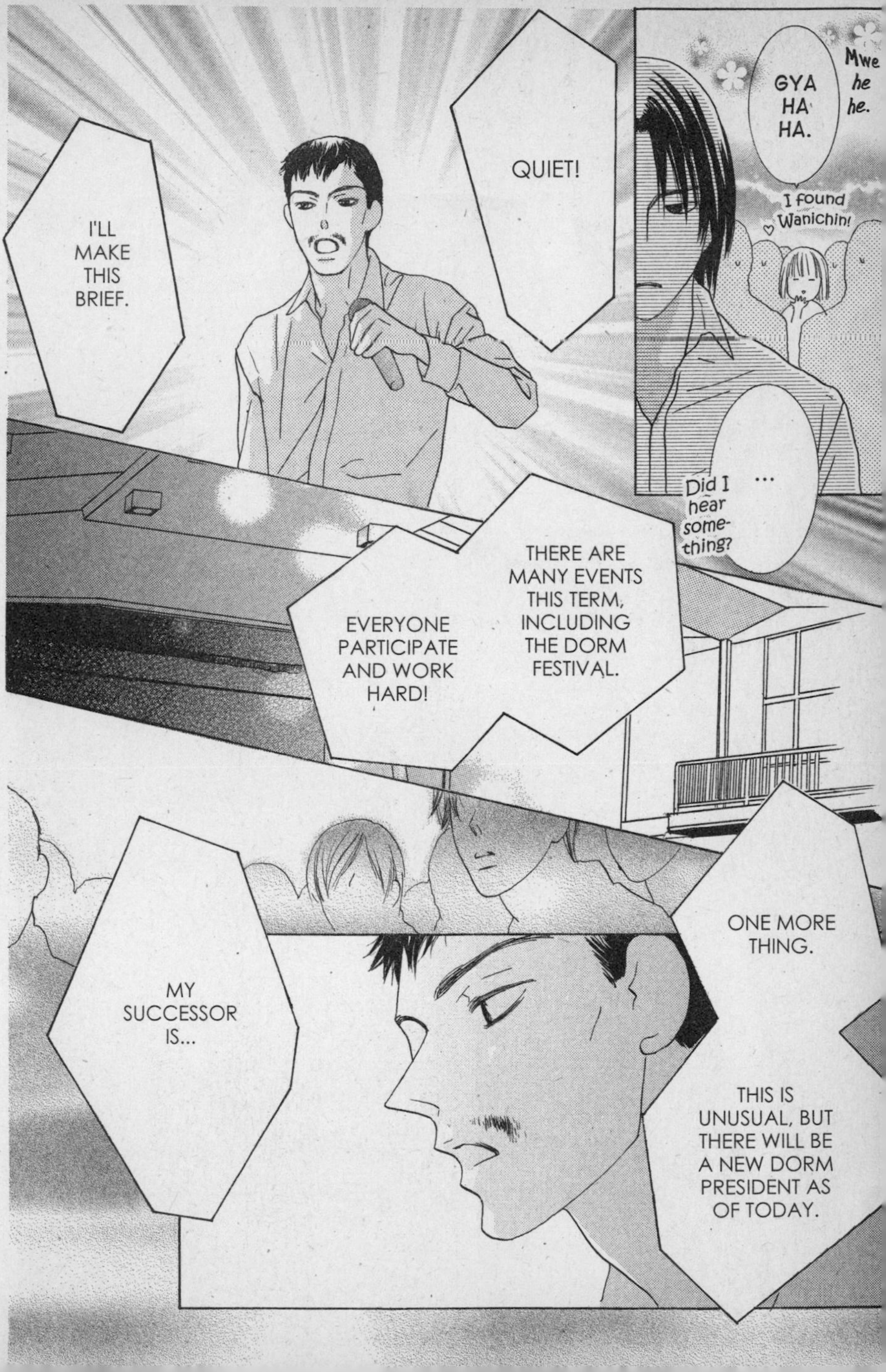
Mwe he he.
GYA HA HA.
I found Wanichin!
...
Did I hear some-thing?
QUIET!
I'LL MAKE THIS BRIEF.
THERE ARE MANY EVENTS THIS TERM, INCLUDING THE DORM FESTIVAL.
EVERYONE PARTICIPATE AND WORK HARD!
ONE MORE THING.
THIS IS UNUSUAL, BUT THERE WILL BE A NEW DORM PRESIDENT AS OF TODAY.
MY SUCCESSOR IS...

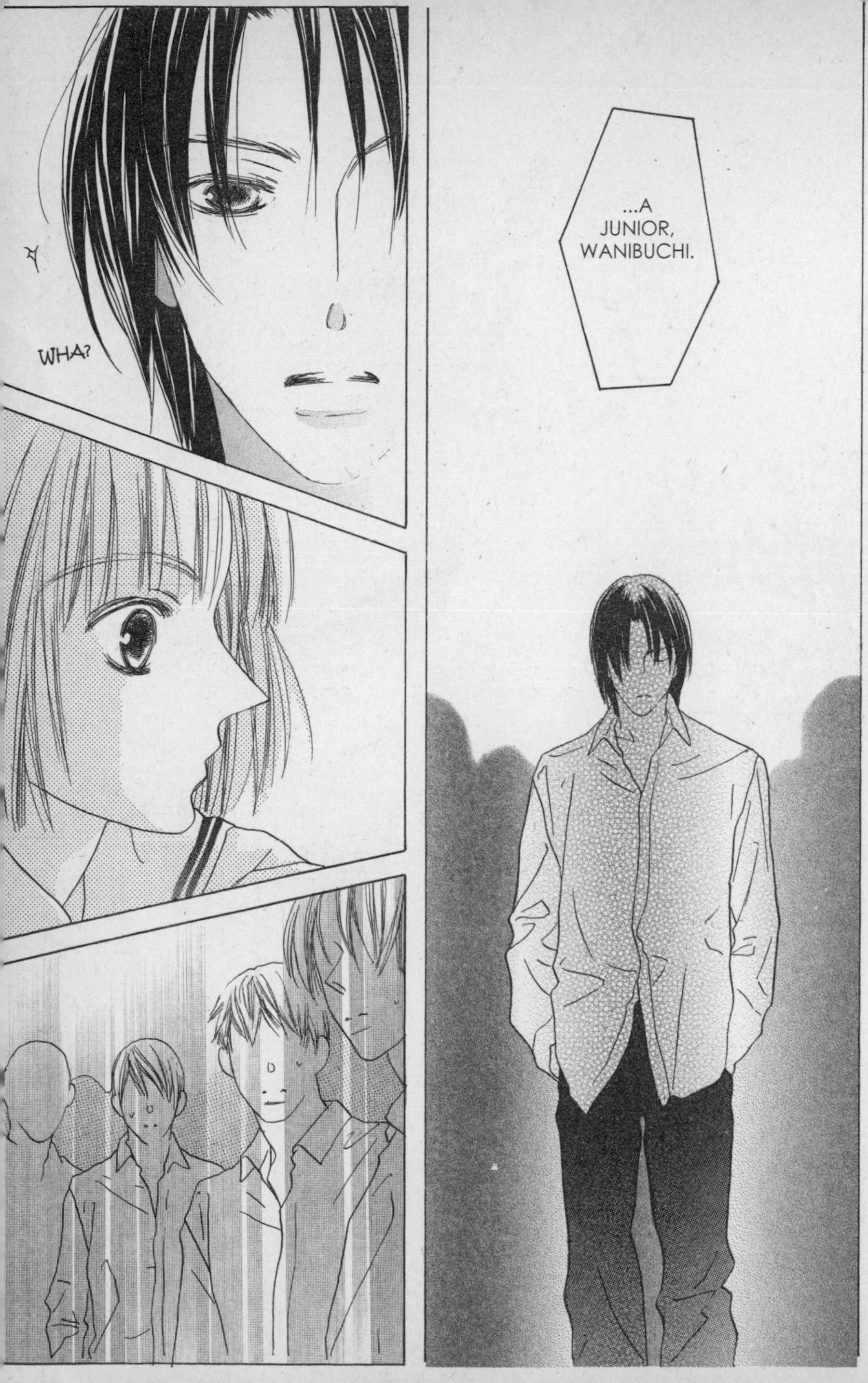
...A JUNIOR, WANIBUCHI.
WHA?

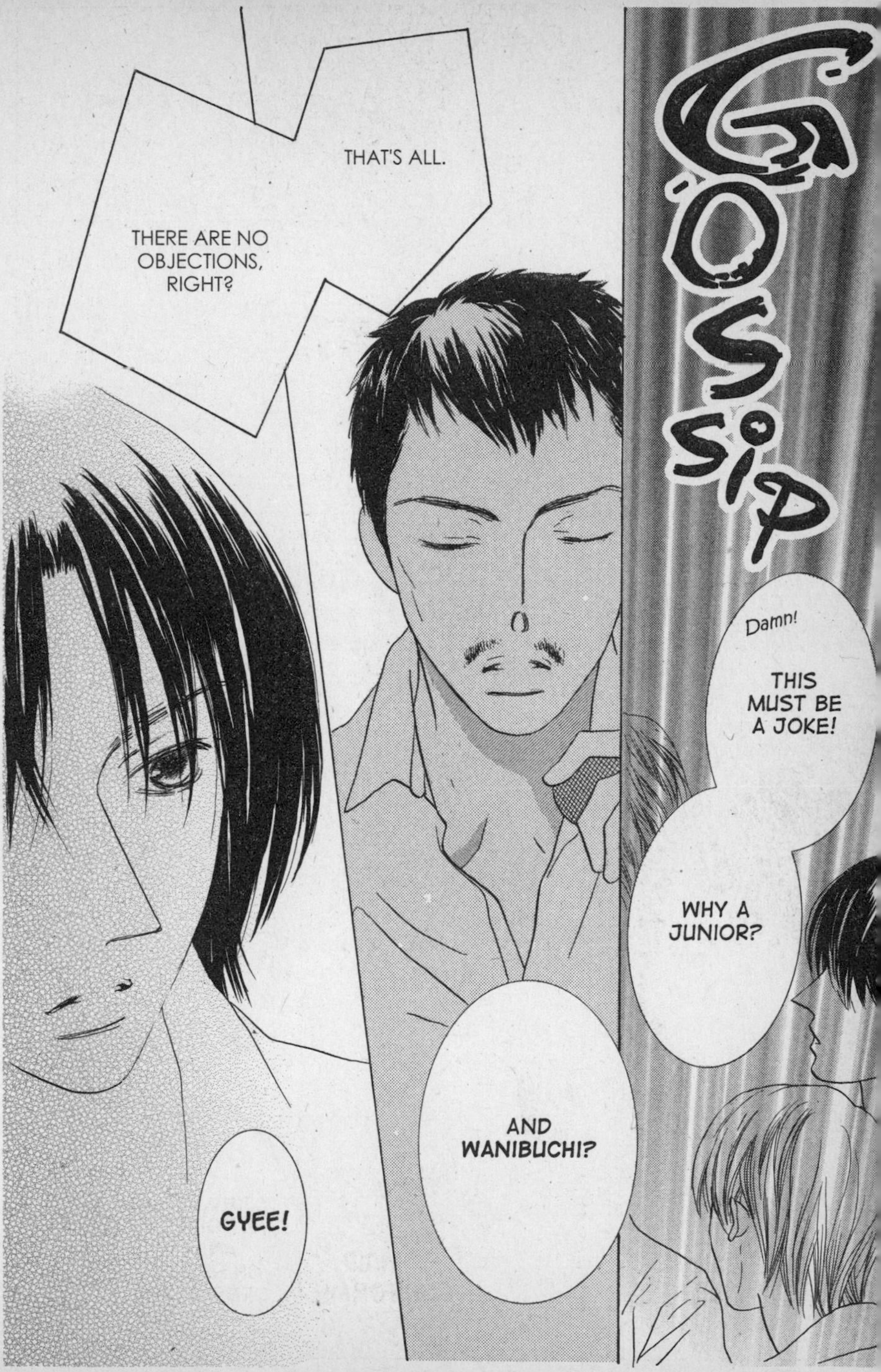
GOSSIP
Damn!
THIS MUST BE A JOKE!
WHY A JUNIOR?
THAT'S ALL.
THERE ARE NO OBJECTIONS, RIGHT?
AND WANIBUCHI?
GYEE!

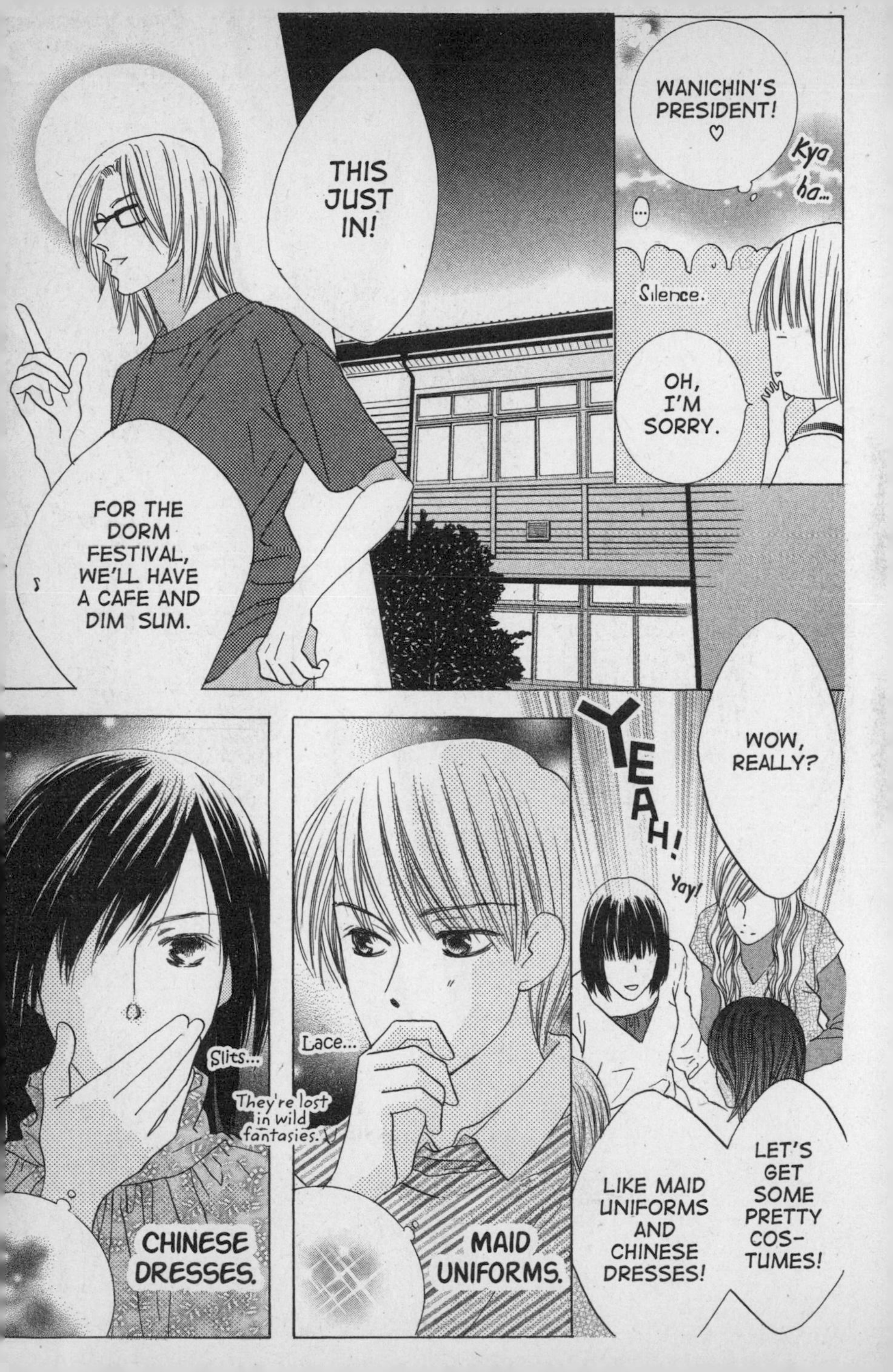
WANICHIN'S PRESIDENT! ♡
Kya ha...
...
Silence.
OH, I'M SORRY.
THIS JUST IN!
FOR THE DORM FESTIVAL, WE'LL HAVE A CAFE AND DIM SUM.
WOW, REALLY?
YEAH!
Yay!
LET'S GET SOME PRETTY COS-TUMES!
LIKE MAID UNIFORMS AND CHINESE DRESSES!
Lace...
MAID UNIFORMS.
They're lost in wild fantasies.
Slits...
CHINESE DRESSES.

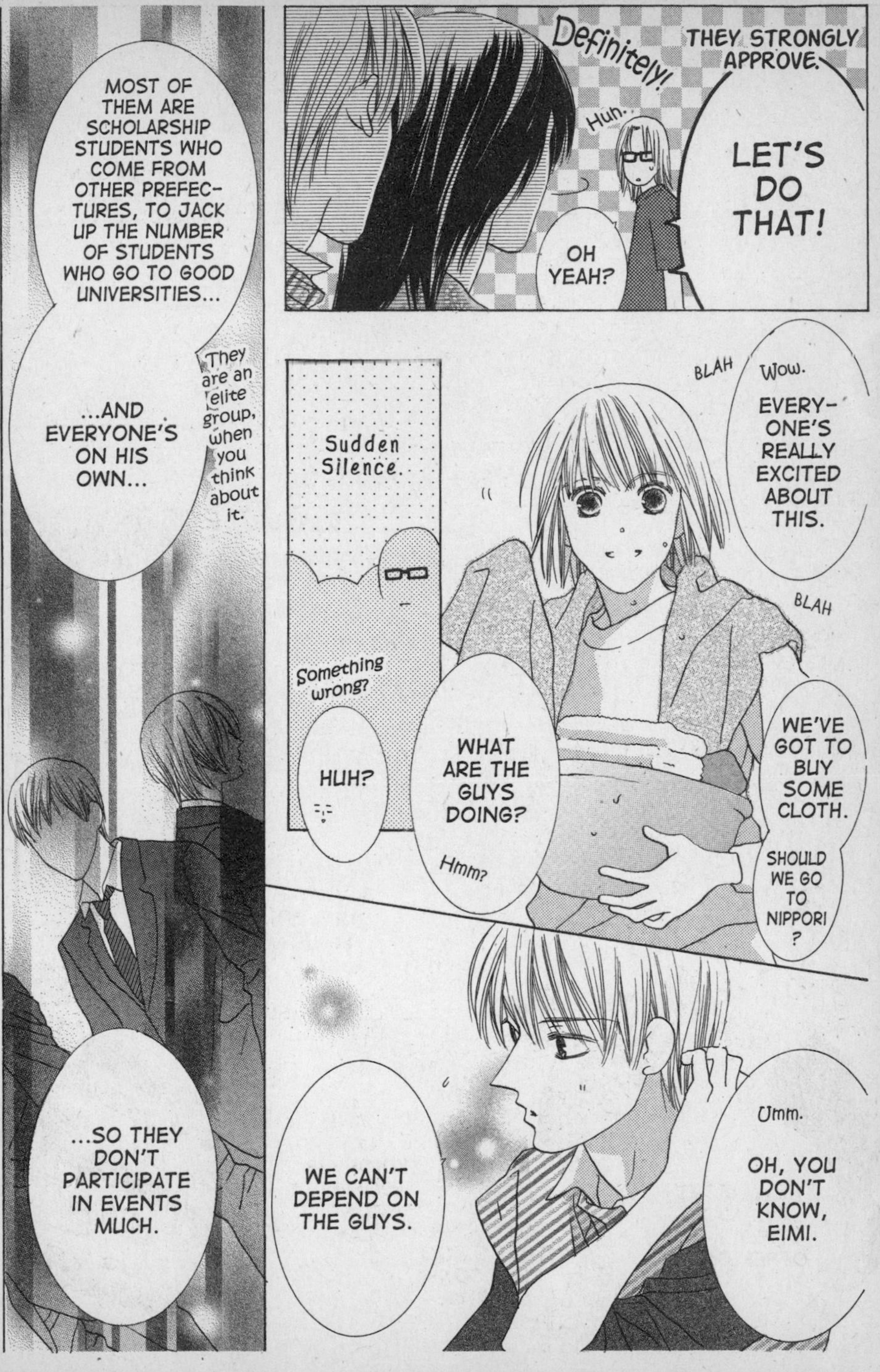

THEY STRONGLY APPROVE.
LET'S DO THAT!
Definitely!
Huh.
OH YEAH?
BLAH
Wow.
EVERYONE'S REALLY EXCITED ABOUT THIS.
BLAH
WE'VE GOT TO BUY SOME CLOTH.
SHOULD WE GO TO NIPPORI?
WHAT ARE THE GUYS DOING?
Hmm?
Sudden Silence.
Something wrong?
HUH?
Umm.
OH, YOU DON'T KNOW, EIMI.
WE CAN'T DEPEND ON THE GUYS.
MOST OF THEM ARE SCHOLARSHIP STUDENTS WHO COME FROM OTHER PREFECTURES, TO JACK UP THE NUMBER OF STUDENTS WHO GO TO GOOD UNIVERSITIES...
They are an elite group, when you think about it.
...AND EVERYONE'S ON HIS OWN...
...SO THEY DON'T PARTICIPATE IN EVENTS MUCH.

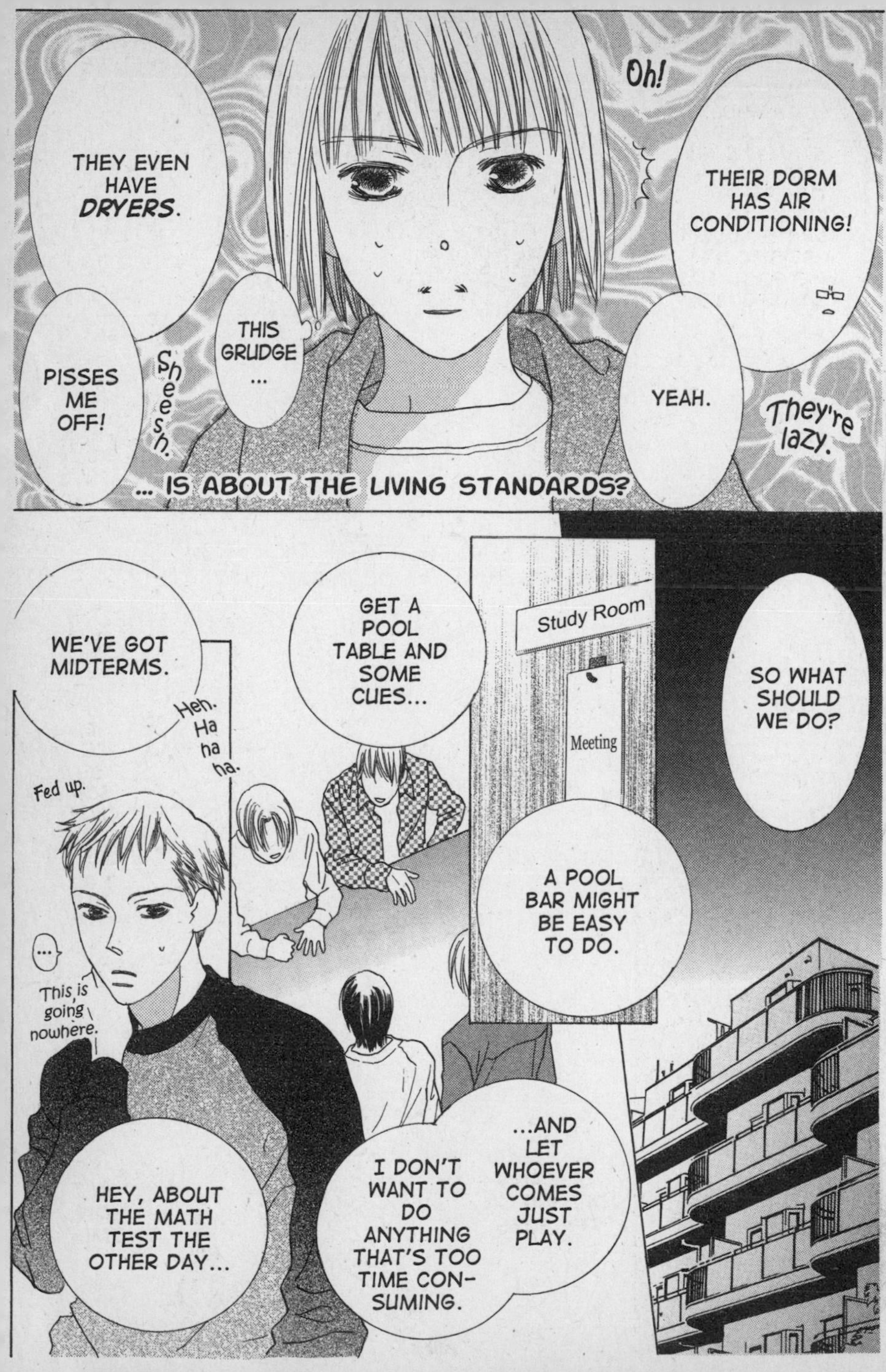

Oh!
THEIR DORM HAS AIR CONDITIONING!
They're lazy.
YEAH.
THEY EVEN HAVE **DRYERS**.
THIS GRUDGE ...
PISSES ME OFF!
Sheesh.
... IS ABOUT THE LIVING STANDARDS?
SO WHAT SHOULD WE DO?
Study Room
Meeting
GET A POOL TABLE AND SOME CUES...
A POOL BAR MIGHT BE EASY TO DO.
WE'VE GOT MIDTERMS.
Heh. Ha ha ha.
Fed up.
...AND LET WHOEVER COMES JUST PLAY.
I DON'T WANT TO DO ANYTHING THAT'S TOO TIME CON-SUMING.
...
This is going nowhere.
HEY, ABOUT THE MATH TEST THE OTHER DAY...

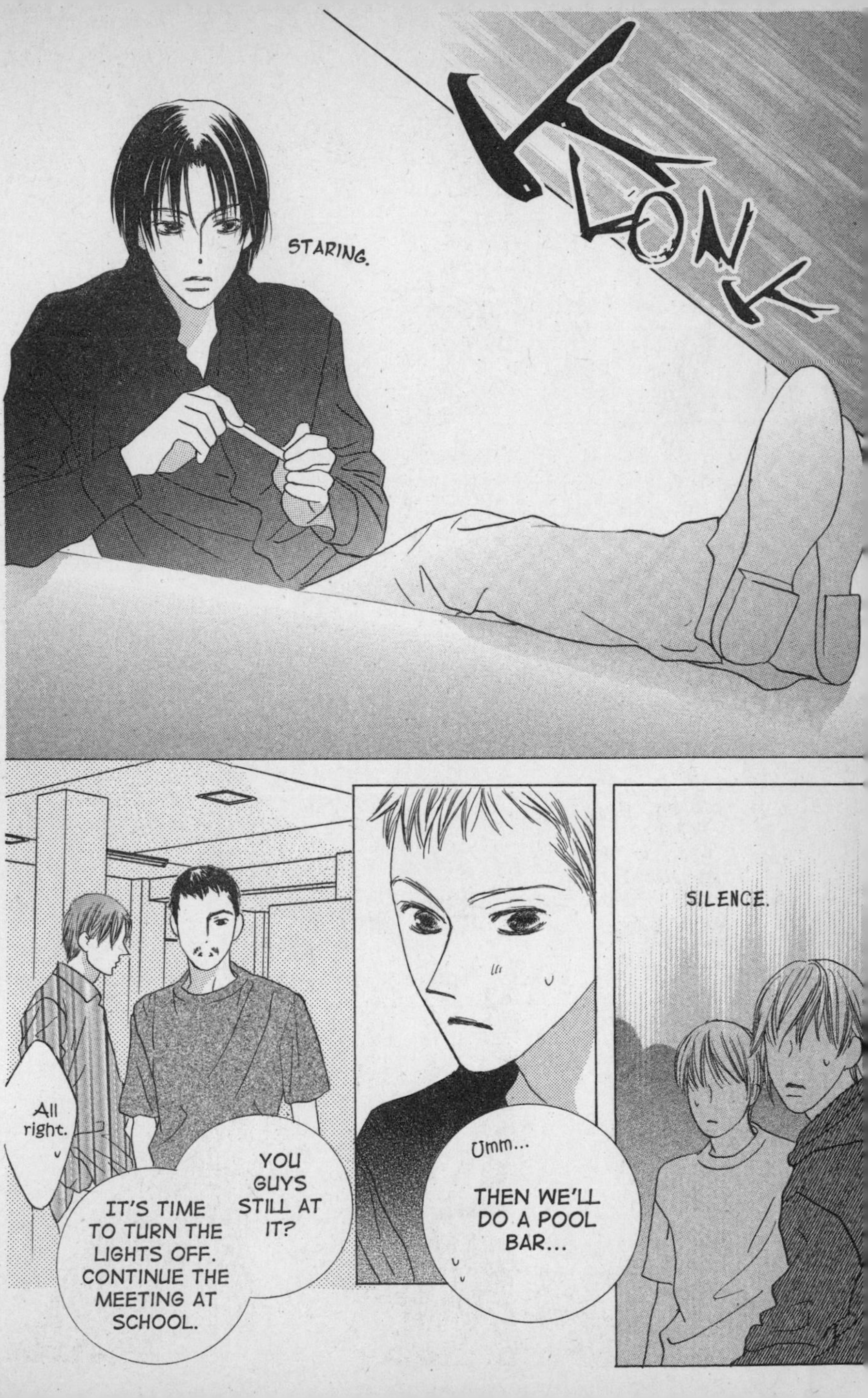
KLONK
STARING.
SILENCE.
Umm...
THEN WE'LL DO A POOL BAR...
YOU GUYS STILL AT IT?
IT'S TIME TO TURN THE LIGHTS OFF. CONTINUE THE MEETING AT SCHOOL.
All right.

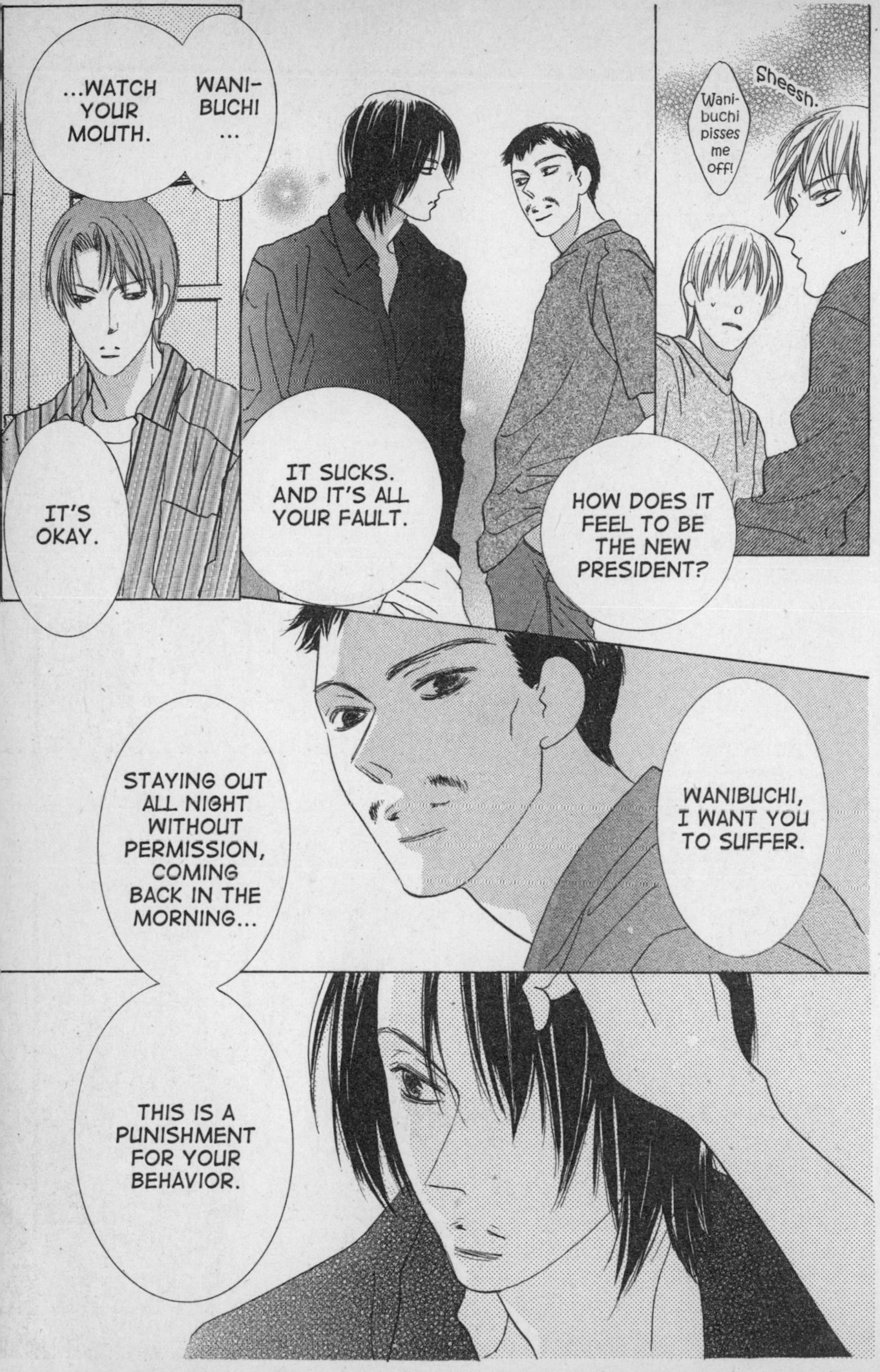
Sheesh.
Wani-buchi pisses me off!
WANI-BUCHI...
...WATCH YOUR MOUTH.
HOW DOES IT FEEL TO BE THE NEW PRESIDENT?
IT SUCKS. AND IT'S ALL YOUR FAULT.
IT'S OKAY.
WANIBUCHI, I WANT YOU TO SUFFER.
STAYING OUT ALL NIGHT WITHOUT PERMISSION, COMING BACK IN THE MORNING...
THIS IS A PUNISHMENT FOR YOUR BEHAVIOR.

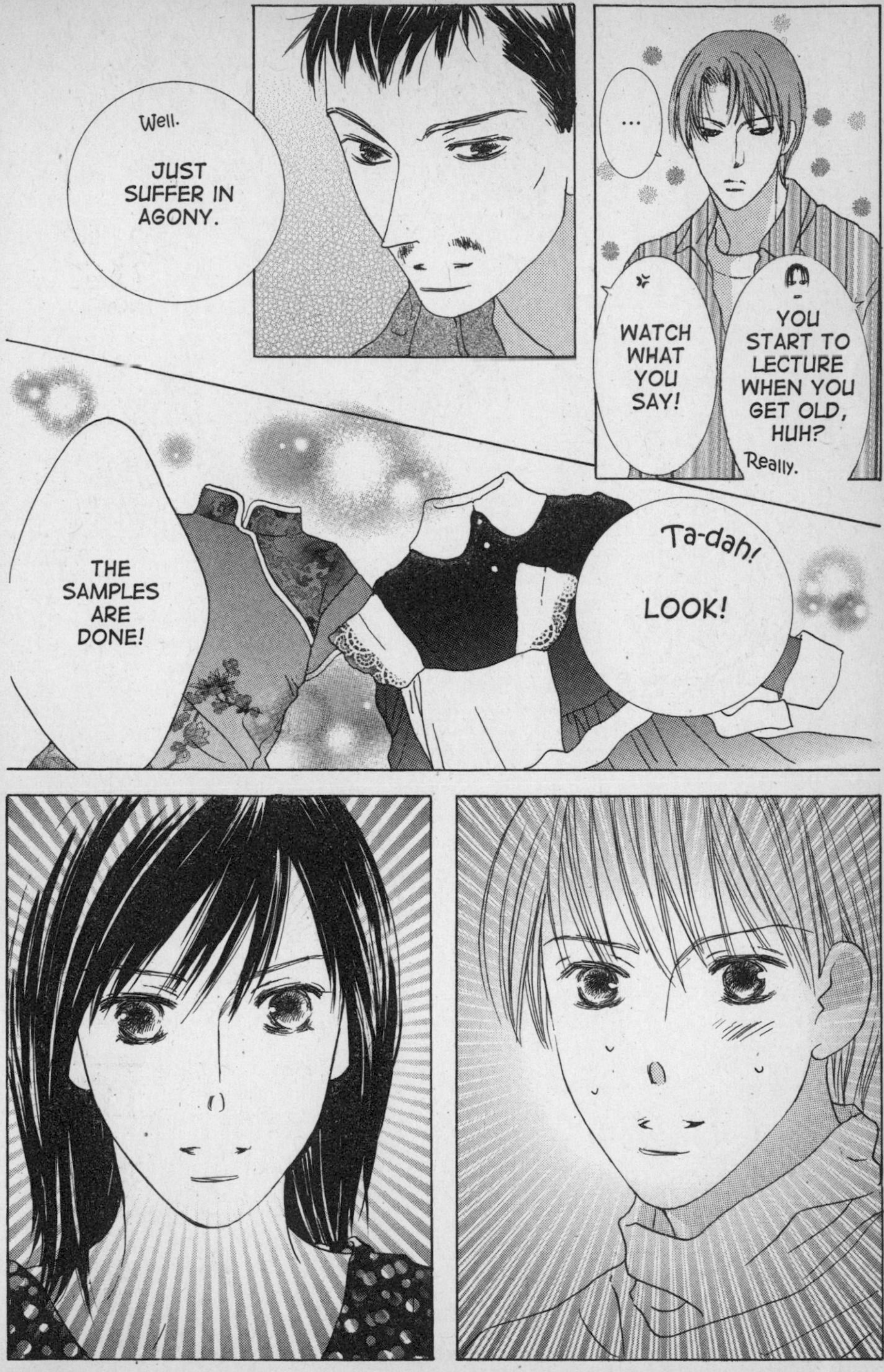
...
YOU START TO LECTURE WHEN YOU GET OLD, HUH?
Really.
WATCH WHAT YOU SAY!
Well.
JUST SUFFER IN AGONY.
Ta-dah!
LOOK!
THE SAMPLES ARE DONE!

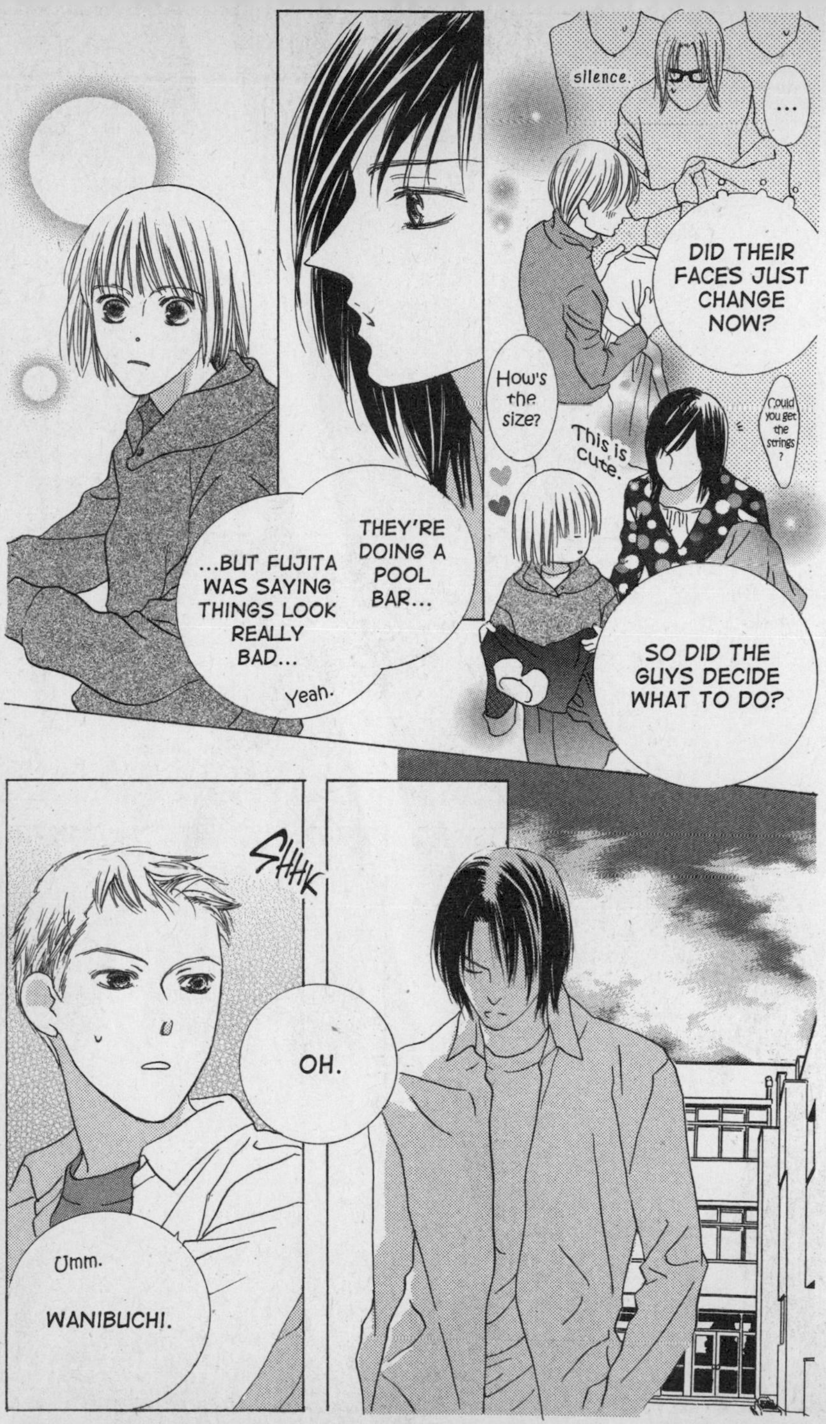
...
silence.
DID THEIR FACES JUST CHANGE NOW?
Could you get the strings?
How's the size?
This is cute.
SO DID THE GUYS DECIDE WHAT TO DO?
THEY'RE DOING A POOL BAR...
...BUT FUJITA WAS SAYING THINGS LOOK REALLY BAD...
Yeah.
SHHK
OH.
Umm.
WANIBUCHI.

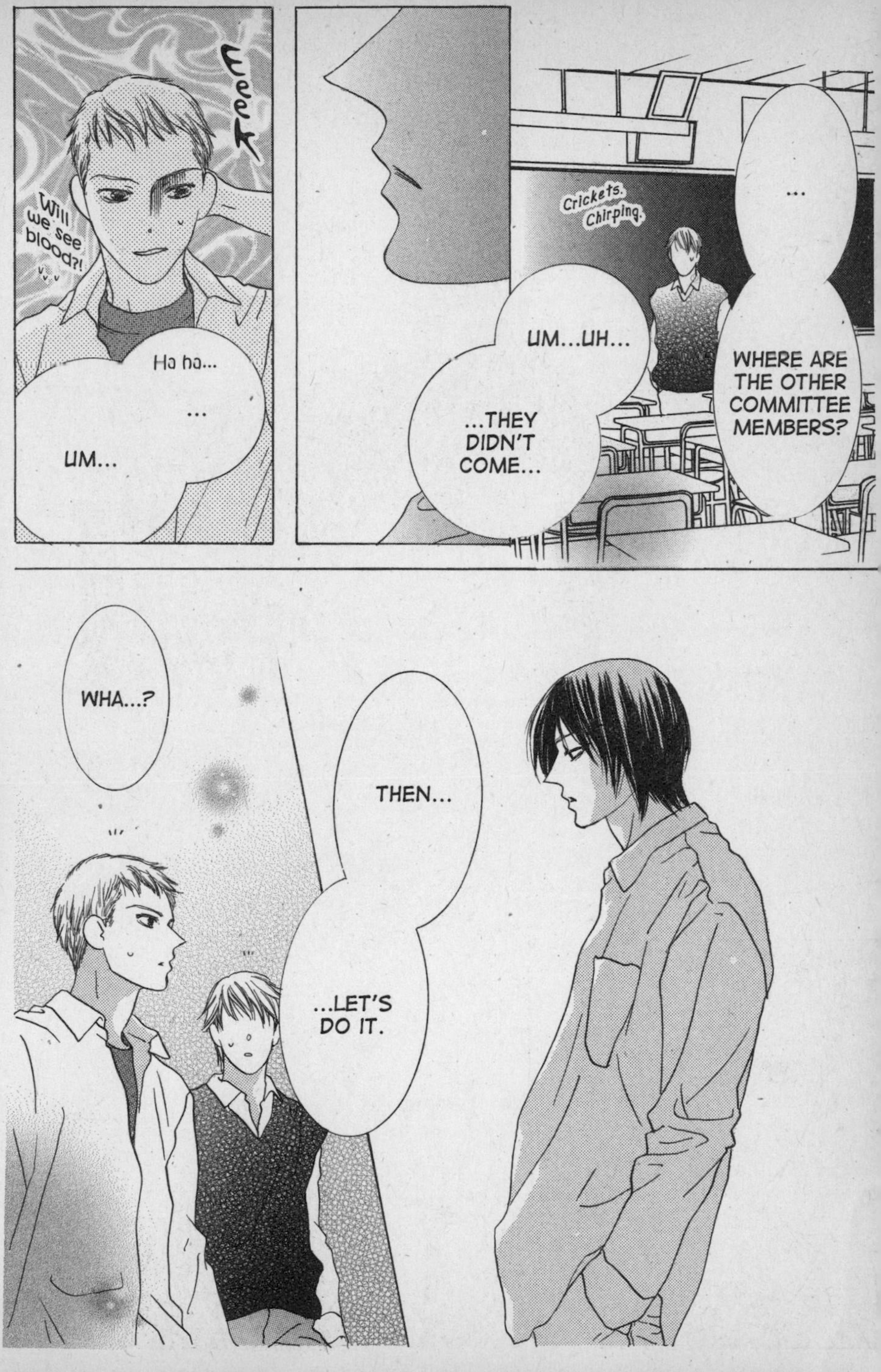
...
WHERE ARE THE OTHER COMMITTEE MEMBERS?
Crickets. Chirping.
UM...UH...
...THEY DIDN'T COME...
Eeek
Will we see blood?!
Ha ha...
...
UM...
THEN...
...LET'S DO IT.
WHA...?

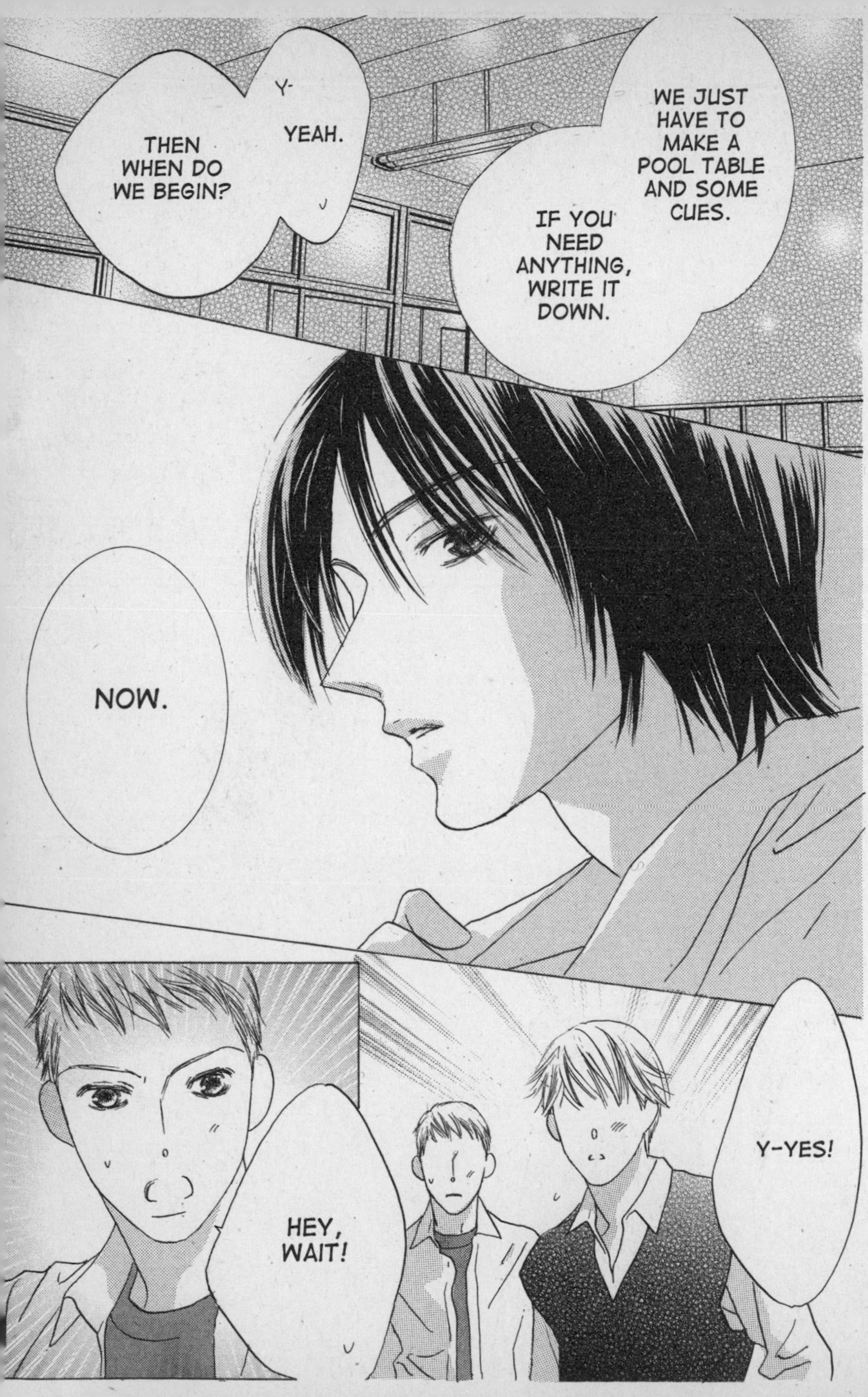
WE JUST HAVE TO MAKE A POOL TABLE AND SOME CUES.
IF YOU NEED ANYTHING, WRITE IT DOWN.
Y-
YEAH.
THEN WHEN DO WE BEGIN?
NOW.
Y-YES!
HEY, WAIT!

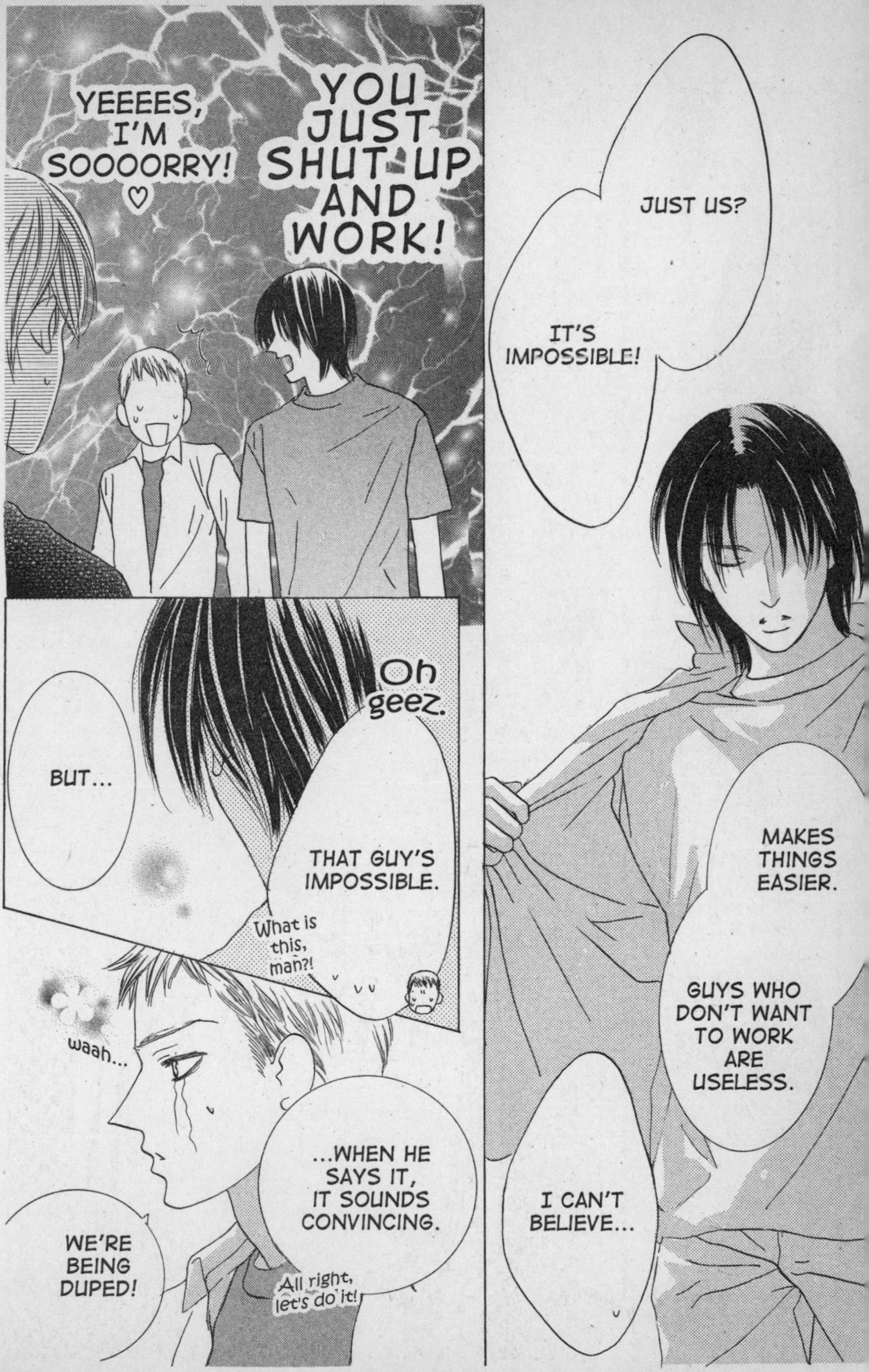
JUST US?
IT'S IMPOSSIBLE!
MAKES THINGS EASIER.
GUYS WHO DON'T WANT TO WORK ARE USELESS.
I CAN'T BELIEVE...
YOU JUST SHUT UP AND WORK!
YEEEES, I'M SOOOORRY! ♡
Oh geez.
THAT GUY'S IMPOSSIBLE.
What is this, man?!
BUT...
...WHEN HE SAYS IT, IT SOUNDS CONVINCING.
waah...
All right, let's do it!
WE'RE BEING DUPED!

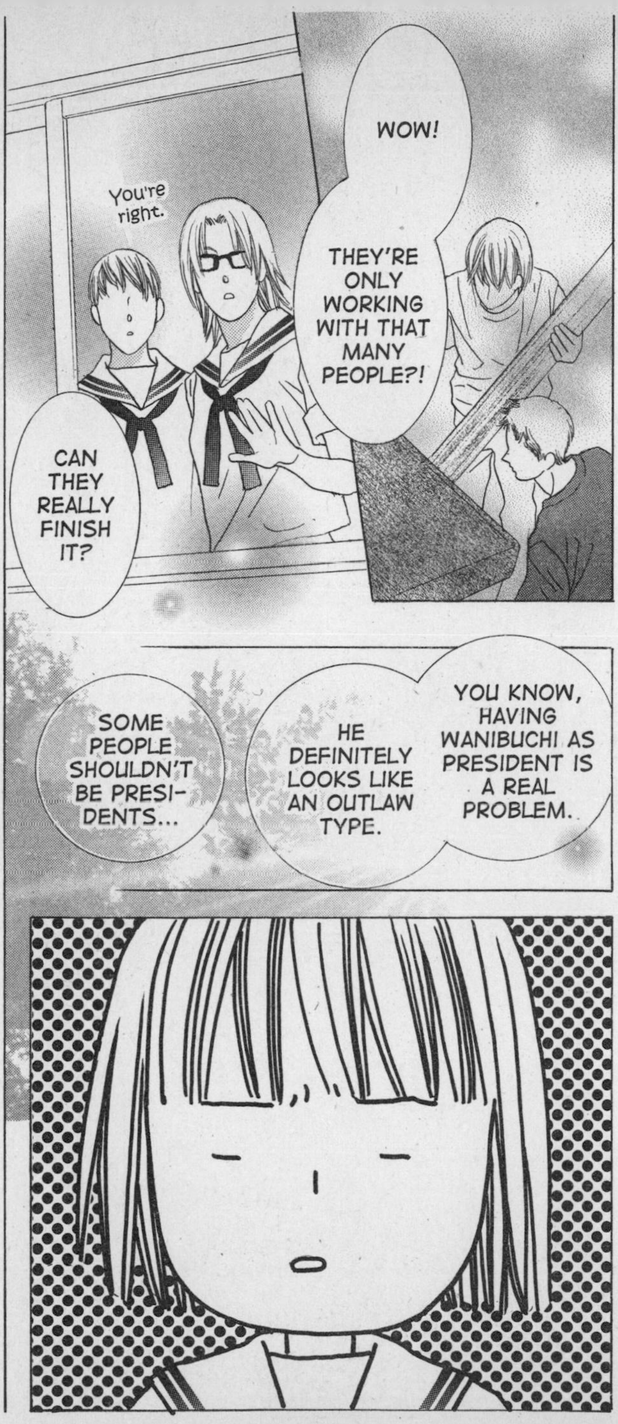
WOW!
THEY'RE ONLY WORKING WITH THAT MANY PEOPLE?!
You're right.
CAN THEY REALLY FINISH IT?
YOU KNOW, HAVING WANIBUCHI AS PRESIDENT IS A REAL PROBLEM.
HE DEFINITELY LOOKS LIKE AN OUTLAW TYPE.
SOME PEOPLE SHOULDN'T BE PRESI-DENTS...

Hello.
I'm Tomo Matsumoto. Thank you very much to everyone who's reading this.

This time, I will write about how I draw my color illustrations. Sometimes, I get questions from my readers about how I do my colors.
A lot of people who write me letters draw illustrations in the letters, and it's fun looking at them!
For everyone who is not interested in drawing, I'm sorry...

So that's how it will be.

Thanks.

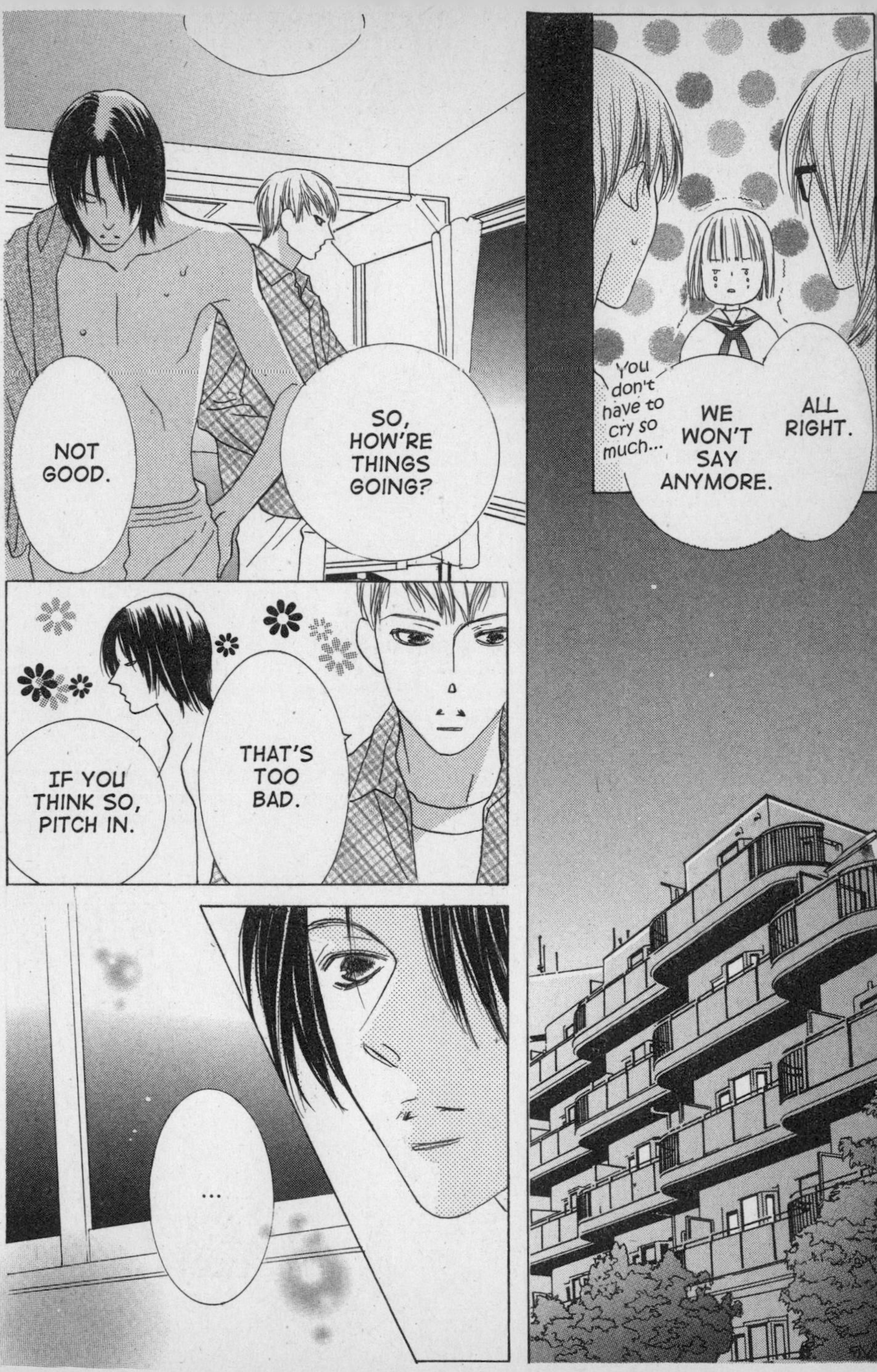
ALL RIGHT.
WE WON'T SAY ANYMORE.
You don't have to cry so much...
SO, HOW'RE THINGS GOING?
NOT GOOD.
THAT'S TOO BAD.
IF YOU THINK SO, PITCH IN.
...

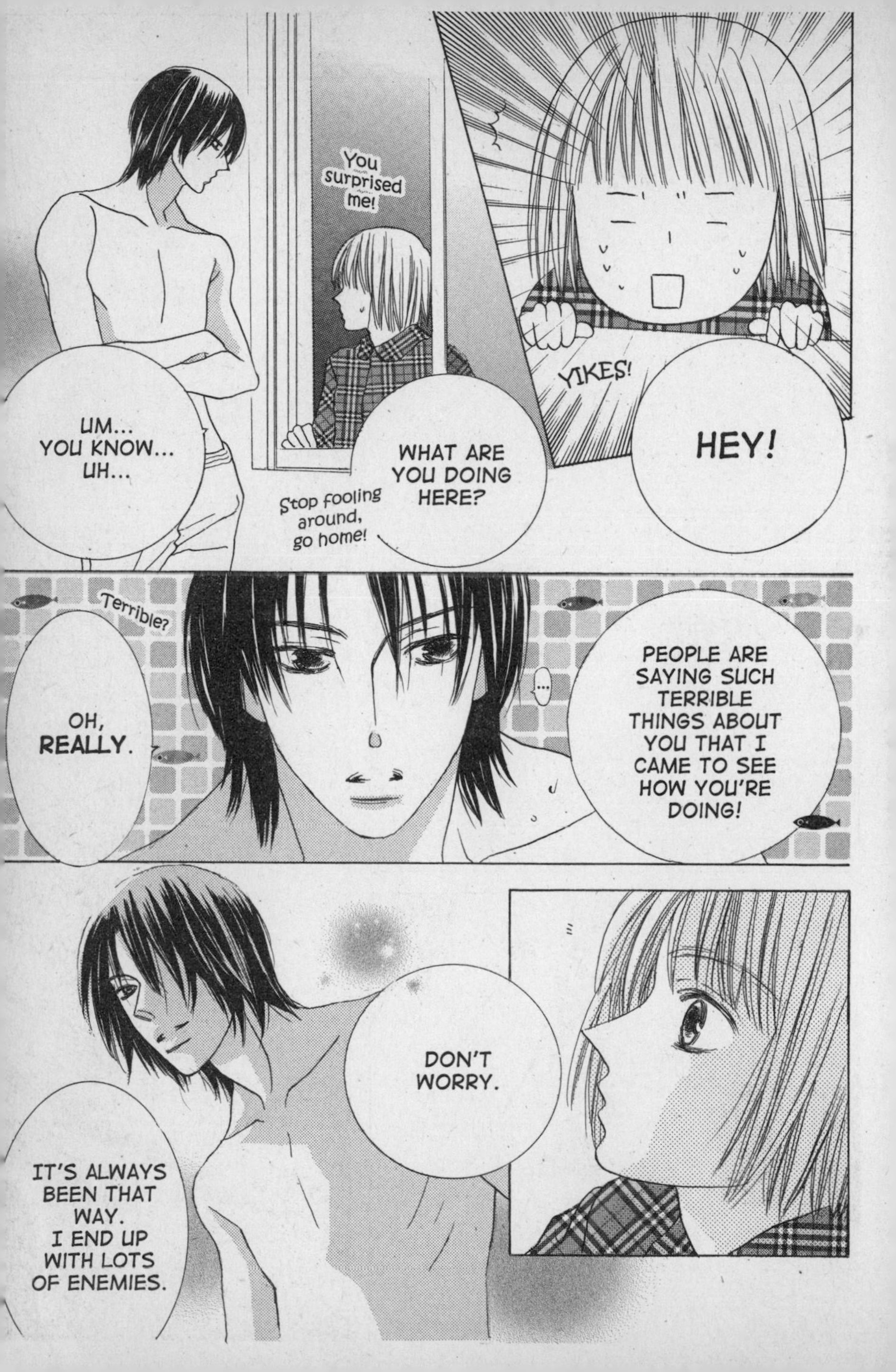
HEY!
YIKES!
You surprised me!
WHAT ARE YOU DOING HERE?
Stop fooling around, go home!
UM... YOU KNOW... UH...
PEOPLE ARE SAYING SUCH TERRIBLE THINGS ABOUT YOU THAT I CAME TO SEE HOW YOU'RE DOING!
...
Terrible?
OH, REALLY.
DON'T WORRY.
IT'S ALWAYS BEEN THAT WAY. I END UP WITH LOTS OF ENEMIES.

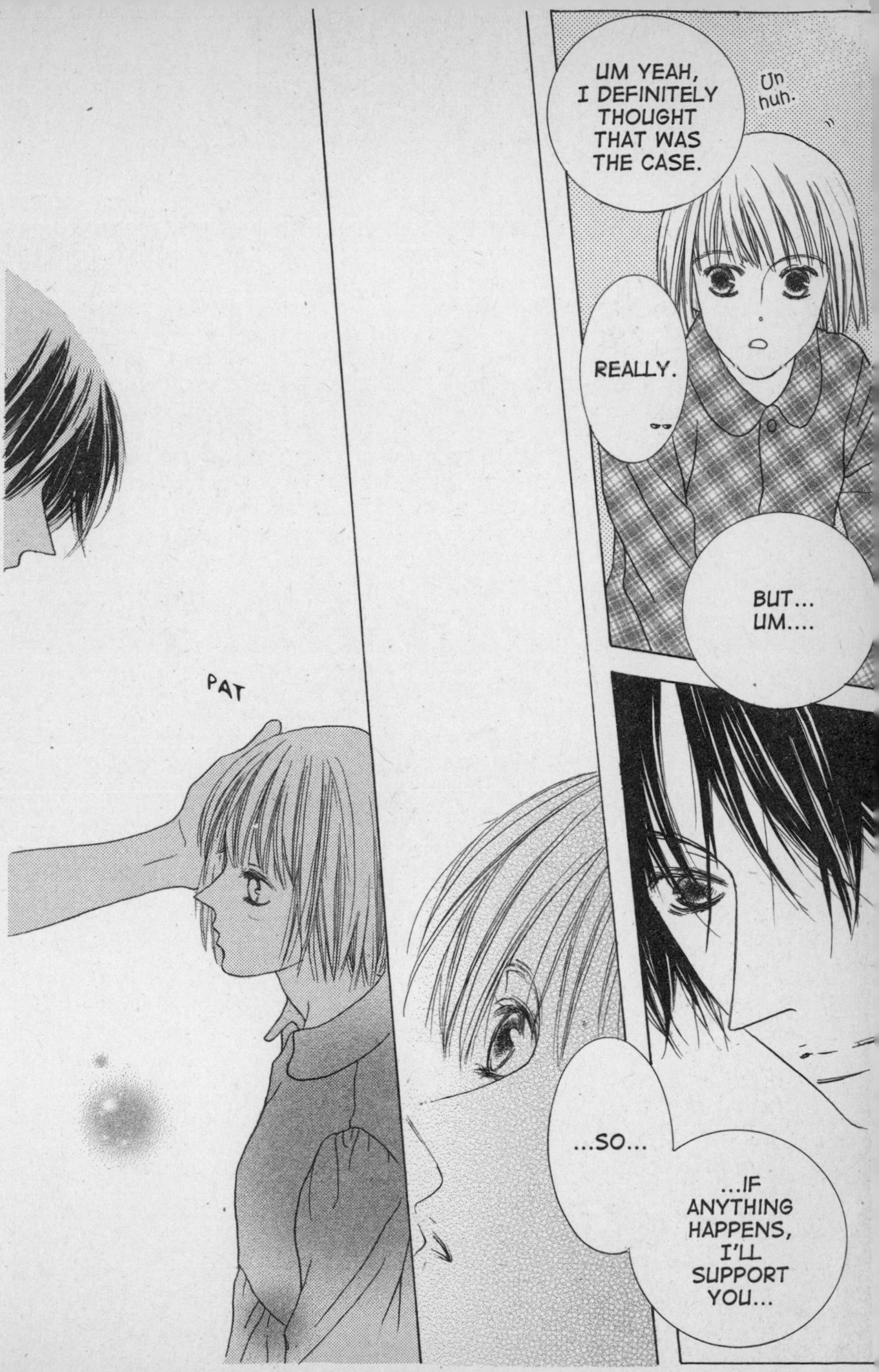
UM YEAH, I DEFINITELY THOUGHT THAT WAS THE CASE.
Un huh.
REALLY.
BUT... UM....
...SO...
...IF ANYTHING HAPPENS, I'LL SUPPORT YOU...
PAT

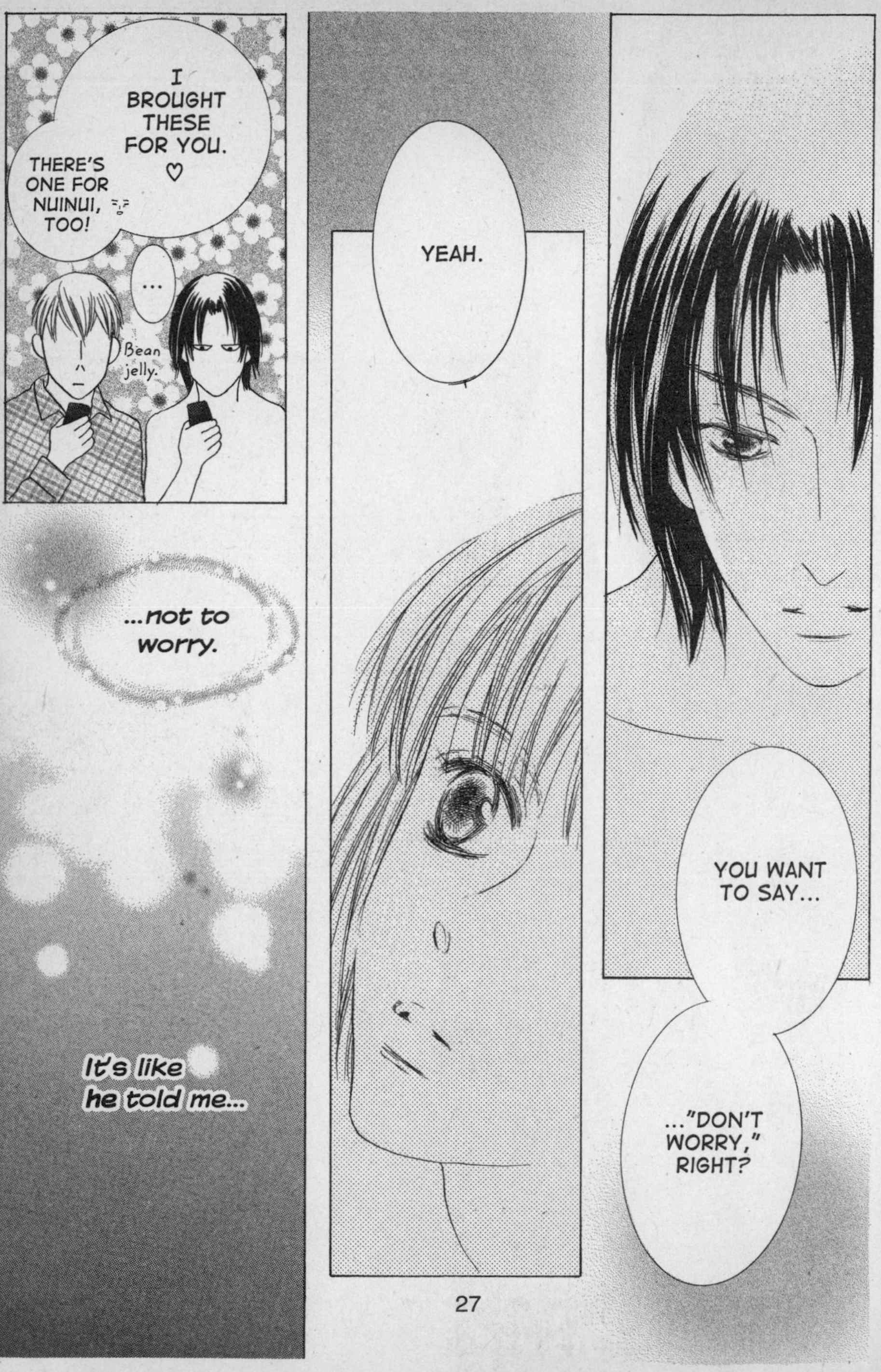

YOU WANT TO SAY...
..."DON'T WORRY," RIGHT?
YEAH.
I BROUGHT THESE FOR YOU. ♡
THERE'S ONE FOR NUINUI, TOO!
...
Bean jelly.
...not to worry.
It's like he told me...

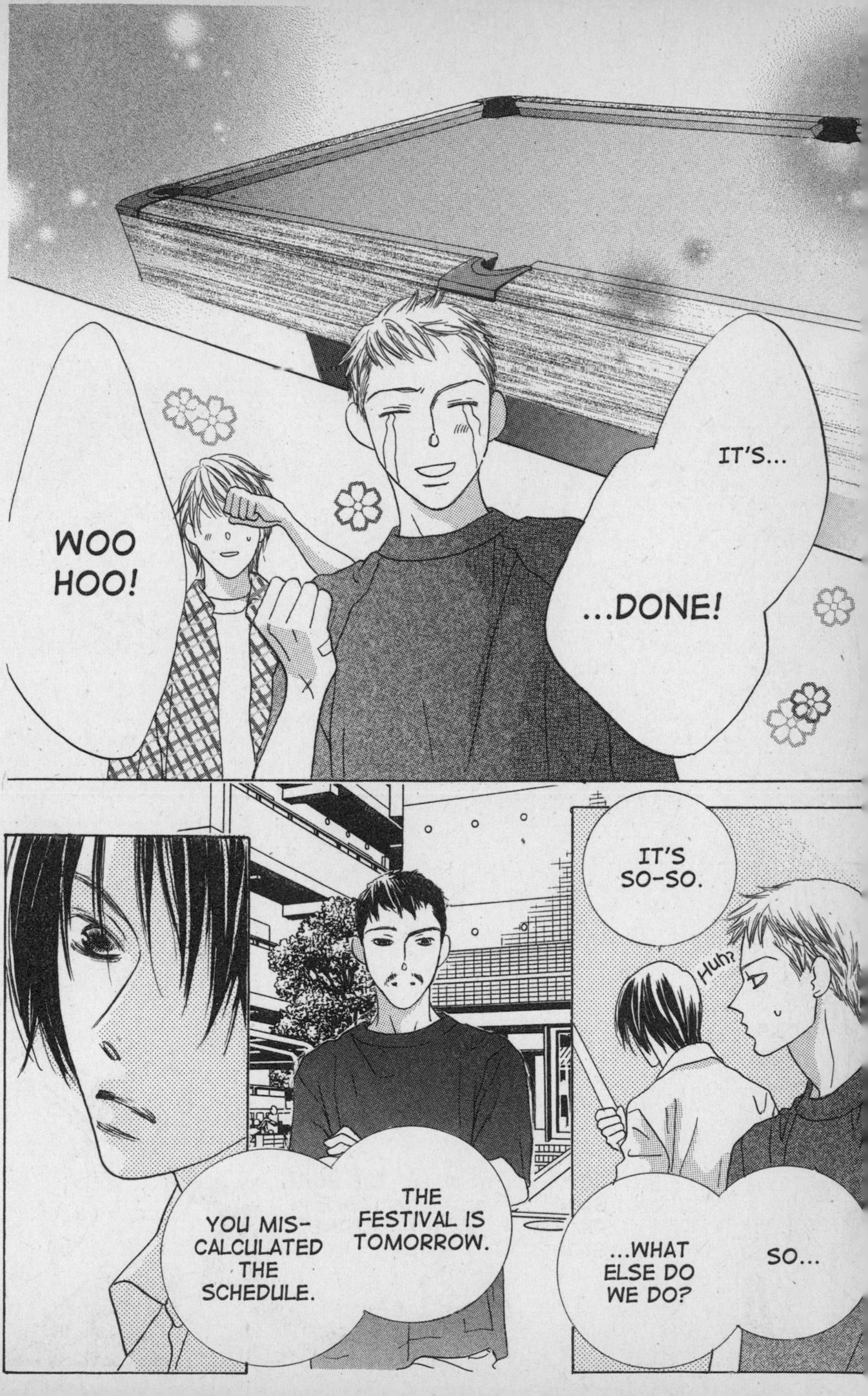
IT'S...
...DONE!
WOO HOO!
IT'S SO-SO.
Huh?
SO...
...WHAT ELSE DO WE DO?
THE FESTIVAL IS TOMORROW.
YOU MIS-CALCULATED THE SCHEDULE.

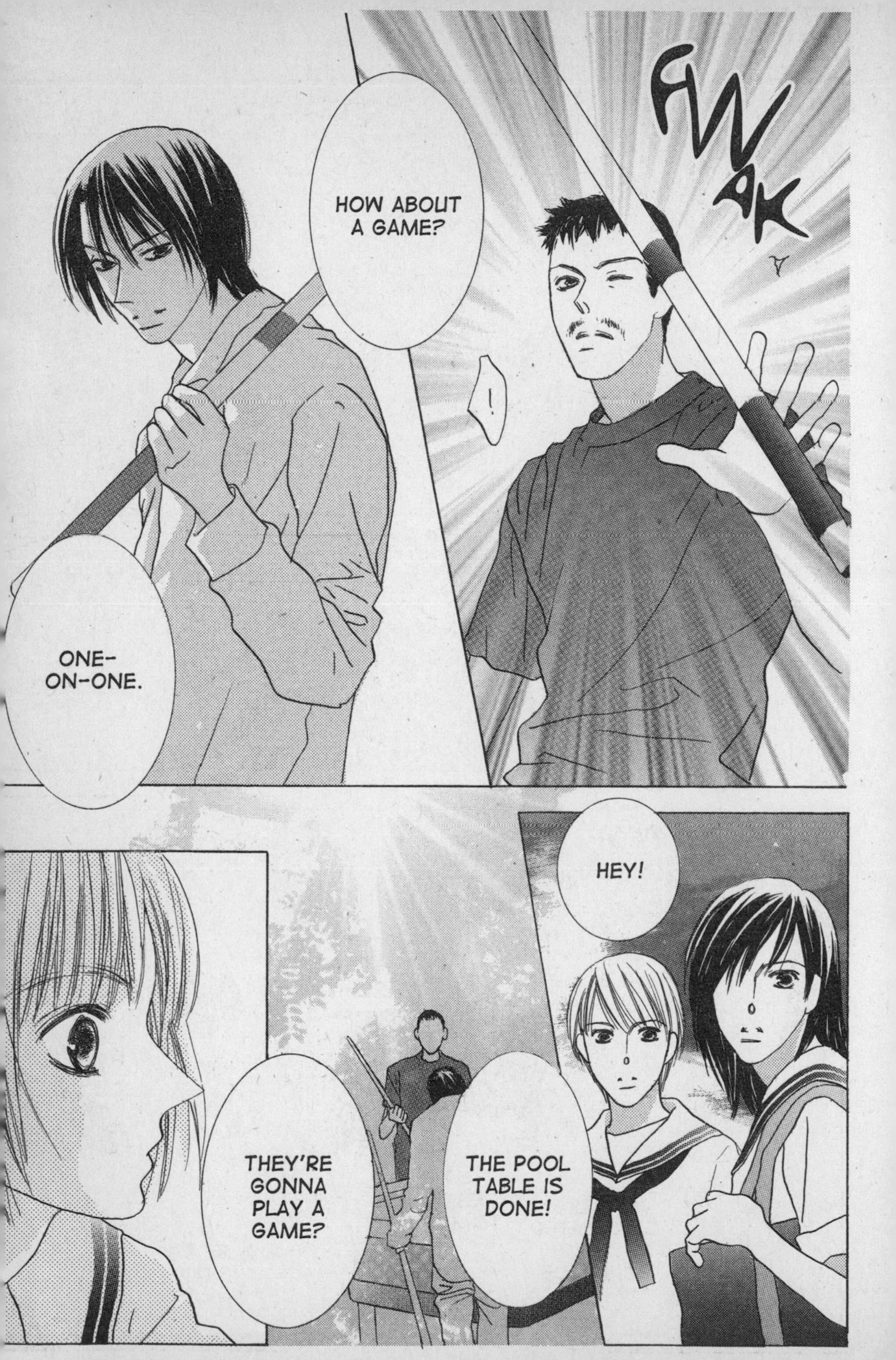
GWAK
!
HOW ABOUT A GAME?
ONE-ON-ONE.
HEY!
THE POOL TABLE IS DONE!
THEY'RE GONNA PLAY A GAME?

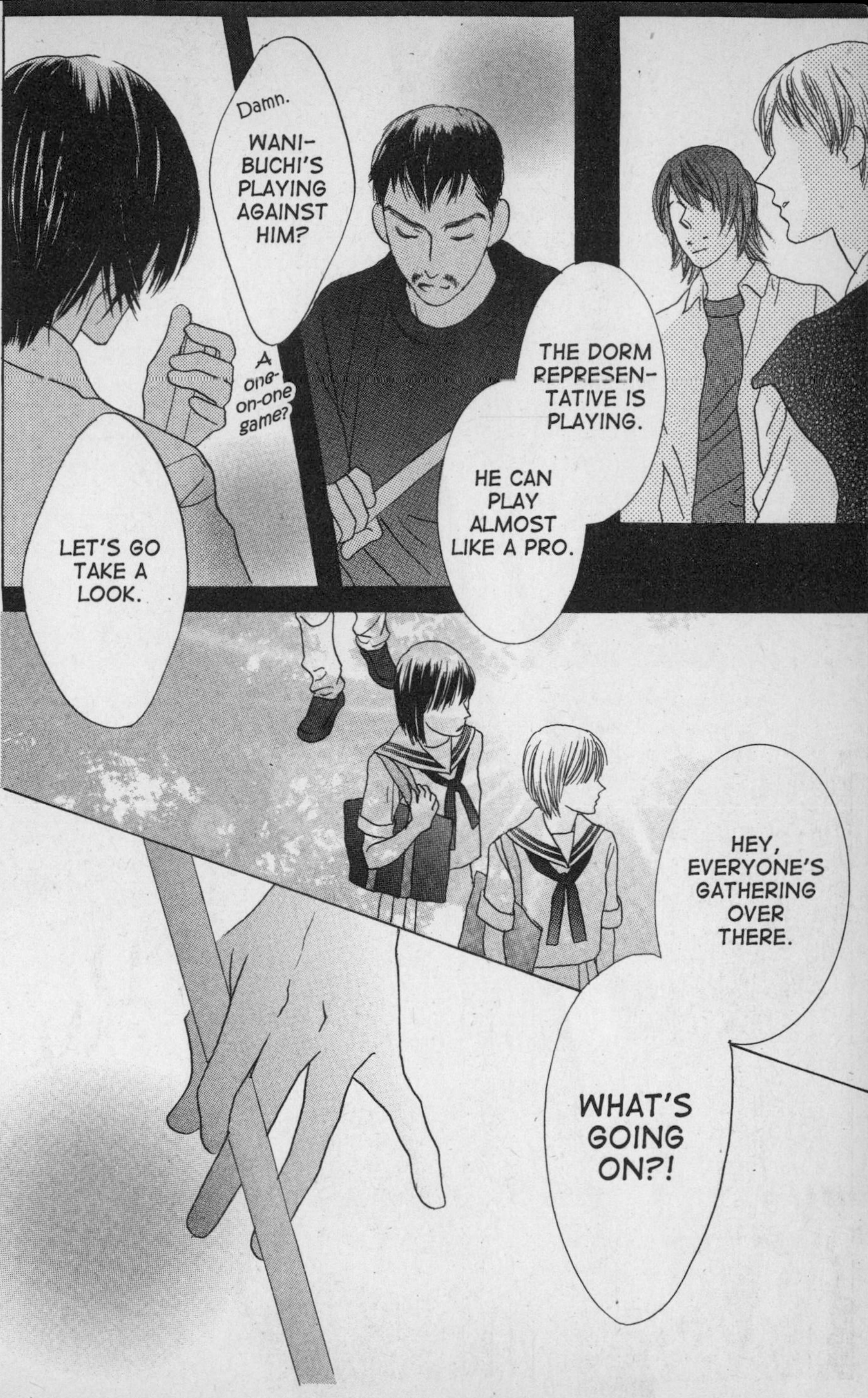
THE DORM REPRESENTATIVE IS PLAYING.
HE CAN PLAY ALMOST LIKE A PRO.
Damn.
WANI-BUCHI'S PLAYING AGAINST HIM?
A one-on-one game?
LET'S GO TAKE A LOOK.
HEY, EVERYONE'S GATHERING OVER THERE.
WHAT'S GOING ON?!

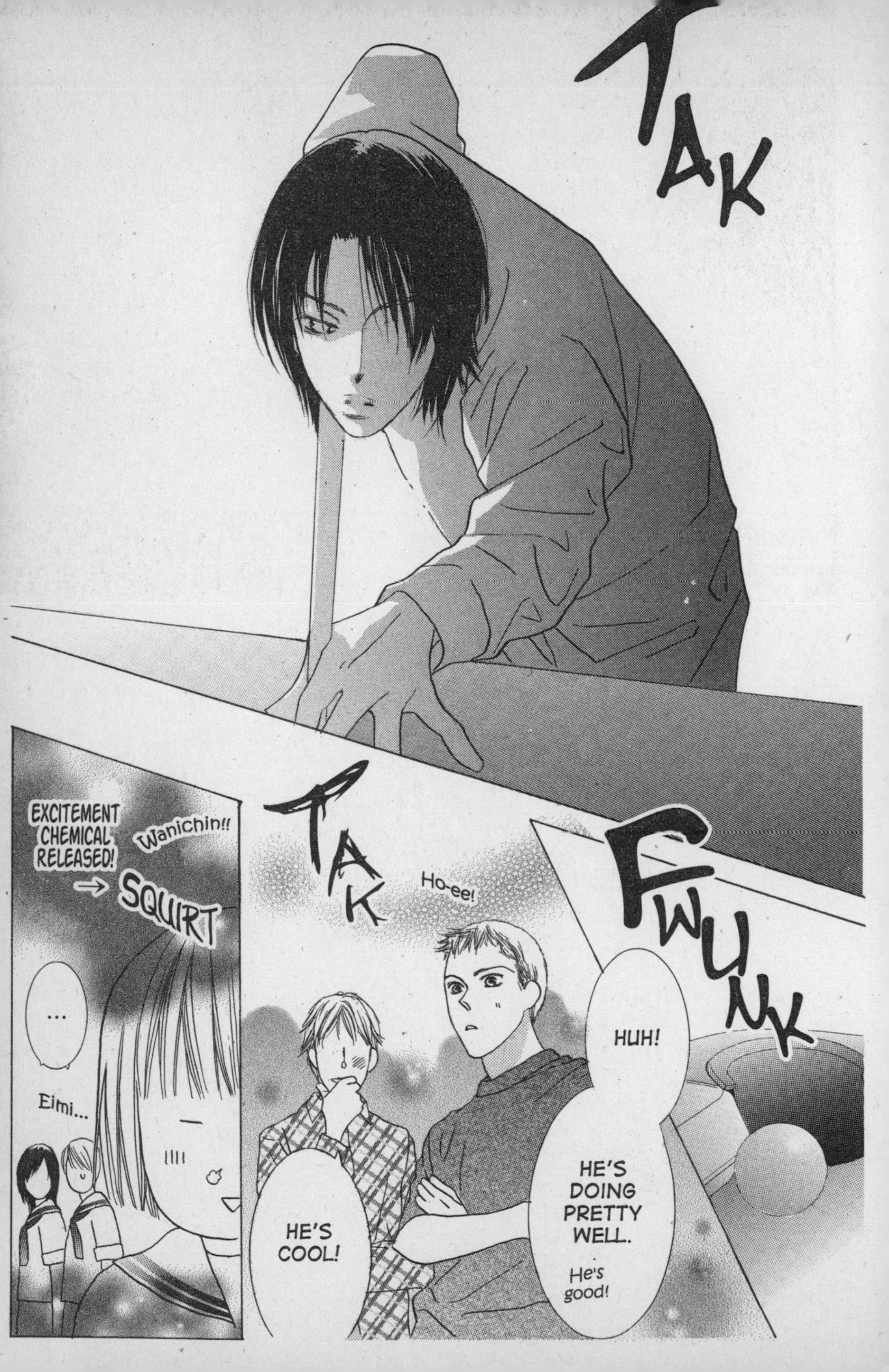
TAK
FWUNK
HUH!
HE'S DOING PRETTY WELL.
He's good!
Ho-ee!
TAK
HE'S COOL!
Wanichin!!
EXCITEMENT CHEMICAL RELEASED!
→ SQUIRT
...
Eimi...

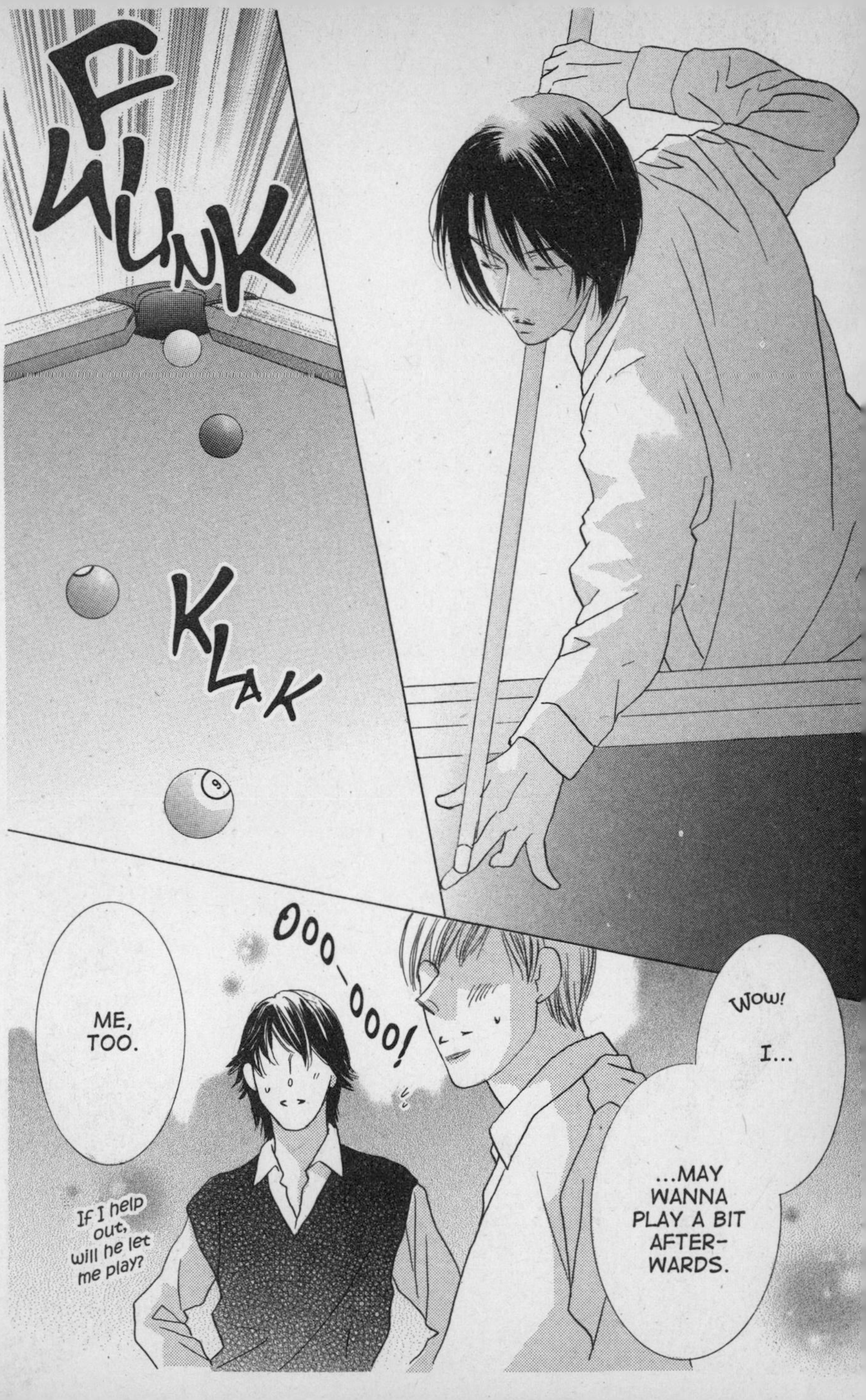
FLUNK
KLAK
WOW!
I...
...MAY WANNA PLAY A BIT AFTER-WARDS.
OOO-OOO!
ME, TOO.
If I help out, will he let me play?

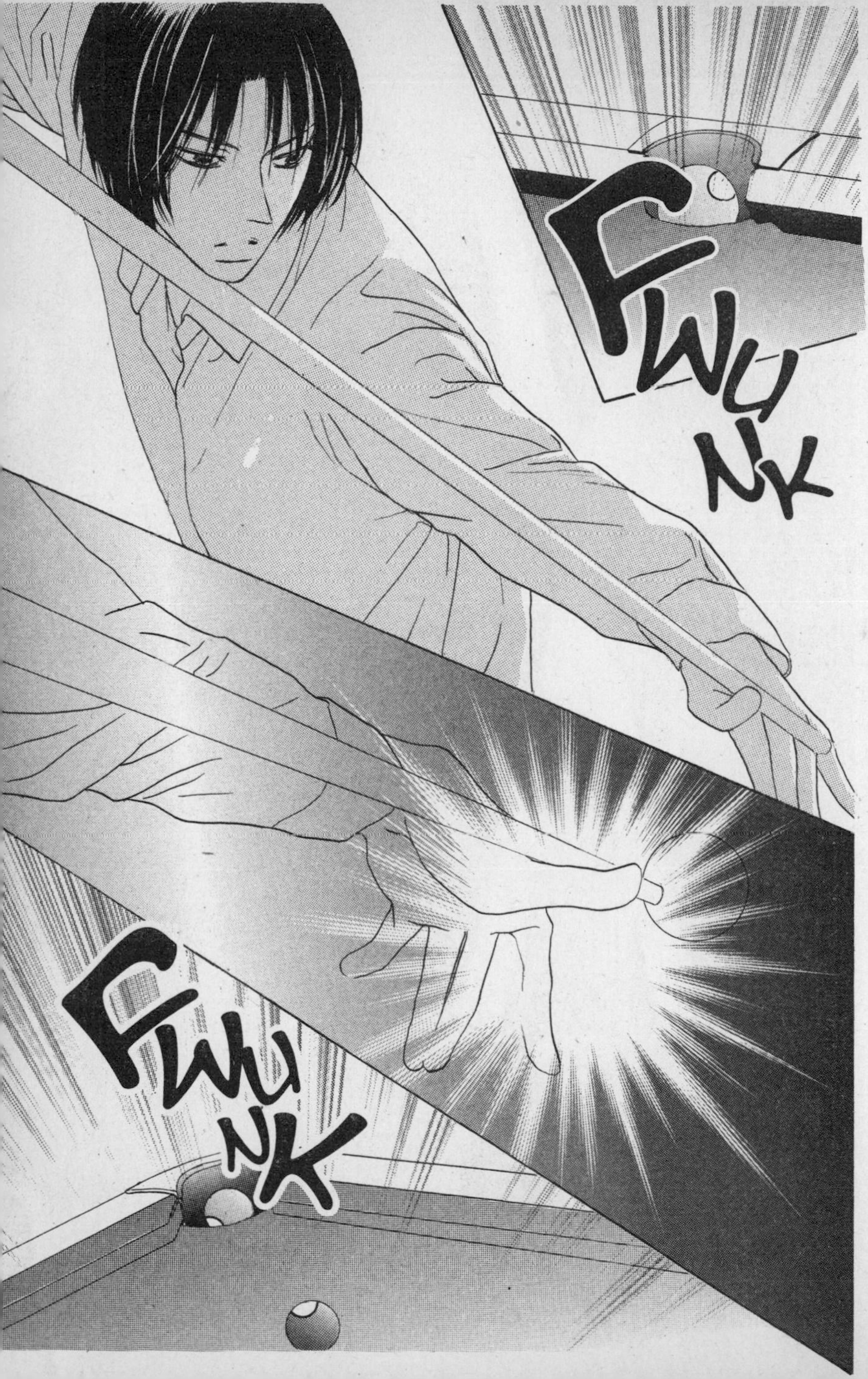
FWUNK
FWUNK

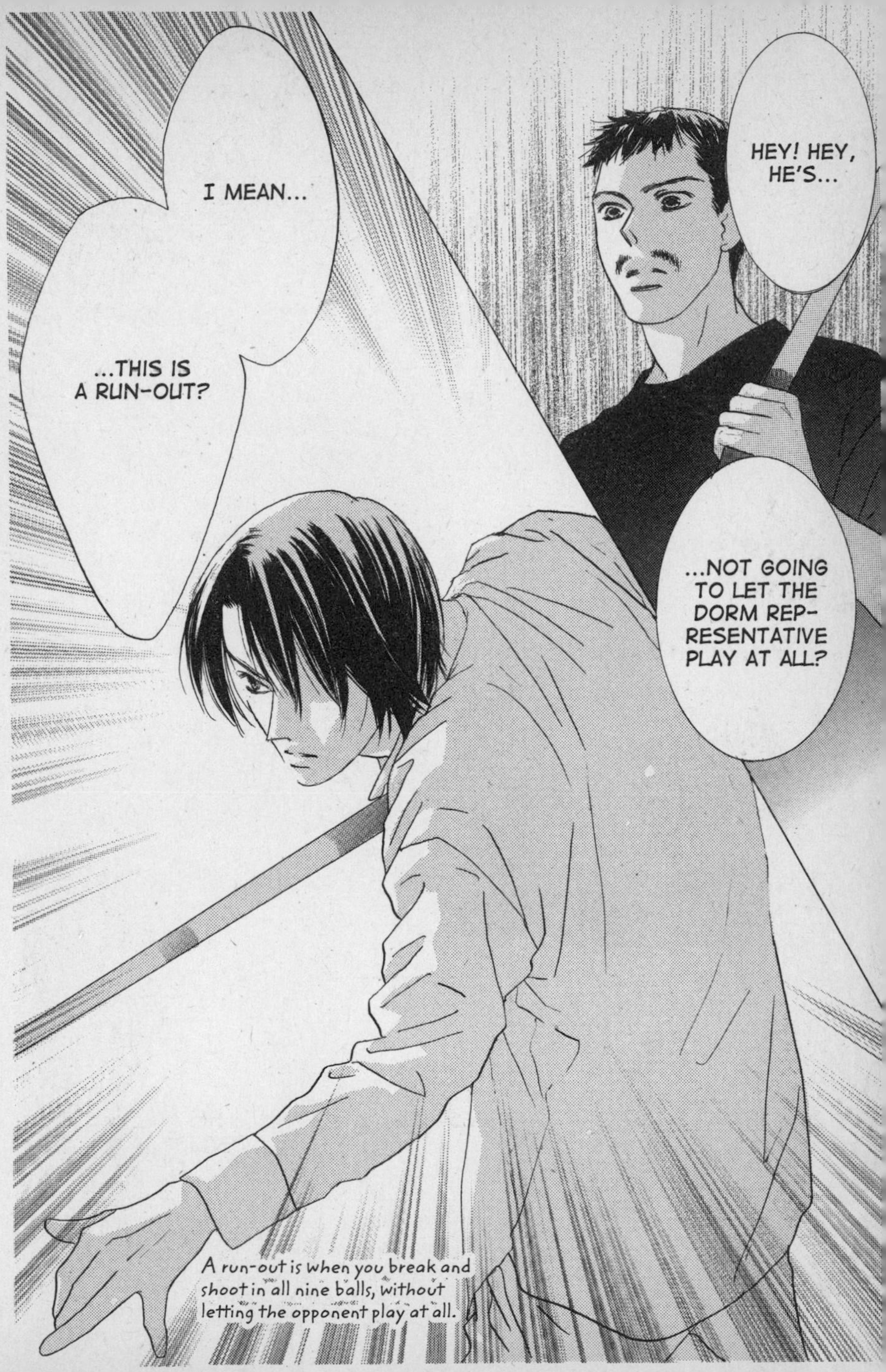
HEY! HEY, HE'S...
...NOT GOING TO LET THE DORM REPRESENTATIVE PLAY AT ALL?
I MEAN...
...THIS IS A RUN-OUT?
A run-out is when you break and shoot in all nine balls, without letting the opponent play at all.

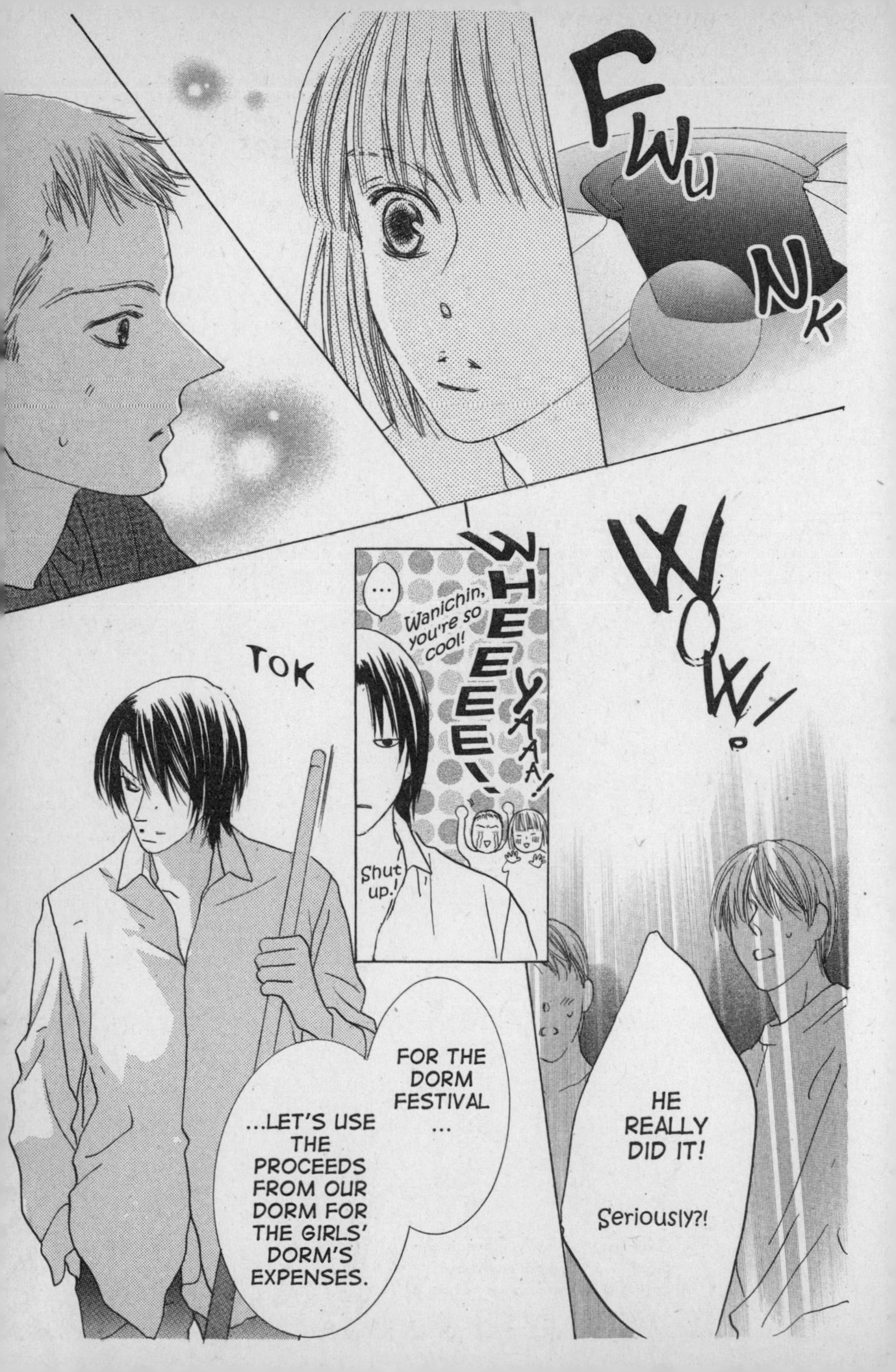
FWUNK
WOW!
HE REALLY DID IT!
Seriously?!
WHEEEEE!
YAAA!
Wanichin, you're so cool!
...
Shut up!
TOK
FOR THE DORM FESTIVAL ...
...LET'S USE THE PROCEEDS FROM OUR DORM FOR THE GIRLS' DORM'S EXPENSES.

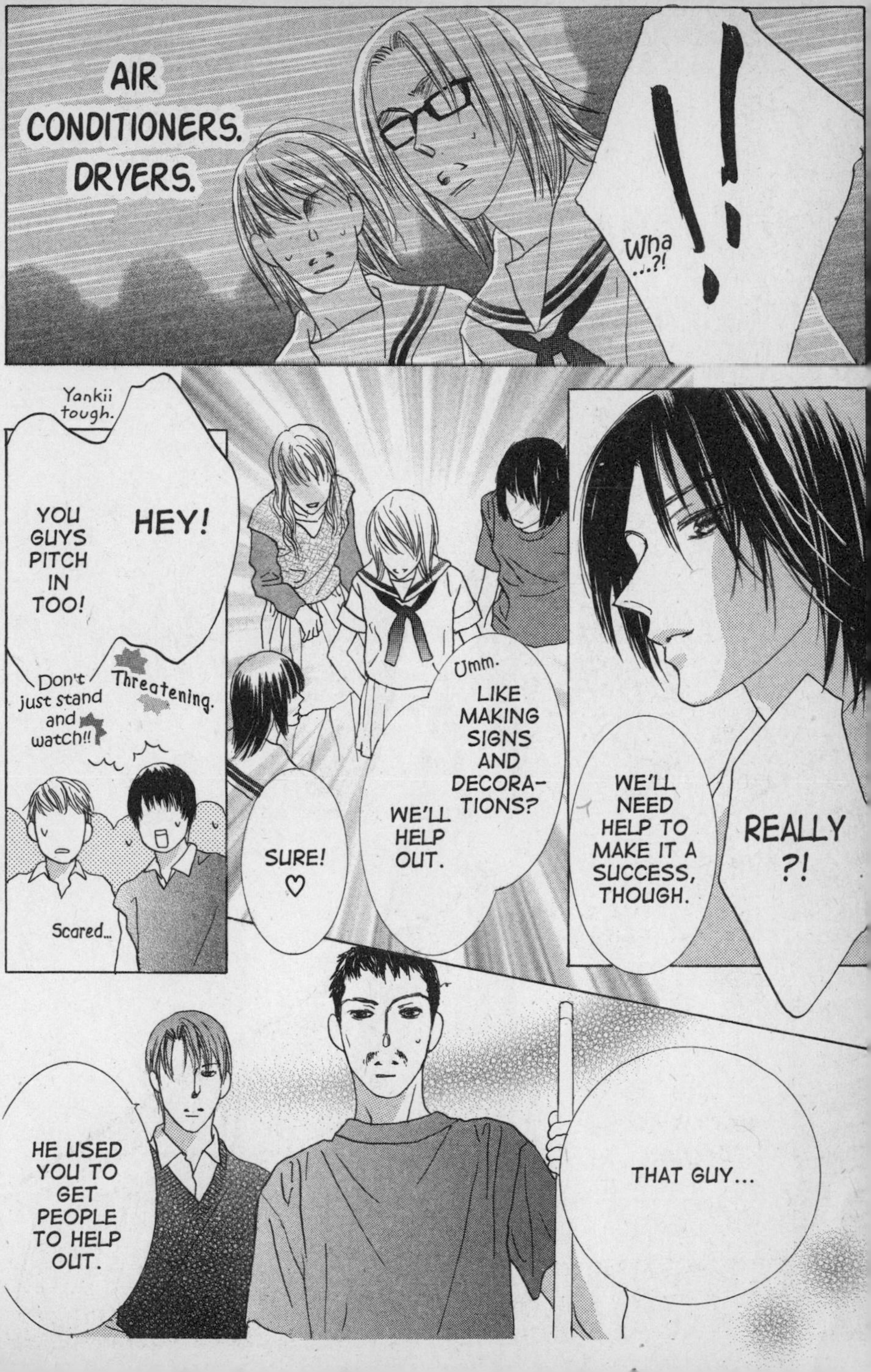
!!
Wha ...?!
AIR CONDITIONERS. DRYERS.
WE'LL NEED HELP TO MAKE IT A SUCCESS, THOUGH.
REALLY ?!
Umm.
LIKE MAKING SIGNS AND DECORATIONS?
WE'LL HELP OUT.
SURE! ♡
HEY!
YOU GUYS PITCH IN TOO!
Yankii tough.
Threatening.
Don't just stand and watch!!
Scared...
THAT GUY...
HE USED YOU TO GET PEOPLE TO HELP OUT.

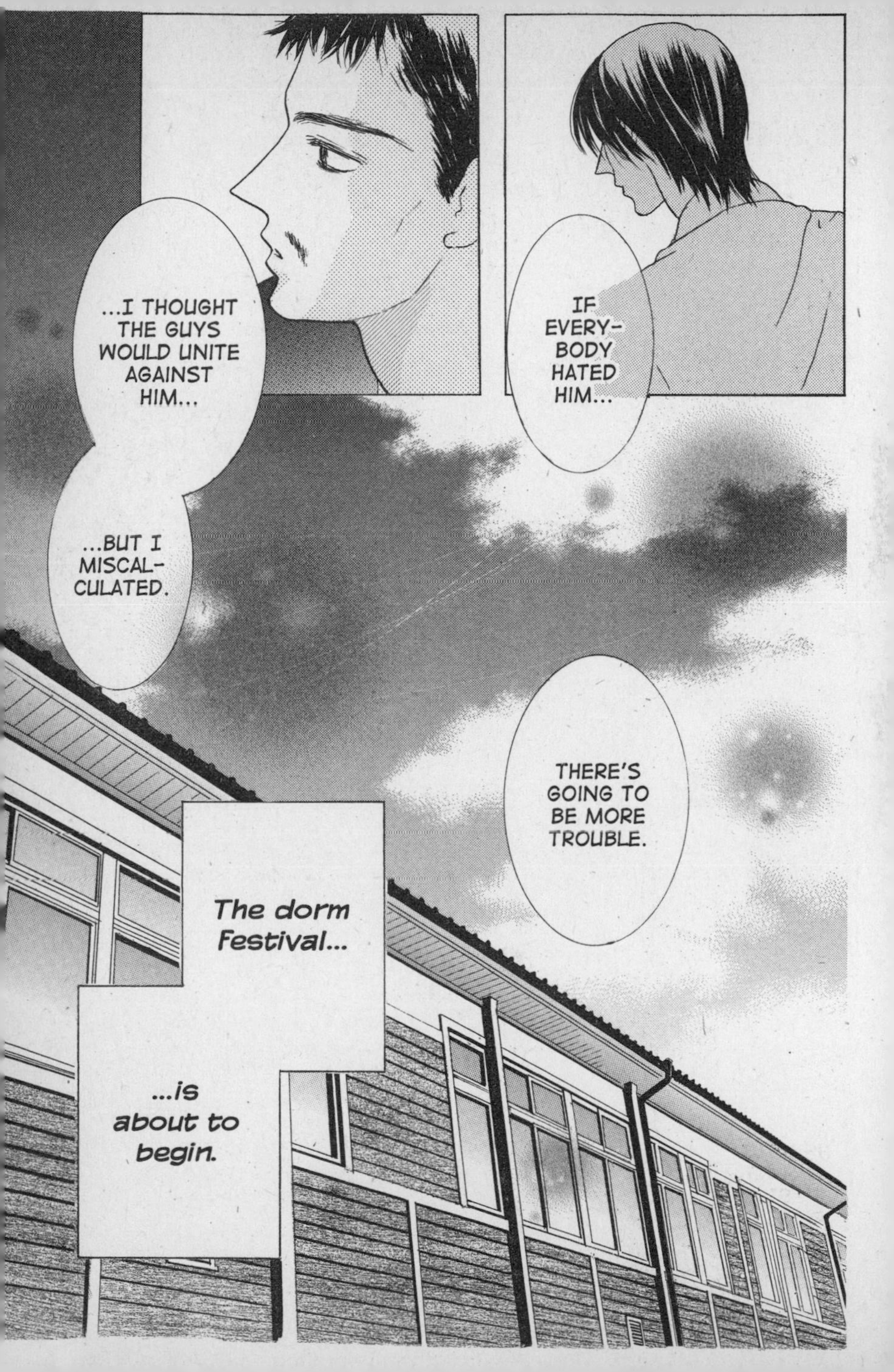
IF EVERY-BODY HATED HIM...
...I THOUGHT THE GUYS WOULD UNITE AGAINST HIM...
...BUT I MISCAL-CULATED.
THERE'S GOING TO BE MORE TROUBLE.
The dorm Festival...
...is about to begin.

BEAUTY
IS THE
BEAST

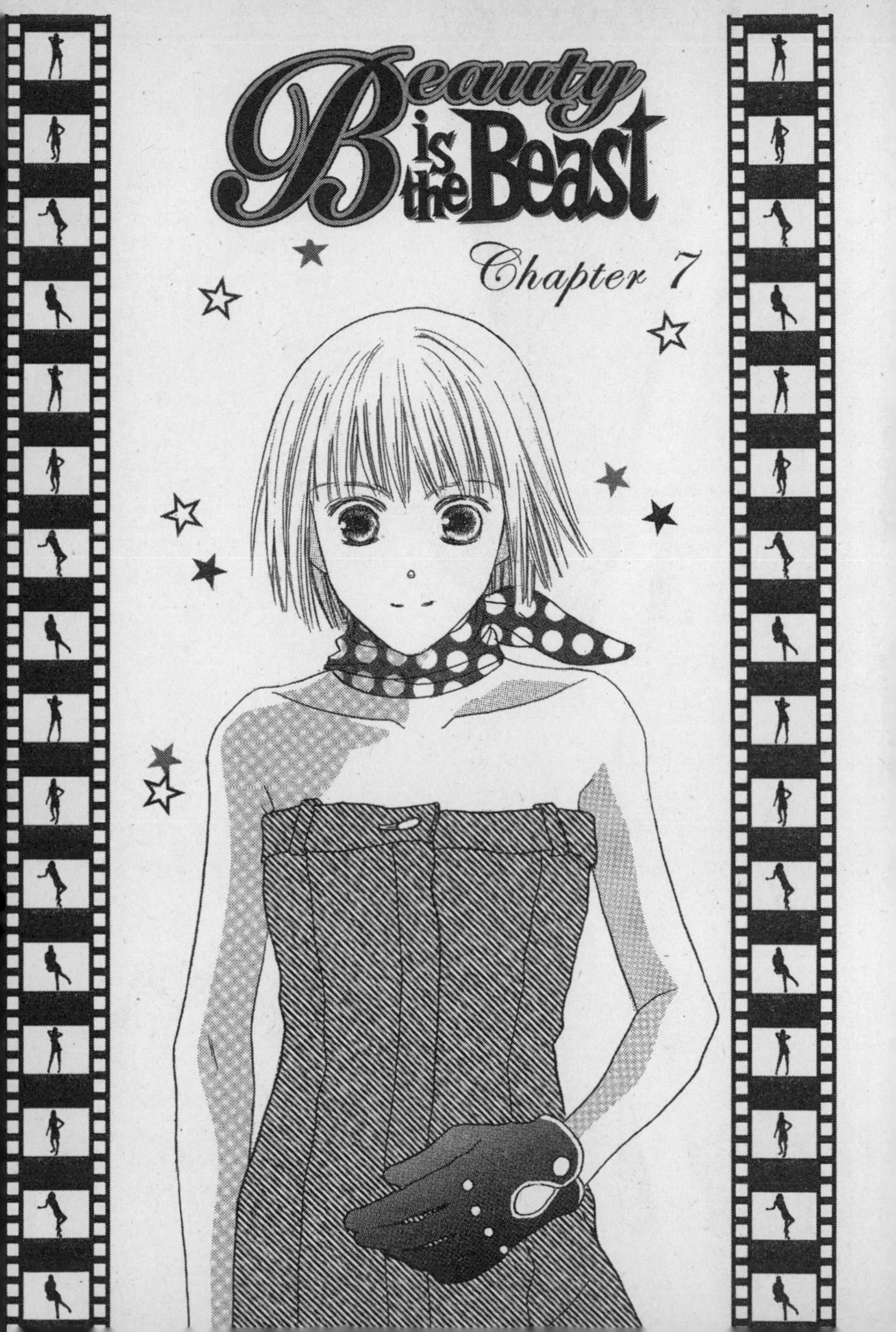
Beauty is the Beast
Chapter 7

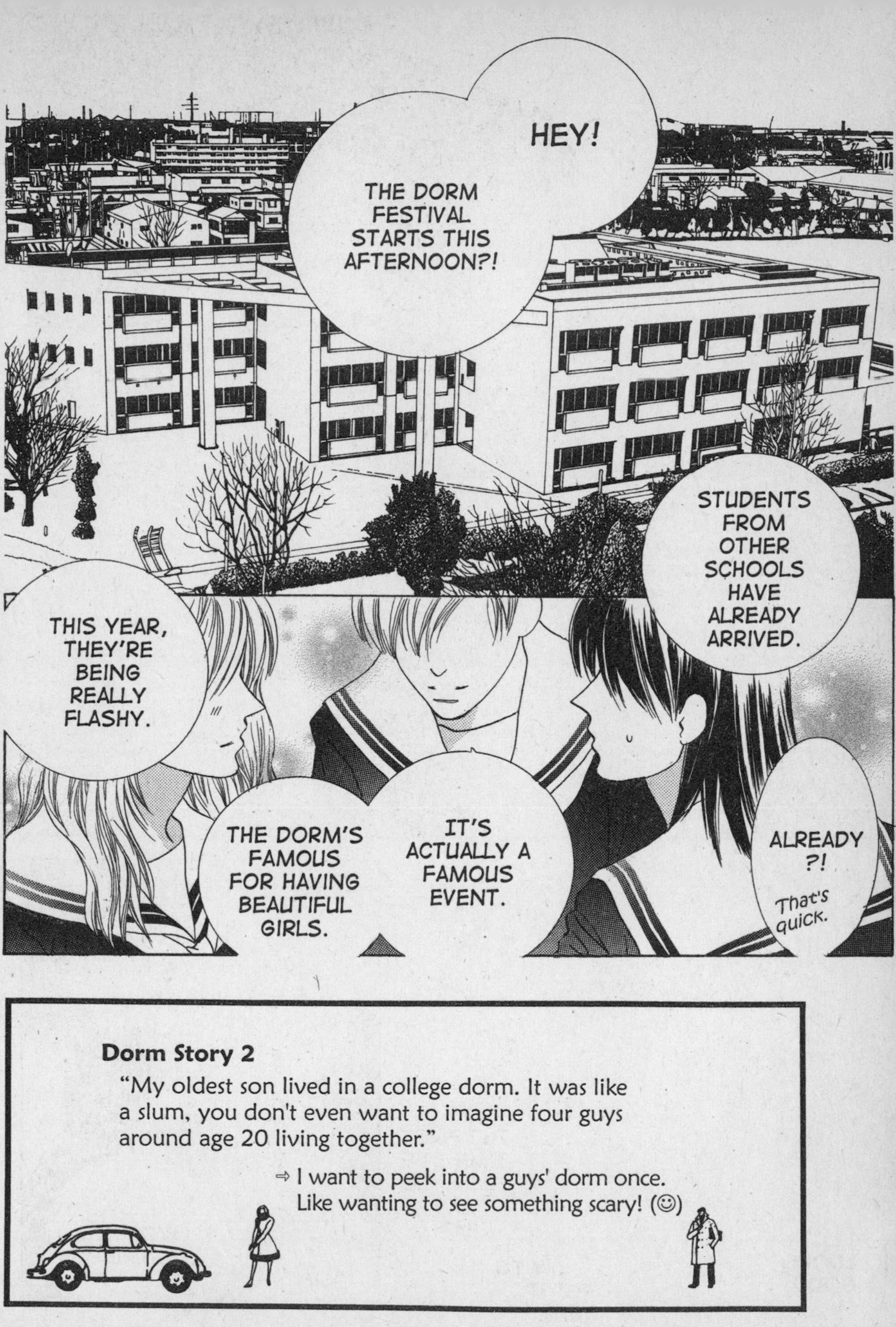
HEY!
THE DORM FESTIVAL STARTS THIS AFTERNOON?!
STUDENTS FROM OTHER SCHOOLS HAVE ALREADY ARRIVED.
ALREADY?!
That's quick.
IT'S ACTUALLY A FAMOUS EVENT.
THE DORM'S FAMOUS FOR HAVING BEAUTIFUL GIRLS.
THIS YEAR, THEY'RE BEING REALLY FLASHY.

Dorm Story 2

"My oldest son lived in a college dorm. It was like a slum, you don't even want to imagine four guys around age 20 living together."

⇨ I want to peek into a guys' dorm once. Like wanting to see something scary! (☺)

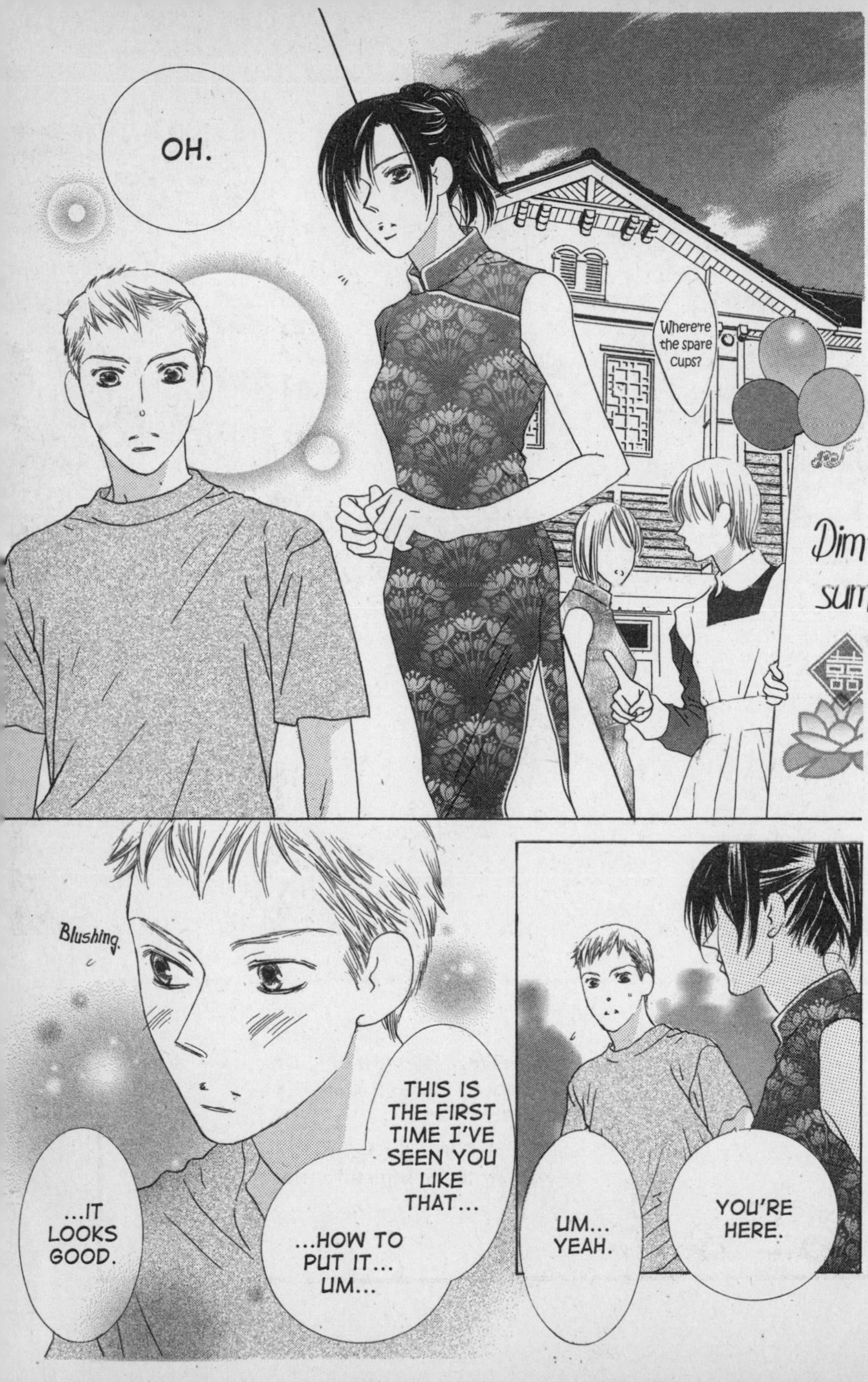
Dim-sum
Where're the spare cups?
OH.
YOU'RE HERE.
UM... YEAH.
THIS IS THE FIRST TIME I'VE SEEN YOU LIKE THAT...
Blushing.
...HOW TO PUT IT... UM...
...IT LOOKS GOOD.

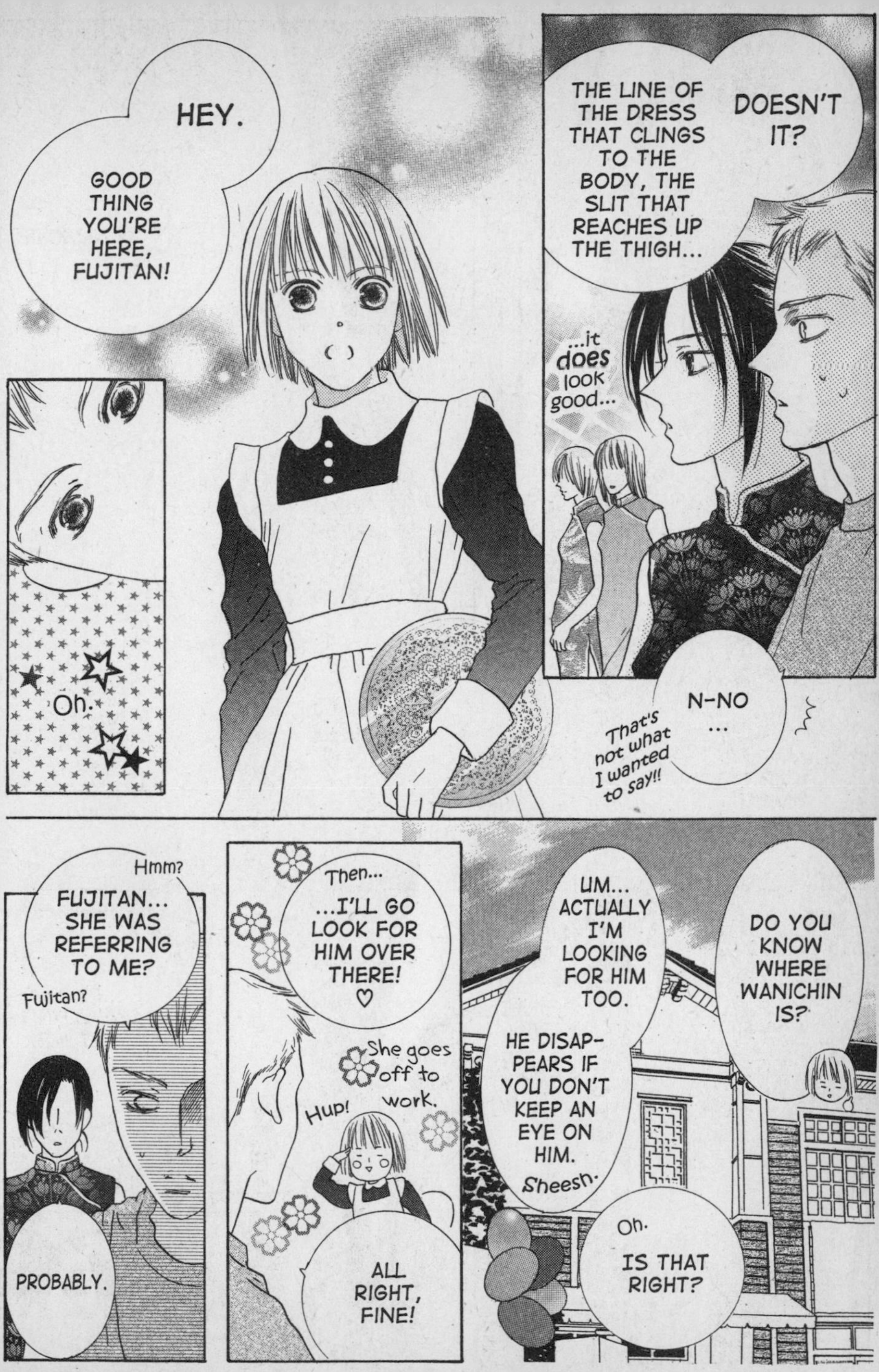
DOESN'T IT?
THE LINE OF THE DRESS THAT CLINGS TO THE BODY, THE SLIT THAT REACHES UP THE THIGH...
...it does look good...
N-NO ...
That's not what I wanted to say!!
HEY.
GOOD THING YOU'RE HERE, FUJITAN!
Oh.
DO YOU KNOW WHERE WANICHIN IS?
UM... ACTUALLY I'M LOOKING FOR HIM TOO.
HE DISAPPEARS IF YOU DON'T KEEP AN EYE ON HIM.
Sheesh.
Oh.
IS THAT RIGHT?
Then...
...I'LL GO LOOK FOR HIM OVER THERE! ♡
She goes off to work.
Hup!
ALL RIGHT, FINE!
Hmm?
FUJITAN... SHE WAS REFERRING TO ME?
Fujitan?
PROBABLY.

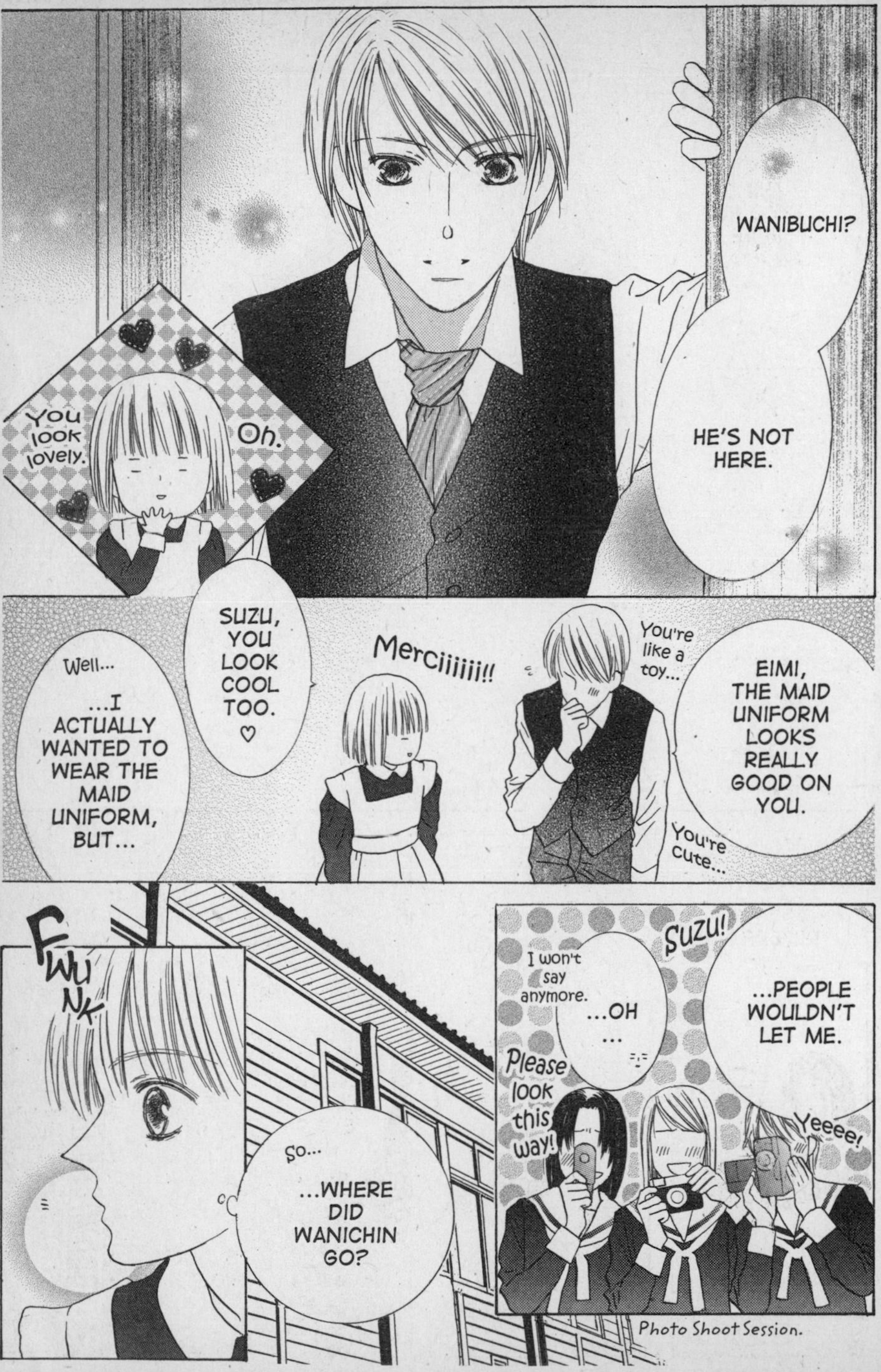
WANIBUCHI?
HE'S NOT HERE.
Oh.
You look lovely.
You're like a toy...
EIMI, THE MAID UNIFORM LOOKS REALLY GOOD ON YOU.
You're cute...
Merciiiiiii!!
SUZU, YOU LOOK COOL TOO. ♡
Well...
...I ACTUALLY WANTED TO WEAR THE MAID UNIFORM, BUT...
...PEOPLE WOULDN'T LET ME.
Suzu!
...OH ...
I won't say anymore.
Please look this way!
Yeeee!
Photo Shoot Session.
FWUNK
So...
...WHERE DID WANICHIN GO?

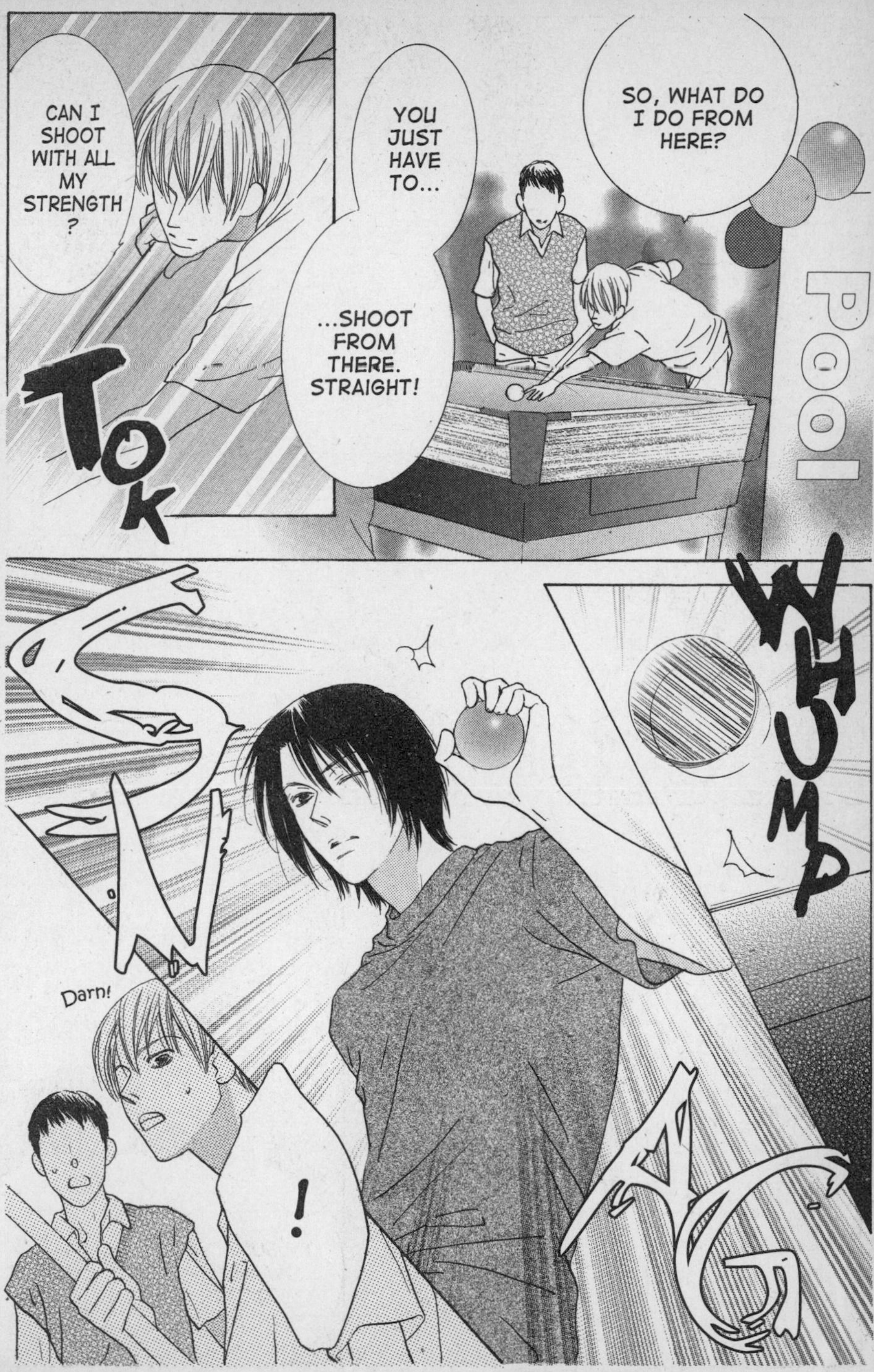

SO, WHAT DO I DO FROM HERE?
YOU JUST HAVE TO...
...SHOOT FROM THERE. STRAIGHT!
POOL
CAN I SHOOT WITH ALL MY STRENGTH?
TOK
WHUMP
!
Darn!

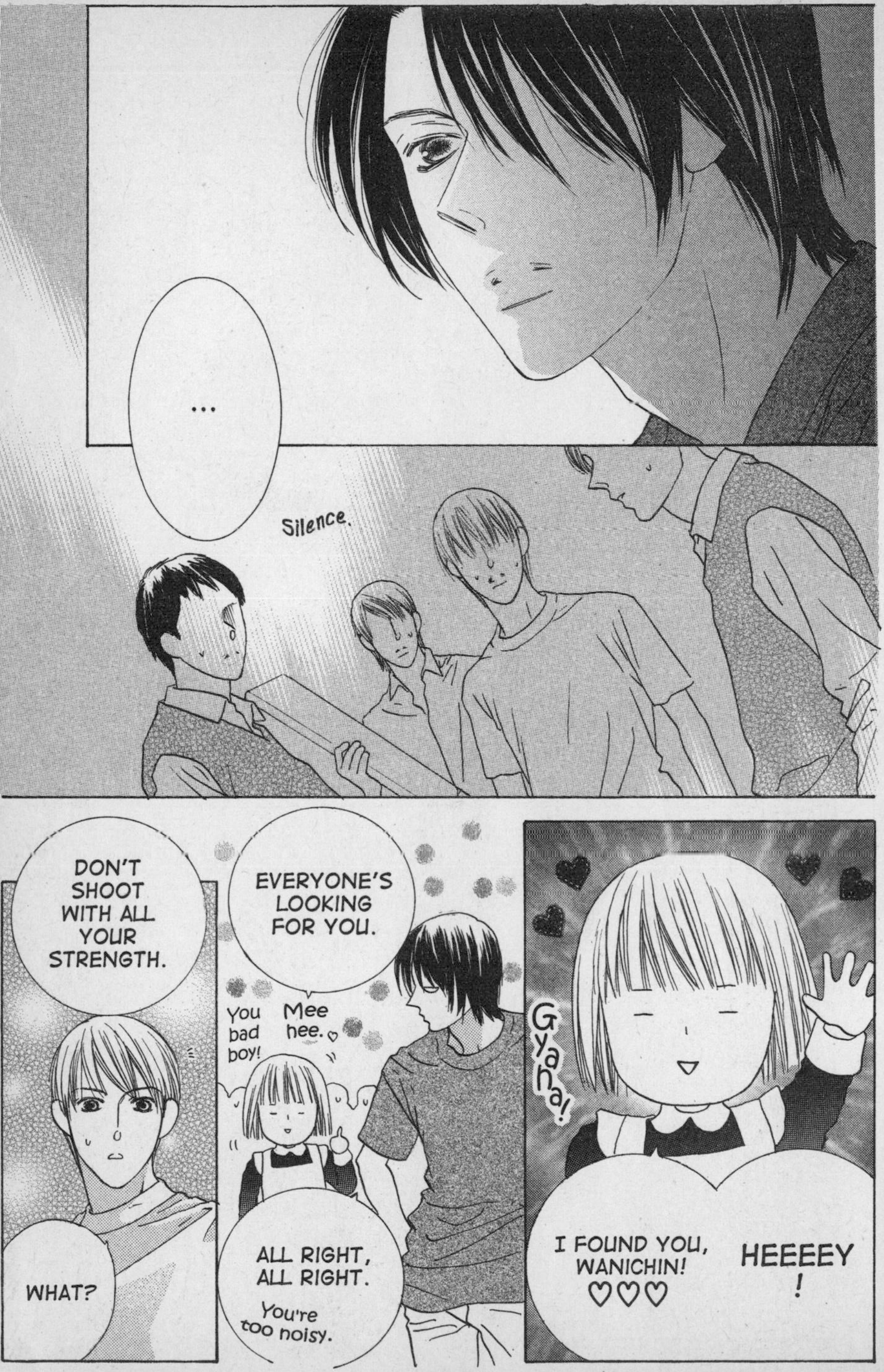
...
Silence.
HEEEEY!
I FOUND YOU, WANICHIN! ♡♡♡
Gyaha!
EVERYONE'S LOOKING FOR YOU.
Mee hee. ♡
You bad boy!
ALL RIGHT, ALL RIGHT.
You're too noisy.
DON'T SHOOT WITH ALL YOUR STRENGTH.
WHAT?

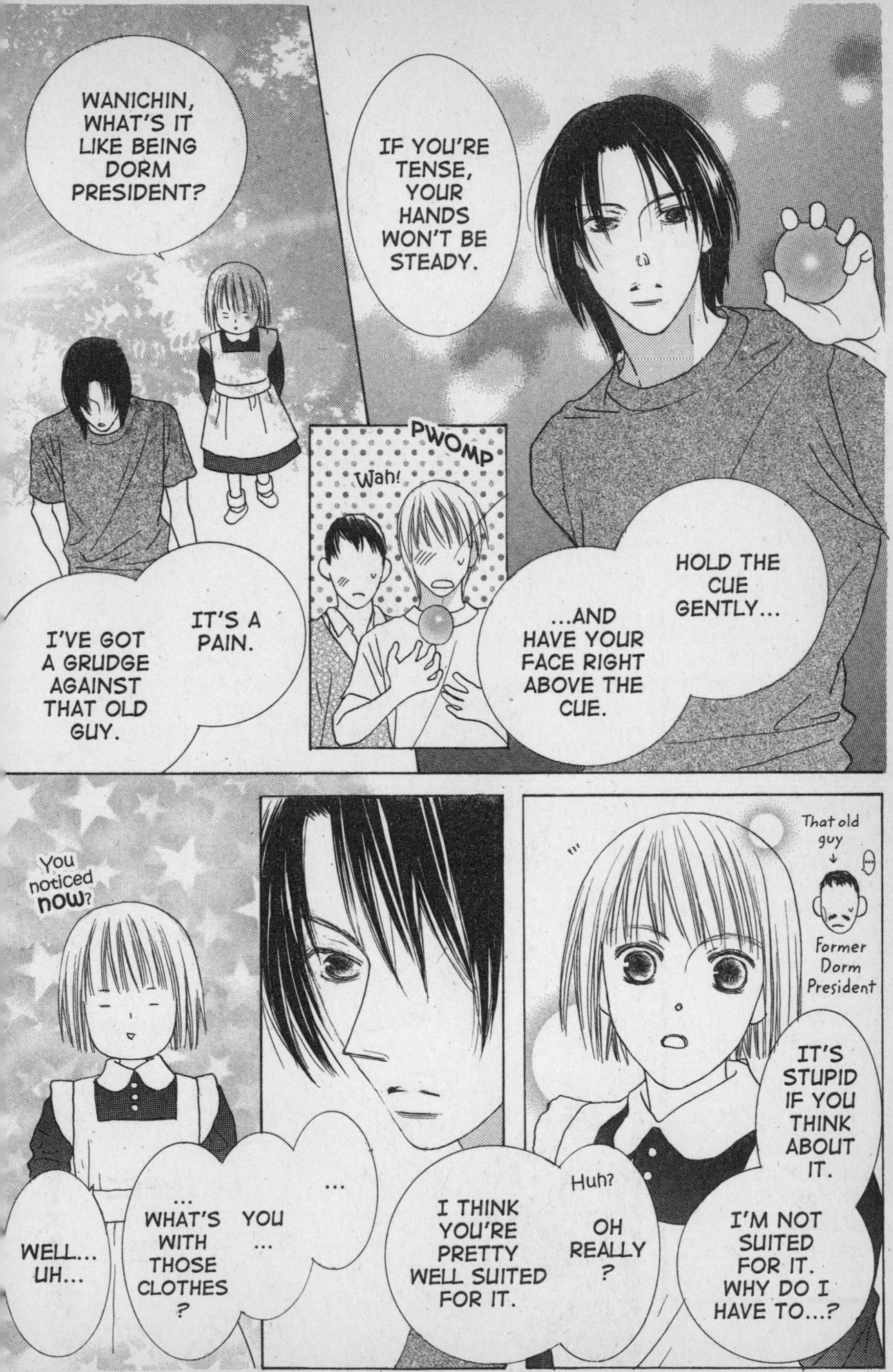

IF YOU'RE TENSE, YOUR HANDS WON'T BE STEADY.
HOLD THE CUE GENTLY...
...AND HAVE YOUR FACE RIGHT ABOVE THE CUE.
PWOMP
Wah!
WANICHIN, WHAT'S IT LIKE BEING DORM PRESIDENT?
IT'S A PAIN.
I'VE GOT A GRUDGE AGAINST THAT OLD GUY.
That old guy
...
Former Dorm President
IT'S STUPID IF YOU THINK ABOUT IT.
I'M NOT SUITED FOR IT. WHY DO I HAVE TO...?
Huh?
OH REALLY?
I THINK YOU'RE PRETTY WELL SUITED FOR IT.
...
You noticed now?
YOU...
...WHAT'S WITH THOSE CLOTHES?
WELL... UH...

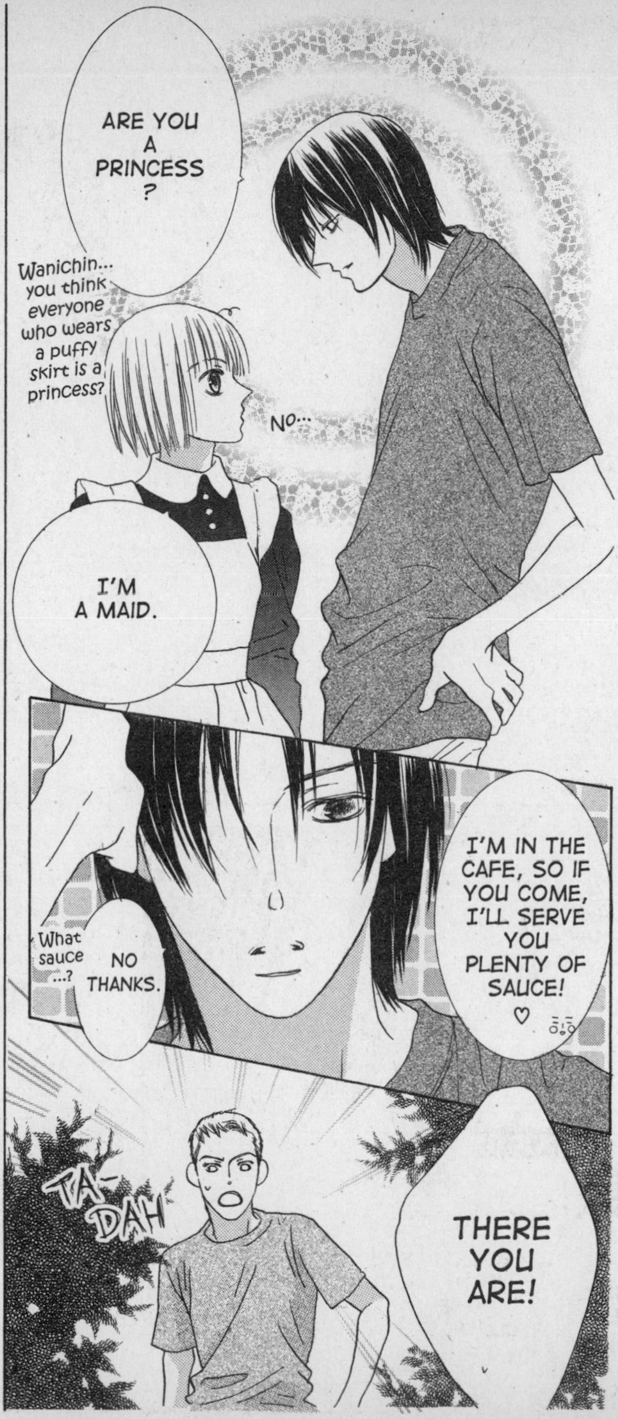
ARE YOU A PRINCESS ?
Wanichin... you think everyone who wears a puffy skirt is a princess?
NO...
I'M A MAID.
I'M IN THE CAFE, SO IF YOU COME, I'LL SERVE YOU PLENTY OF SAUCE! ♡
NO THANKS.
What sauce ...?
THERE YOU ARE!
TA-DAH

① **Draw the rough sketch.**

I do the rough sketch on some paper lying around.
This is to decide on the character's pose and other things, but it actually takes time.
I tend to hesitate a lot.

And if it's the cover illustration for LaLa (the magazine), there are lots of letters printed on the cover, so I put my heart in drawing the character's expression. In contrast, for the comics, I draw with the background blank spaces being the main focus.

In any case, if I can't make decisions about things, I feel irritated, and binge on snacks. Sigh.

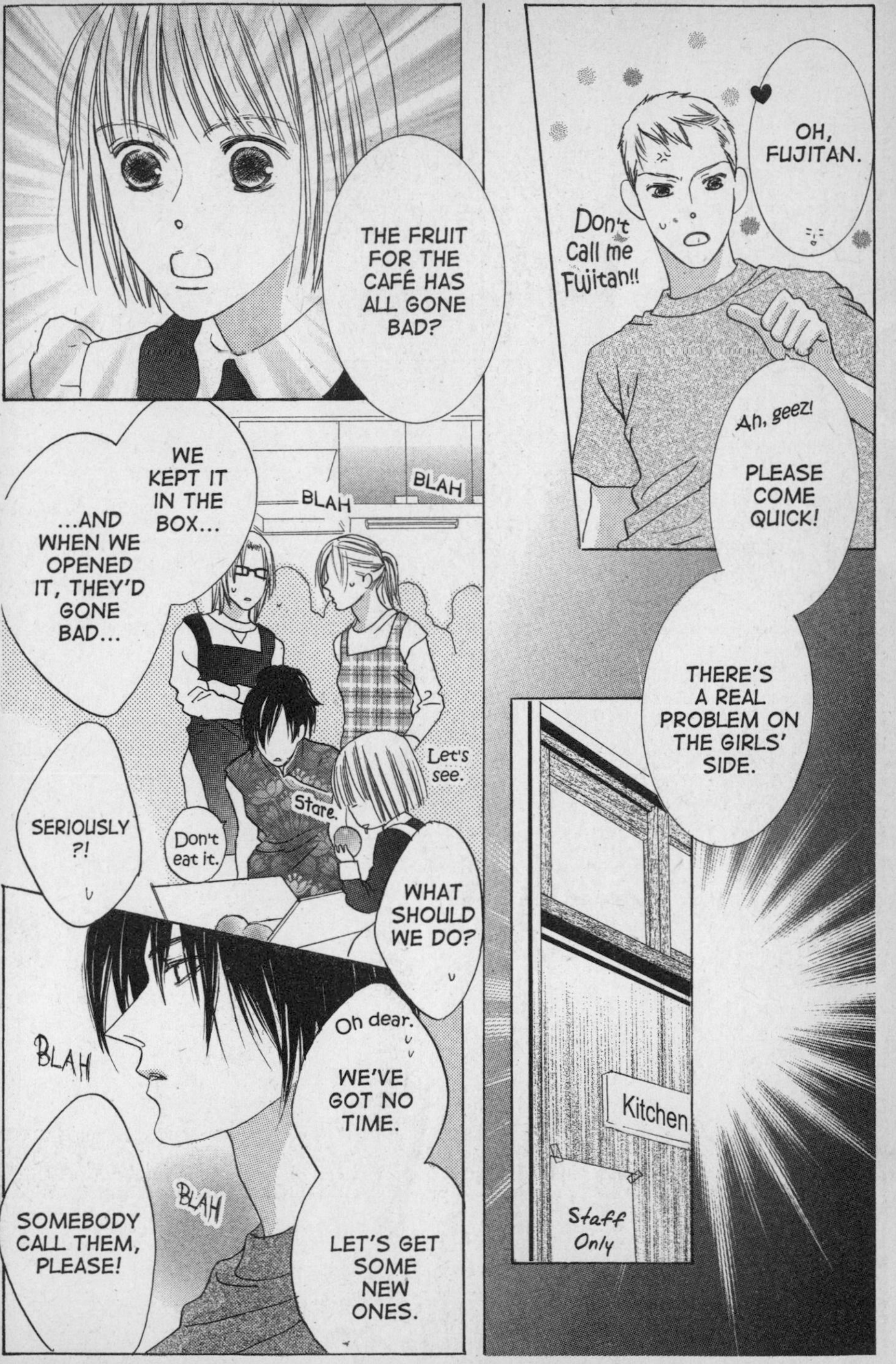
OH, FUJITAN.
Don't call me Fujitan!!
Ah, geez!
PLEASE COME QUICK!
THERE'S A REAL PROBLEM ON THE GIRLS' SIDE.
Kitchen
Staff Only
THE FRUIT FOR THE CAFÉ HAS ALL GONE BAD?
WE KEPT IT IN THE BOX...
...AND WHEN WE OPENED IT, THEY'D GONE BAD...
BLAH
BLAH
Let's see.
Stare.
Don't eat it.
SERIOUSLY ?!
WHAT SHOULD WE DO?
Oh dear.
WE'VE GOT NO TIME.
LET'S GET SOME NEW ONES.
SOMEBODY CALL THEM, PLEASE!
BLAH
BLAH

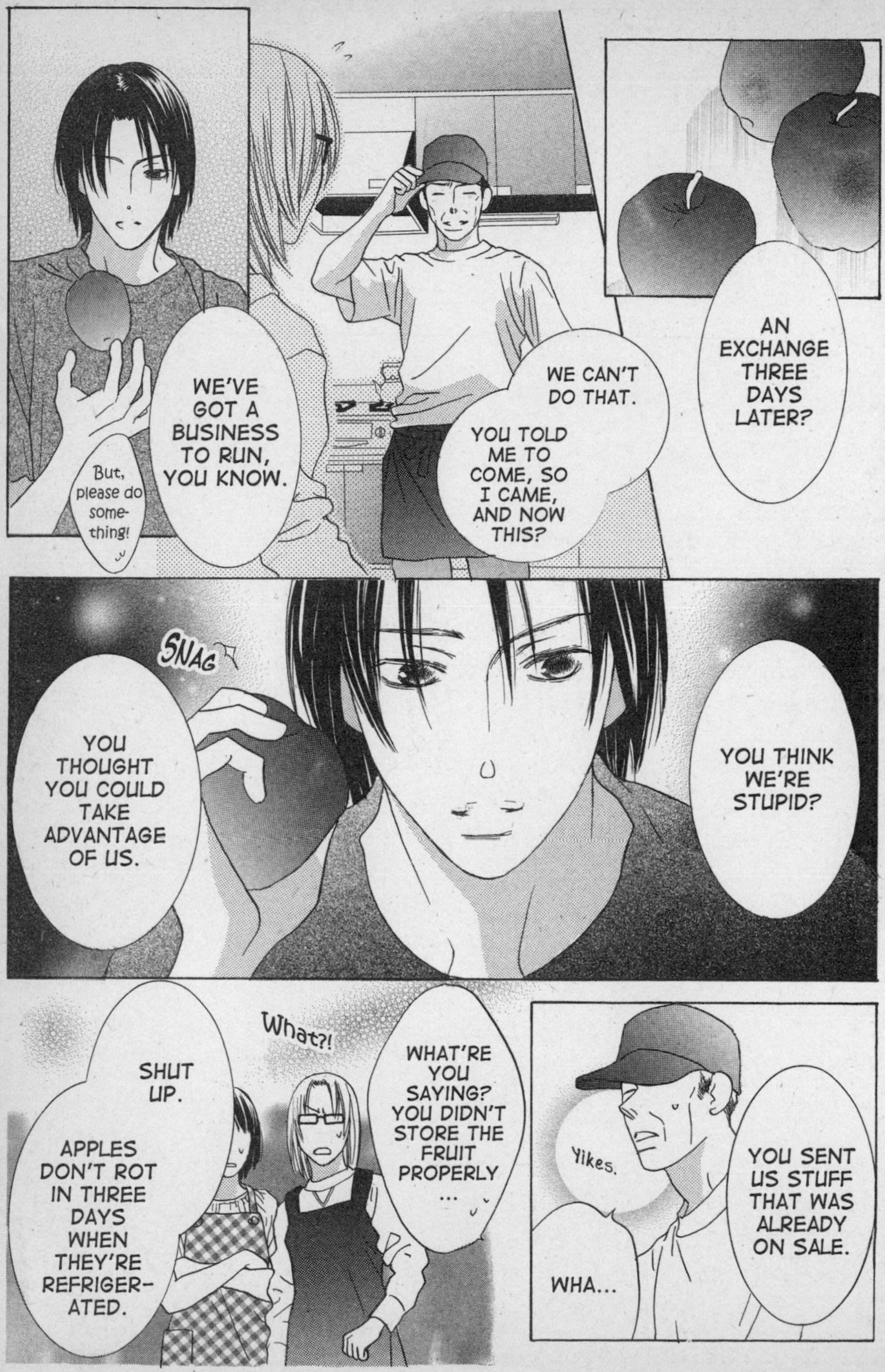
AN EXCHANGE THREE DAYS LATER?
WE CAN'T DO THAT.
YOU TOLD ME TO COME, SO I CAME, AND NOW THIS?
WE'VE GOT A BUSINESS TO RUN, YOU KNOW.
But, please do some-thing!
YOU THINK WE'RE STUPID?
SNAG
YOU THOUGHT YOU COULD TAKE ADVANTAGE OF US.
YOU SENT US STUFF THAT WAS ALREADY ON SALE.
Yikes.
WHA...
WHAT'RE YOU SAYING? YOU DIDN'T STORE THE FRUIT PROPERLY...
What?!
SHUT UP.
APPLES DON'T ROT IN THREE DAYS WHEN THEY'RE REFRIGER-ATED.

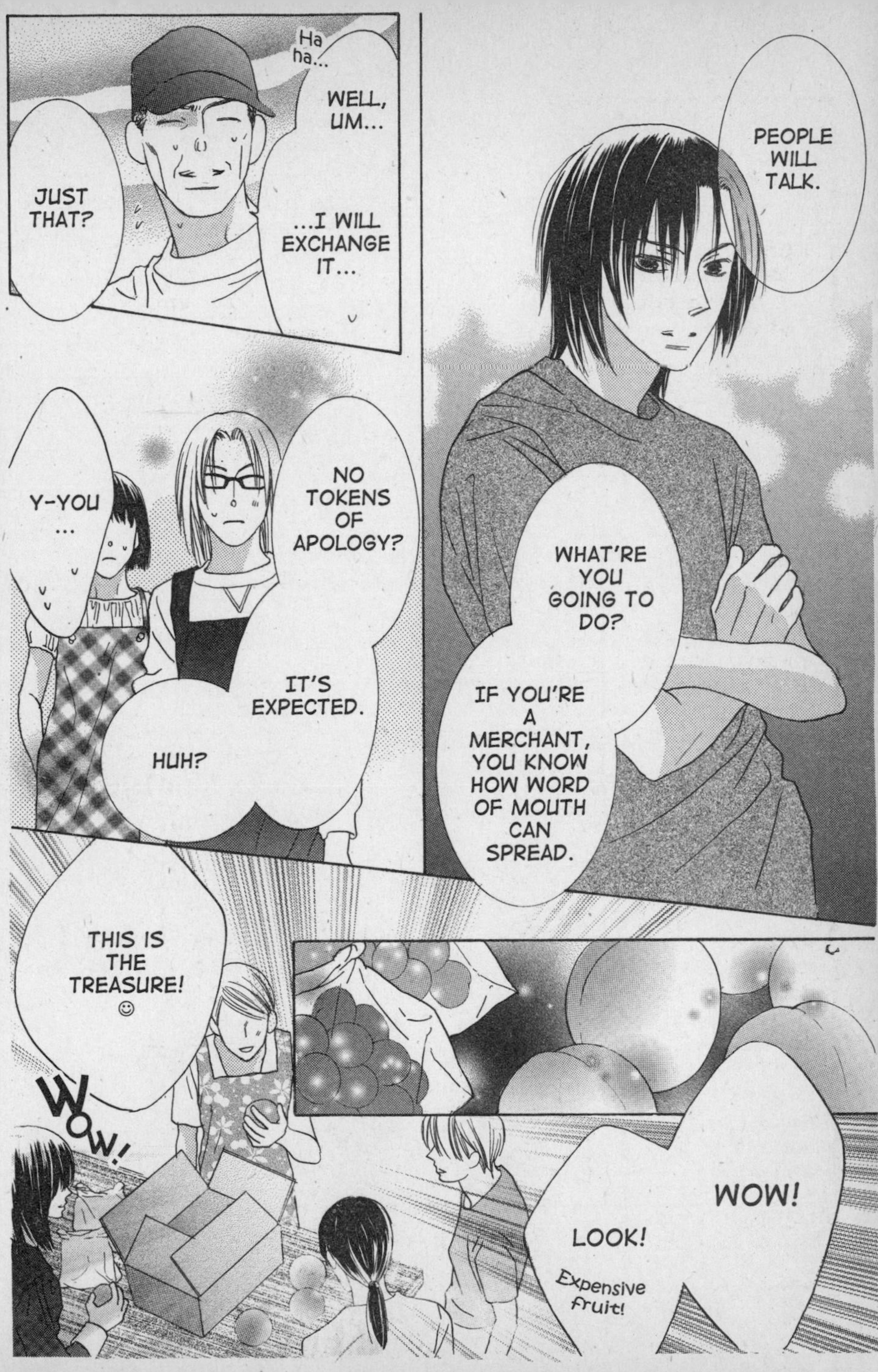
PEOPLE WILL TALK.
WHAT'RE YOU GOING TO DO?
IF YOU'RE A MERCHANT, YOU KNOW HOW WORD OF MOUTH CAN SPREAD.
Ha ha...
WELL, UM...
...I WILL EXCHANGE IT...
JUST THAT?
NO TOKENS OF APOLOGY?
IT'S EXPECTED.
Y-YOU ...
HUH?
WOW!
LOOK!
Expensive fruit!
THIS IS THE TREASURE! ☺
WOW!

② Copy the illustration on a clean sheet of paper.

I use KMK Kent paper, which you can get at an art supply store.

Then, I copy the illustration by shining light through my rough sketch. Now I use a lightbox, which is a tool just for this purpose, but a long time ago, I used to do it using a window on a sunny day. Ha ha. (You can tell I was poor then.)

By the way, I am really not good at doing this part of the process, and no matter how hard I try, the rough sketch and the clean sketch doesn't turn out the same.
It must be my looseness.
(Declaration!)

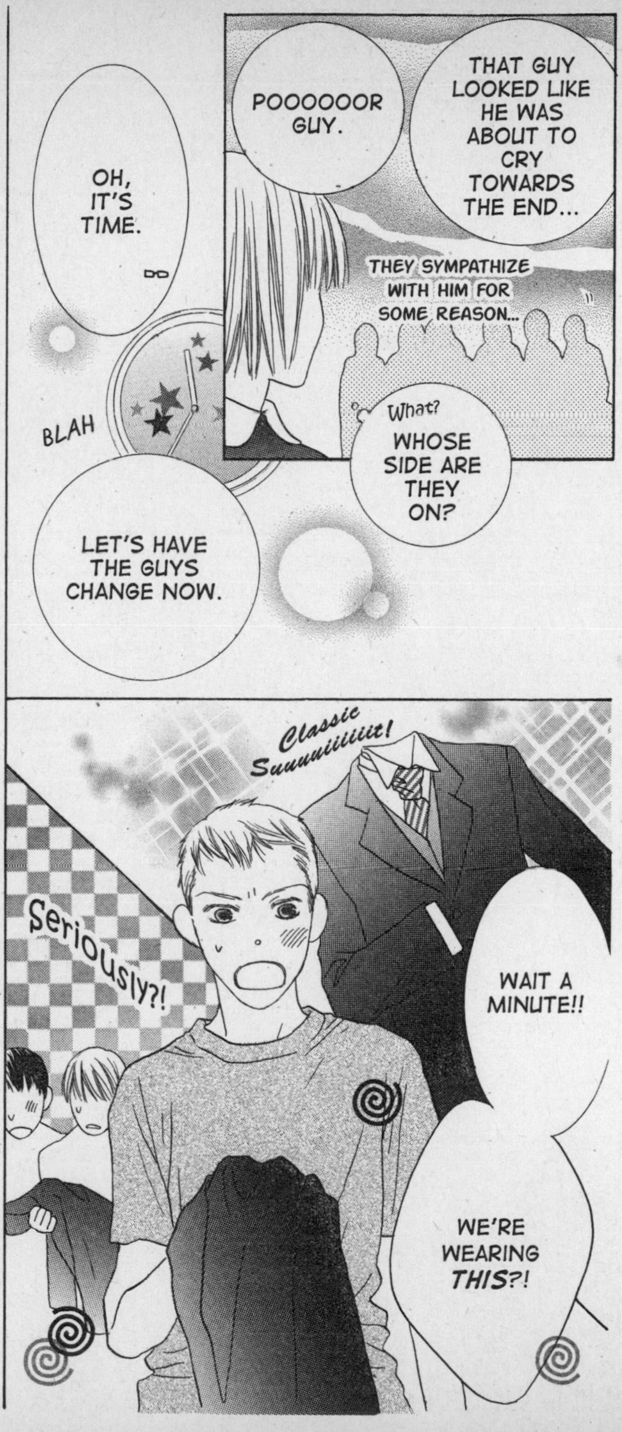
THAT GUY LOOKED LIKE HE WAS ABOUT TO CRY TOWARDS THE END...
POOOOOOR GUY.
THEY SYMPATHIZE WITH HIM FOR SOME REASON...
What?
WHOSE SIDE ARE THEY ON?
OH, IT'S TIME.
BLAH
LET'S HAVE THE GUYS CHANGE NOW.
Classic Suuuuiiiiiit!
WAIT A MINUTE!!
WE'RE WEARING *THIS*?!
Seriously?!

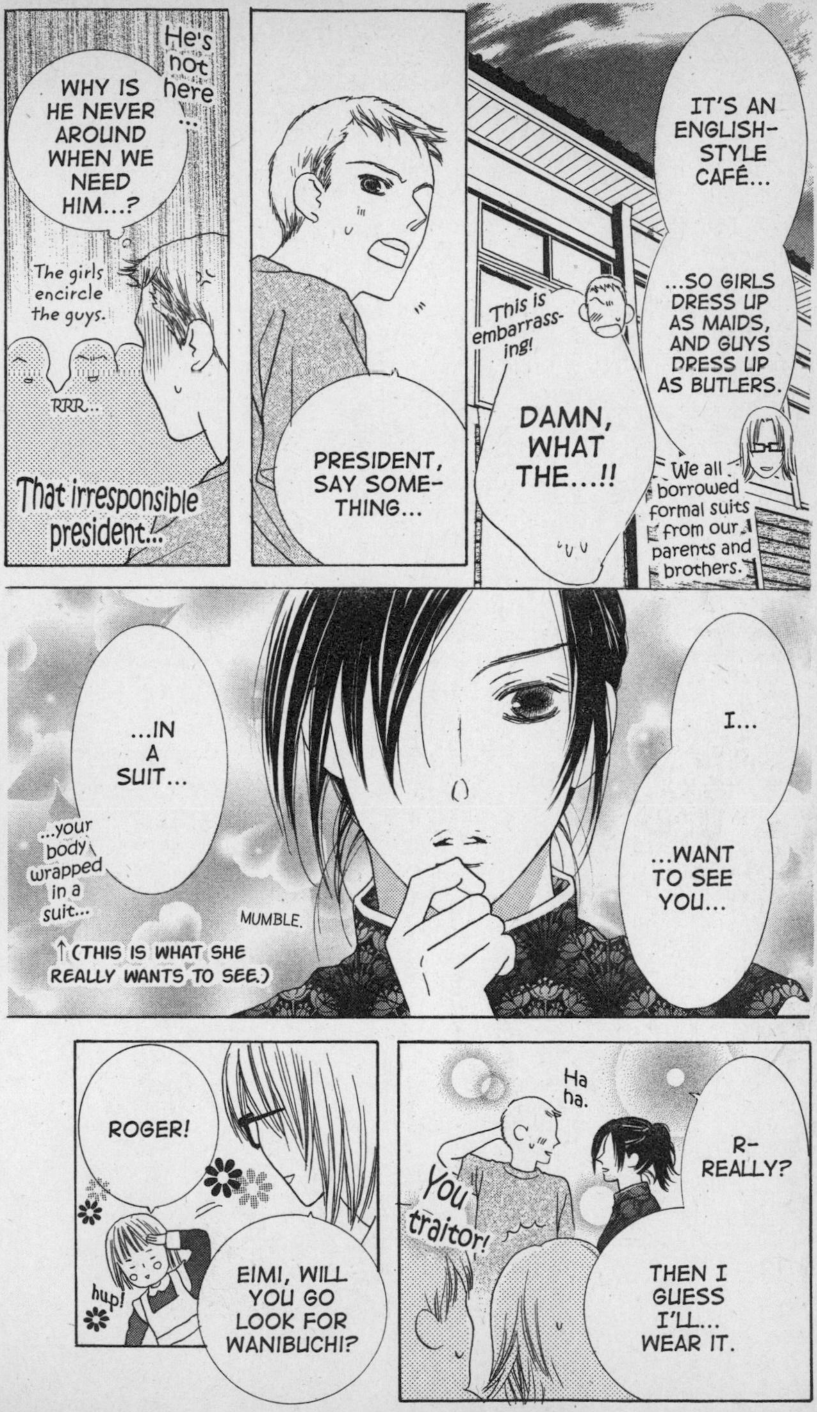
IT'S AN ENGLISH-STYLE CAFÉ...
...SO GIRLS DRESS UP AS MAIDS, AND GUYS DRESS UP AS BUTLERS.
We all borrowed formal suits from our parents and brothers.
This is embarrassing!
DAMN, WHAT THE...!!
PRESIDENT, SAY SOME-THING...
He's not here...
WHY IS HE NEVER AROUND WHEN WE NEED HIM...?
The girls encircle the guys.
RRR...
That irresponsible president...
I...
...WANT TO SEE YOU...
...IN A SUIT...
...your body wrapped in a suit...
MUMBLE.
↑(THIS IS WHAT SHE REALLY WANTS TO SEE.)
R-REALLY?
THEN I GUESS I'LL... WEAR IT.
Ha ha.
You traitor!
EIMI, WILL YOU GO LOOK FOR WANIBUCHI?
ROGER!
hup!

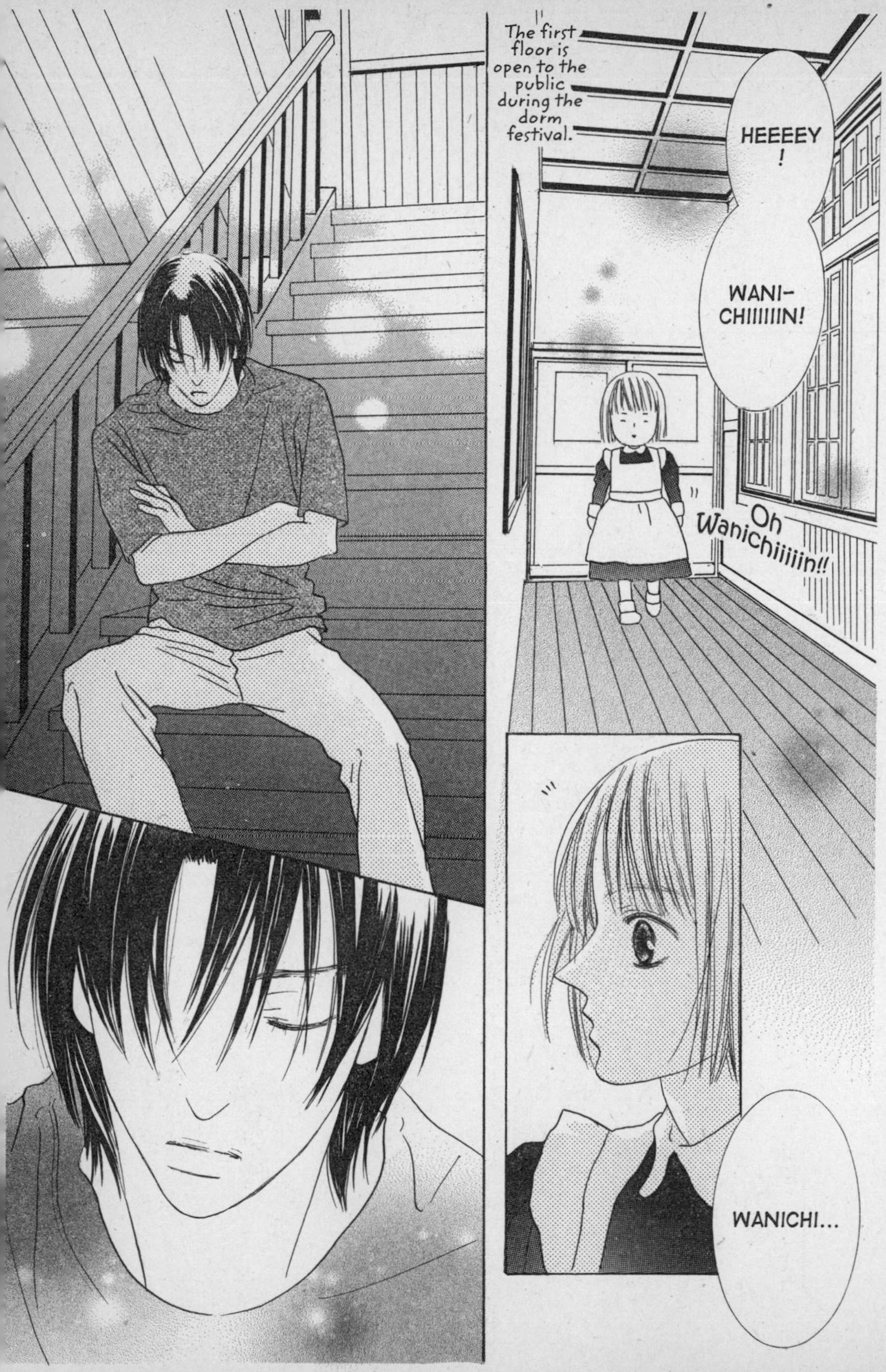
The first floor is open to the public during the dorm festival.
HEEEEY!
WANI-CHIIIIIIN!
Oh Wanichiiiiiin!!
WANICHI...

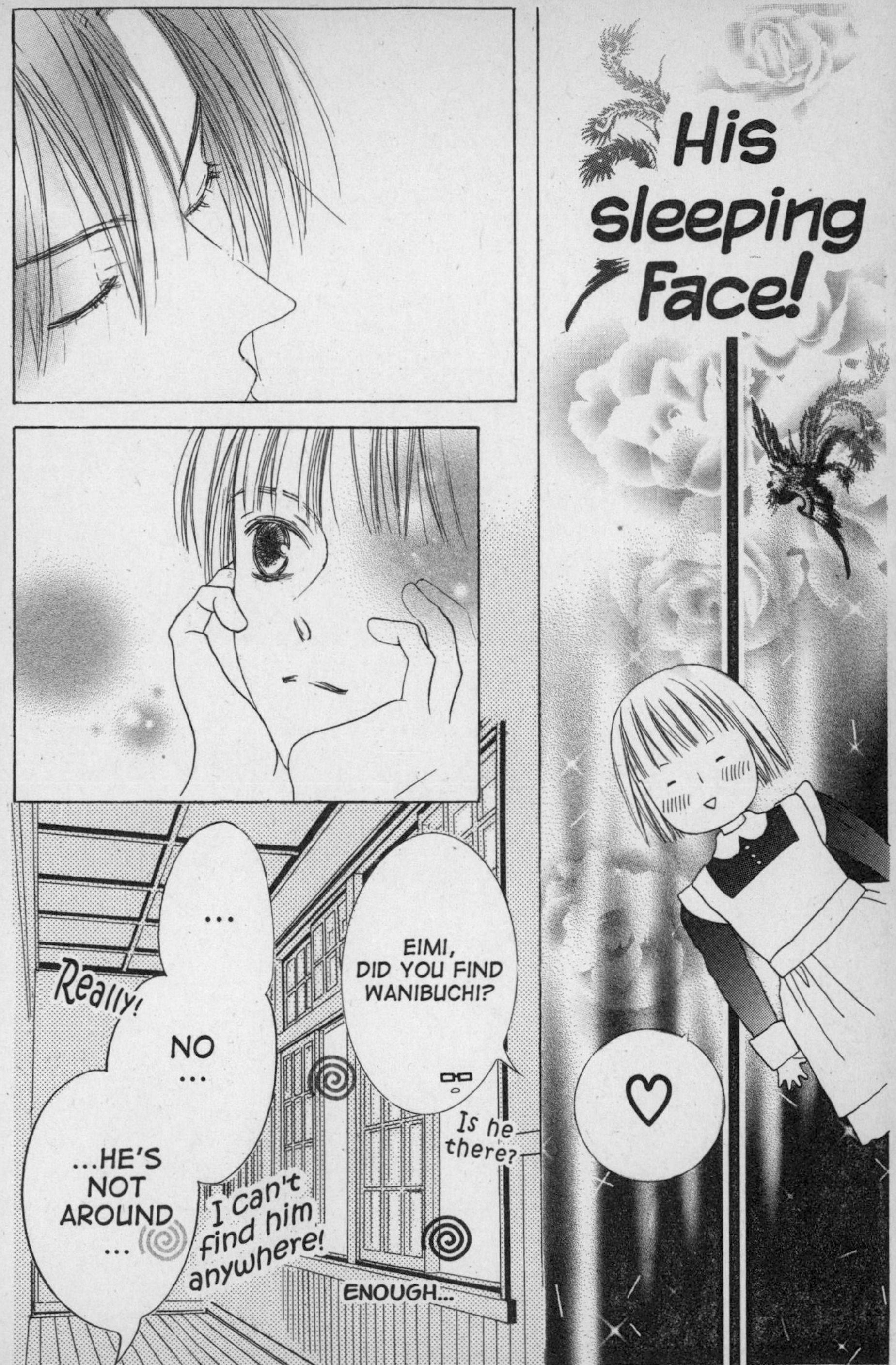
His sleeping Face!
♡
EIMI, DID YOU FIND WANIBUCHI?
Is he there?
...
Really!
NO ...
...HE'S NOT AROUND ...
I can't find him anywhere!
ENOUGH...

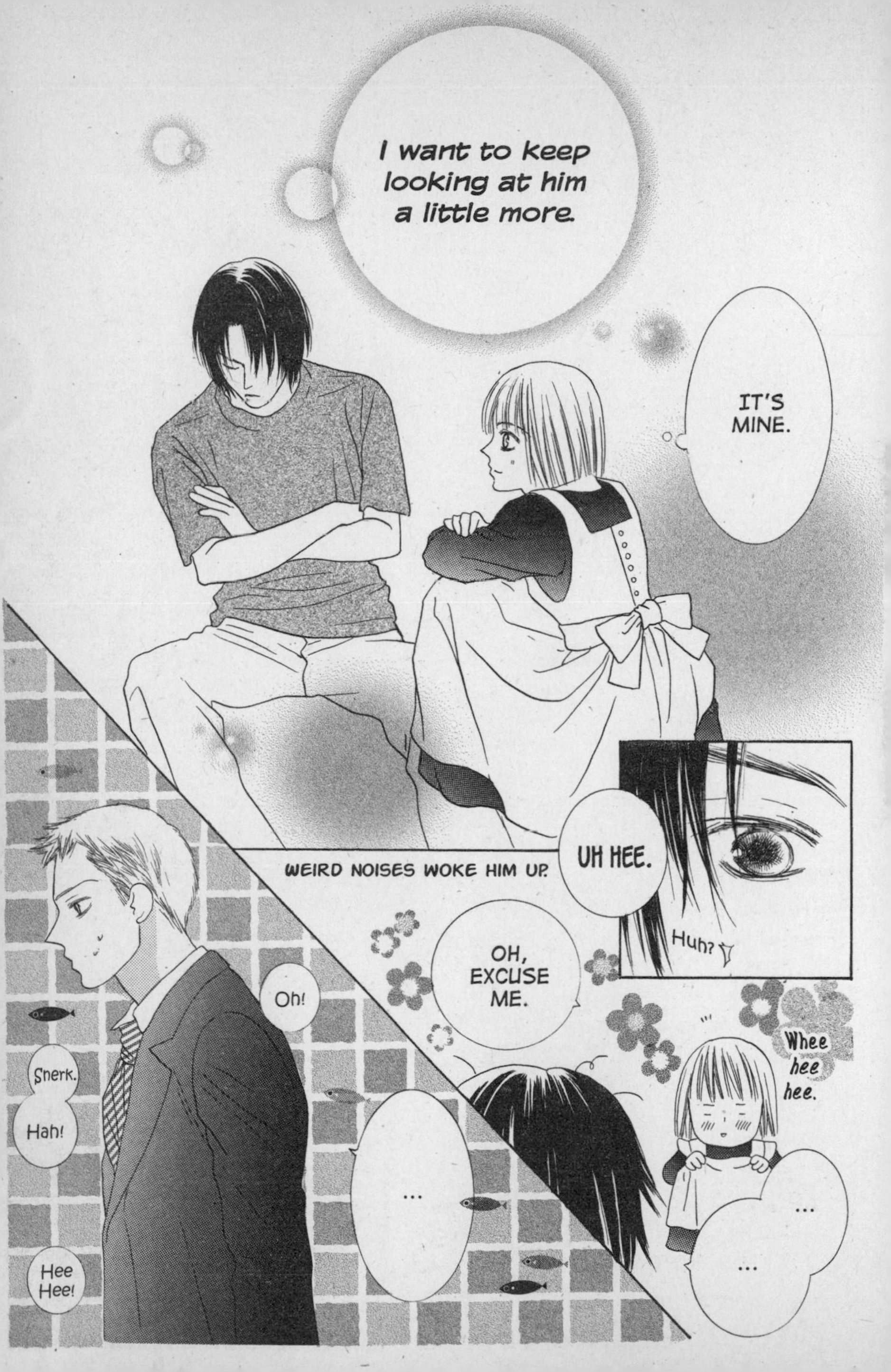
I want to keep looking at him a little more.
IT'S MINE.
WEIRD NOISES WOKE HIM UP.
UH HEE.
Huh?
OH, EXCUSE ME.
Whee hee hee.
...
...
...
Oh!
Snerk.
Hah!
Hee Hee!

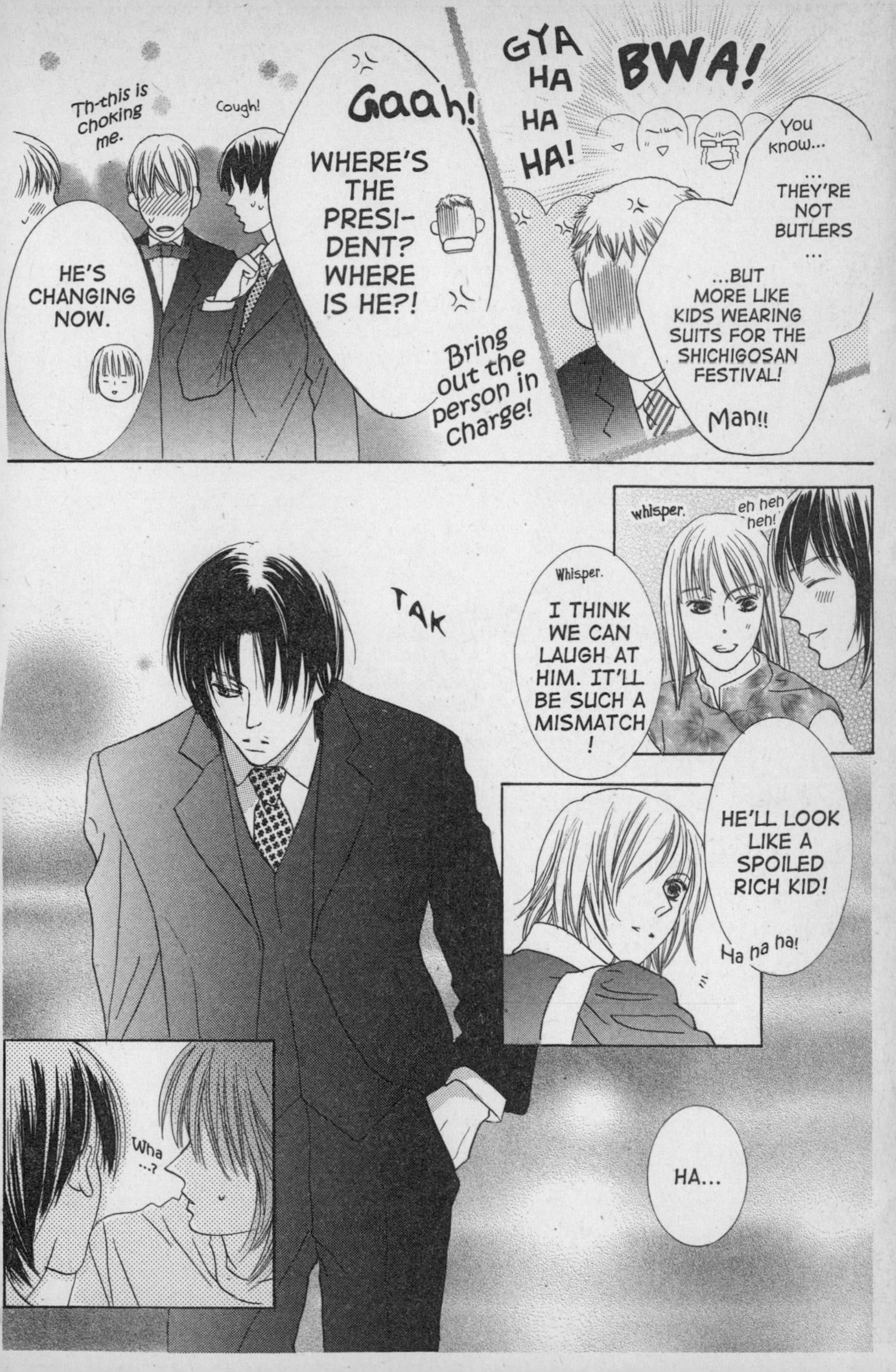
GYA HA HA HA!
BWA!
You know... ...THEY'RE NOT BUTLERS...
...BUT MORE LIKE KIDS WEARING SUITS FOR THE SHICHIGOSAN FESTIVAL!
Man!!
Gaah!
WHERE'S THE PRESI-DENT? WHERE IS HE?!
Bring out the person in charge!
Cough!
Th-this is choking me.
HE'S CHANGING NOW.
whisper.
eh heh heh!
Whisper.
I THINK WE CAN LAUGH AT HIM. IT'LL BE SUCH A MISMATCH!
HE'LL LOOK LIKE A SPOILED RICH KID!
Ha ha ha!
TAK
HA...
Wha...?

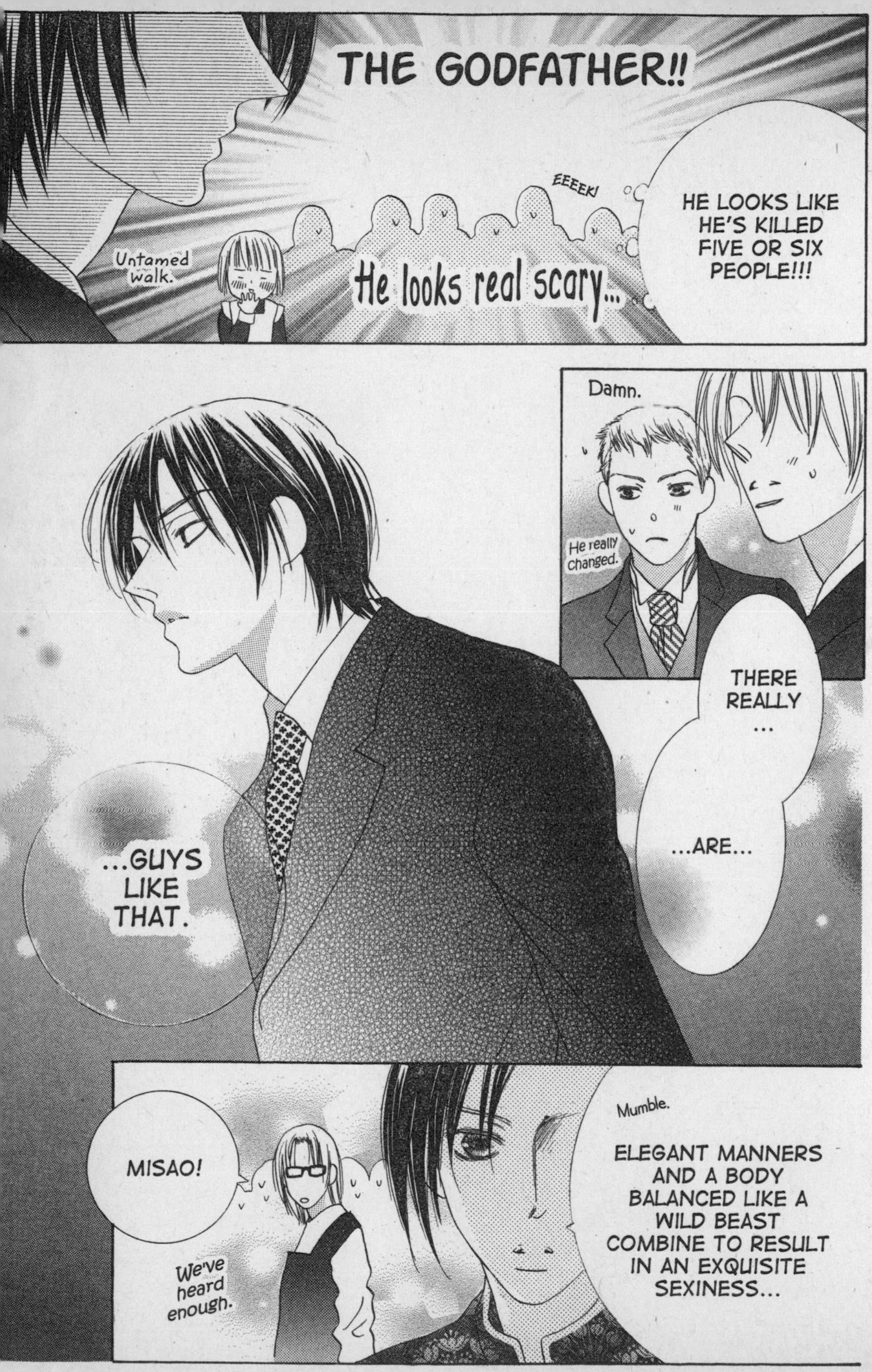
THE GODFATHER!!
HE LOOKS LIKE HE'S KILLED FIVE OR SIX PEOPLE!!!
EEEEK!
He looks real scary...
Untamed walk.
Damn.
He really changed.
THERE REALLY ...
...ARE...
...GUYS LIKE THAT.
Mumble.
ELEGANT MANNERS AND A BODY BALANCED LIKE A WILD BEAST COMBINE TO RESULT IN AN EXQUISITE SEXINESS...
MISAO!
We've heard enough.

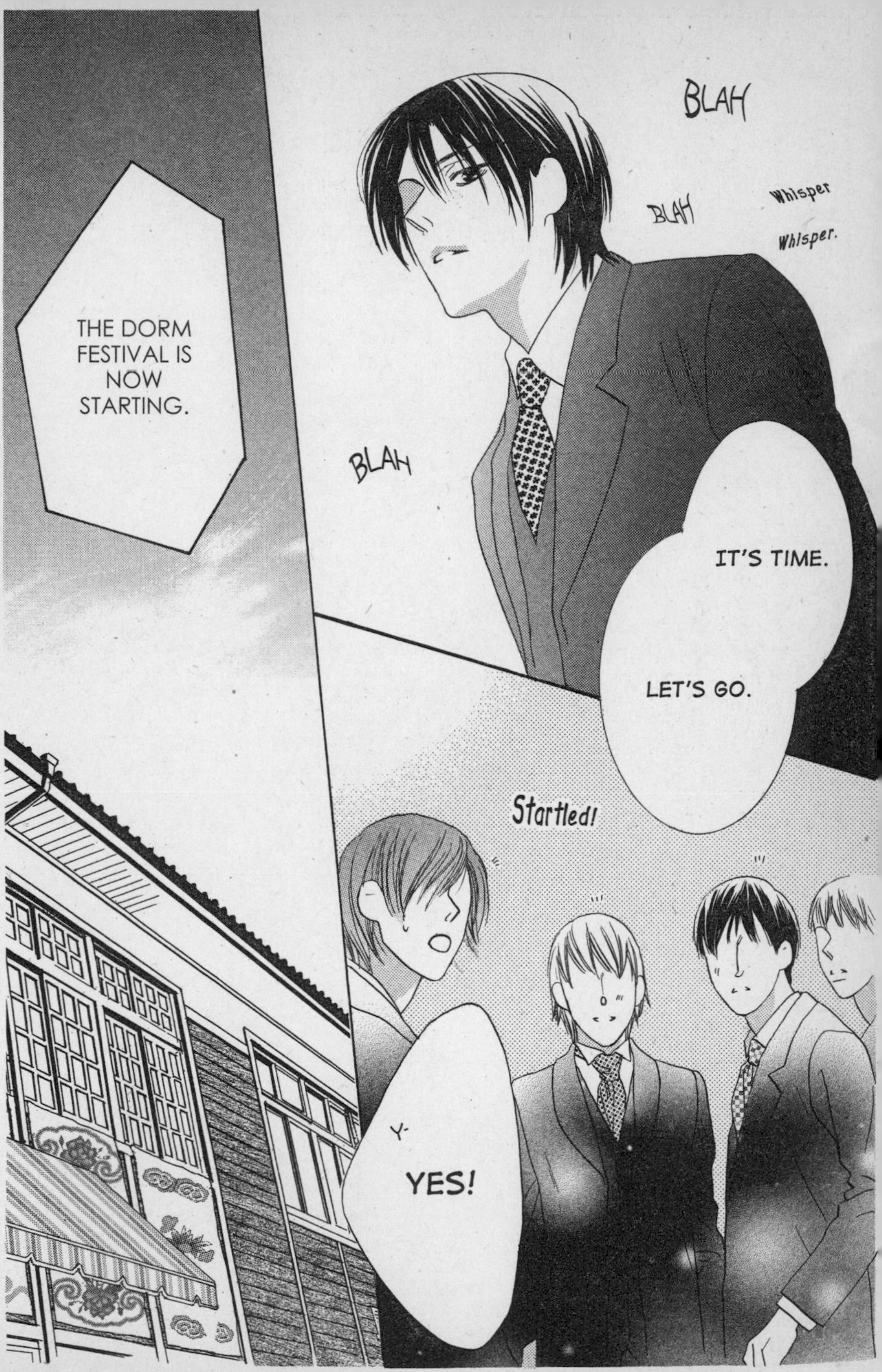
BLAH
BLAH
Whisper
Whisper.
BLAH
IT'S TIME.
LET'S GO.
Startled!
Y-
YES!
THE DORM FESTIVAL IS NOW STARTING.

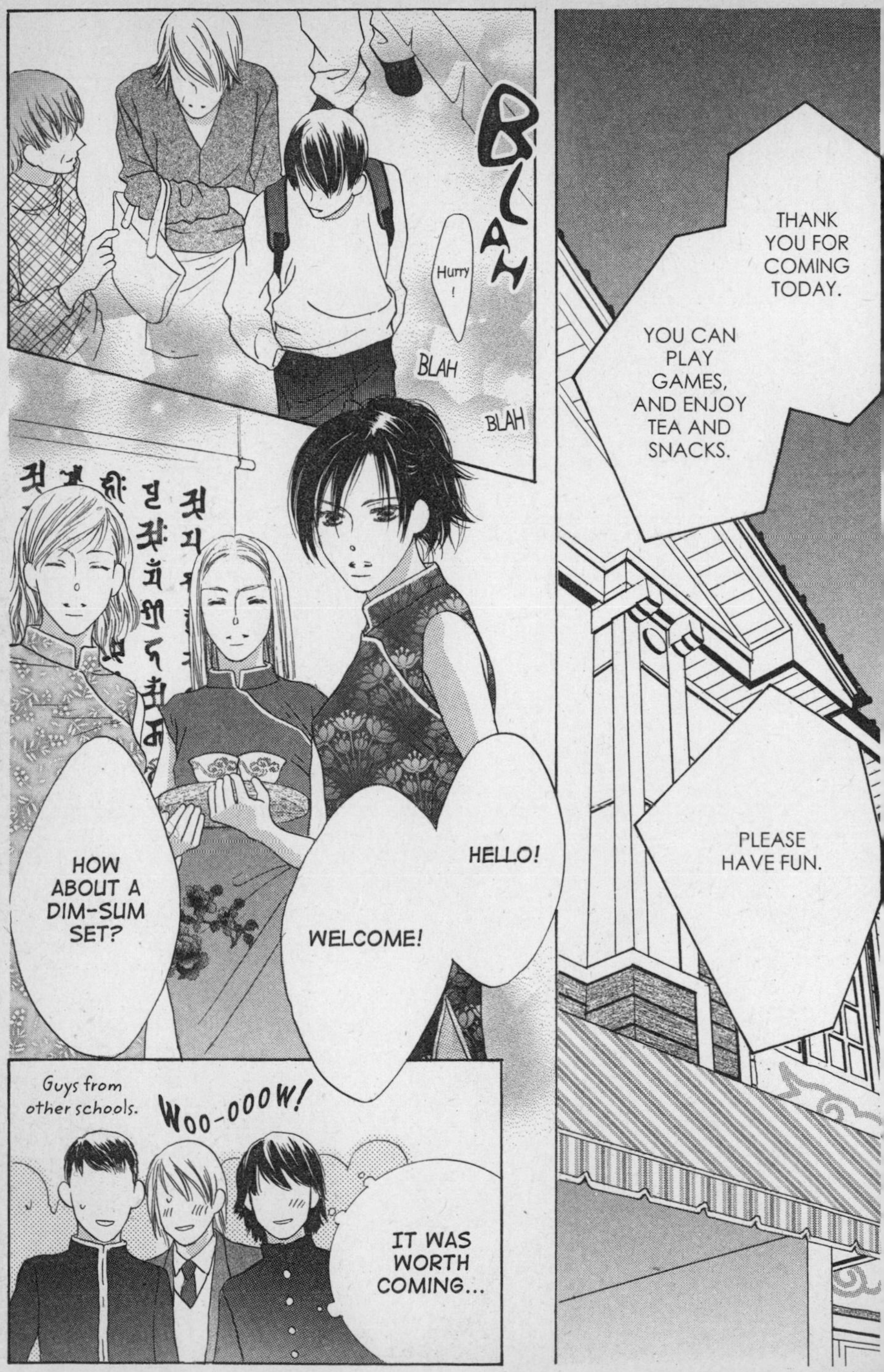
THANK YOU FOR COMING TODAY.
YOU CAN PLAY GAMES, AND ENJOY TEA AND SNACKS.
PLEASE HAVE FUN.
BLAH
Hurry!
BLAH
BLAH
HELLO!
WELCOME!
HOW ABOUT A DIM-SUM SET?
WOO-OOOW!
Guys from other schools.
IT WAS WORTH COMING...

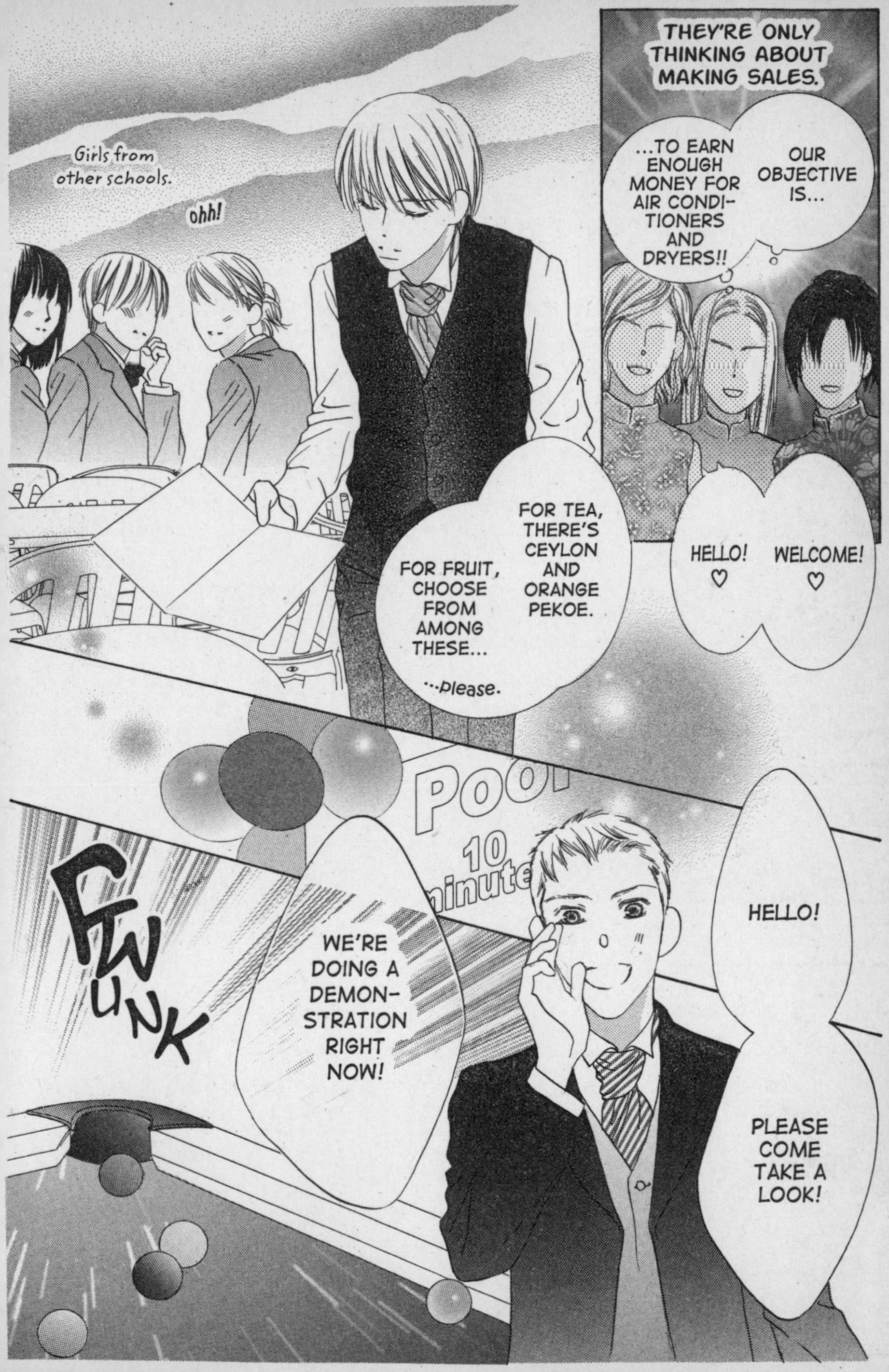
THEY'RE ONLY THINKING ABOUT MAKING SALES.
OUR OBJECTIVE IS...
...TO EARN ENOUGH MONEY FOR AIR CONDITIONERS AND DRYERS!!
WELCOME! ♡
HELLO! ♡
Girls from other schools.
ohh!
FOR TEA, THERE'S CEYLON AND ORANGE PEKOE.
FOR FRUIT, CHOOSE FROM AMONG THESE...
...please.
HELLO!
PLEASE COME TAKE A LOOK!
10
WE'RE DOING A DEMONSTRATION RIGHT NOW!
FWUNK

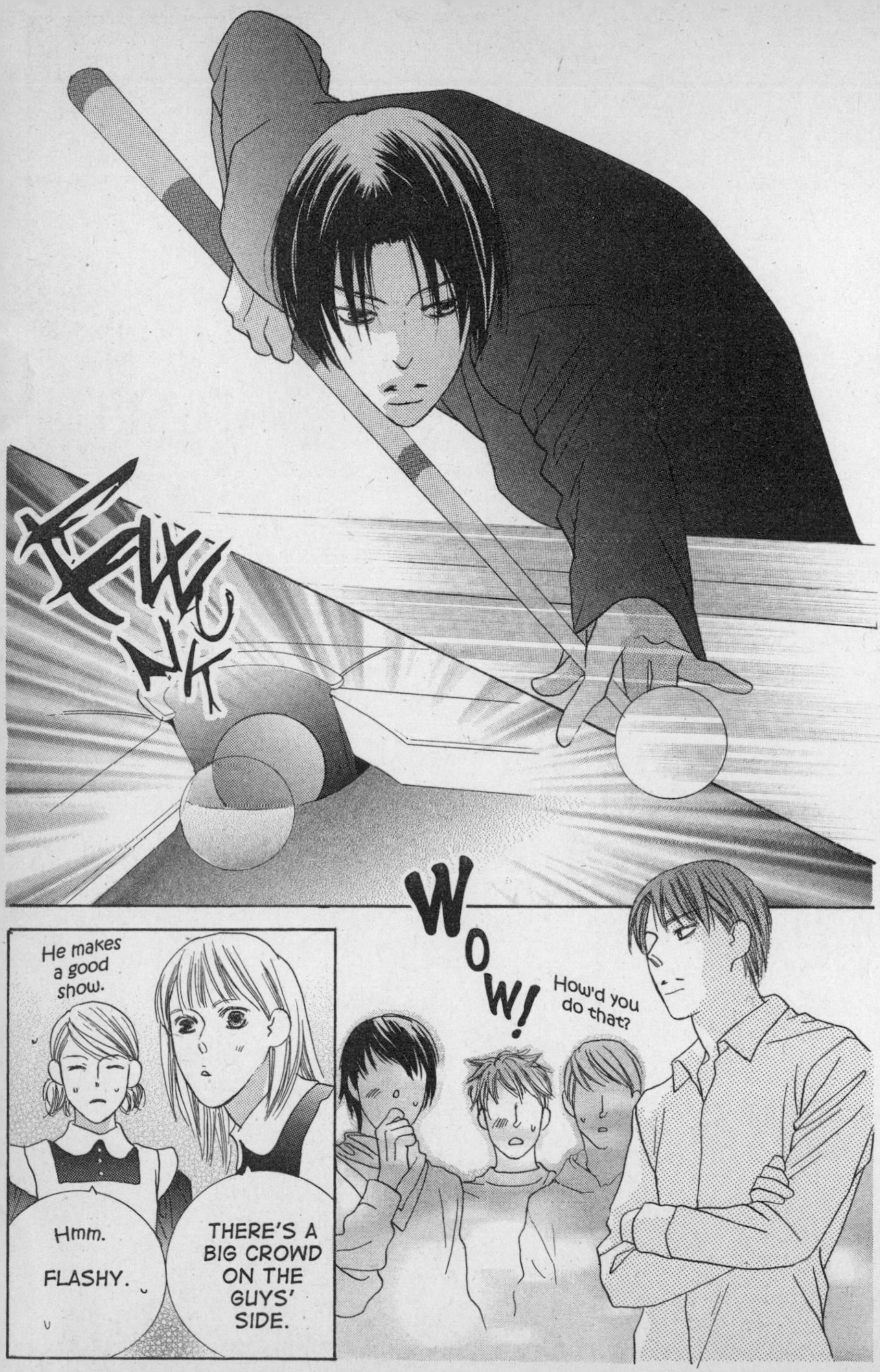
THWUNK
WOW!
How'd you do that?
THERE'S A BIG CROWD ON THE GUYS' SIDE.
Hmm.
FLASHY.
He makes a good show.

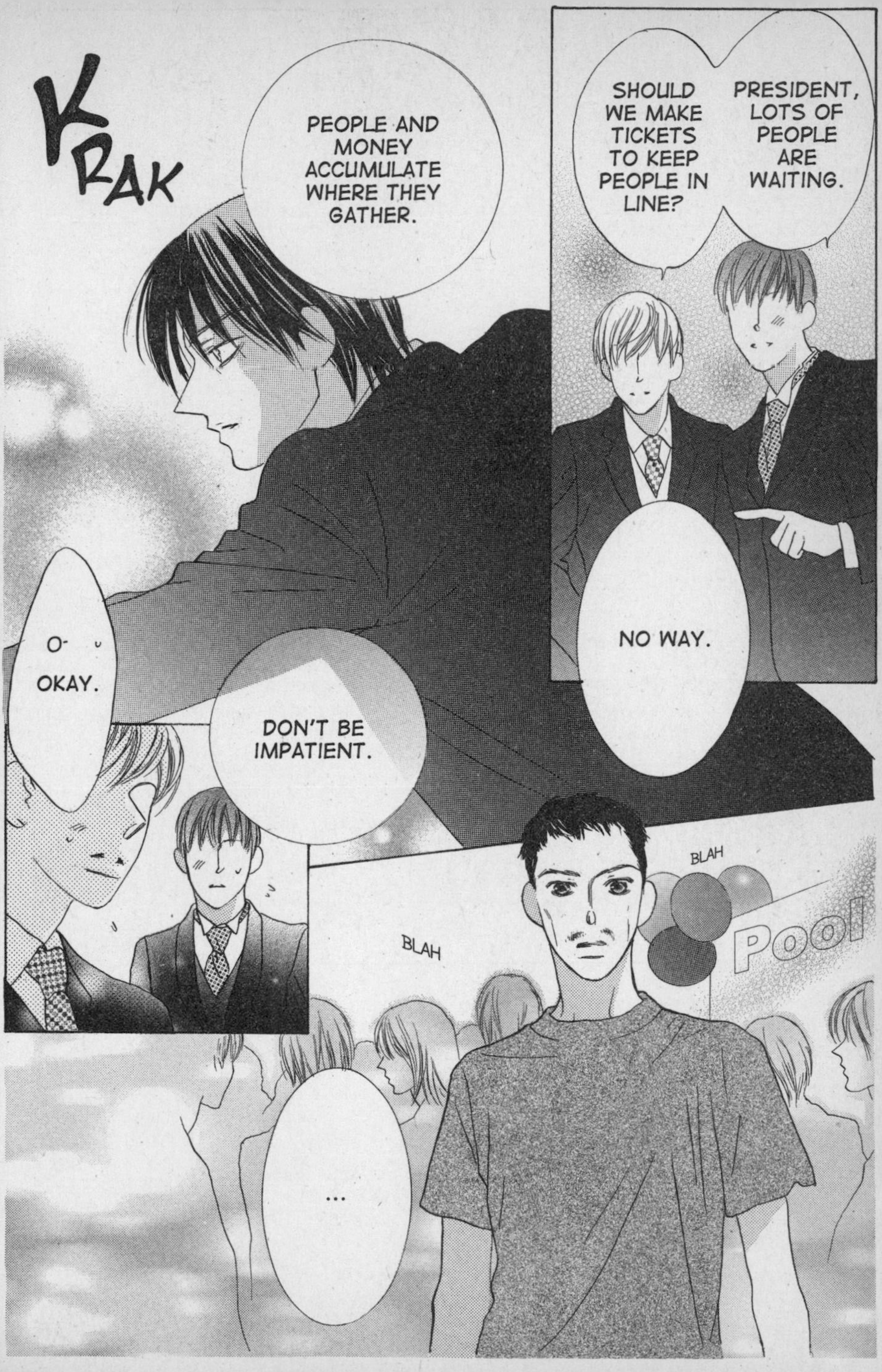
PRESIDENT, LOTS OF PEOPLE ARE WAITING.
SHOULD WE MAKE TICKETS TO KEEP PEOPLE IN LINE?
NO WAY.
KRAK
PEOPLE AND MONEY ACCUMULATE WHERE THEY GATHER.
DON'T BE IMPATIENT.
O- OKAY.
BLAH
Pool
BLAH
...

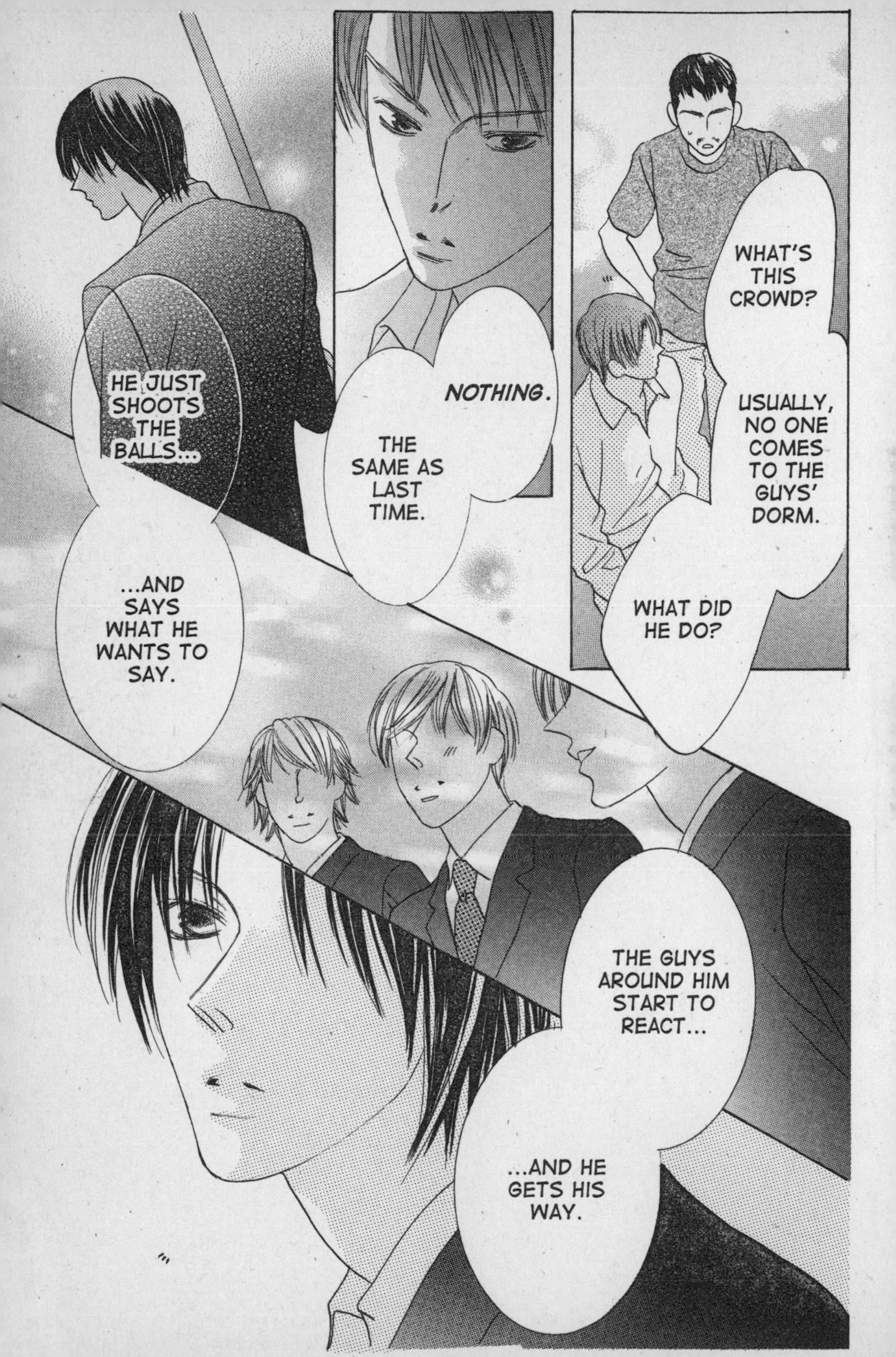
WHAT'S THIS CROWD?
USUALLY, NO ONE COMES TO THE GUYS' DORM.
WHAT DID HE DO?
NOTHING.
THE SAME AS LAST TIME.
HE JUST SHOOTS THE BALLS...
...AND SAYS WHAT HE WANTS TO SAY.
THE GUYS AROUND HIM START TO REACT...
...AND HE GETS HIS WAY.

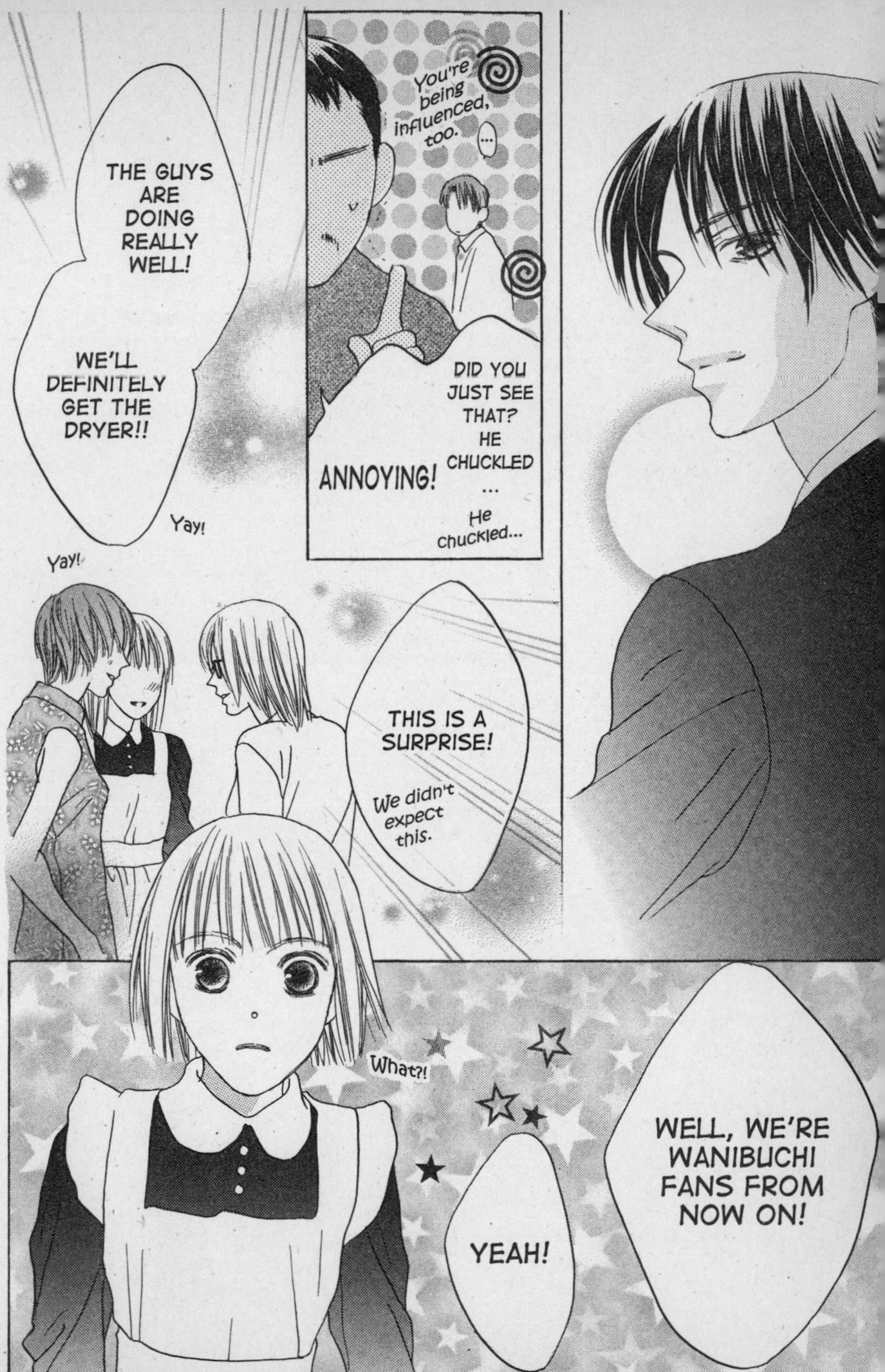
You're being influenced, too.
...
DID YOU JUST SEE THAT? HE CHUCKLED ...
He chuckled...
ANNOYING!
THE GUYS ARE DOING REALLY WELL!
WE'LL DEFINITELY GET THE DRYER!!
Yay!
Yay!
THIS IS A SURPRISE!
We didn't expect this.
WELL, WE'RE WANIBUCHI FANS FROM NOW ON!
YEAH!
What?!

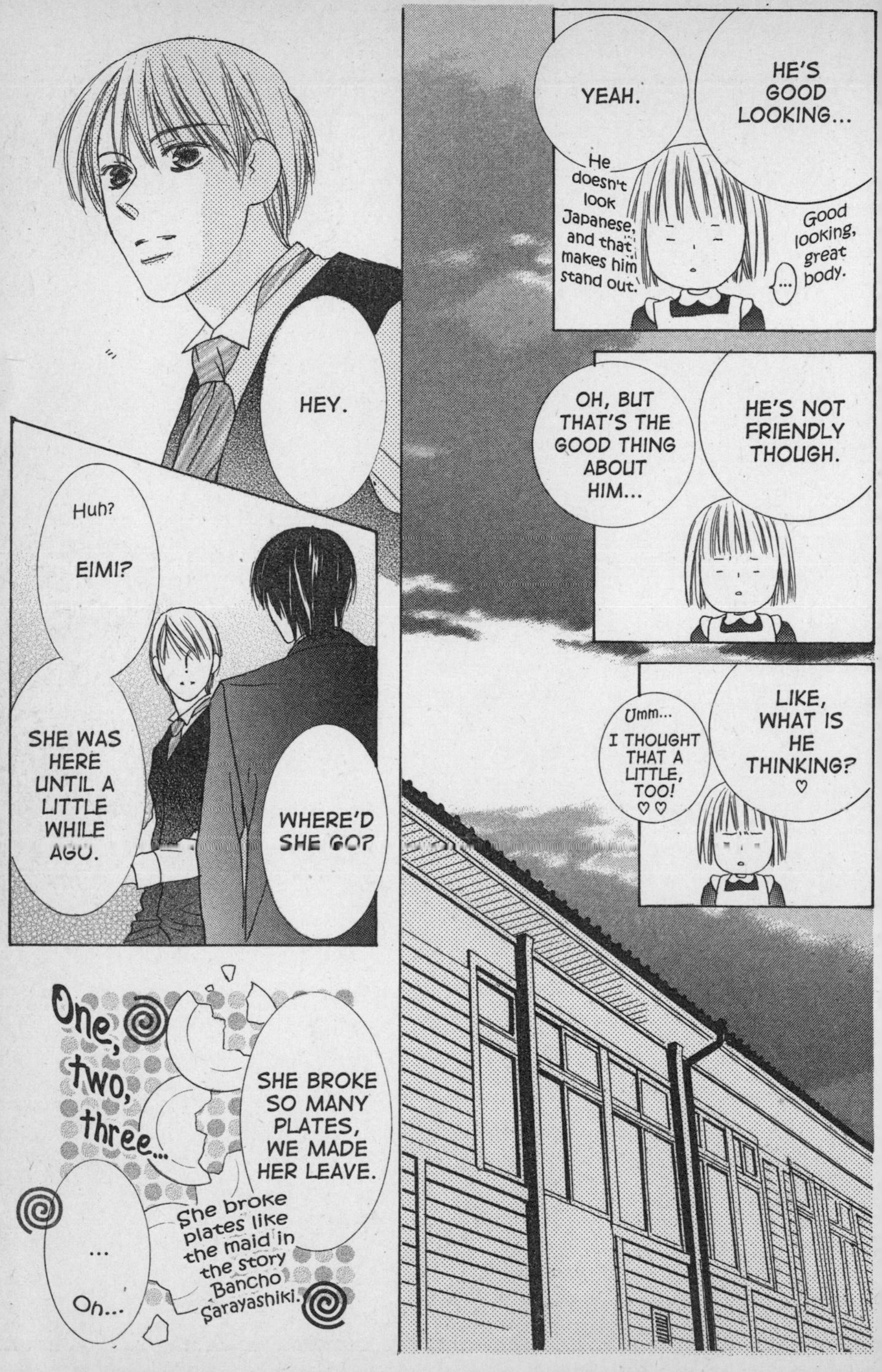
HE'S GOOD LOOKING...
YEAH.
Good looking, great body.
...
He doesn't look Japanese, and that makes him stand out.
HE'S NOT FRIENDLY THOUGH.
OH, BUT THAT'S THE GOOD THING ABOUT HIM...
LIKE, WHAT IS HE THINKING? ♡
Umm... I THOUGHT THAT A LITTLE, TOO! ♡ ♡
HEY.
Huh?
EIMI?
WHERE'D SHE GO?
SHE WAS HERE UNTIL A LITTLE WHILE AGO.
SHE BROKE SO MANY PLATES, WE MADE HER LEAVE.
One, two, three...
...
Oh...
She broke plates like the maid in the story Bancho Sarayashiki.

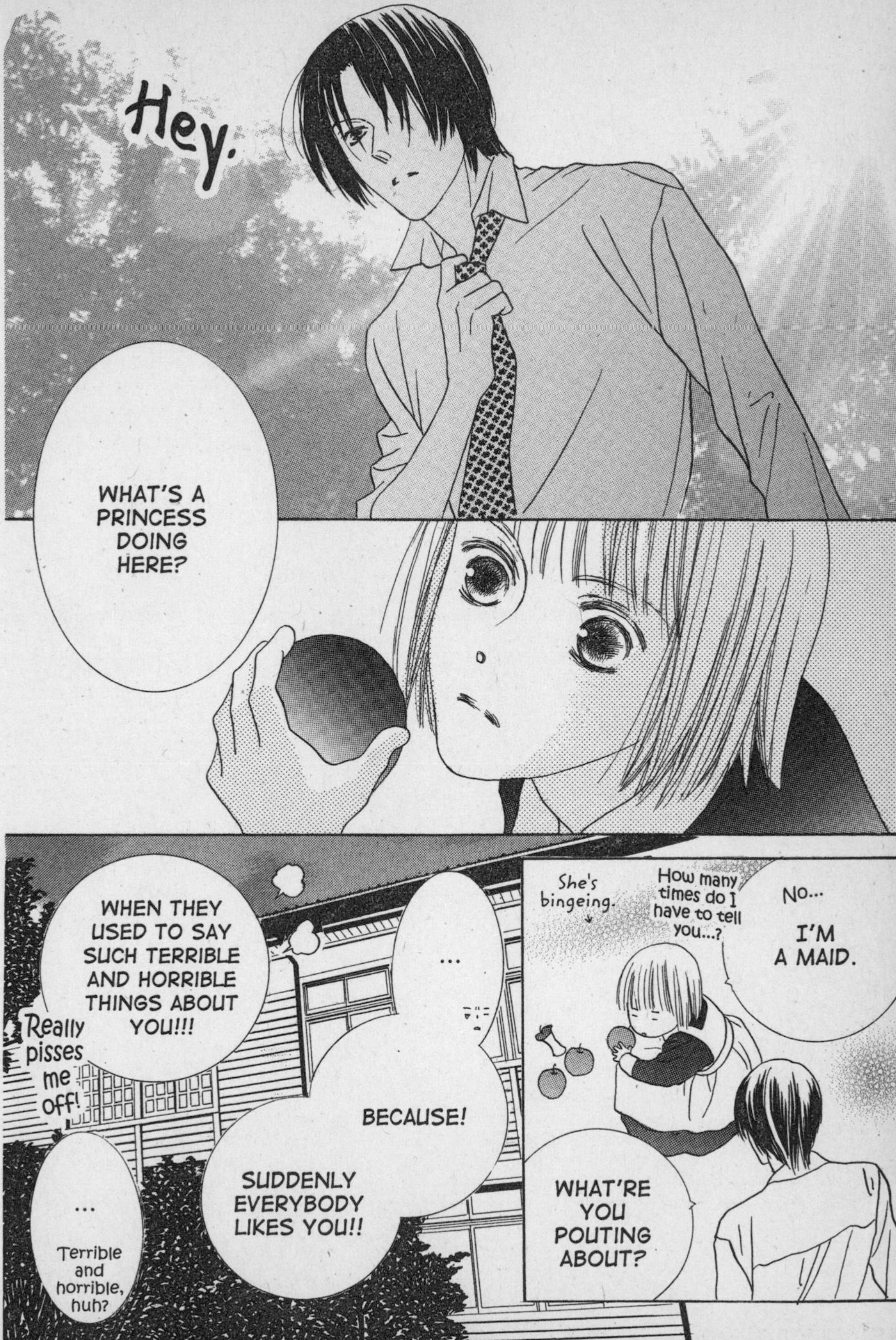
Hey.
WHAT'S A PRINCESS DOING HERE?
No... I'M A MAID.
How many times do I have to tell you...?
She's bingeing.
WHAT'RE YOU POUTING ABOUT?
...
BECAUSE!
SUDDENLY EVERYBODY LIKES YOU!!
WHEN THEY USED TO SAY SUCH TERRIBLE AND HORRIBLE THINGS ABOUT YOU!!!
Really pisses me off!
...
Terrible and horrible, huh?

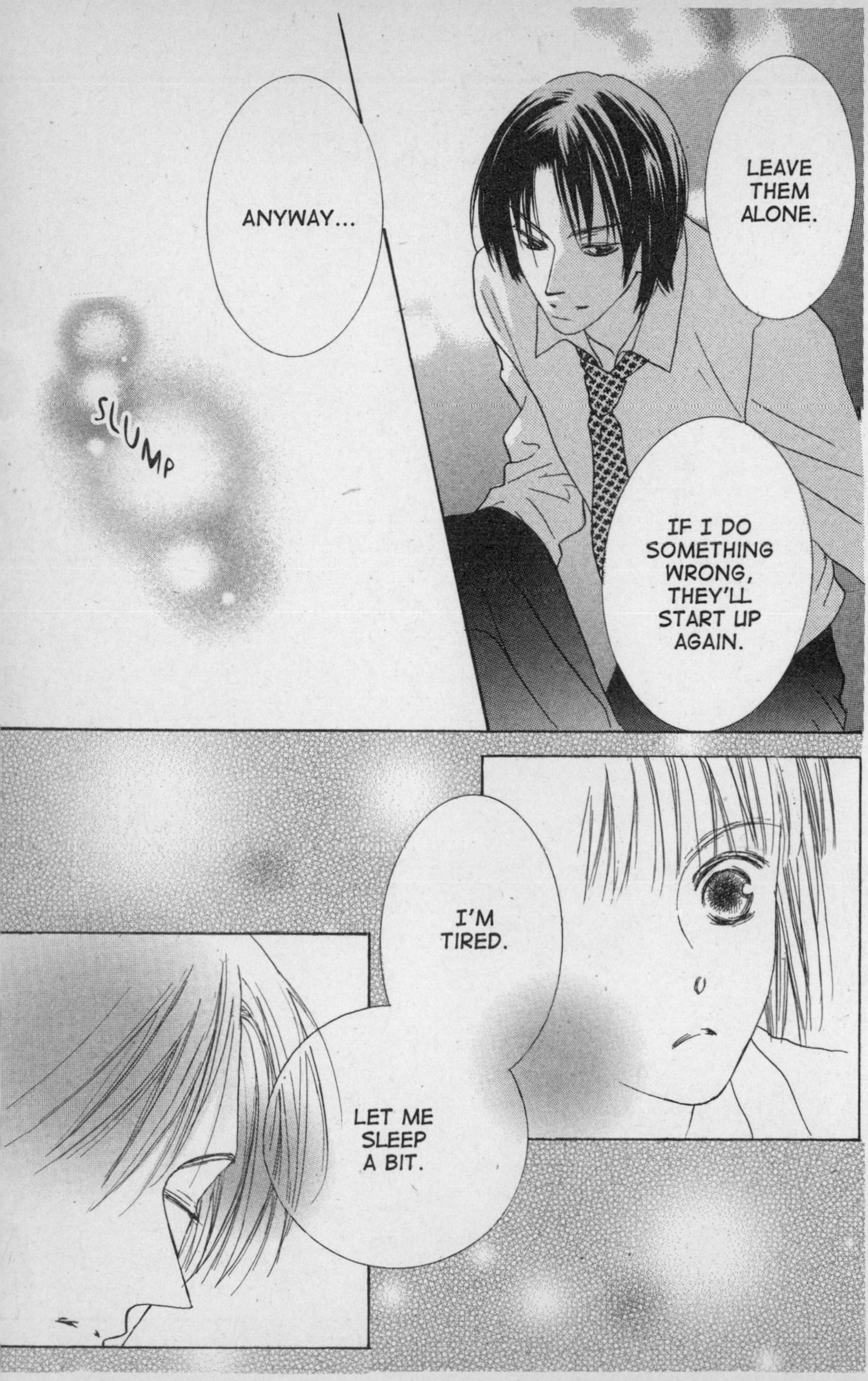
LEAVE THEM ALONE.
IF I DO SOMETHING WRONG, THEY'LL START UP AGAIN.
ANYWAY...
SLUMP
I'M TIRED.
LET ME SLEEP A BIT.

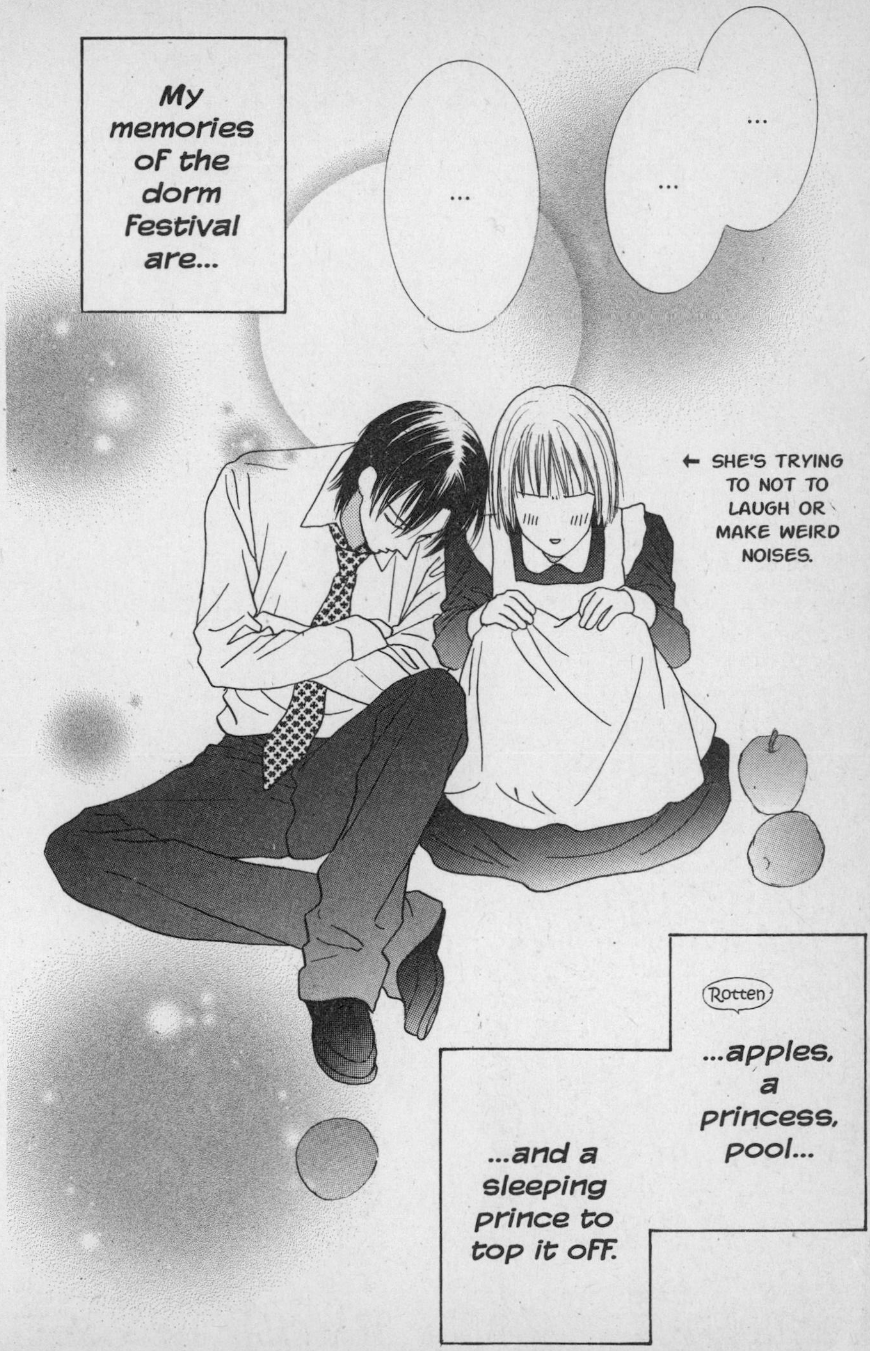
...
...
...
My memories of the dorm festival are...
← SHE'S TRYING TO NOT TO LAUGH OR MAKE WEIRD NOISES.
Rotten
...apples, a princess, pool...
...and a sleeping prince to top it off.

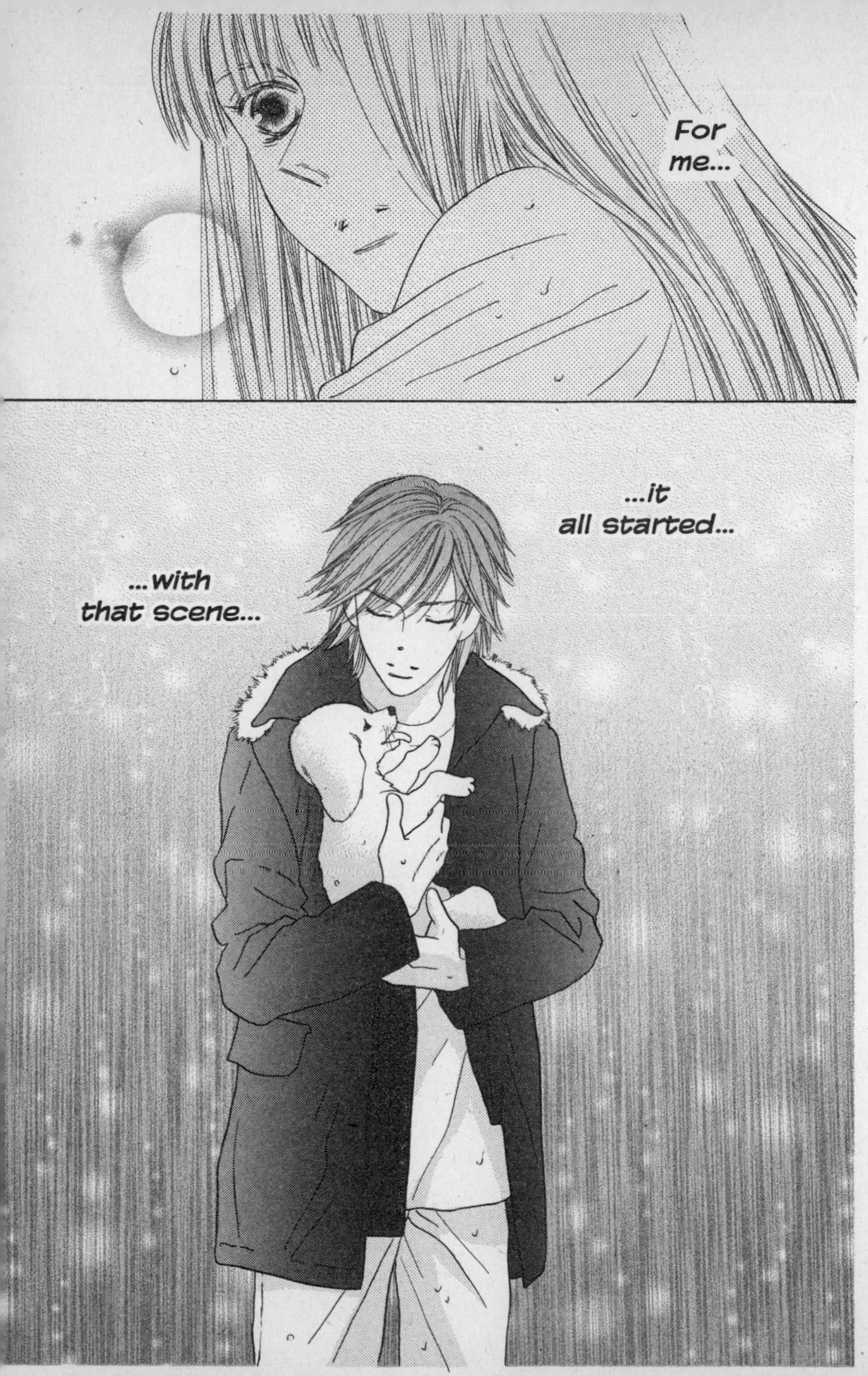
For me...
...it all started...
...with that scene...

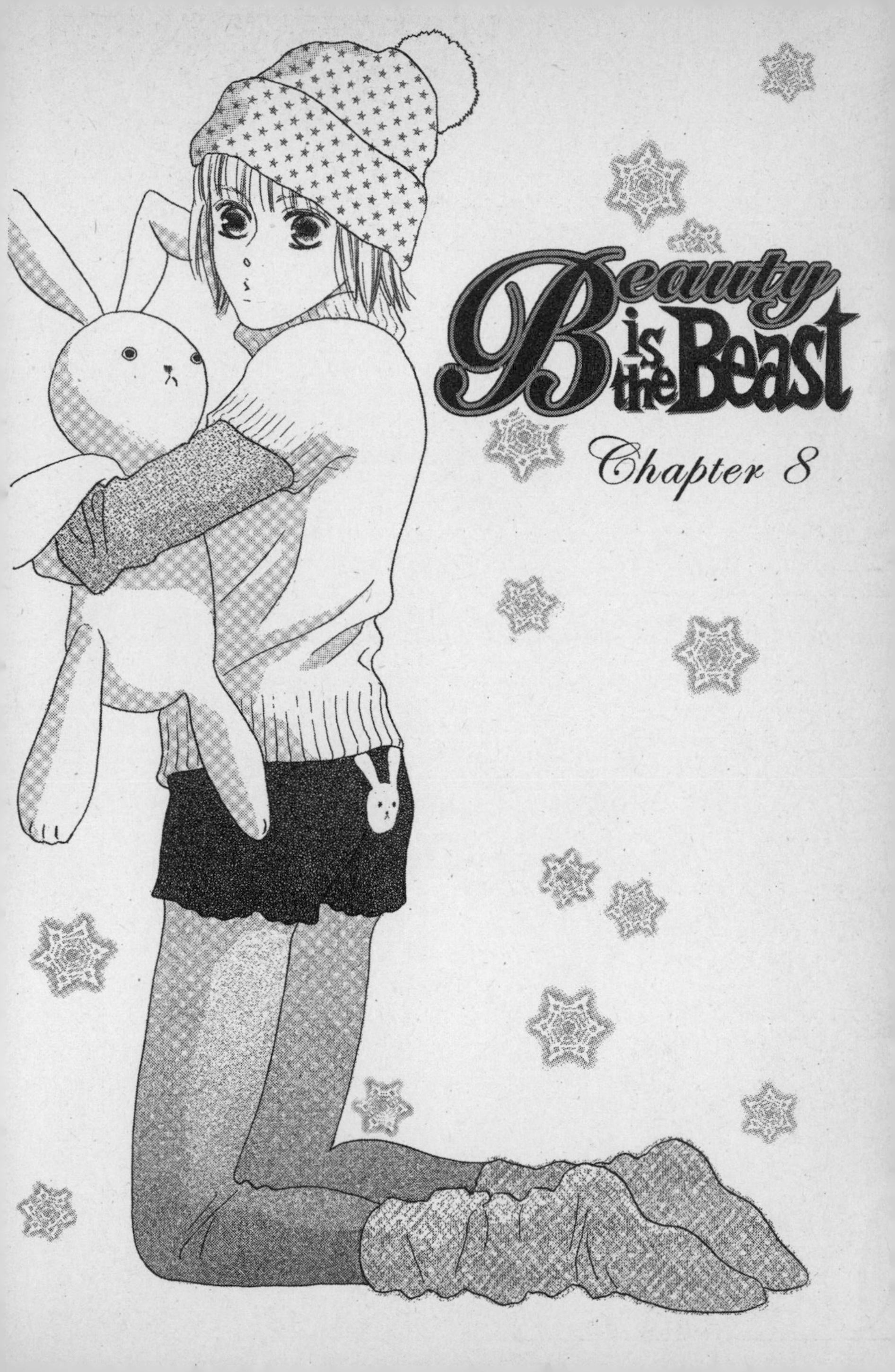
Beauty is the Beast
Chapter 8

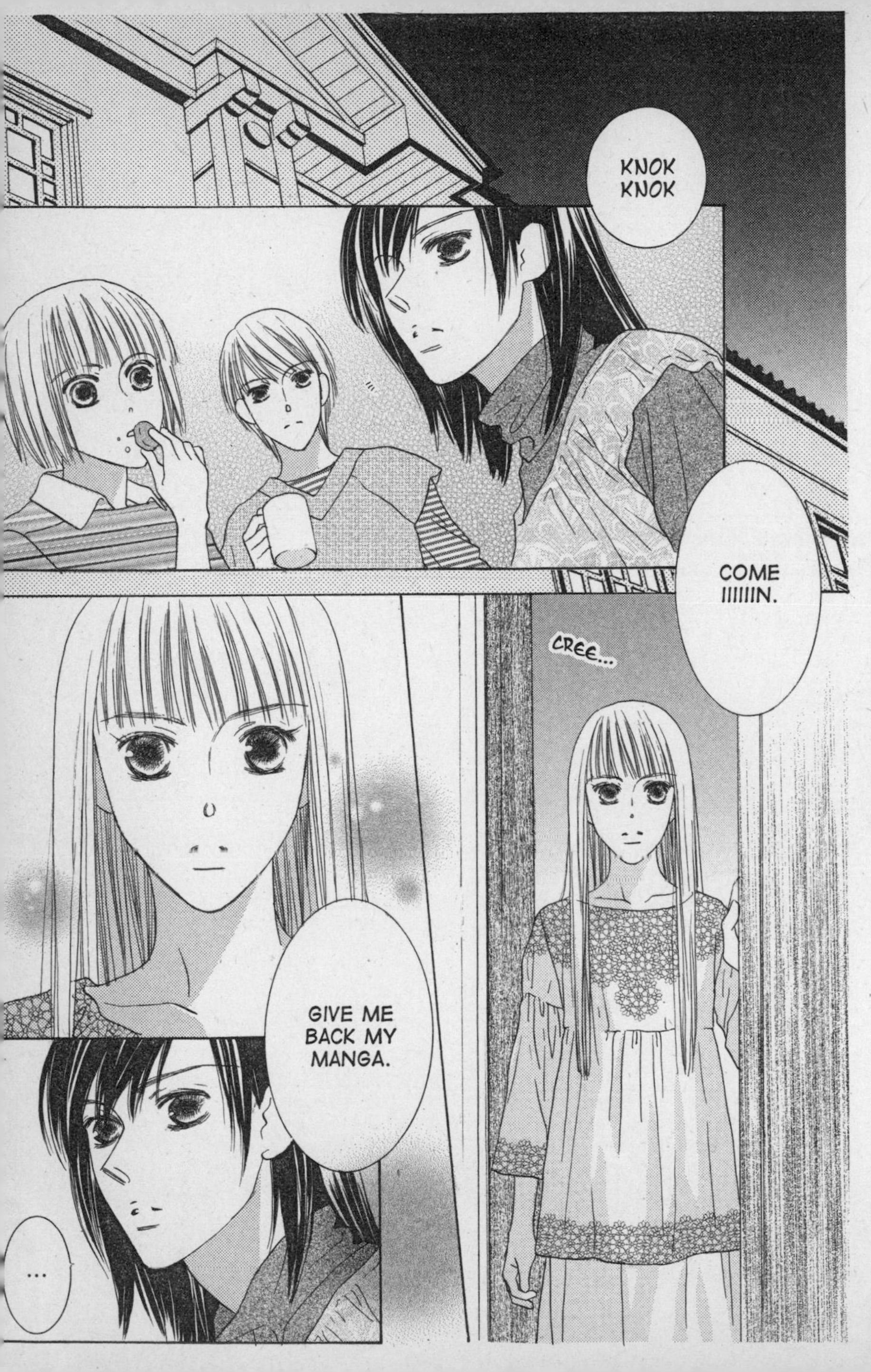
KNOK KNOK
COME IIIIIIN.
CREE...
GIVE ME BACK MY MANGA.
...

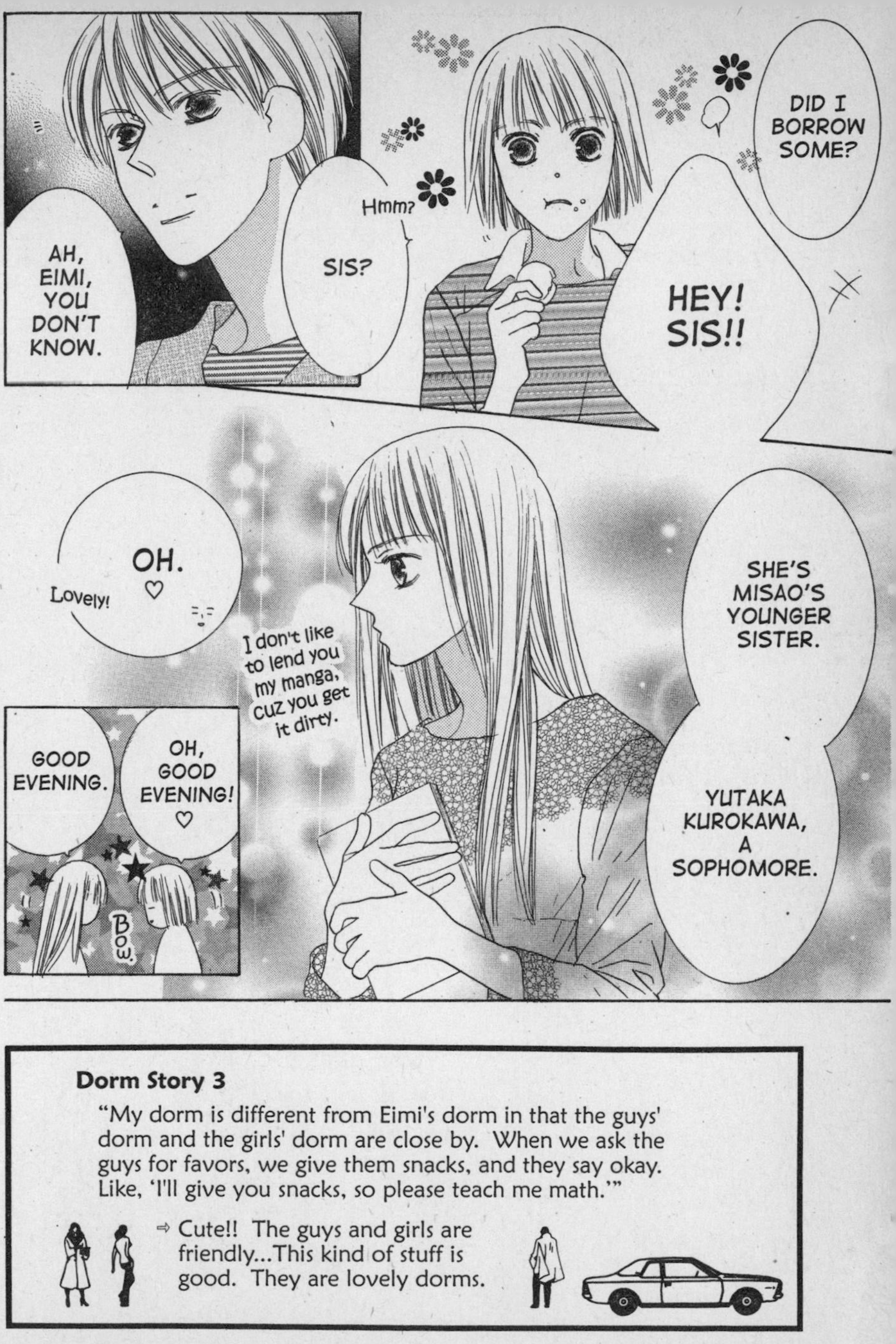
DID I BORROW SOME?
HEY! SIS!!
Hmm?
SIS?
AH, EIMI, YOU DON'T KNOW.
SHE'S MISAO'S YOUNGER SISTER.
YUTAKA KUROKAWA, A SOPHOMORE.
I don't like to lend you my manga, cuz you get it dirty.
OH. ♡
Lovely!
OH, GOOD EVENING! ♡
GOOD EVENING.
Bow.

Dorm Story 3

"My dorm is different from Eimi's dorm in that the guys' dorm and the girls' dorm are close by. When we ask the guys for favors, we give them snacks, and they say okay. Like, 'I'll give you snacks, so please teach me math.'"

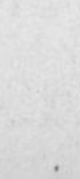

⇨ Cute!! The guys and girls are friendly...This kind of stuff is good. They are lovely dorms.

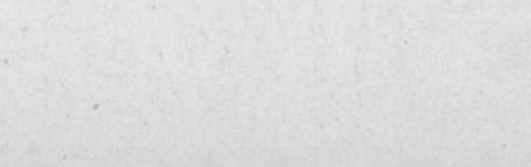

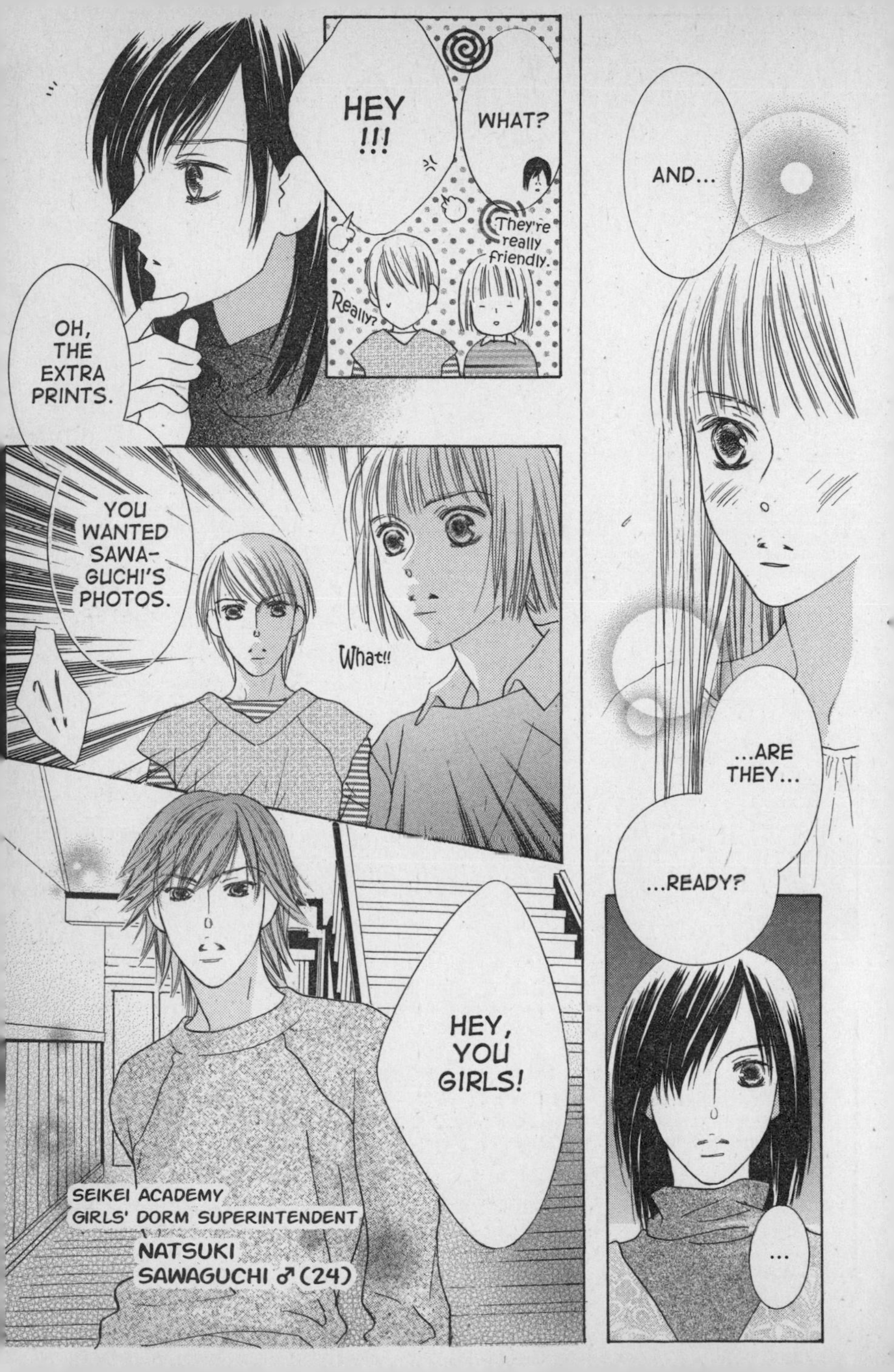
AND...
...ARE THEY...
...READY?
...
WHAT?
HEY !!!
They're really friendly.
Really?
OH, THE EXTRA PRINTS.
YOU WANTED SAWAGUCHI'S PHOTOS.
What!!
HEY, YOU GIRLS!
SEIKEI ACADEMY GIRLS' DORM SUPERINTENDENT
NATSUKI SAWAGUCHI ♂ (24)

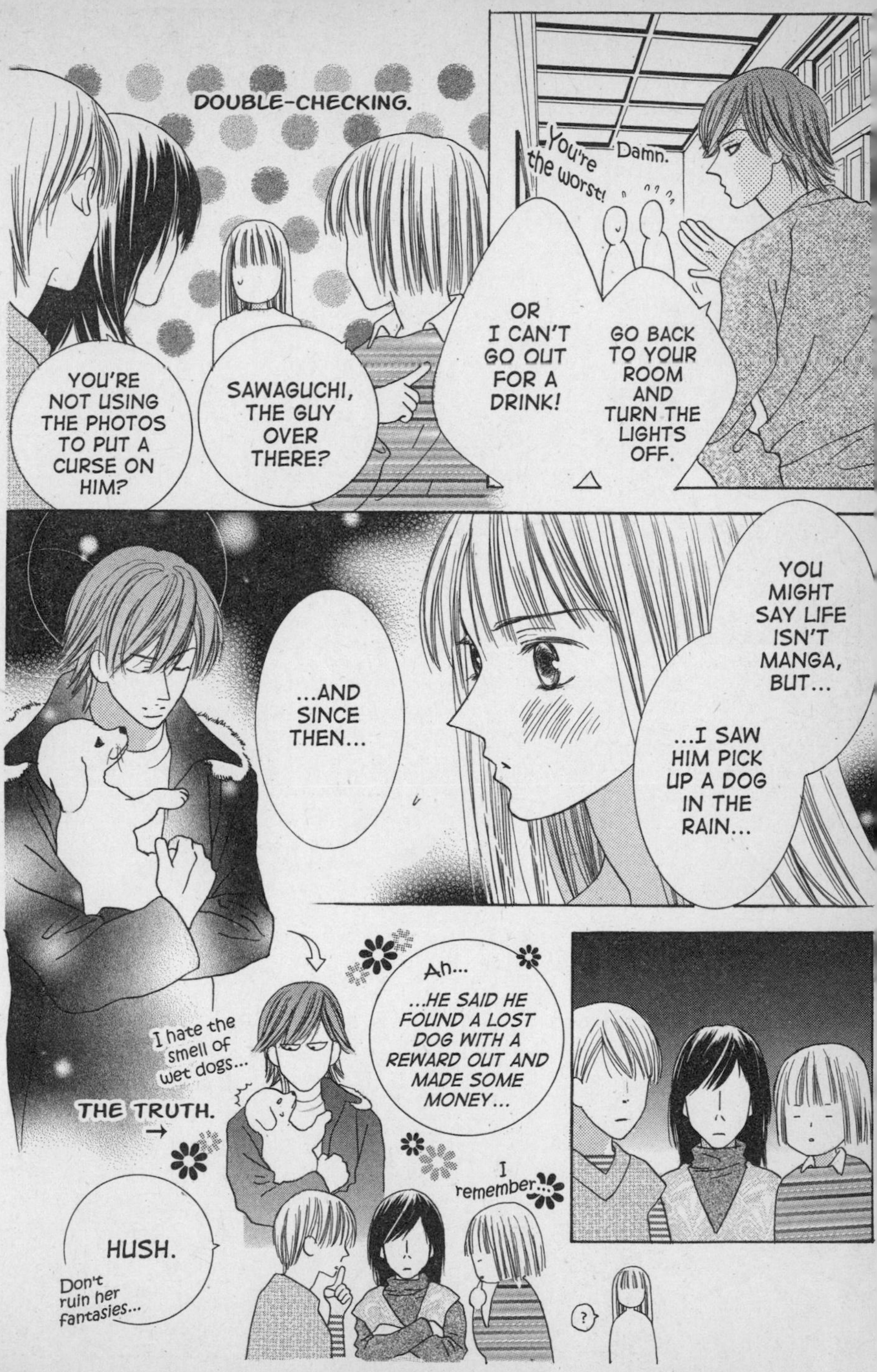
Damn.
You're the worst!
GO BACK TO YOUR ROOM AND TURN THE LIGHTS OFF.
OR I CAN'T GO OUT FOR A DRINK!
DOUBLE-CHECKING.
SAWAGUCHI, THE GUY OVER THERE?
YOU'RE NOT USING THE PHOTOS TO PUT A CURSE ON HIM?
YOU MIGHT SAY LIFE ISN'T MANGA, BUT...
...I SAW HIM PICK UP A DOG IN THE RAIN...
...AND SINCE THEN...
Ah...
...HE SAID HE FOUND A LOST DOG WITH A REWARD OUT AND MADE SOME MONEY...
I remember...
I hate the smell of wet dogs...
THE TRUTH. →
HUSH.
Don't ruin her fantasies...
?

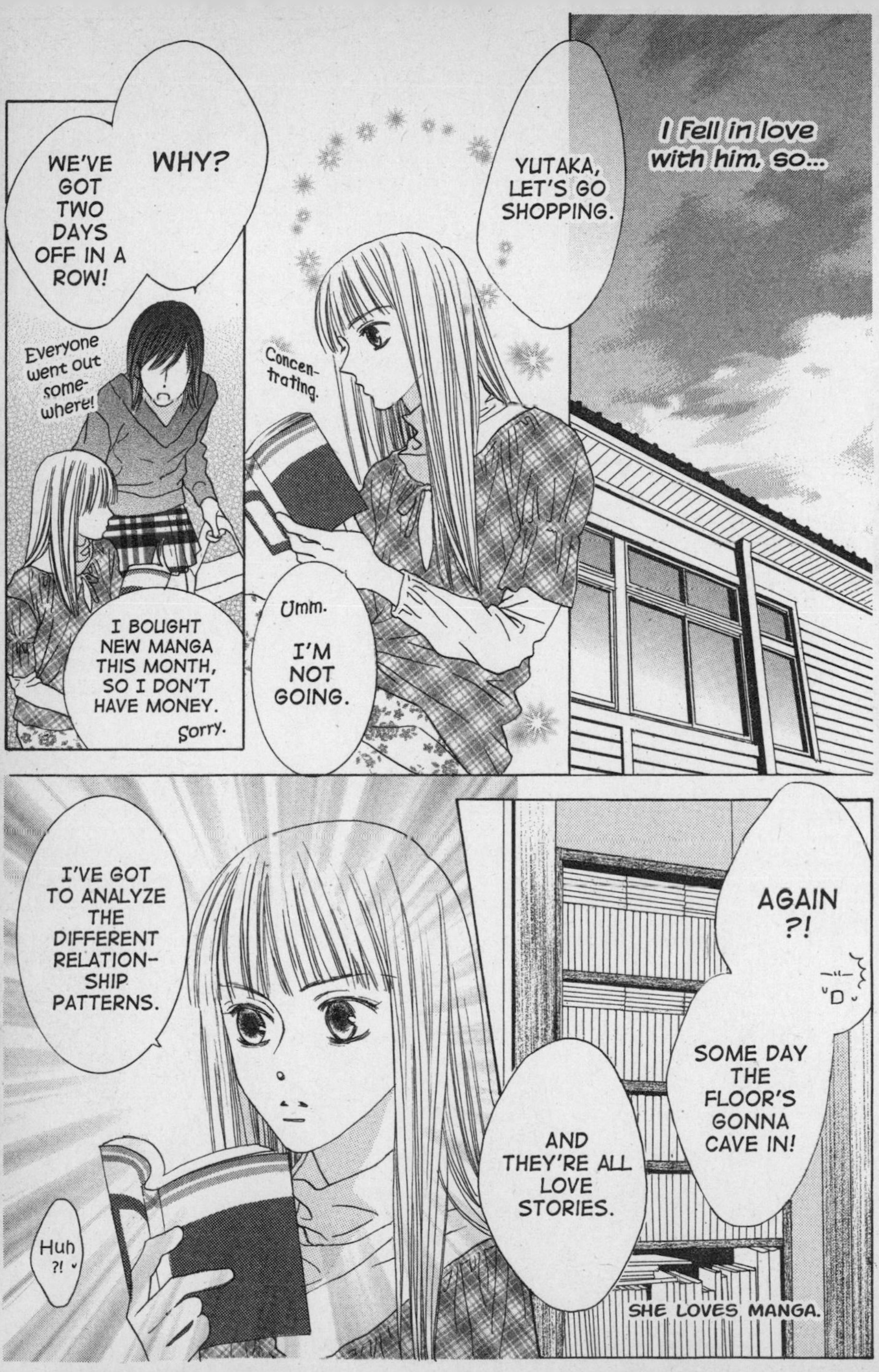
I Fell in love with him, so...
YUTAKA, LET'S GO SHOPPING.
Concen-trating.
Umm.
I'M NOT GOING.
WHY?
WE'VE GOT TWO DAYS OFF IN A ROW!
Everyone went out some-where!
I BOUGHT NEW MANGA THIS MONTH, SO I DON'T HAVE MONEY.
Sorry.
AGAIN ?!
SOME DAY THE FLOOR'S GONNA CAVE IN!
AND THEY'RE ALL LOVE STORIES.
SHE LOVES MANGA.
I'VE GOT TO ANALYZE THE DIFFERENT RELATION-SHIP PATTERNS.
Huh ?!

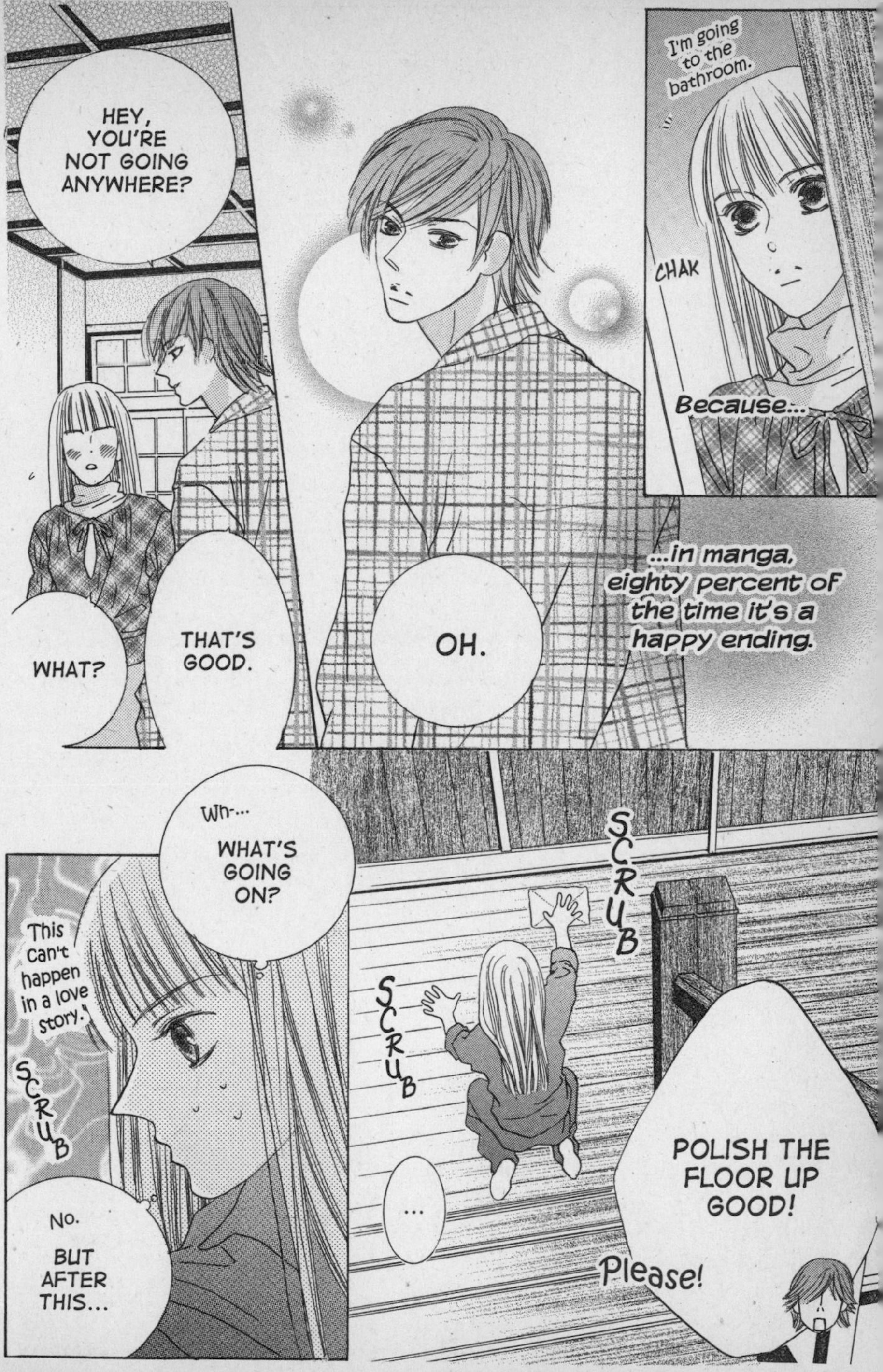

I'm going to the bathroom.
CHAK
Because...
...in manga, eighty percent of the time it's a happy ending.
OH.
HEY, YOU'RE NOT GOING ANYWHERE?
THAT'S GOOD.
WHAT?
SCRUB
SCRUB
POLISH THE FLOOR UP GOOD!
...
Please!
Wh-... WHAT'S GOING ON?
This can't happen in a love story.
SCRUB
No.
BUT AFTER THIS...

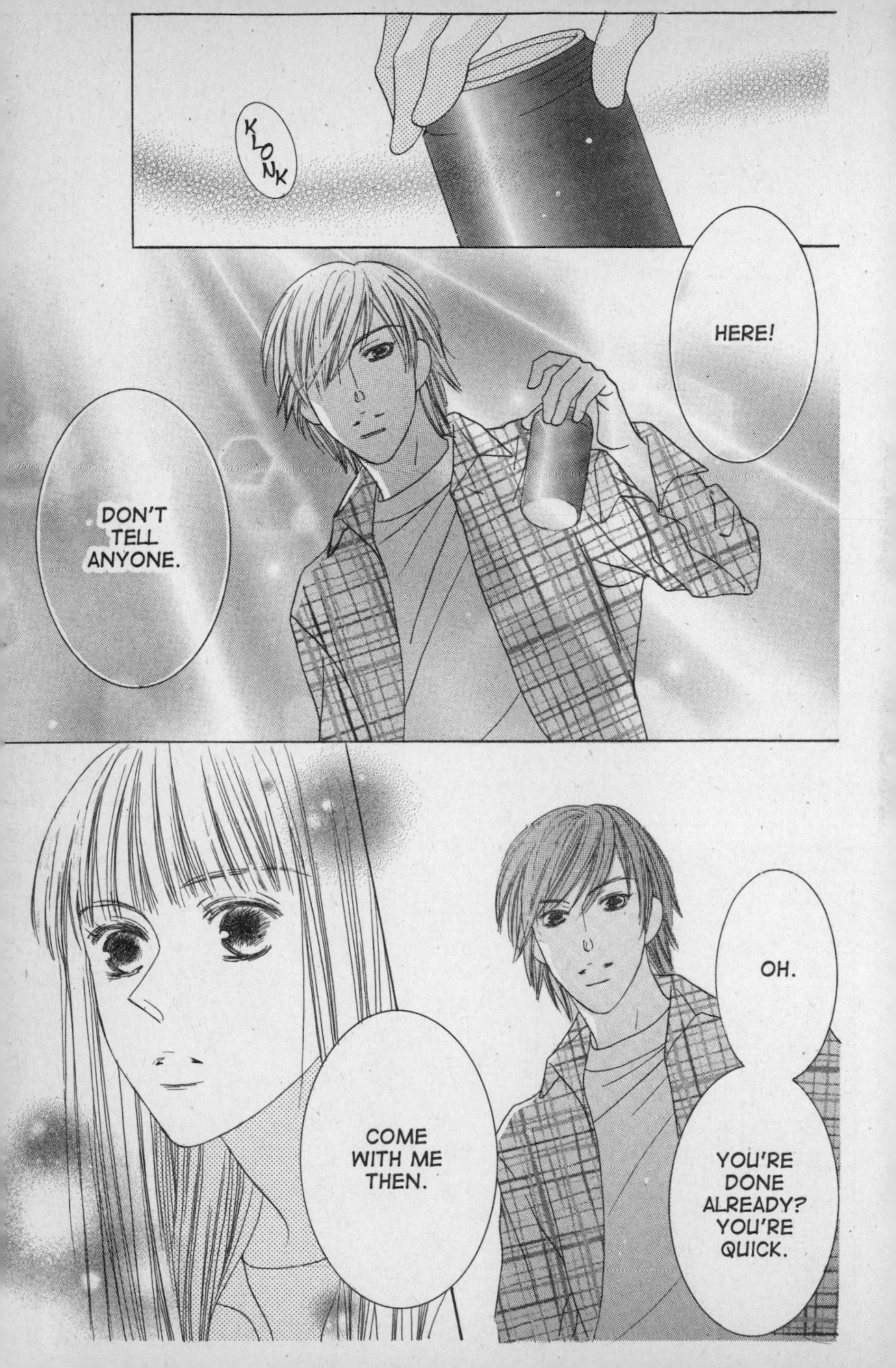
KLONK
HERE!
DON'T TELL ANYONE.
OH.
YOU'RE DONE ALREADY? YOU'RE QUICK.
COME WITH ME THEN.

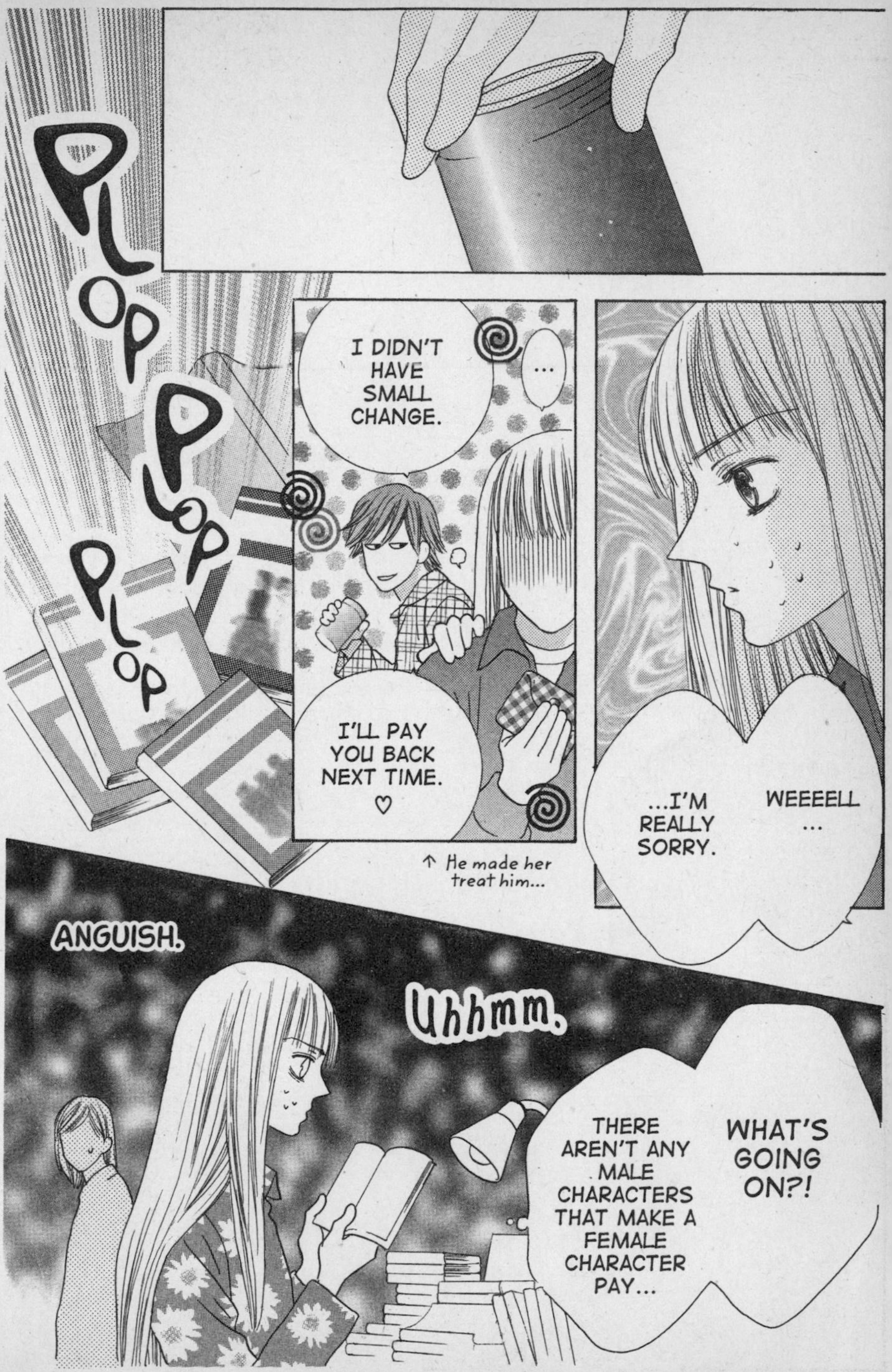
PLOP
WEEEELL...
...I'M REALLY SORRY.
...
I DIDN'T HAVE SMALL CHANGE.
I'LL PAY YOU BACK NEXT TIME. ♡
↑ He made her treat him...
PLOP PLOP PLOP
WHAT'S GOING ON?!
THERE AREN'T ANY MALE CHARACTERS THAT MAKE A FEMALE CHARACTER PAY...
Uhhmm.
ANGUISH.

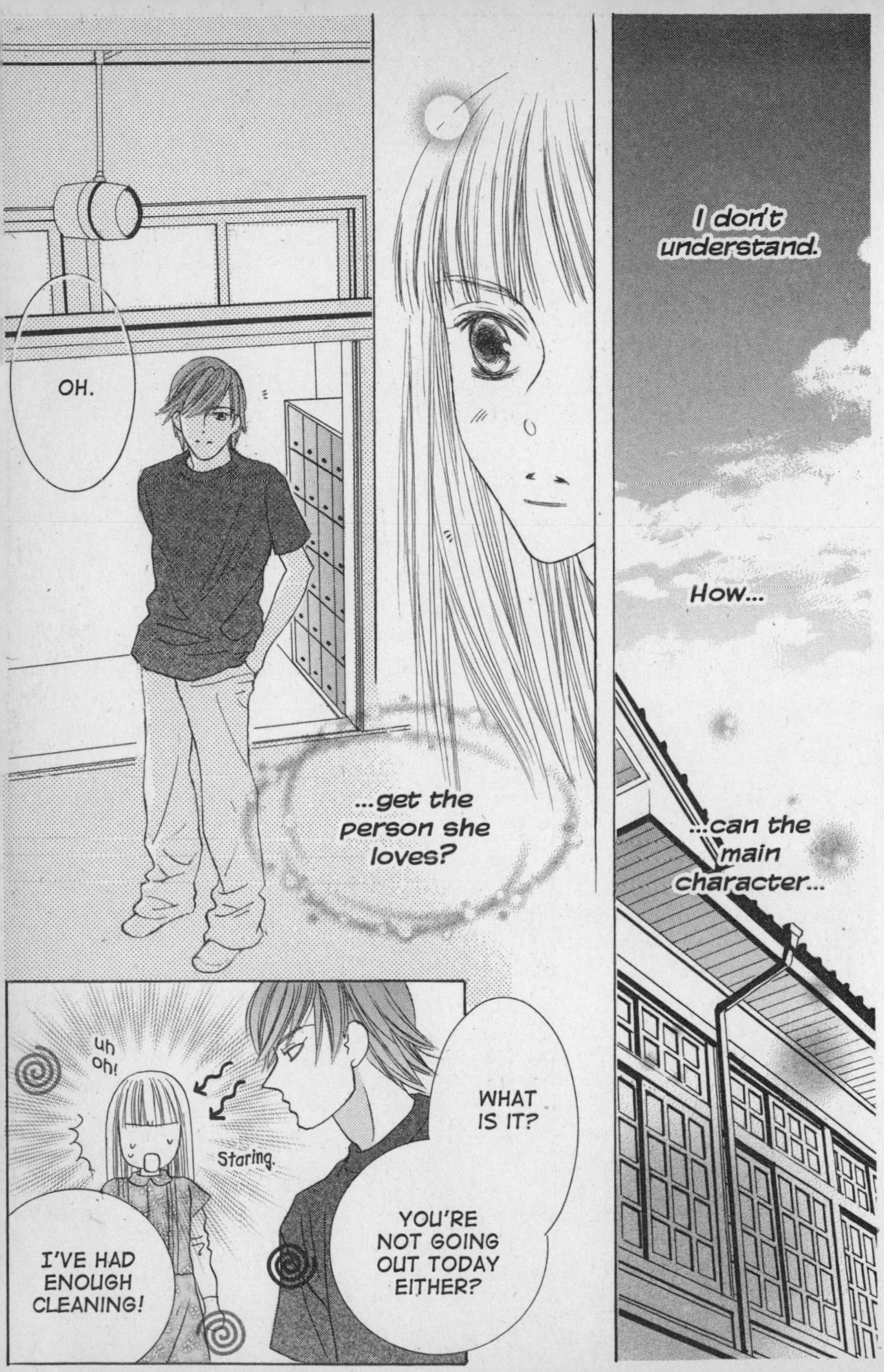
I don't understand.
How...
...can the main character...
...get the person she loves?
OH.
WHAT IS IT?
YOU'RE NOT GOING OUT TODAY EITHER?
Staring.
uh oh!
I'VE HAD ENOUGH CLEANING!

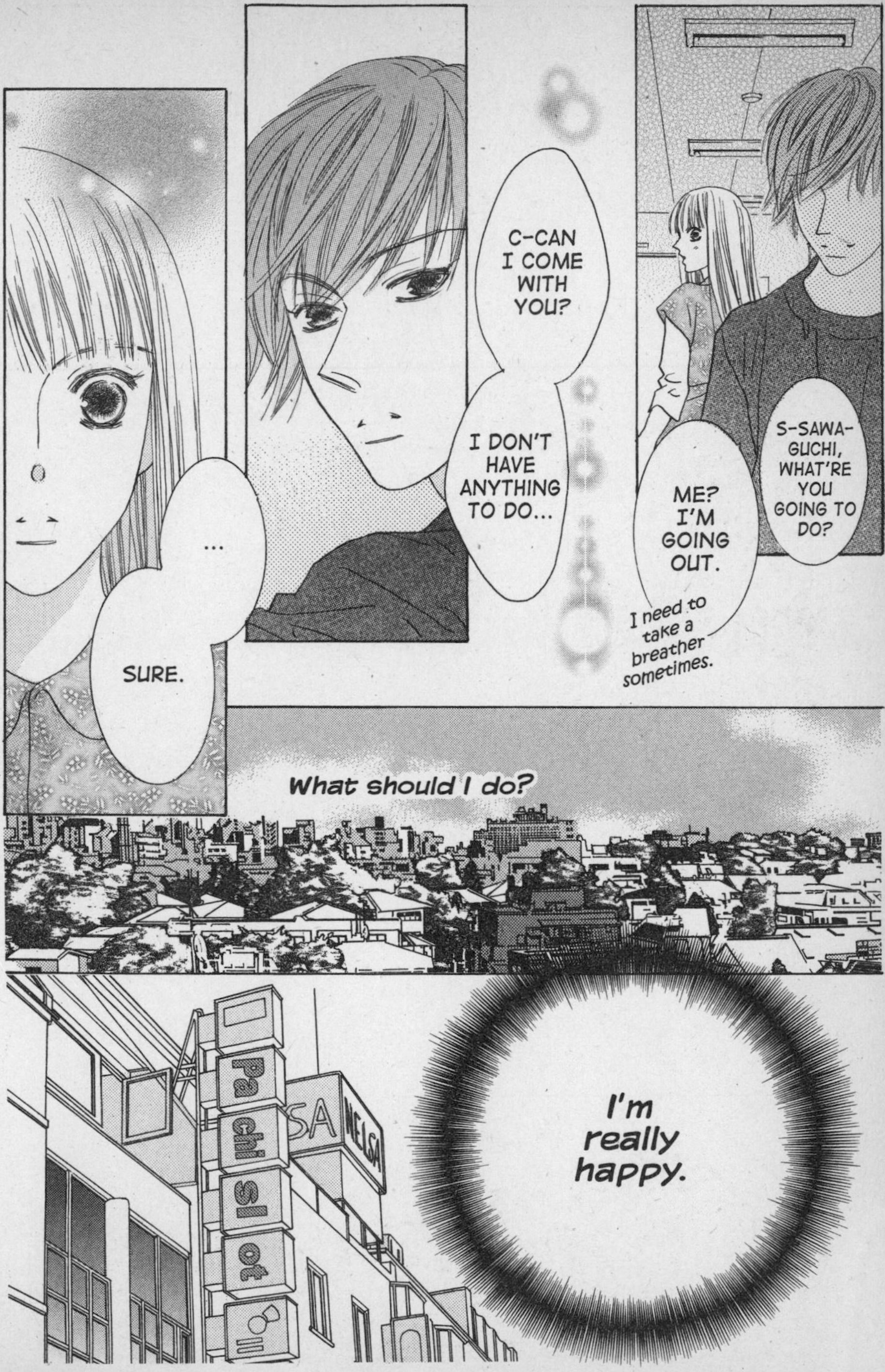
S-SAWAGUCHI, WHAT'RE YOU GOING TO DO?
ME? I'M GOING OUT.
I need to take a breather sometimes.
C-CAN I COME WITH YOU?
I DON'T HAVE ANYTHING TO DO...
...
SURE.
What should I do?
NELSA
I'm really happy.

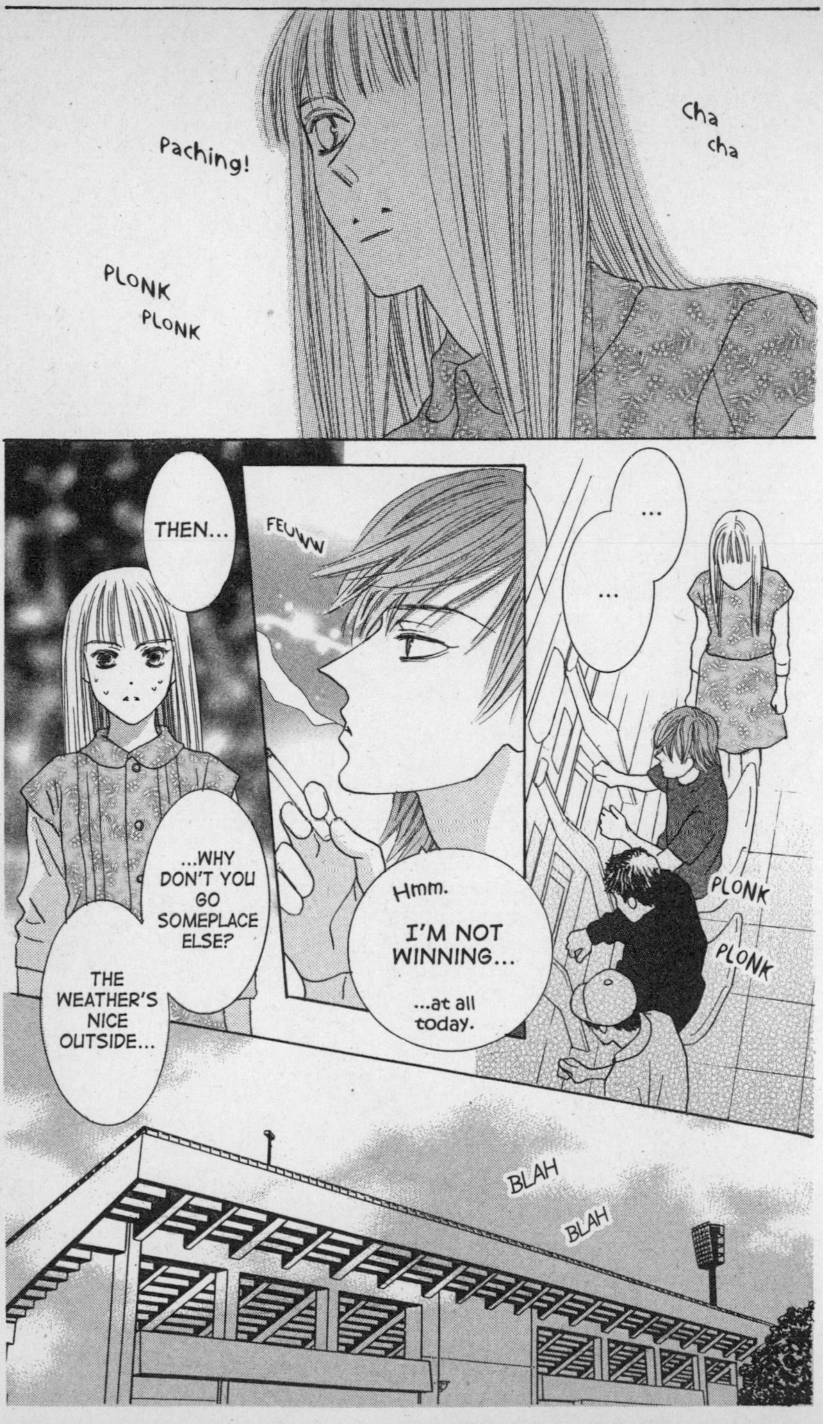
Cha
cha
Paching!
PLONK
PLONK
...
...
PLONK
PLONK
FEUWW
Hmm.
I'M NOT WINNING...
...at all today.
THEN...
...WHY DON'T YOU GO SOMEPLACE ELSE?
THE WEATHER'S NICE OUTSIDE...
BLAH
BLAH

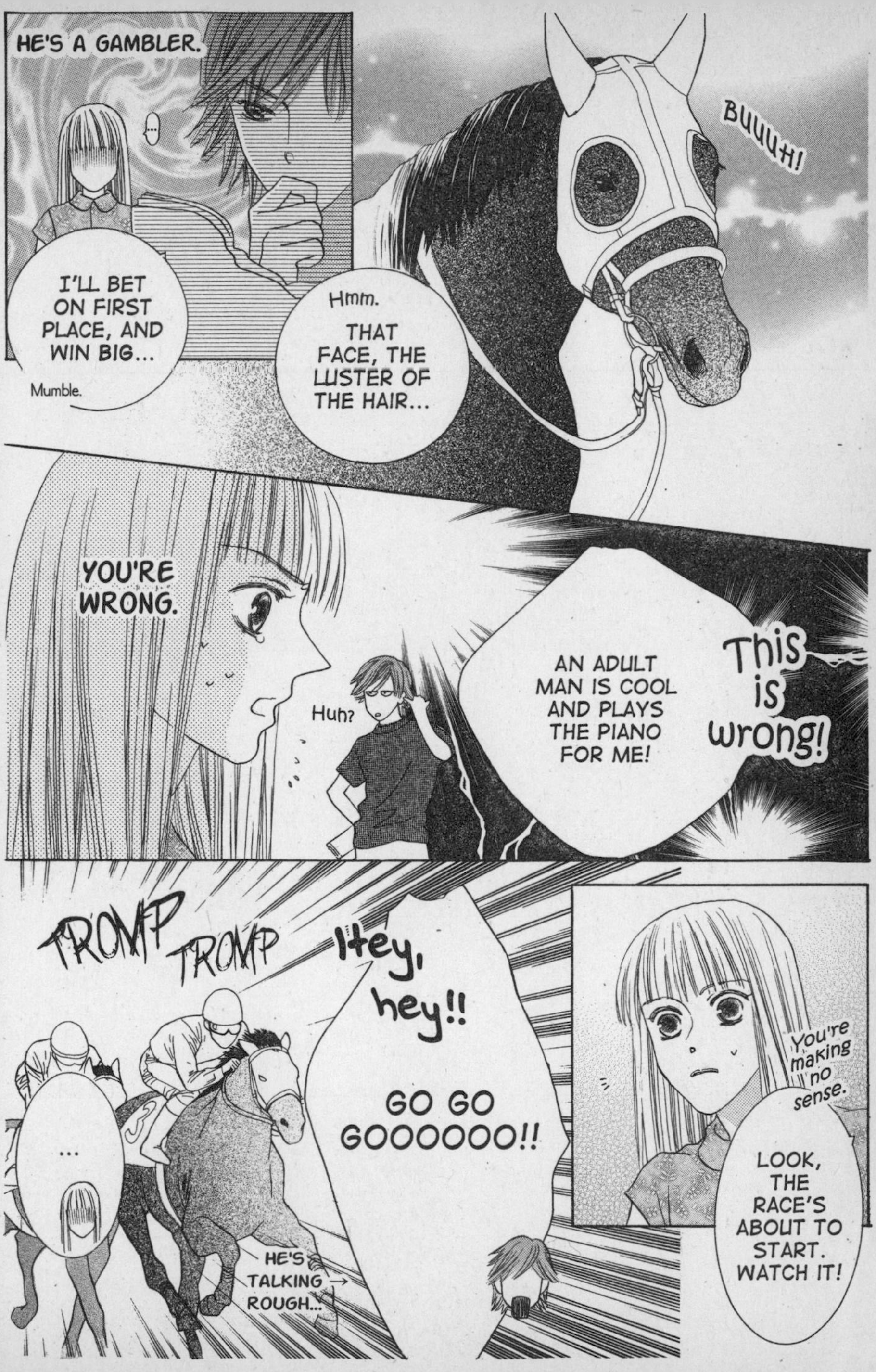
BUUUH!
HE'S A GAMBLER.
...
Hmm.
THAT FACE, THE LUSTER OF THE HAIR...
I'LL BET ON FIRST PLACE, AND WIN BIG...
Mumble.
This is wrong!
AN ADULT MAN IS COOL AND PLAYS THE PIANO FOR ME!
Huh?
YOU'RE WRONG.
You're making no sense.
LOOK, THE RACE'S ABOUT TO START. WATCH IT!
Hey, hey!!
GO GO GOOOOOO!!
TROMP TROMP
...
HE'S TALKING ROUGH...

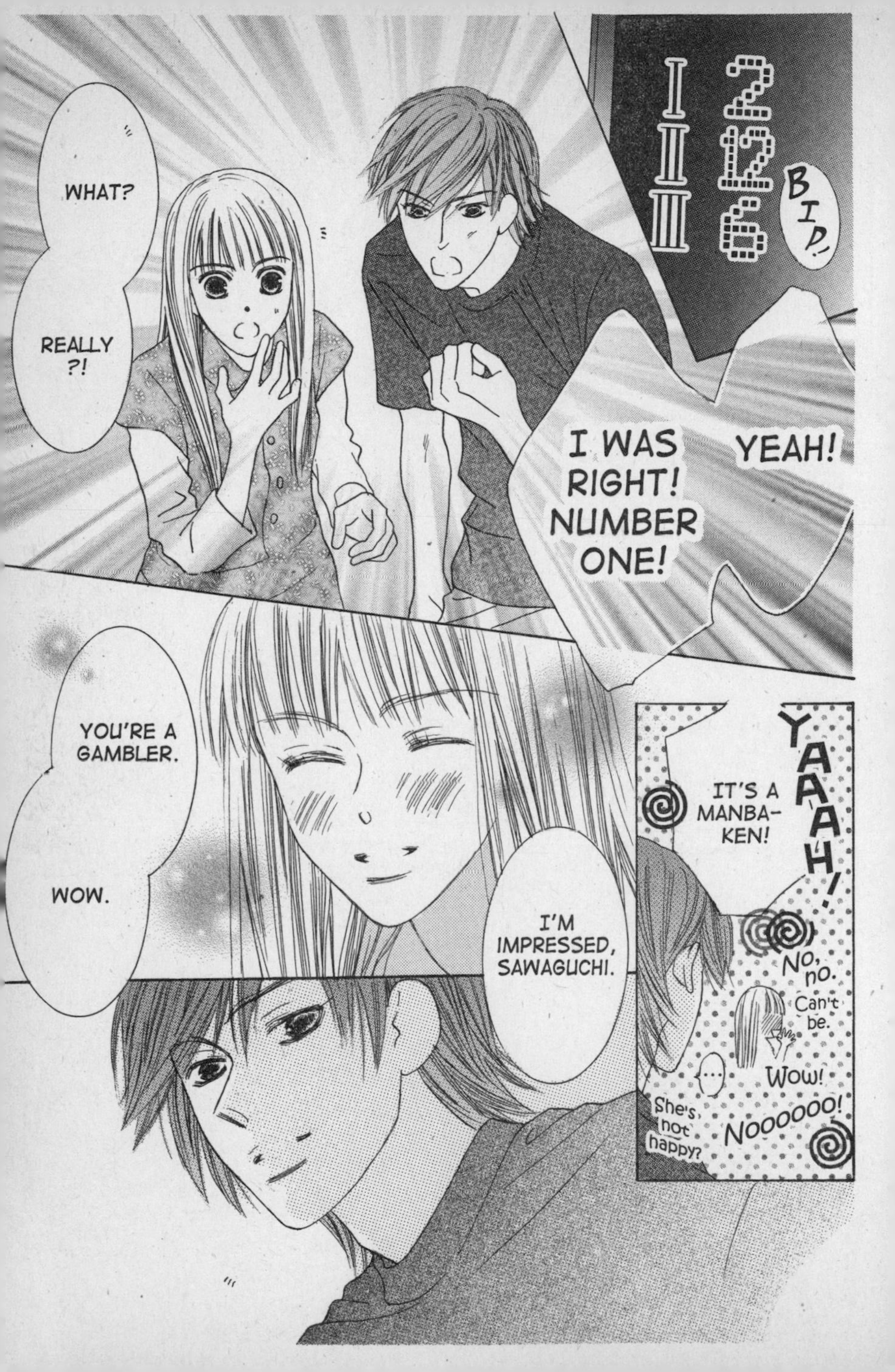
BIP!
YEAH!
I WAS RIGHT! NUMBER ONE!
WHAT? REALLY ?!
YAAAAH!
IT'S A MANBA-KEN!
No, no. Can't be.
Wow!
...
She's not happy?
Noooooo!
I'M IMPRESSED, SAWAGUCHI.
YOU'RE A GAMBLER. WOW.

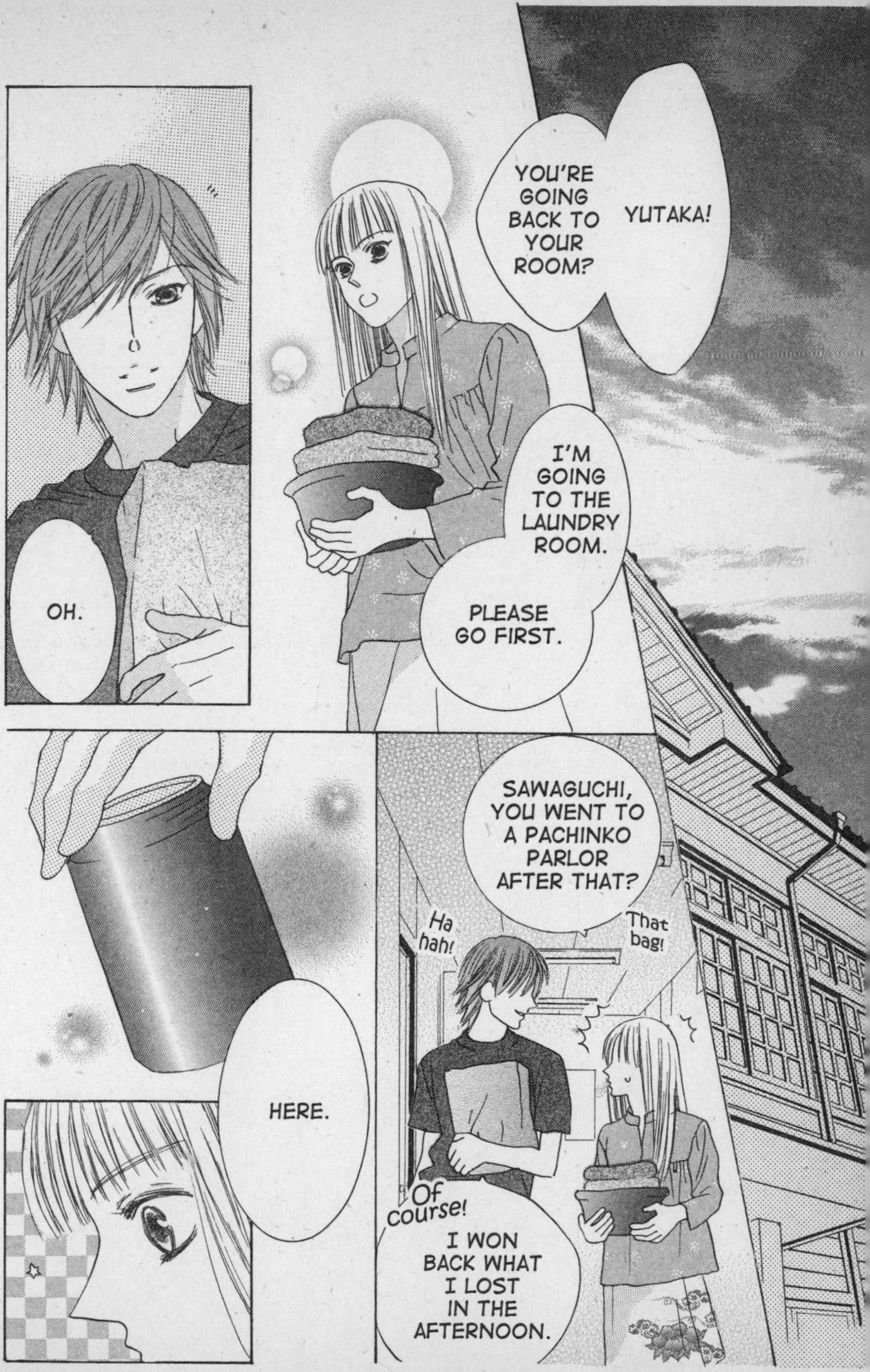
YUTAKA!
YOU'RE GOING BACK TO YOUR ROOM?
I'M GOING TO THE LAUNDRY ROOM.
PLEASE GO FIRST.
OH.
SAWAGUCHI, YOU WENT TO A PACHINKO PARLOR AFTER THAT?
That bag!
Ha hah!
Of course!
I WON BACK WHAT I LOST IN THE AFTERNOON.
HERE.

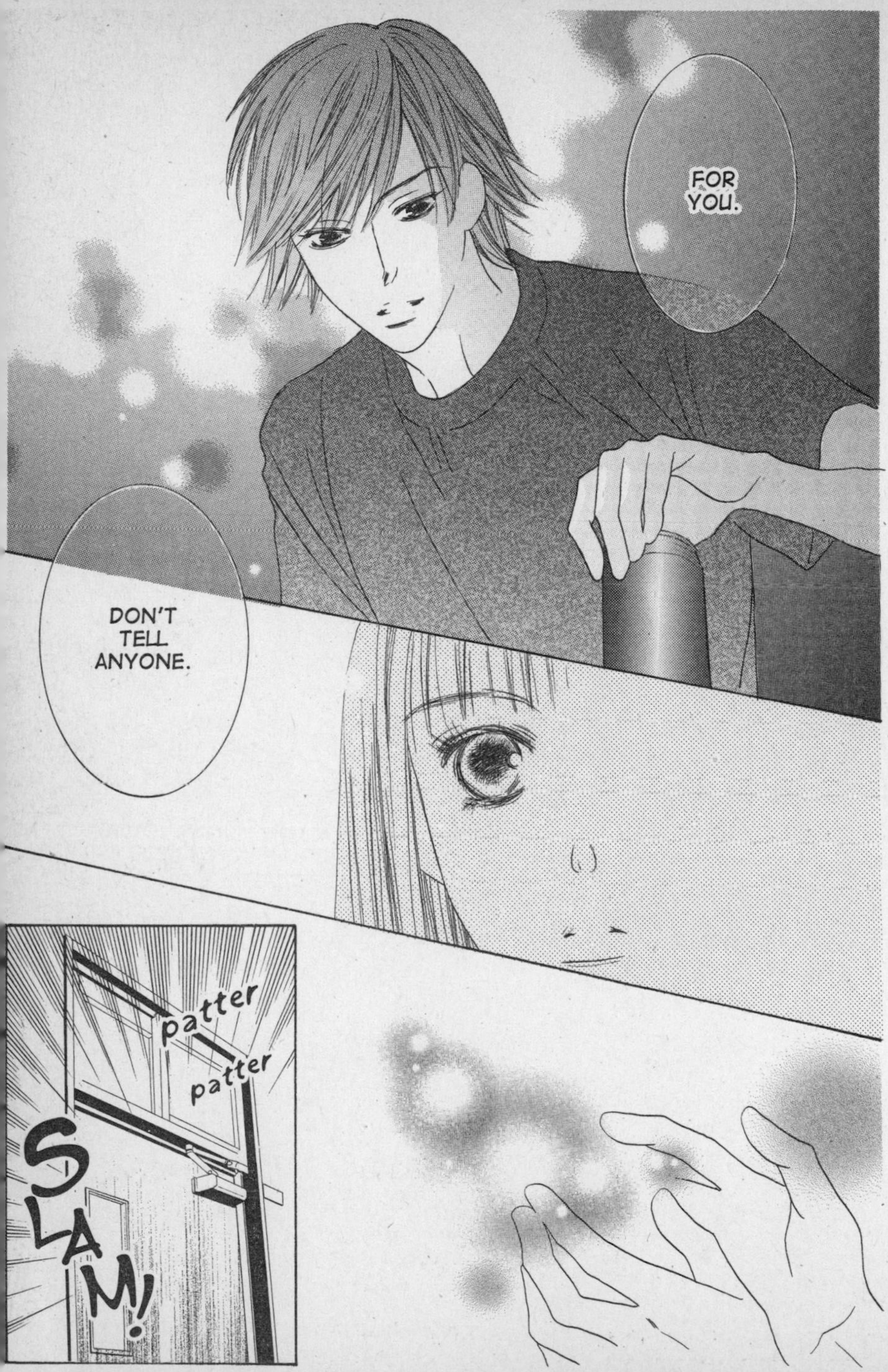
FOR YOU.
DON'T TELL ANYONE.
patter
patter
SLAM!

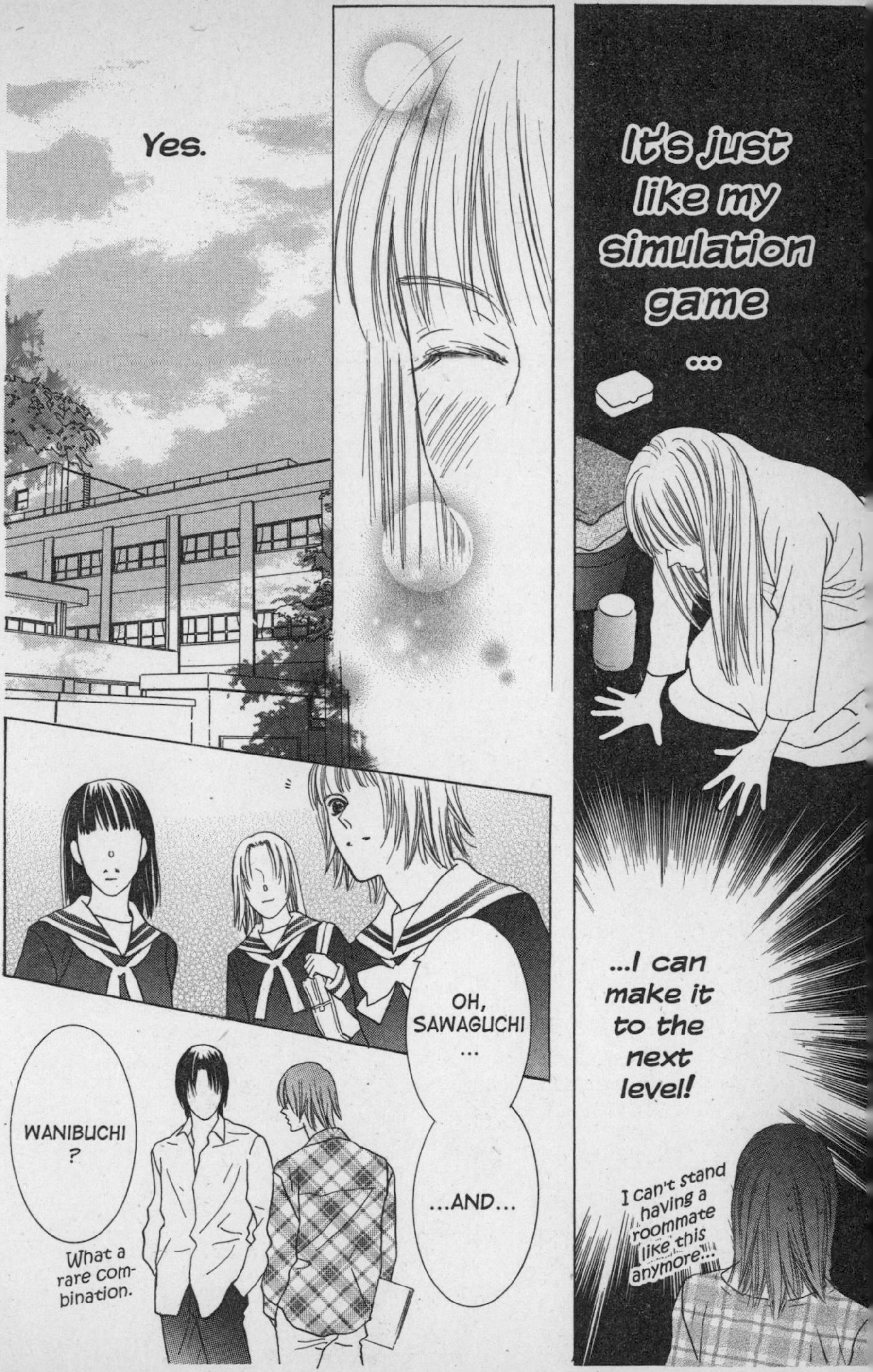
It's just like my simulation game...
...I can make it to the next level!
I can't stand having a roommate like this anymore...
Yes.
OH, SAWAGUCHI...
...AND...
WANIBUCHI?
What a rare combination.

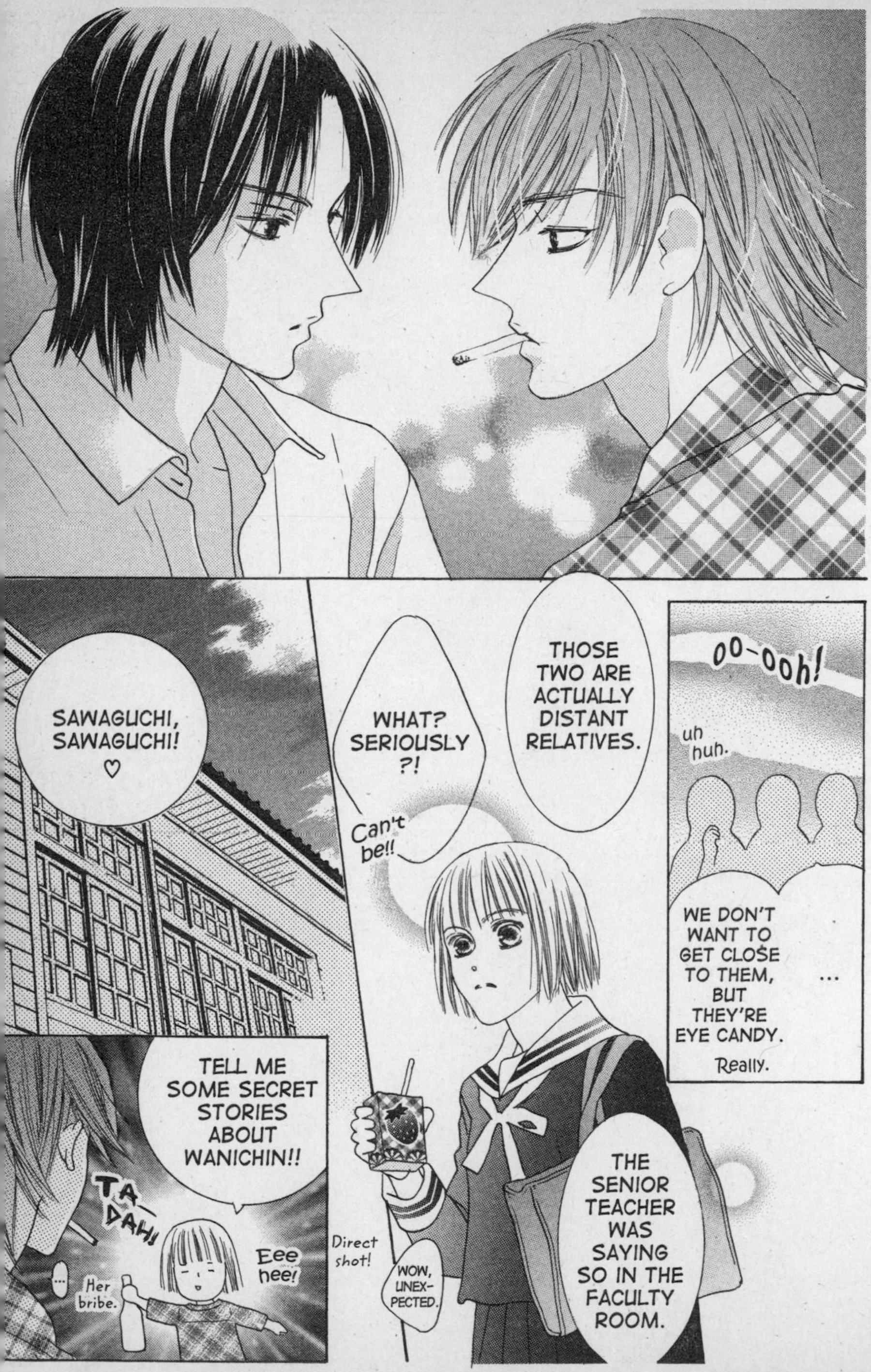
OO-OOH!
uh huh.
WE DON'T WANT TO GET CLOSE TO THEM, BUT THEY'RE EYE CANDY.
...
Really.
THOSE TWO ARE ACTUALLY DISTANT RELATIVES.
WHAT? SERIOUSLY?!
Can't be!!
THE SENIOR TEACHER WAS SAYING SO IN THE FACULTY ROOM.
WOW, UNEXPECTED.
Direct shot!
SAWAGUCHI, SAWAGUCHI! ♡
TELL ME SOME SECRET STORIES ABOUT WANICHIN!!
TA-DAH!
Eee hee!
...
Her bribe.

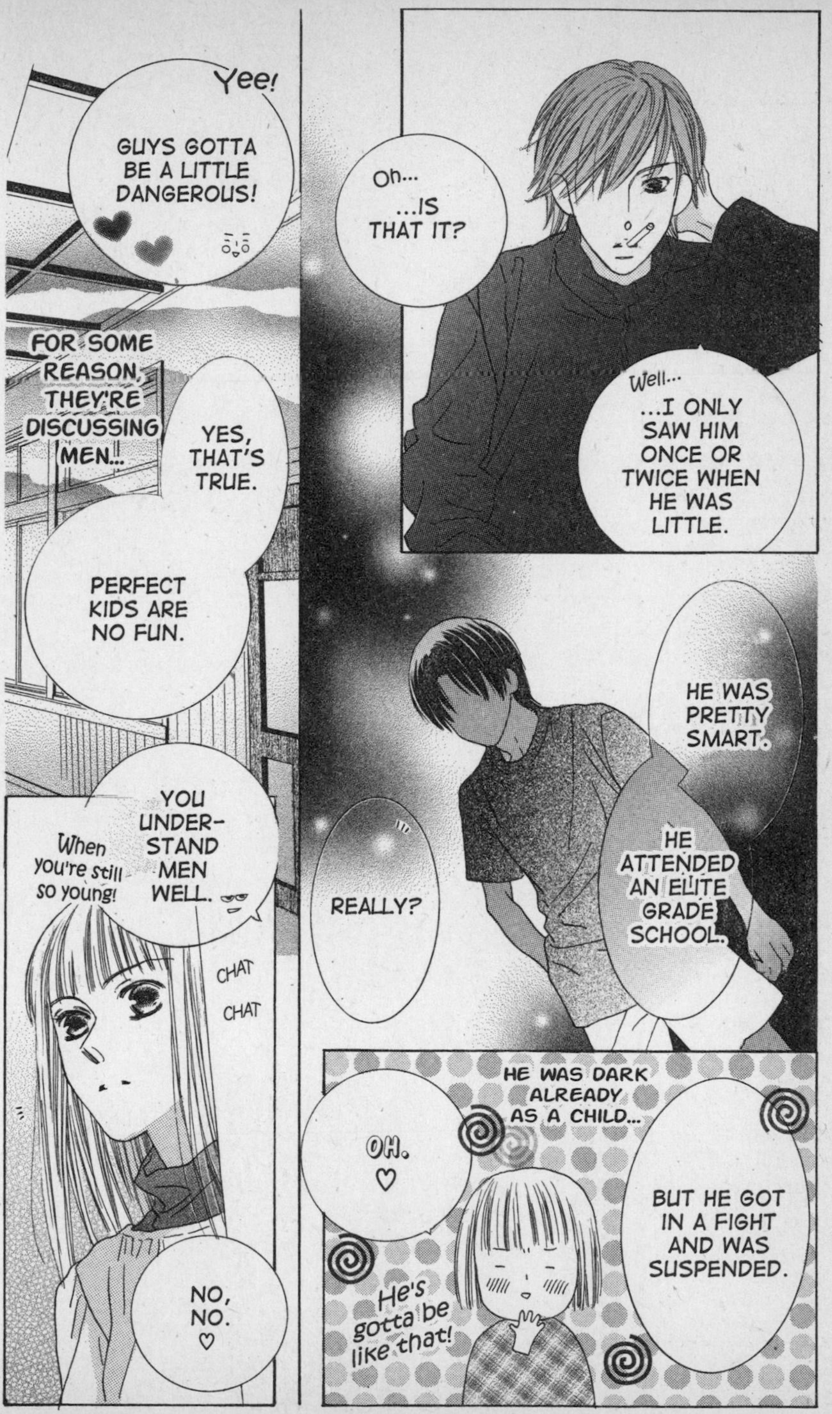
Oh...
...IS THAT IT?
Well...
...I ONLY SAW HIM ONCE OR TWICE WHEN HE WAS LITTLE.
HE WAS PRETTY SMART.
HE ATTENDED AN ELITE GRADE SCHOOL.
REALLY?
HE WAS DARK ALREADY AS A CHILD...
BUT HE GOT IN A FIGHT AND WAS SUSPENDED.
OH. ♡
He's gotta be like that!
Yee!
GUYS GOTTA BE A LITTLE DANGEROUS!
YES, THAT'S TRUE.
FOR SOME REASON, THEY'RE DISCUSSING MEN...
PERFECT KIDS ARE NO FUN.
YOU UNDER-STAND MEN WELL.
When you're still so young!
CHAT
CHAT
NO, NO. ♡

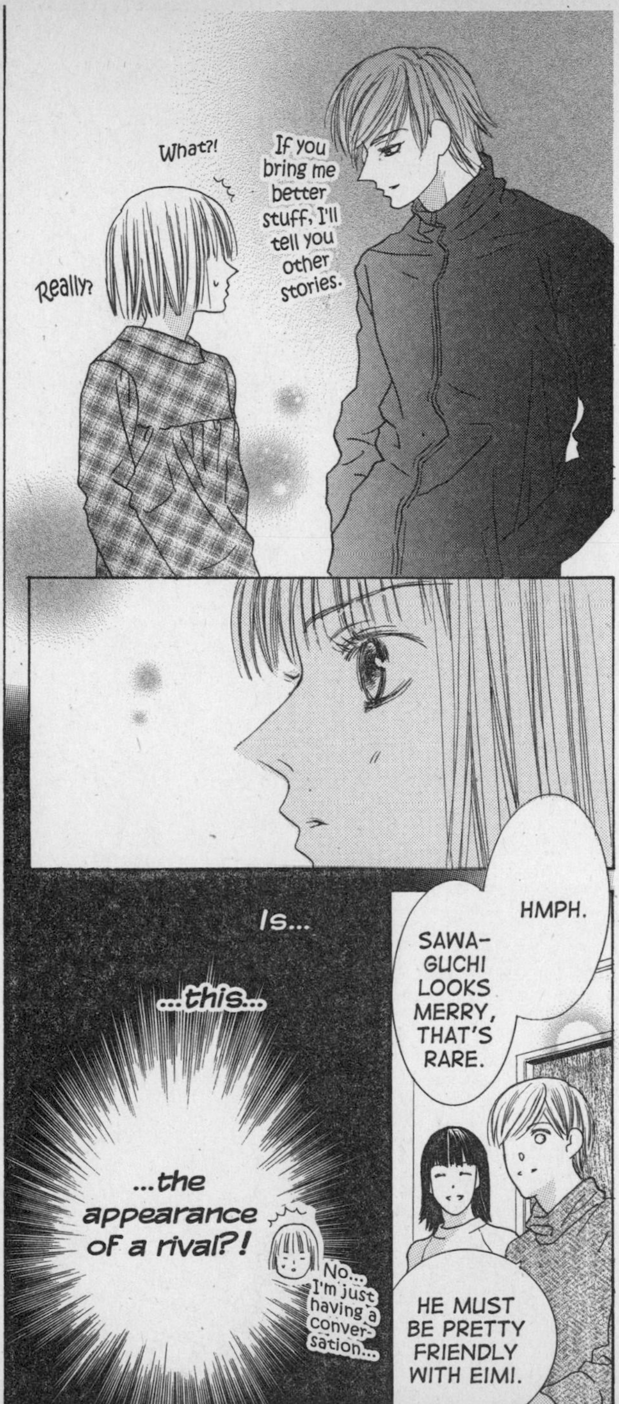
If you bring me better stuff, I'll tell you other stories.
What?!
Really?
HMPH.
SAWAGUCHI LOOKS MERRY, THAT'S RARE.
HE MUST BE PRETTY FRIENDLY WITH EIMI.
Is...
...this...
...the appearance of a rival?!
No... I'm just having a conversation...

③ Do the Inking.

I use a crow quill pen for inking. When I do my black-and-white manuscripts, I only use a crow quill pen.

For the ink, I use Pilot's ink for bonds. I thin it with water three to five times. You can use color inks (sepia or gray), but I haven't really tried it. (I would actually like to try different methods.)

But at this point, I try to change the composition on a whim, and fail... so depressing.

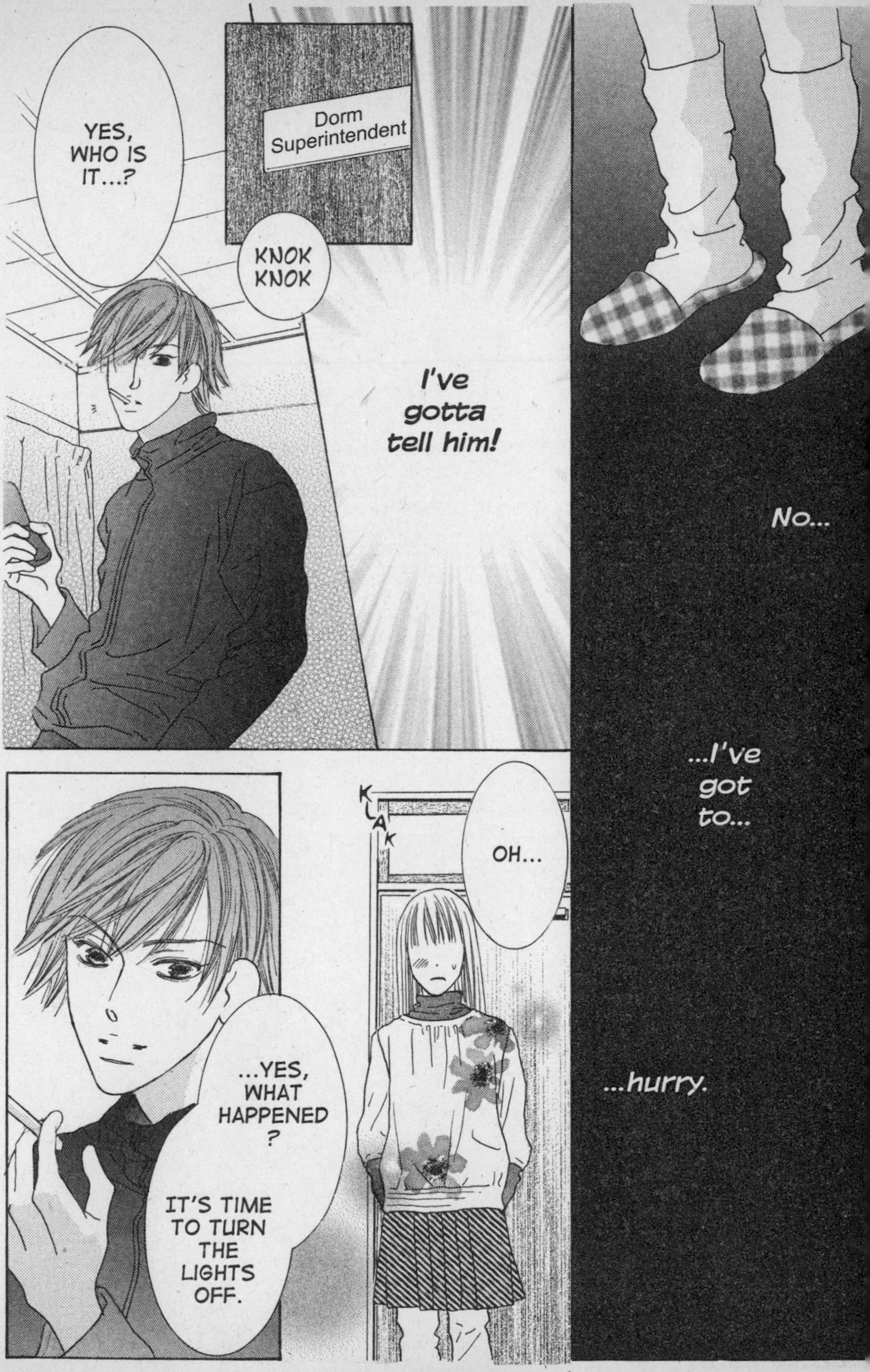
No...
...I've got to...
...hurry.
Dorm Superintendent
KNOK KNOK
I've gotta tell him!
YES, WHO IS IT...?
KLAK
OH...
...YES, WHAT HAPPENED?
IT'S TIME TO TURN THE LIGHTS OFF.

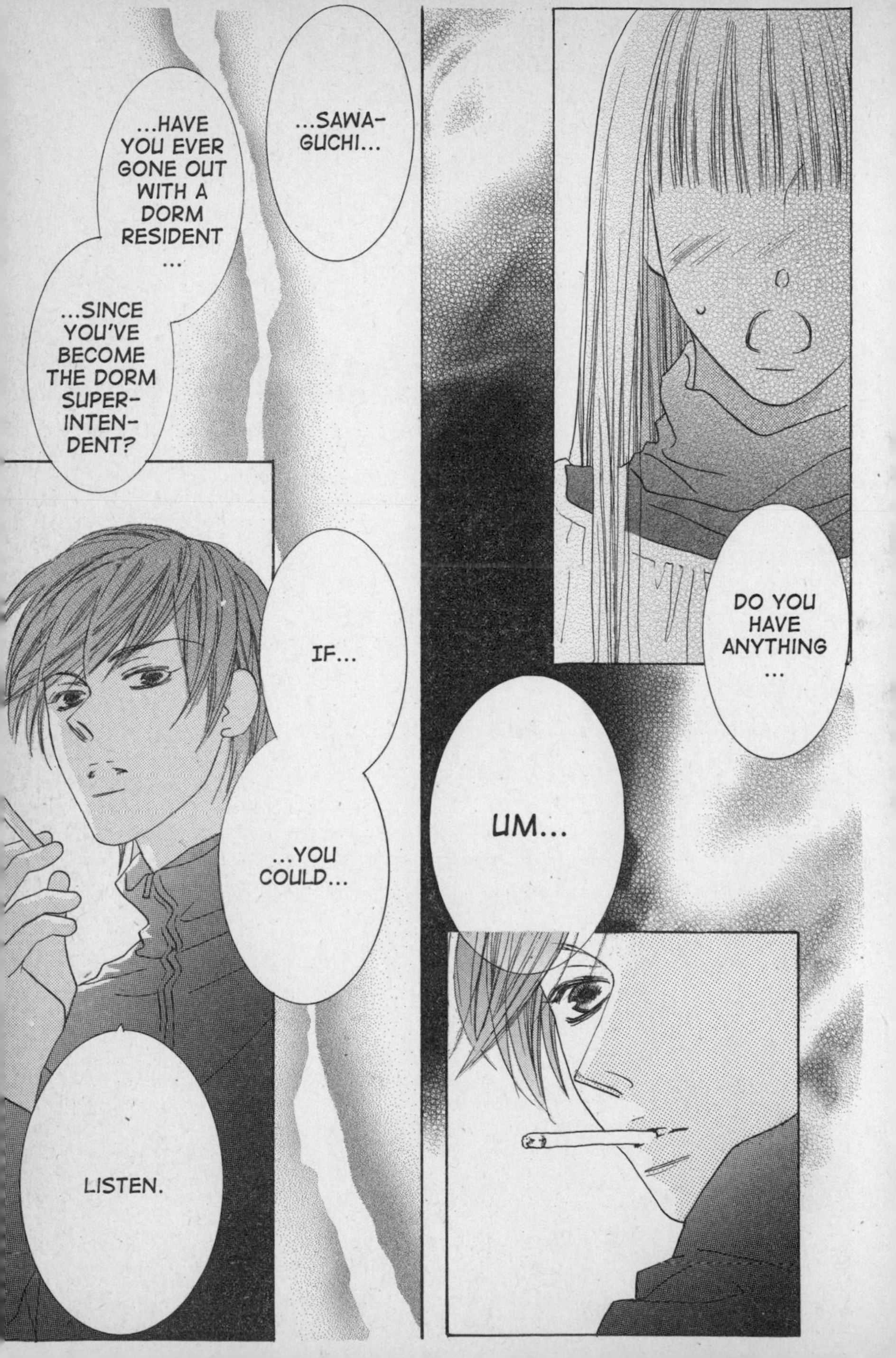
DO YOU HAVE ANYTHING ...
UM...
...SAWA-GUCHI...
...HAVE YOU EVER GONE OUT WITH A DORM RESIDENT ...
...SINCE YOU'VE BECOME THE DORM SUPER-INTEN-DENT?
IF...
...YOU COULD...
LISTEN.

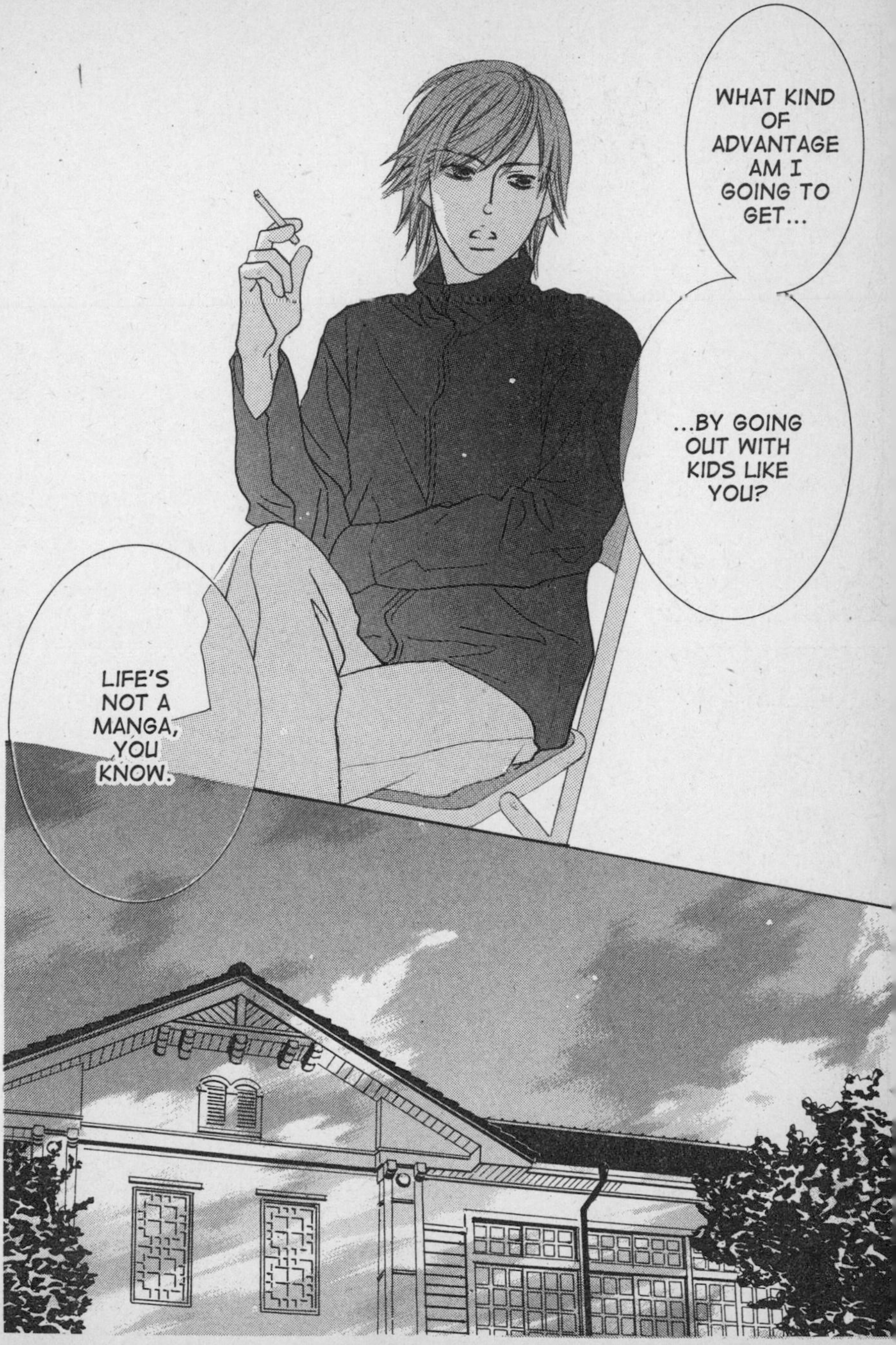
WHAT KIND OF ADVANTAGE AM I GOING TO GET...
...BY GOING OUT WITH KIDS LIKE YOU?
LIFE'S NOT A MANGA, YOU KNOW.

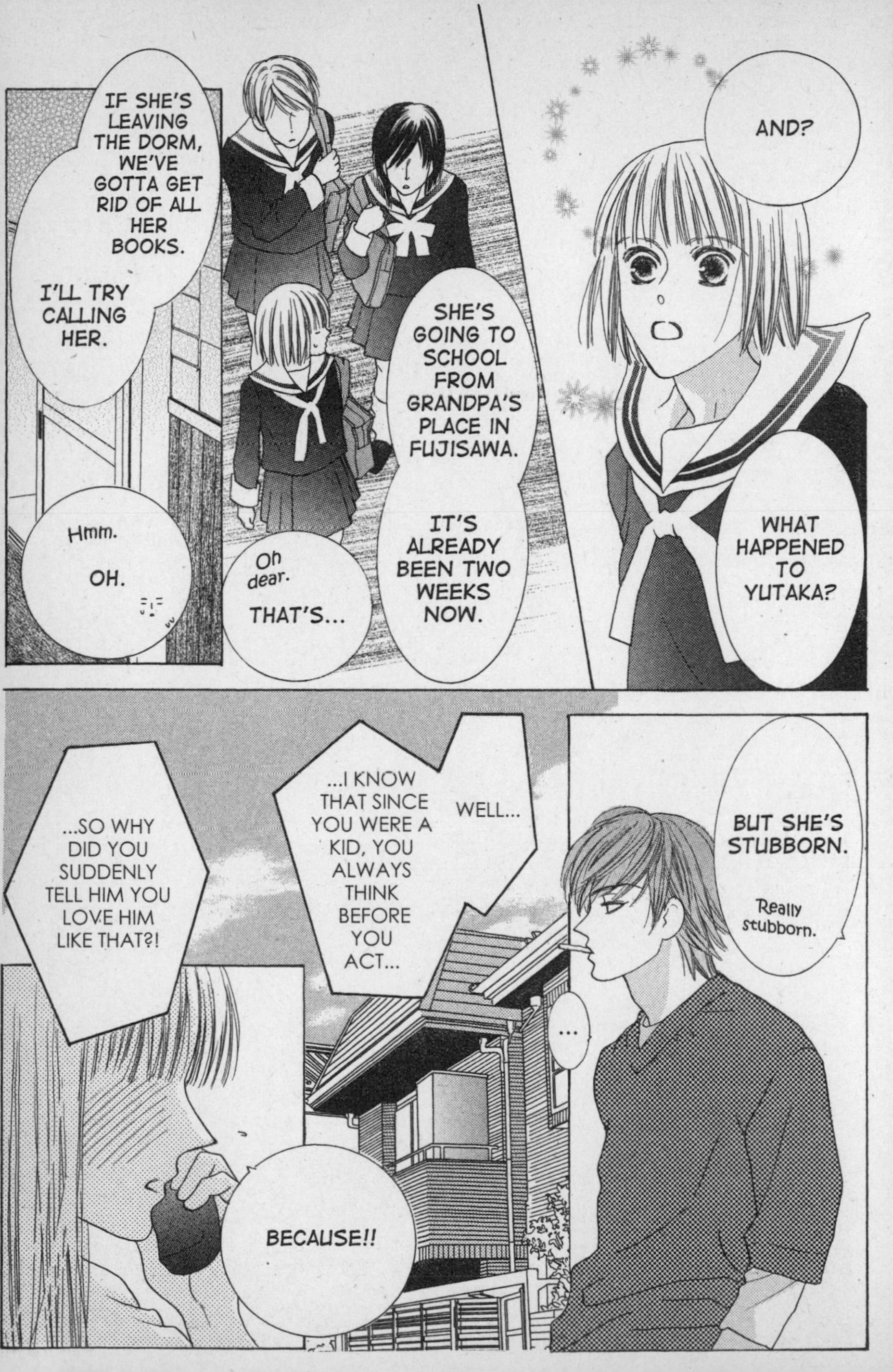
AND?
WHAT HAPPENED TO YUTAKA?
SHE'S GOING TO SCHOOL FROM GRANDPA'S PLACE IN FUJISAWA.
IT'S ALREADY BEEN TWO WEEKS NOW.
IF SHE'S LEAVING THE DORM, WE'VE GOTTA GET RID OF ALL HER BOOKS.
I'LL TRY CALLING HER.
Oh dear.
THAT'S...
Hmm.
OH.
BUT SHE'S STUBBORN.
Really stubborn.
...
WELL...
...I KNOW THAT SINCE YOU WERE A KID, YOU ALWAYS THINK BEFORE YOU ACT...
...SO WHY DID YOU SUDDENLY TELL HIM YOU LOVE HIM LIKE THAT?!
BECAUSE!!

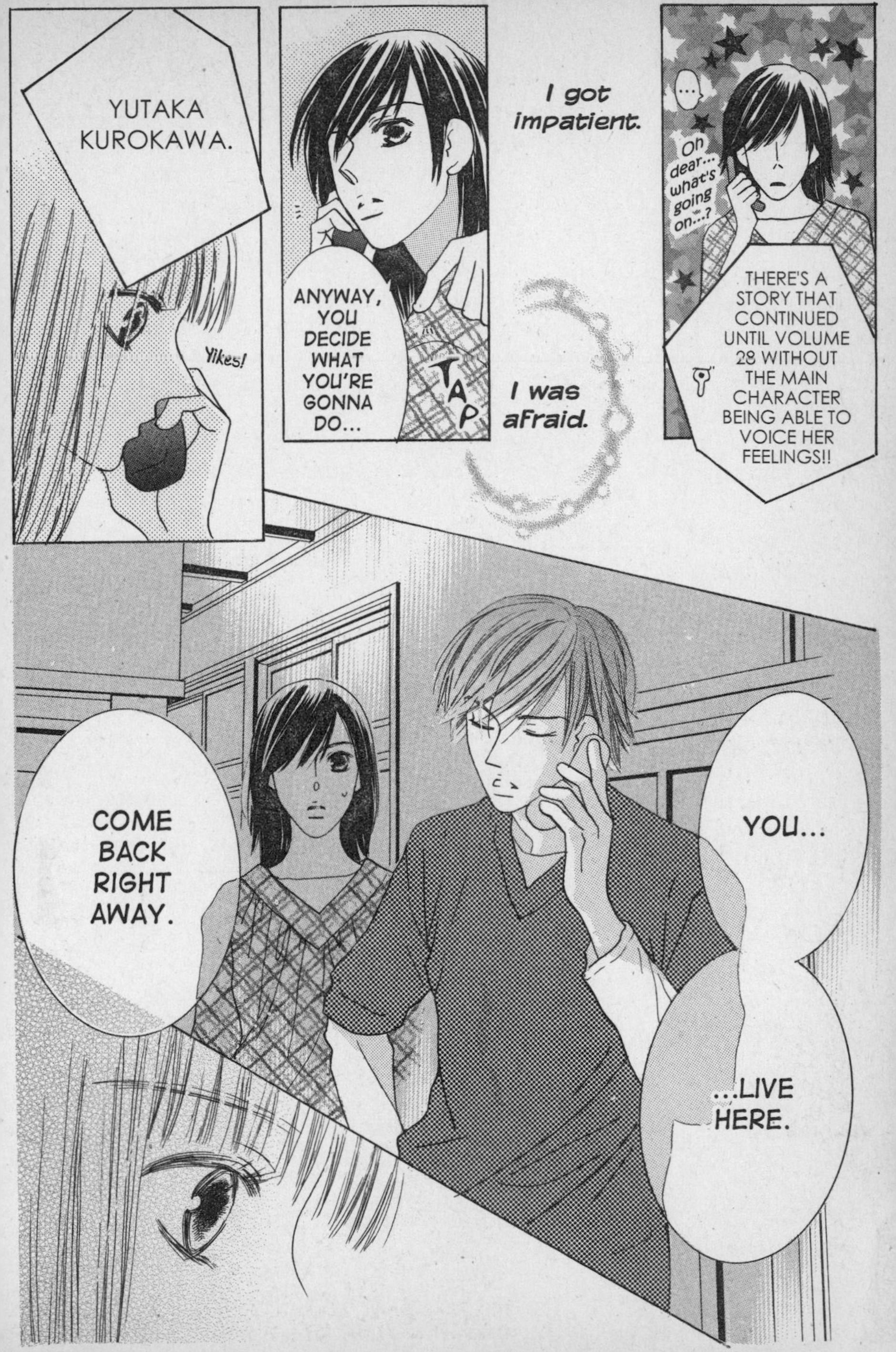
...
Oh dear... what's going on...?
THERE'S A STORY THAT CONTINUED UNTIL VOLUME 28 WITHOUT THE MAIN CHARACTER BEING ABLE TO VOICE HER FEELINGS!!
I got impatient.
ANYWAY, YOU DECIDE WHAT YOU'RE GONNA DO...
TAP
I was afraid.
YUTAKA KUROKAWA.
Yikes!
YOU...
...LIVE HERE.
COME BACK RIGHT AWAY.

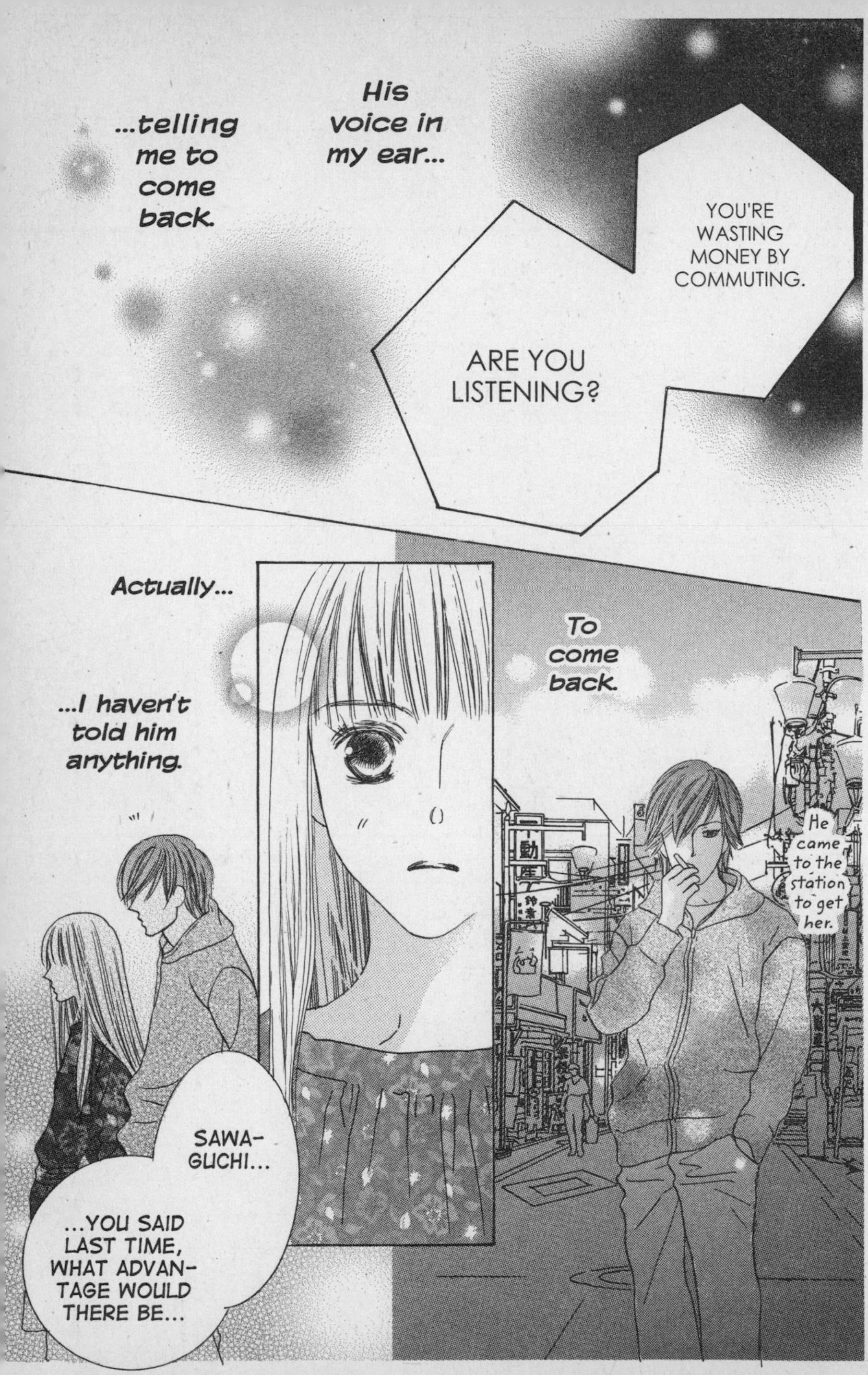
YOU'RE WASTING MONEY BY COMMUTING.
ARE YOU LISTENING?
His voice in my ear...
...telling me to come back.
To come back.
He came to the station to get her.
Actually...
...I haven't told him anything.
SAWA-GUCHI...
...YOU SAID LAST TIME, WHAT ADVAN-TAGE WOULD THERE BE...

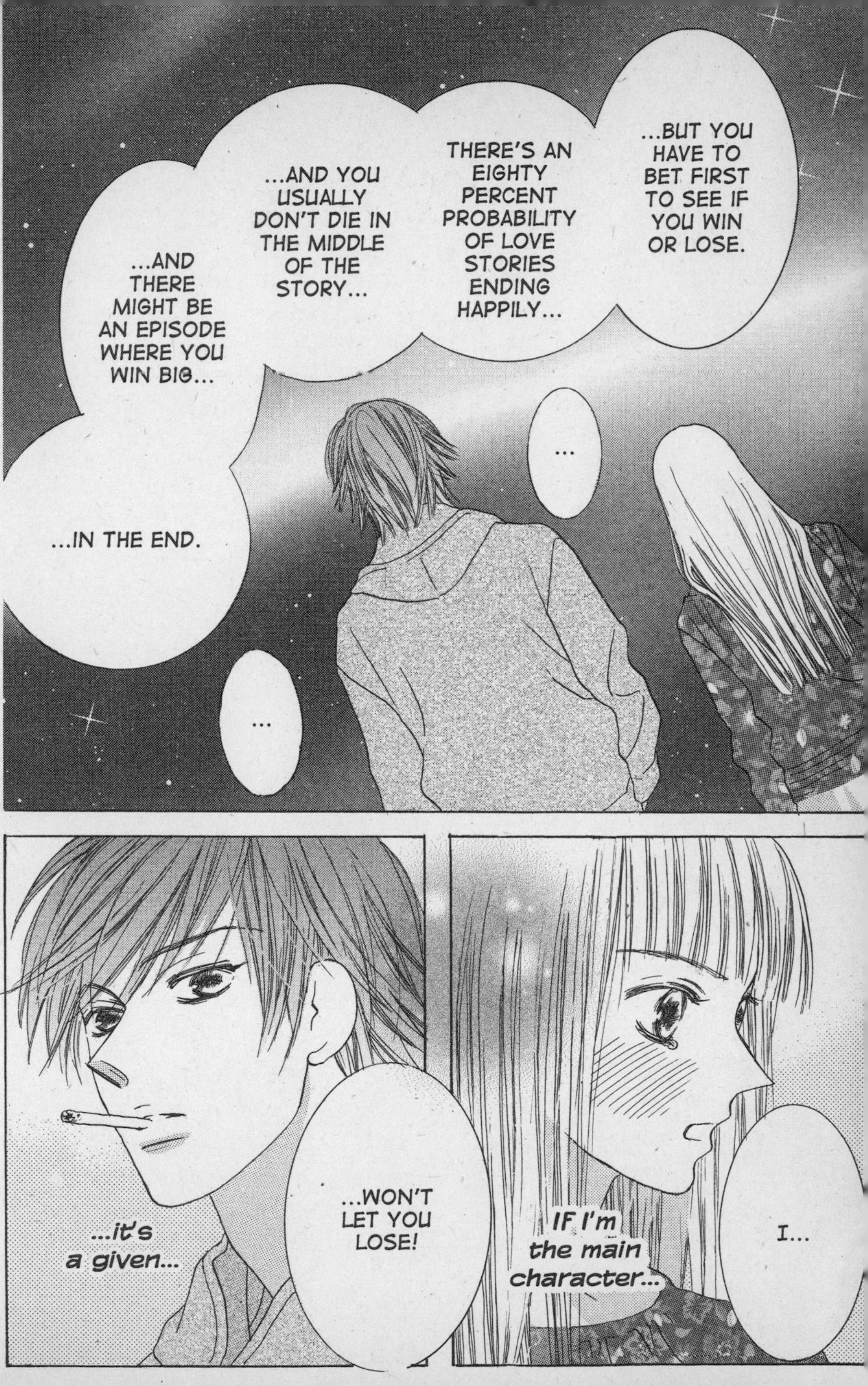
...BUT YOU HAVE TO BET FIRST TO SEE IF YOU WIN OR LOSE.
THERE'S AN EIGHTY PERCENT PROBABILITY OF LOVE STORIES ENDING HAPPILY...
...AND YOU USUALLY DON'T DIE IN THE MIDDLE OF THE STORY...
...AND THERE MIGHT BE AN EPISODE WHERE YOU WIN BIG...
...IN THE END.
...
...
I...
IF I'm the main character...
...WON'T LET YOU LOSE!
...it's a given...

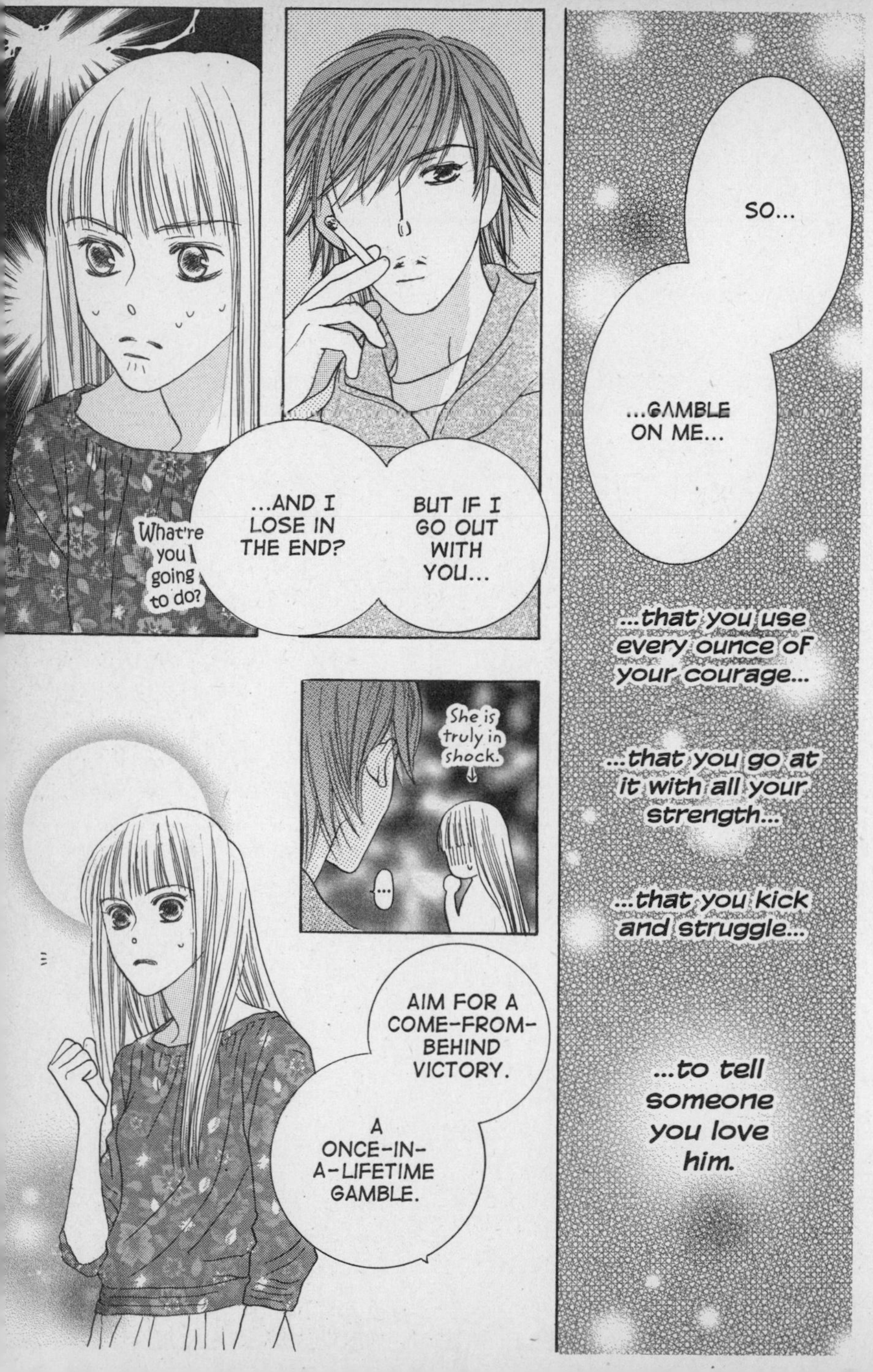
SO...
...GAMBLE ON ME...
...that you use every ounce of your courage...
...that you go at it with all your strength...
...that you kick and struggle...
...to tell someone you love him.
BUT IF I GO OUT WITH YOU...
...AND I LOSE IN THE END?
What're you going to do?
She is truly in shock.
...
AIM FOR A COME-FROM-BEHIND VICTORY.
A ONCE-IN-A-LIFETIME GAMBLE.

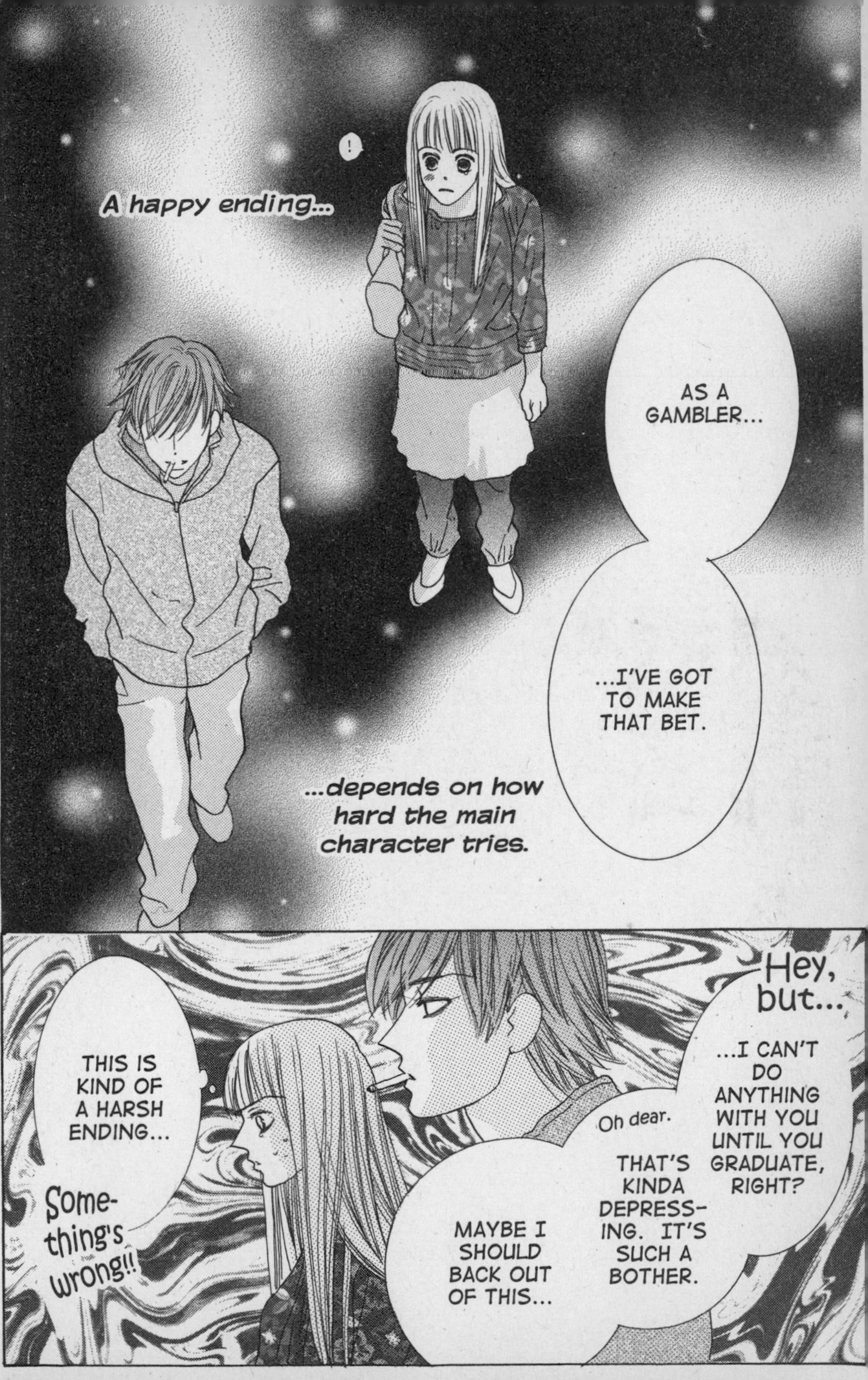
!
A happy ending...
AS A GAMBLER...
...I'VE GOT TO MAKE THAT BET.
...depends on how hard the main character tries.
Hey, but...
...I CAN'T DO ANYTHING WITH YOU UNTIL YOU GRADUATE, RIGHT?
Oh dear.
THAT'S KINDA DEPRESSING. IT'S SUCH A BOTHER.
MAYBE I SHOULD BACK OUT OF THIS...
THIS IS KIND OF A HARSH ENDING...
Something's wrong!!

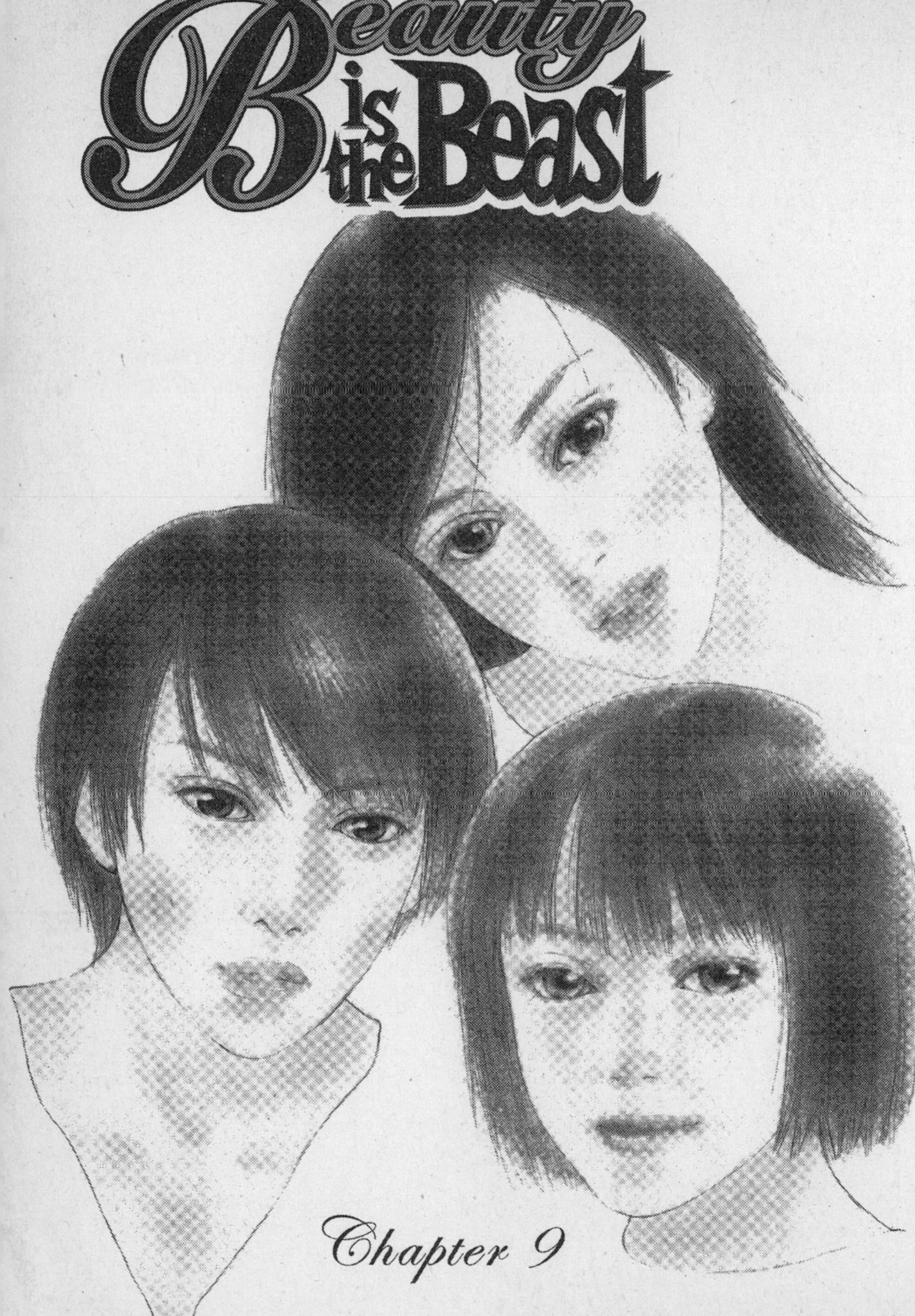
Beauty is the Beast
Chapter 9

BEAUTY
IS THE
BEAST

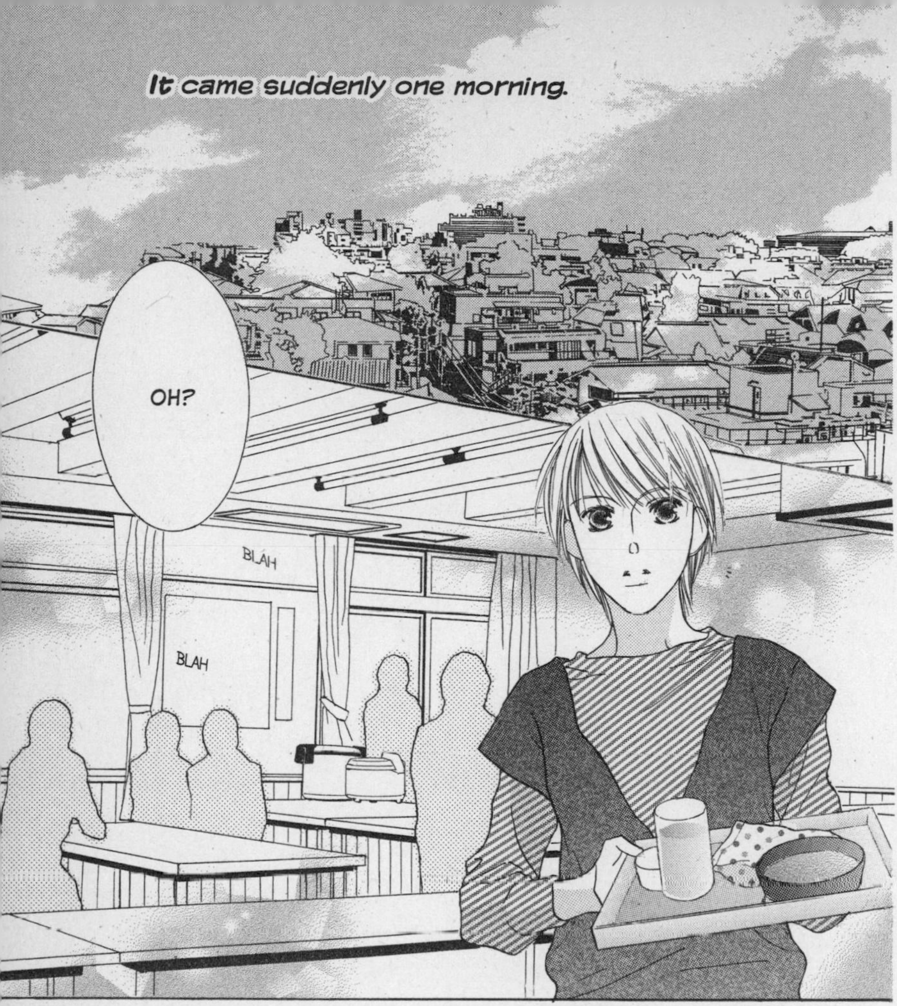
It came suddenly one morning.
OH?
BLAH
BLAH

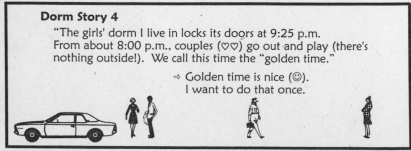

Dorm Story 4

"The girls' dorm I live in locks its doors at 9:25 p.m. From about 8:00 p.m., couples (♡♡) go out and play (there's nothing outside!). We call this time the "golden time."

⇨ Golden time is nice (☺). I want to do that once.

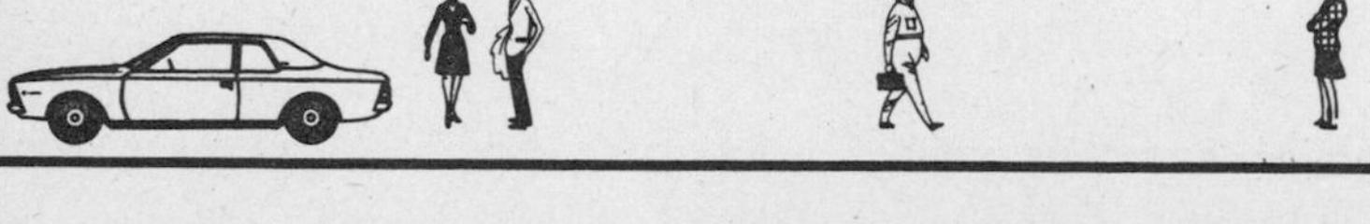

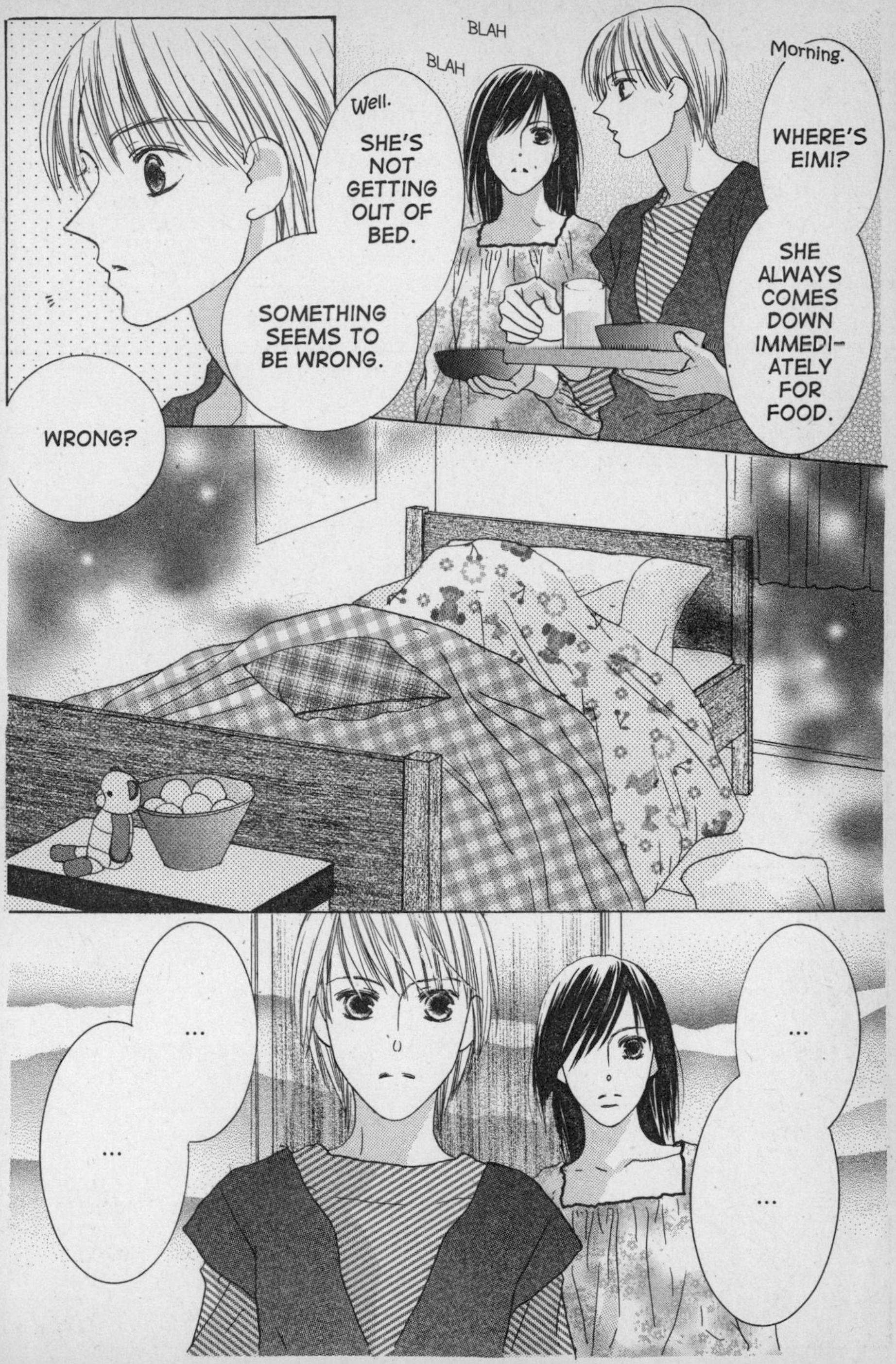
Morning.
WHERE'S EIMI?
SHE ALWAYS COMES DOWN IMMEDI-ATELY FOR FOOD.
BLAH
BLAH
Well.
SHE'S NOT GETTING OUT OF BED.
SOMETHING SEEMS TO BE WRONG.
WRONG?
...
...
...
...

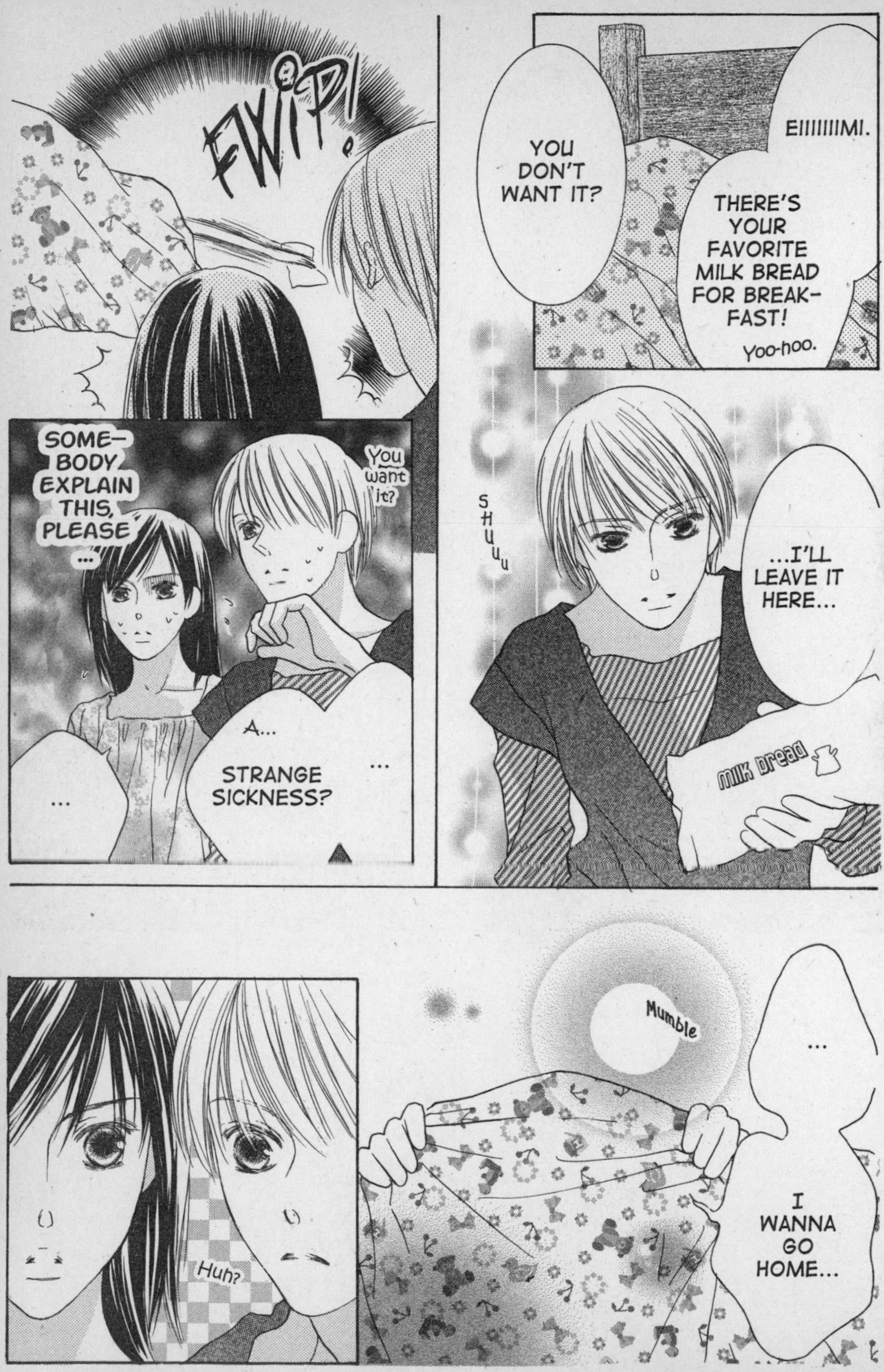

EIIIIIIIMI.
THERE'S YOUR FAVORITE MILK BREAD FOR BREAK-FAST!
Yoo-hoo.
YOU DON'T WANT IT?
...I'LL LEAVE IT HERE...
SHUUU
MILK bread
FWIP!
You want it?
SOME-BODY EXPLAIN THIS, PLEASE...
...
A... STRANGE SICKNESS?
...
...
I WANNA GO HOME...
Mumble
Huh?

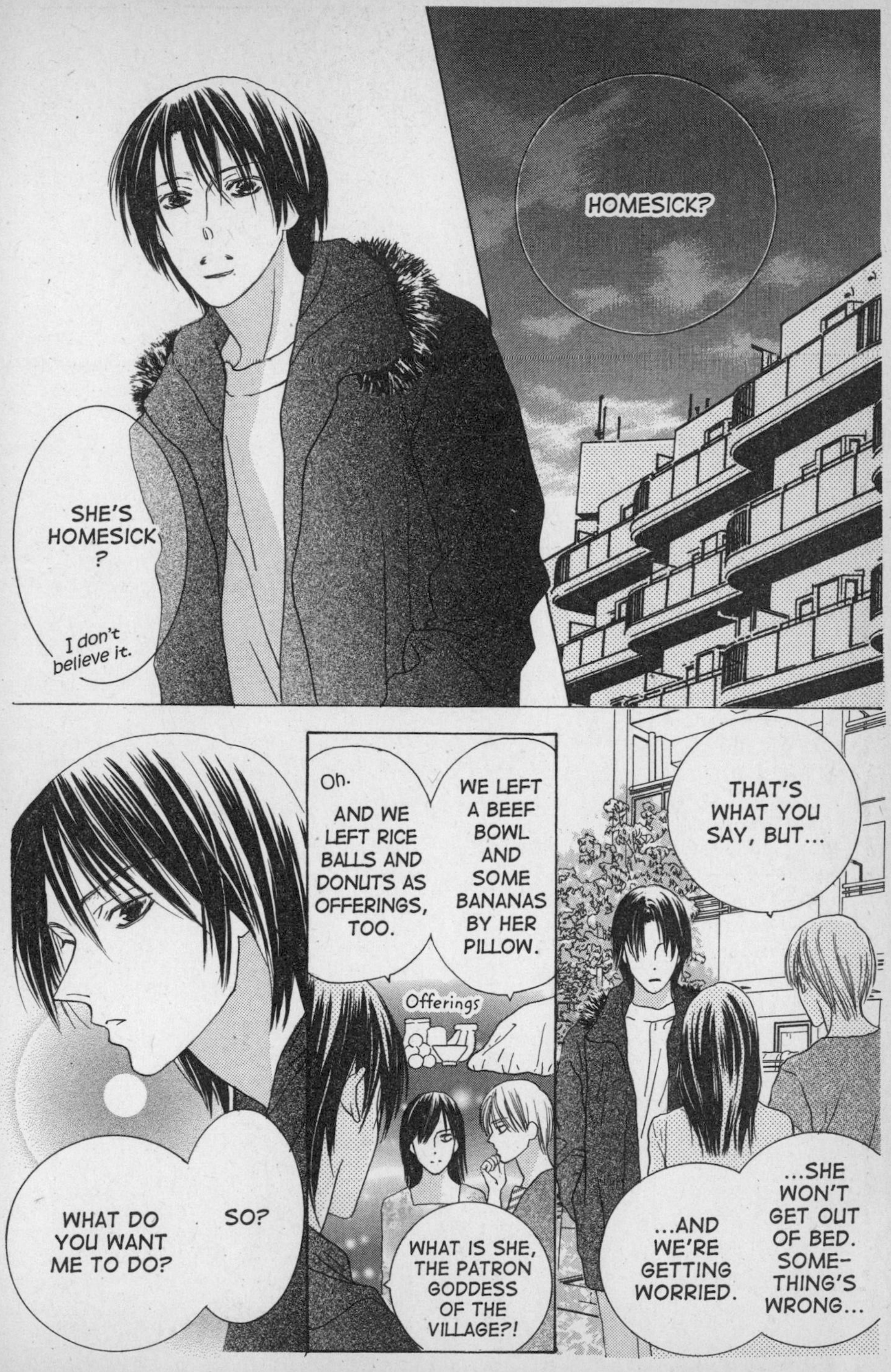
HOMESICK?
SHE'S HOMESICK?
I don't believe it.
THAT'S WHAT YOU SAY, BUT...
...SHE WON'T GET OUT OF BED. SOME-THING'S WRONG...
...AND WE'RE GETTING WORRIED.
WE LEFT A BEEF BOWL AND SOME BANANAS BY HER PILLOW.
Oh.
AND WE LEFT RICE BALLS AND DONUTS AS OFFERINGS, TOO.
Offerings
WHAT IS SHE, THE PATRON GODDESS OF THE VILLAGE?!
SO?
WHAT DO YOU WANT ME TO DO?

④ **Decide Which Colors to Use.**

Sometimes, I get a little down because things work better if I don't spend too much time on them.

For coloring, I use color tones, markers, and inks. For finishing, I use pastels. For skin color, I mix Luma's color ink, vermillion, and lemon.

↑ But this is not being sold now, so I'm worried about what to do when my inks run out. Oh dear...

(I'm sorry this information isn't of any use at all.)

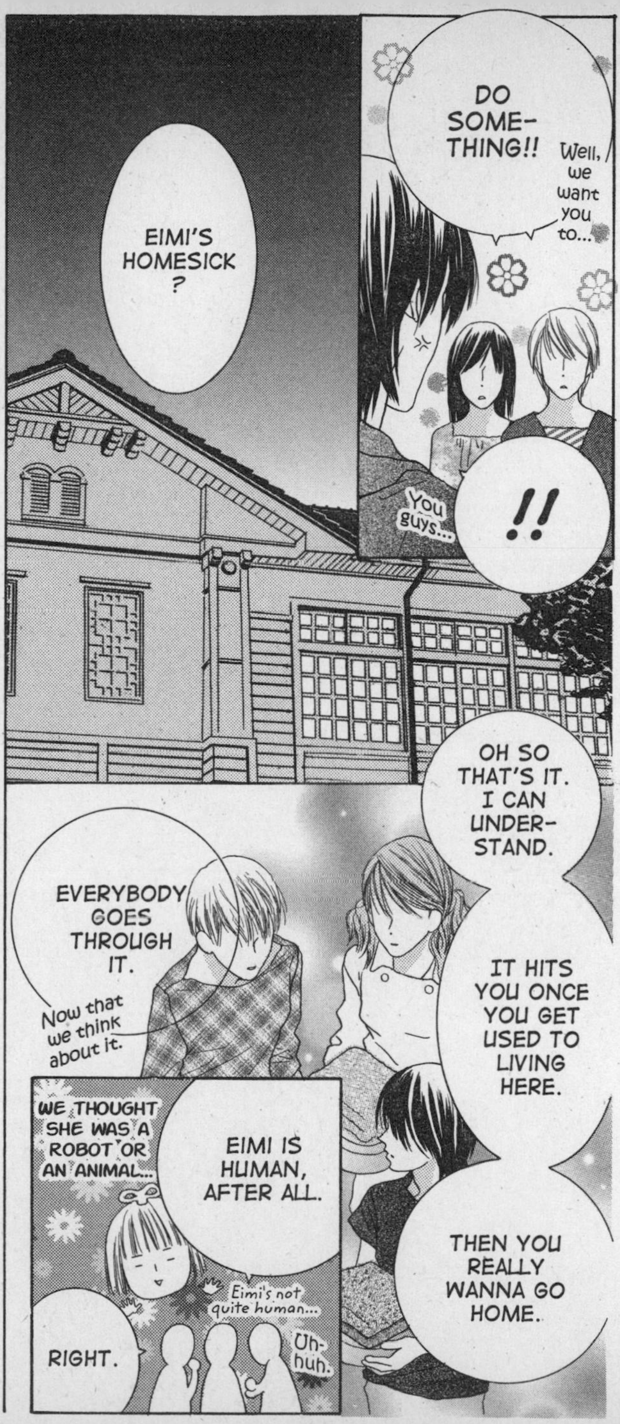
Well, we want you to...
DO SOME-THING!!
!!
You guys...
EIMI'S HOMESICK?
OH SO THAT'S IT. I CAN UNDER-STAND.
EVERYBODY GOES THROUGH IT.
Now that we think about it.
IT HITS YOU ONCE YOU GET USED TO LIVING HERE.
THEN YOU REALLY WANNA GO HOME.
EIMI IS HUMAN, AFTER ALL.
WE THOUGHT SHE WAS A ROBOT OR AN ANIMAL...
Eimi's not quite human...
Uh-huh.
RIGHT.

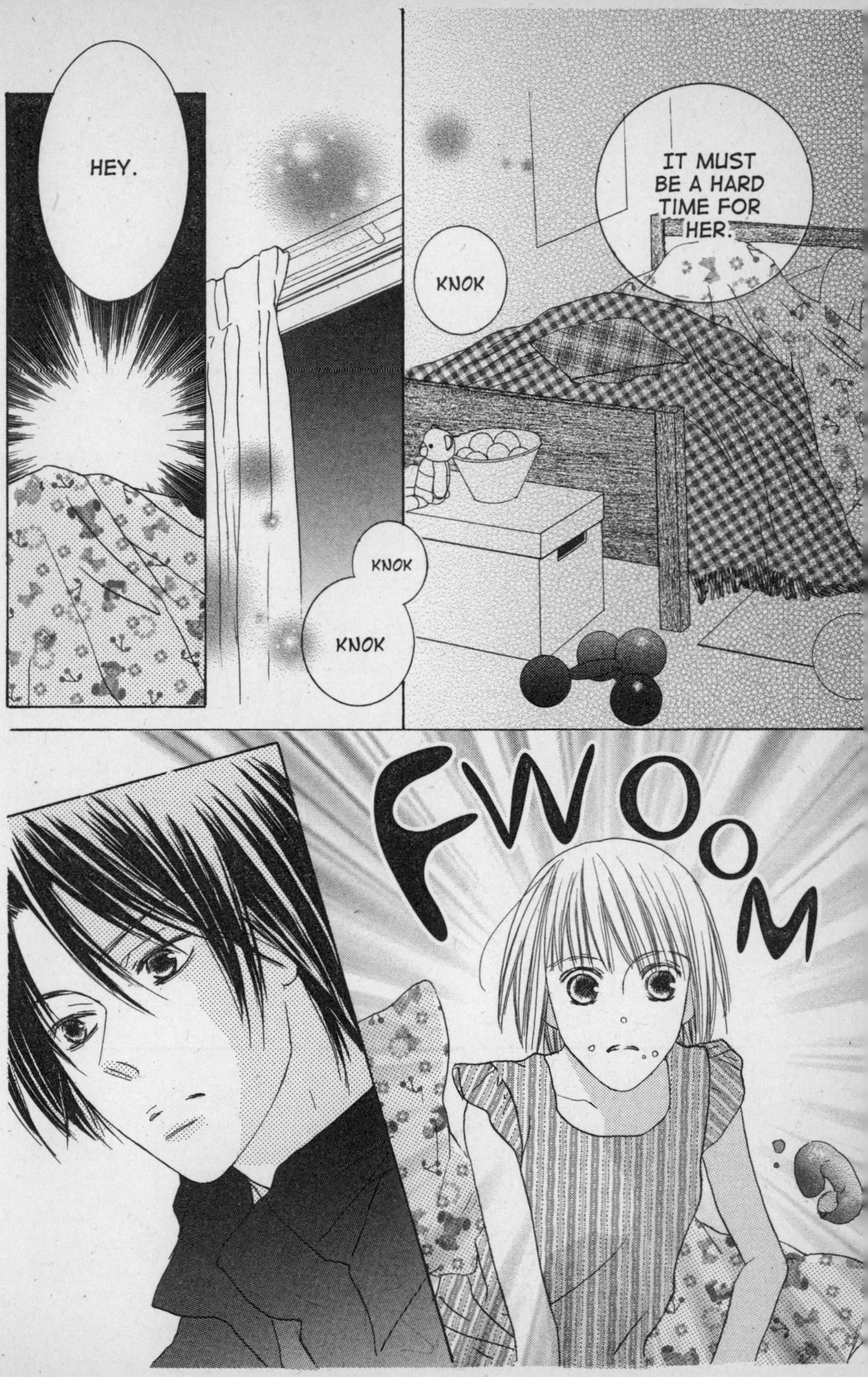
IT MUST BE A HARD TIME FOR HER.
KNOK
KNOK
KNOK
HEY.
FWOOM

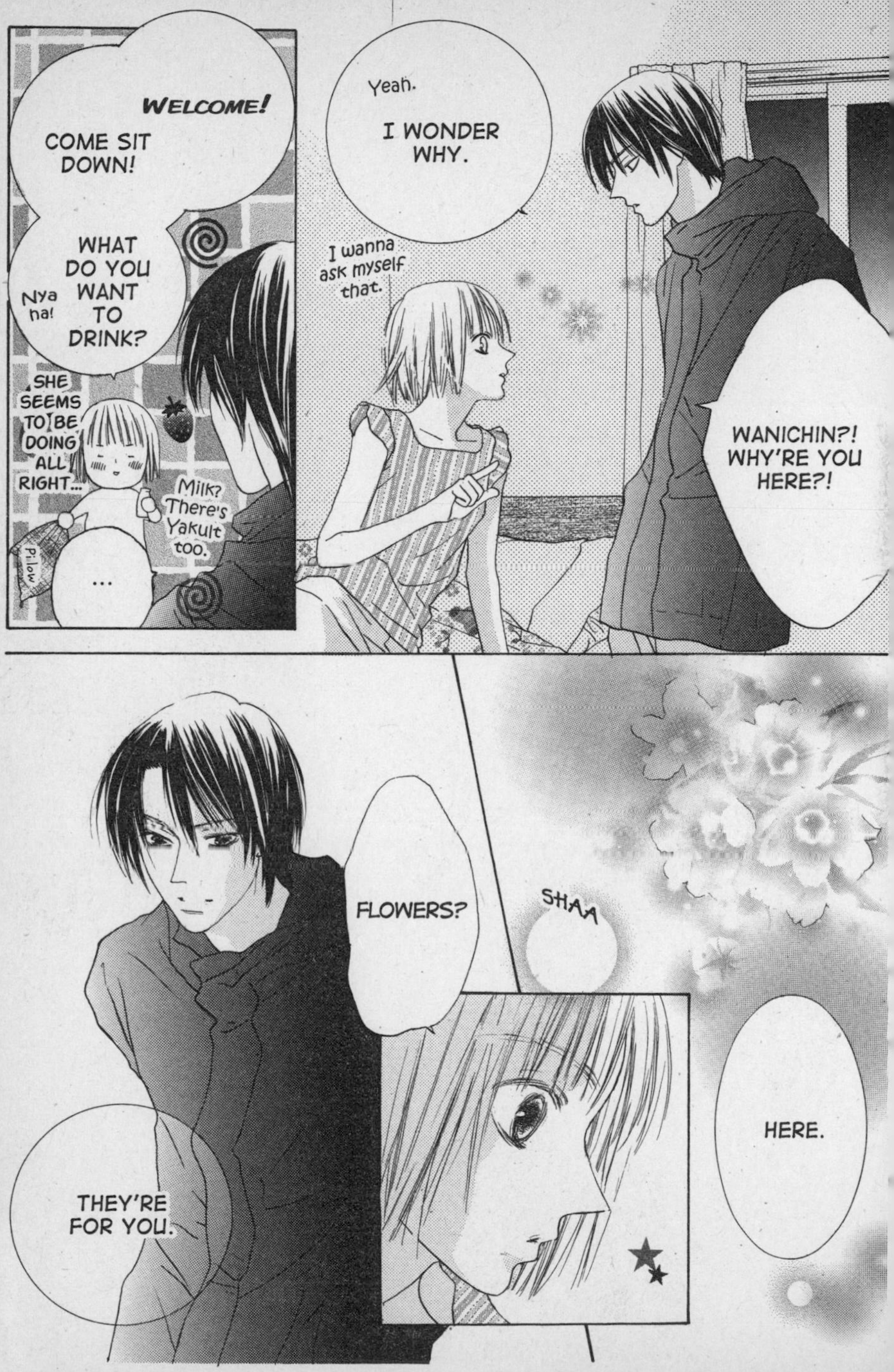
WANICHIN?! WHY'RE YOU HERE?!
Yeah.
I WONDER WHY.
I wanna ask myself that.
WELCOME!
COME SIT DOWN!
WHAT DO YOU WANT TO DRINK?
Nya na!
SHE SEEMS TO BE DOING ALL RIGHT...
Milk? There's Yakult too.
...
Pilow
SHAA
HERE.
FLOWERS?
THEY'RE FOR YOU.

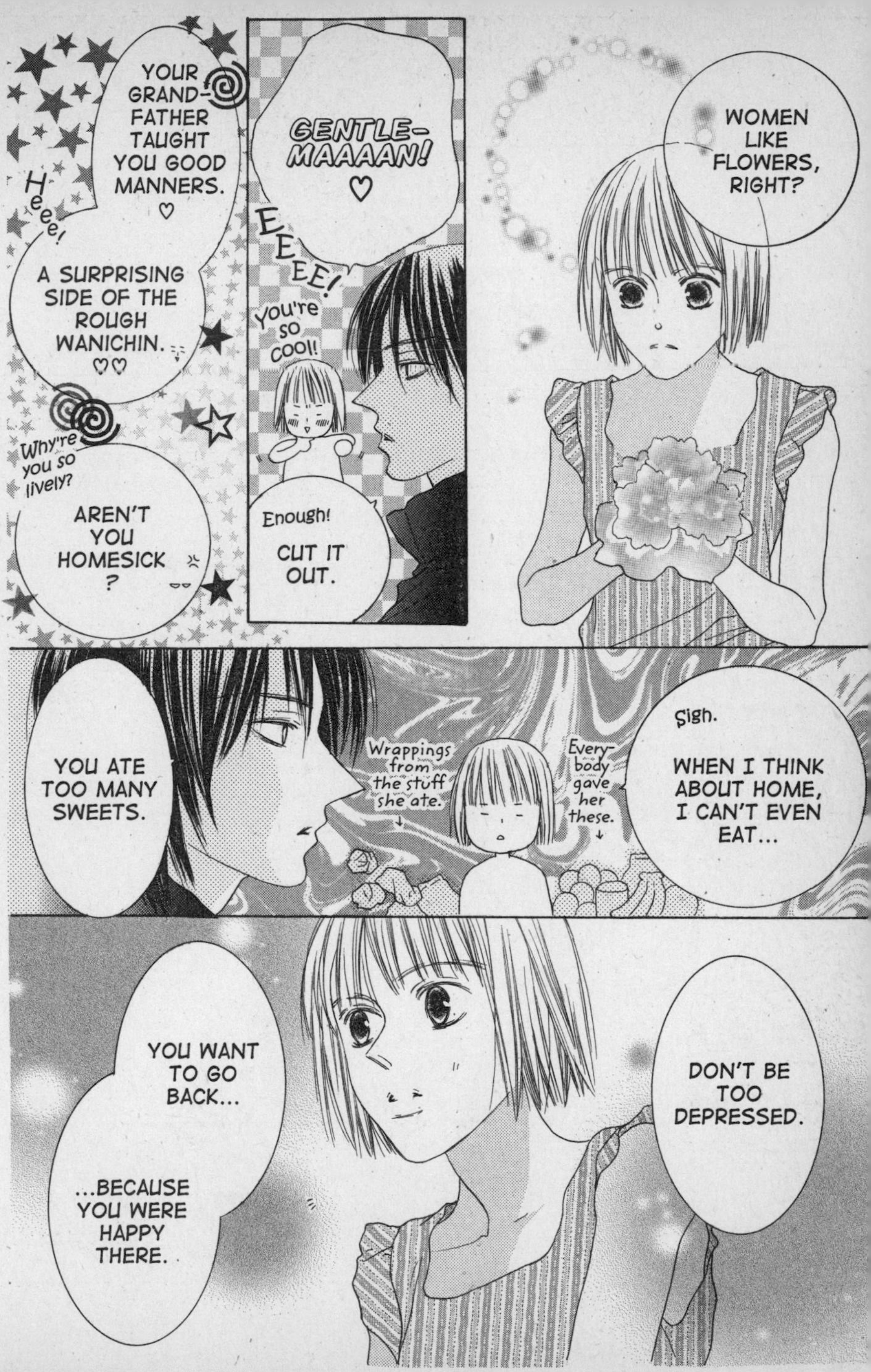
WOMEN LIKE FLOWERS, RIGHT?
GENTLE-MAAAAN! ♡
EEEEE!
You're so cool!
Enough!
CUT IT OUT.
YOUR GRAND-FATHER TAUGHT YOU GOOD MANNERS. ♡
Heee!
A SURPRISING SIDE OF THE ROUGH WANICHIN. ♡♡
Why're you so lively?
AREN'T YOU HOMESICK?
Sigh.
WHEN I THINK ABOUT HOME, I CAN'T EVEN EAT...
Every-body gave her these.
Wrappings from the stuff she ate.
YOU ATE TOO MANY SWEETS.
DON'T BE TOO DEPRESSED.
YOU WANT TO GO BACK...
...BECAUSE YOU WERE HAPPY THERE.

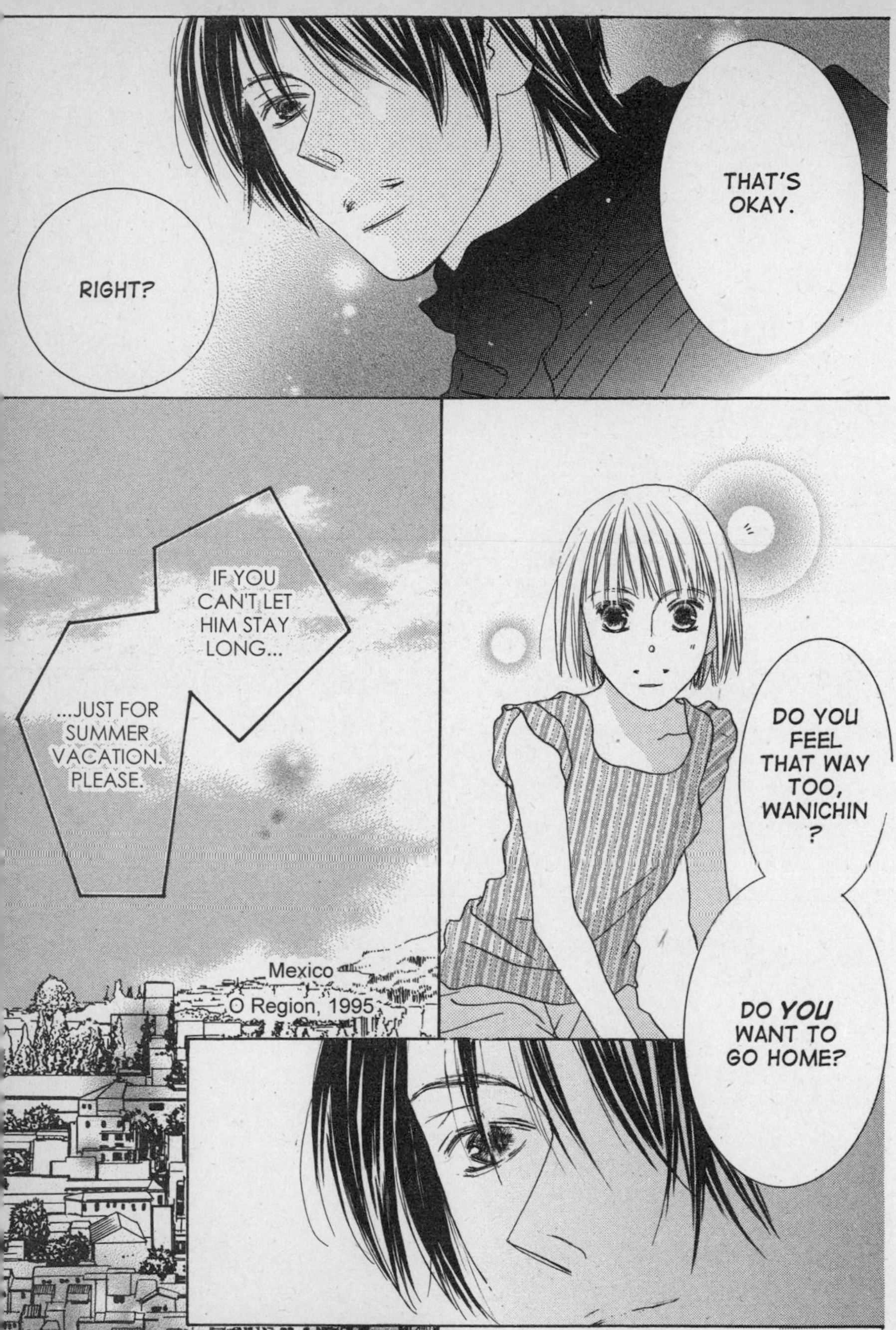
THAT'S OKAY.
RIGHT?
DO YOU FEEL THAT WAY TOO, WANICHIN?
DO *YOU* WANT TO GO HOME?
IF YOU CAN'T LET HIM STAY LONG...
...JUST FOR SUMMER VACATION. PLEASE.
Mexico
O Region, 1995

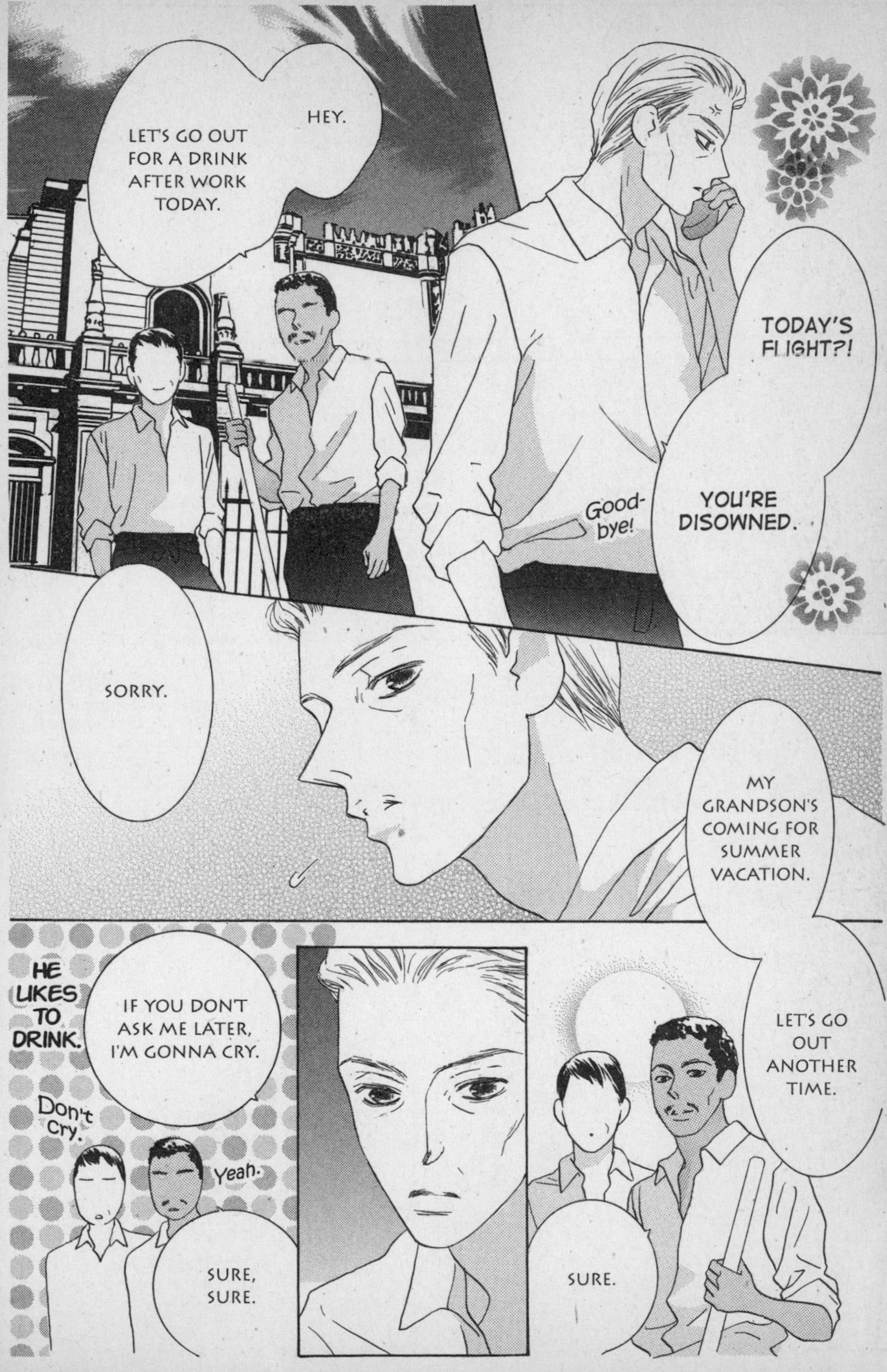
TODAY'S FLIGHT?!
YOU'RE DISOWNED.
Good-bye!
HEY.
LET'S GO OUT FOR A DRINK AFTER WORK TODAY.
SORRY.
MY GRANDSON'S COMING FOR SUMMER VACATION.
LET'S GO OUT ANOTHER TIME.
SURE.
IF YOU DON'T ASK ME LATER, I'M GONNA CRY.
HE LIKES TO DRINK.
Don't cry.
Yeah.
SURE, SURE.

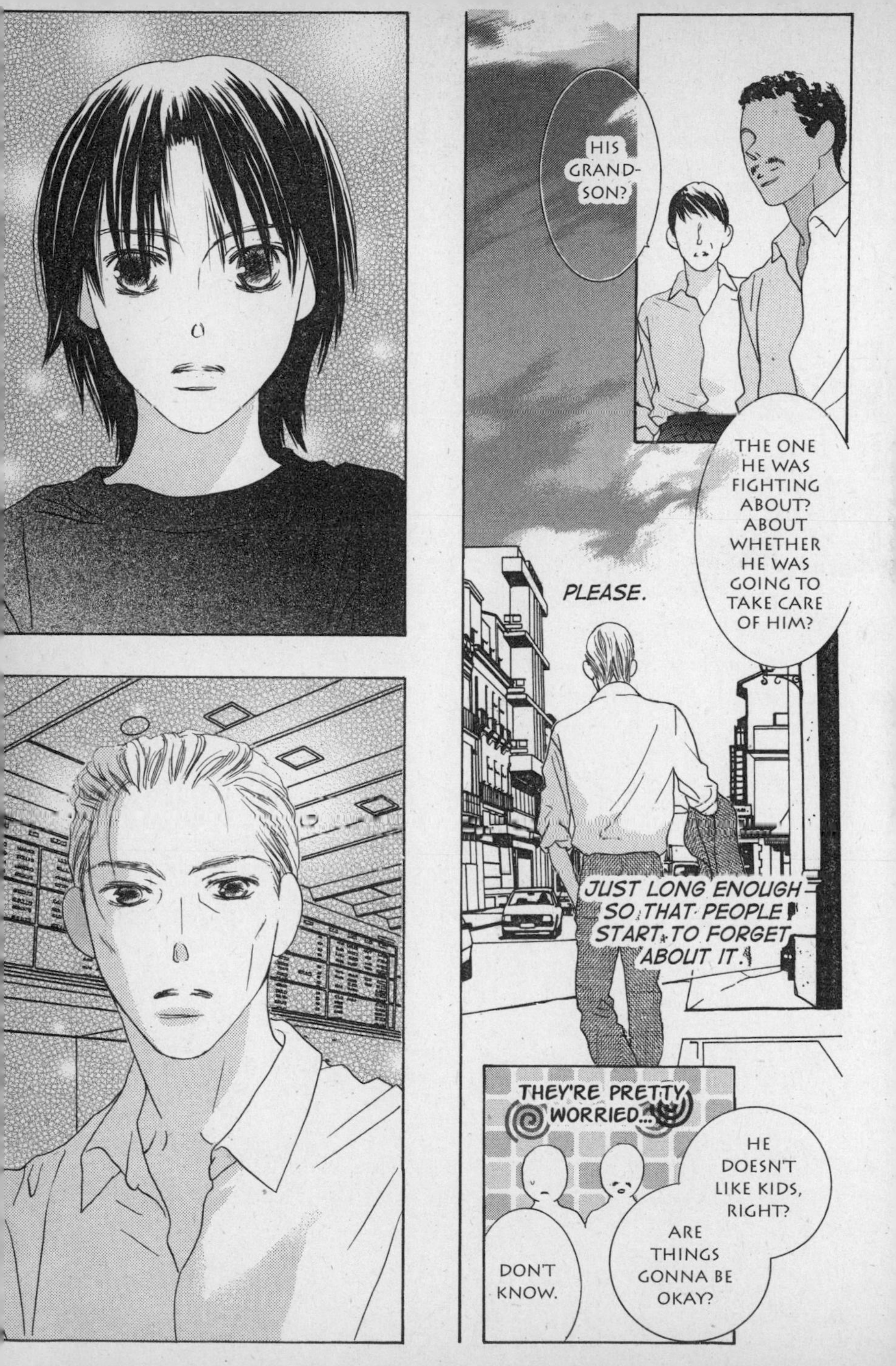
HIS GRAND-SON?
THE ONE HE WAS FIGHTING ABOUT? ABOUT WHETHER HE WAS GOING TO TAKE CARE OF HIM?
PLEASE.
JUST LONG ENOUGH SO THAT PEOPLE START TO FORGET ABOUT IT.
THEY'RE PRETTY WORRIED...
HE DOESN'T LIKE KIDS, RIGHT?
ARE THINGS GONNA BE OKAY?
DON'T KNOW.

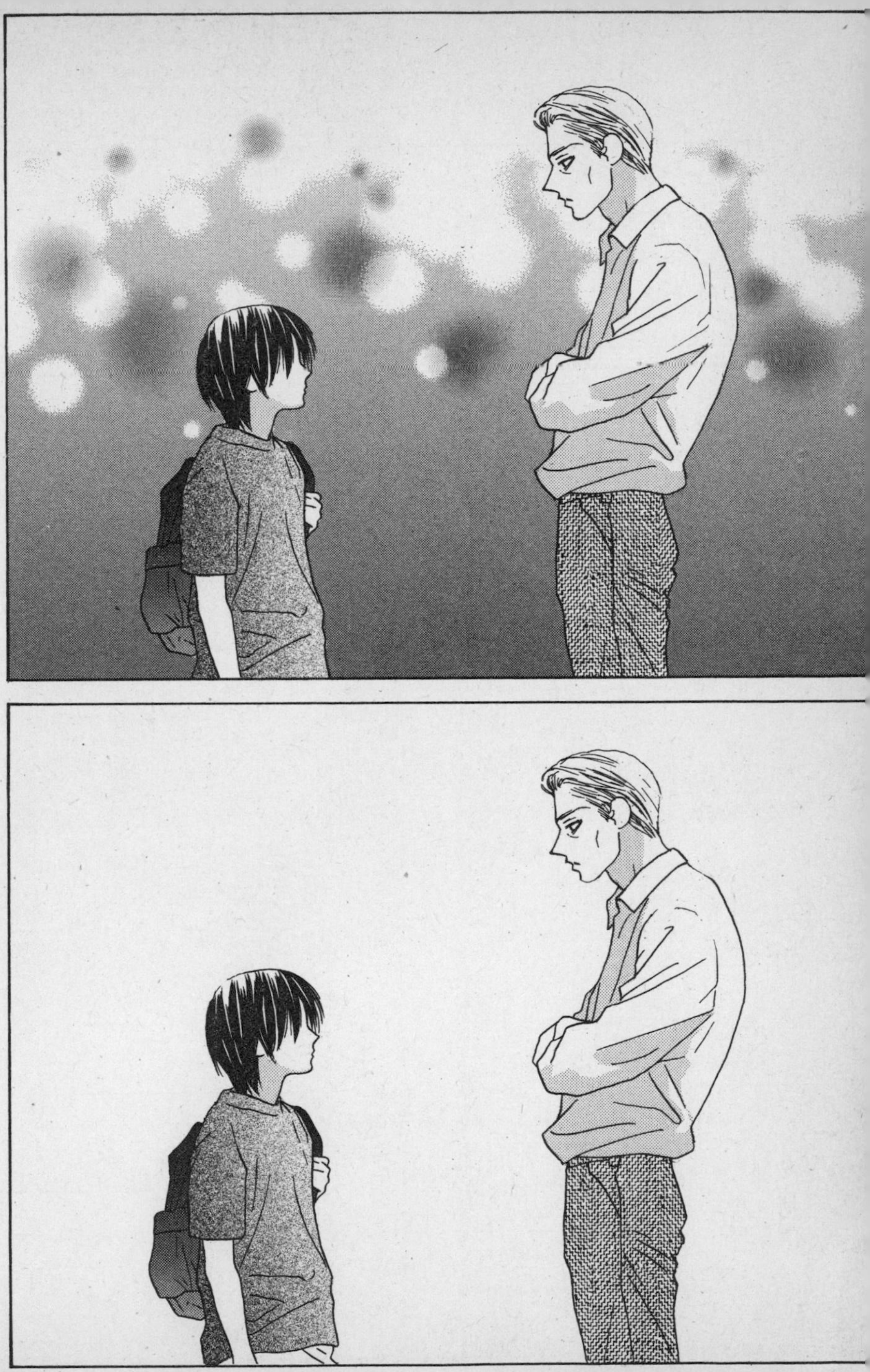

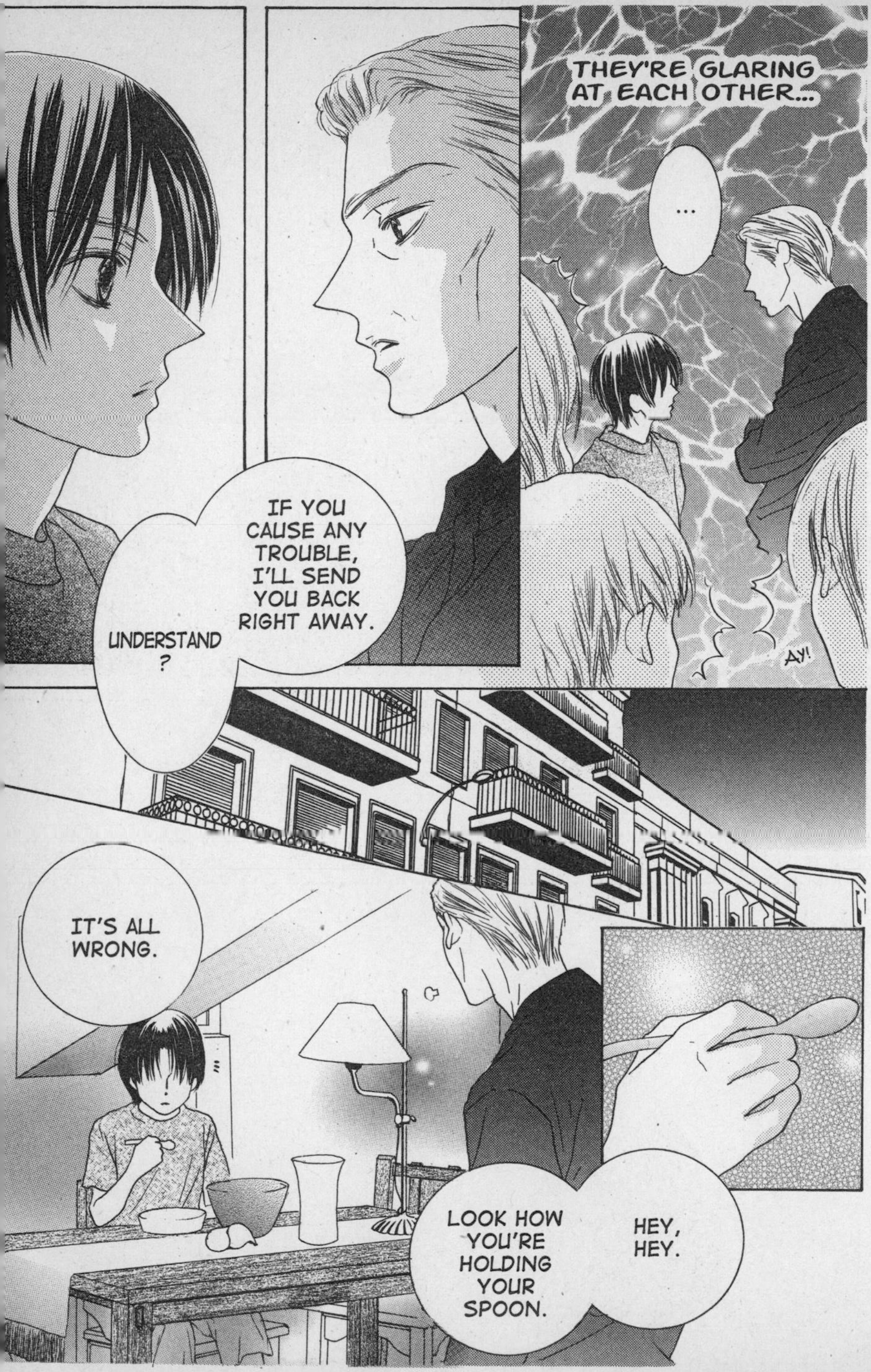
THEY'RE GLARING AT EACH OTHER...
...
AY!
IF YOU CAUSE ANY TROUBLE, I'LL SEND YOU BACK RIGHT AWAY.
UNDERSTAND ?
HEY, HEY.
LOOK HOW YOU'RE HOLDING YOUR SPOON.
IT'S ALL WRONG.

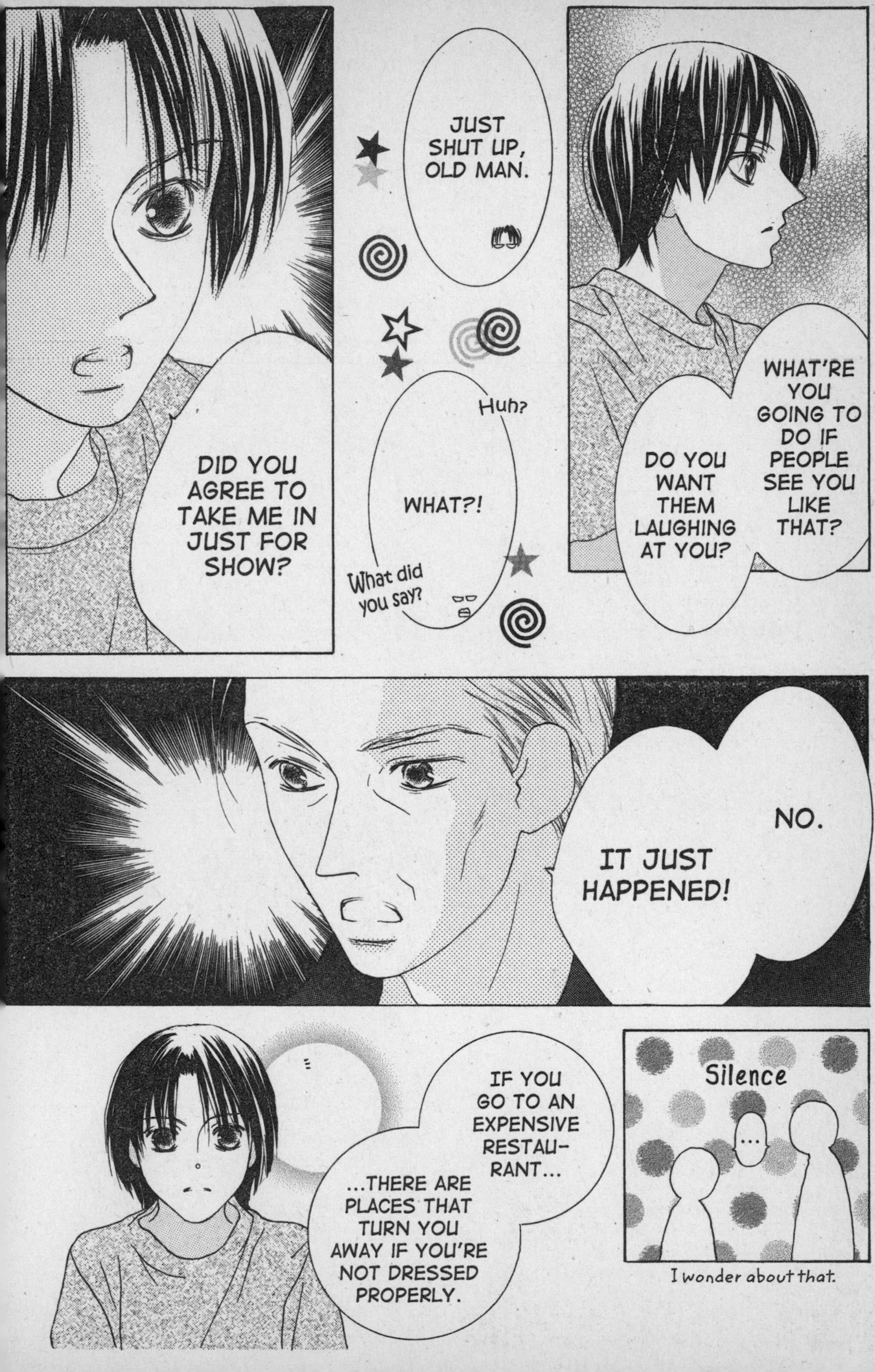
WHAT'RE YOU GOING TO DO IF PEOPLE SEE YOU LIKE THAT?
DO YOU WANT THEM LAUGHING AT YOU?
JUST SHUT UP, OLD MAN.
Huh?
WHAT?!
What did you say?
DID YOU AGREE TO TAKE ME IN JUST FOR SHOW?
NO.
IT JUST HAPPENED!
Silence
...
I wonder about that.
IF YOU GO TO AN EXPENSIVE RESTAU-RANT...
...THERE ARE PLACES THAT TURN YOU AWAY IF YOU'RE NOT DRESSED PROPERLY.

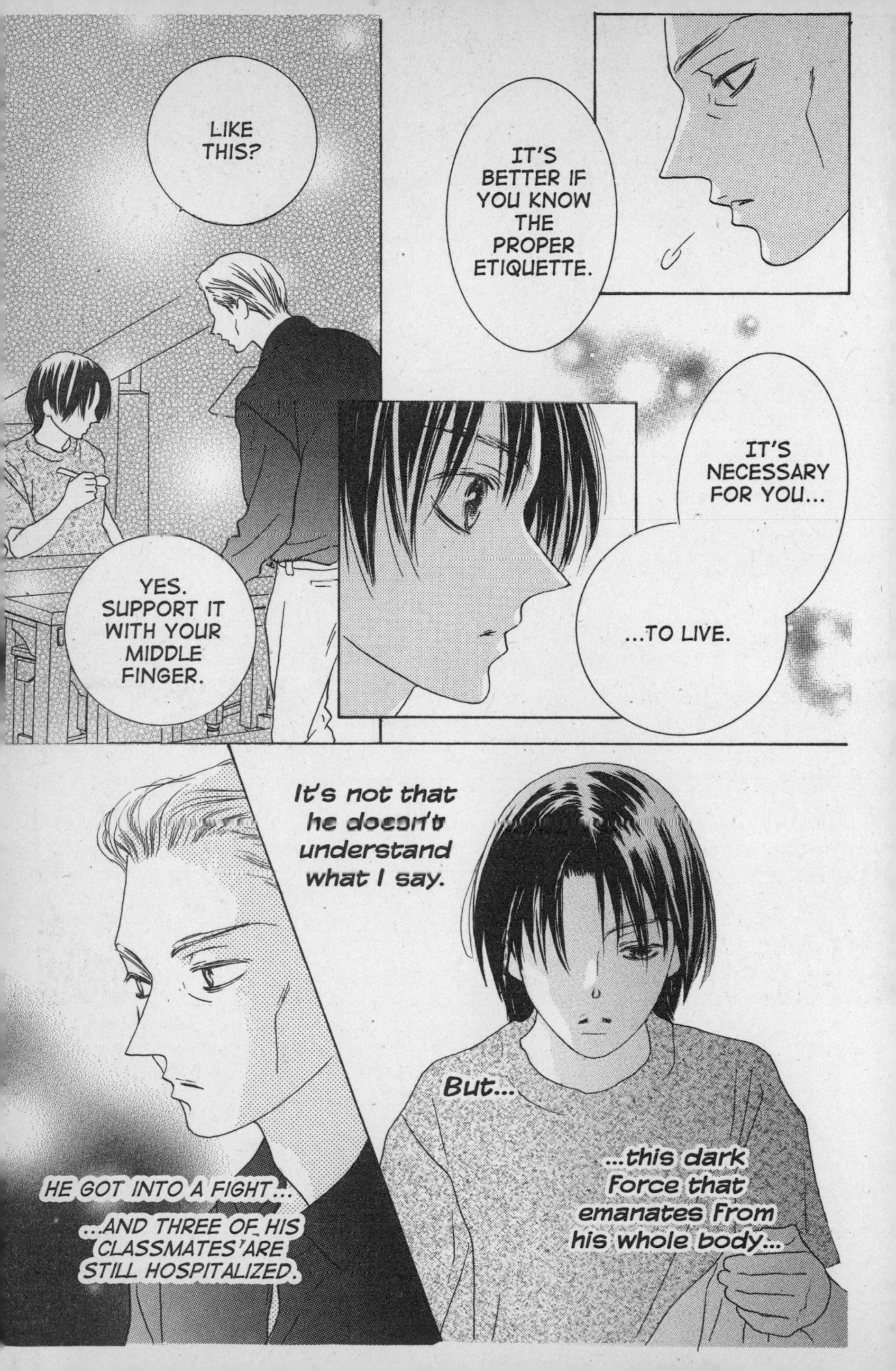
IT'S BETTER IF YOU KNOW THE PROPER ETIQUETTE.
IT'S NECESSARY FOR YOU...
...TO LIVE.
LIKE THIS?
YES. SUPPORT IT WITH YOUR MIDDLE FINGER.
It's not that he doesn't understand what I say.
But...
...this dark force that emanates from his whole body...
HE GOT INTO A FIGHT...
...AND THREE OF HIS CLASSMATES ARE STILL HOSPITALIZED.

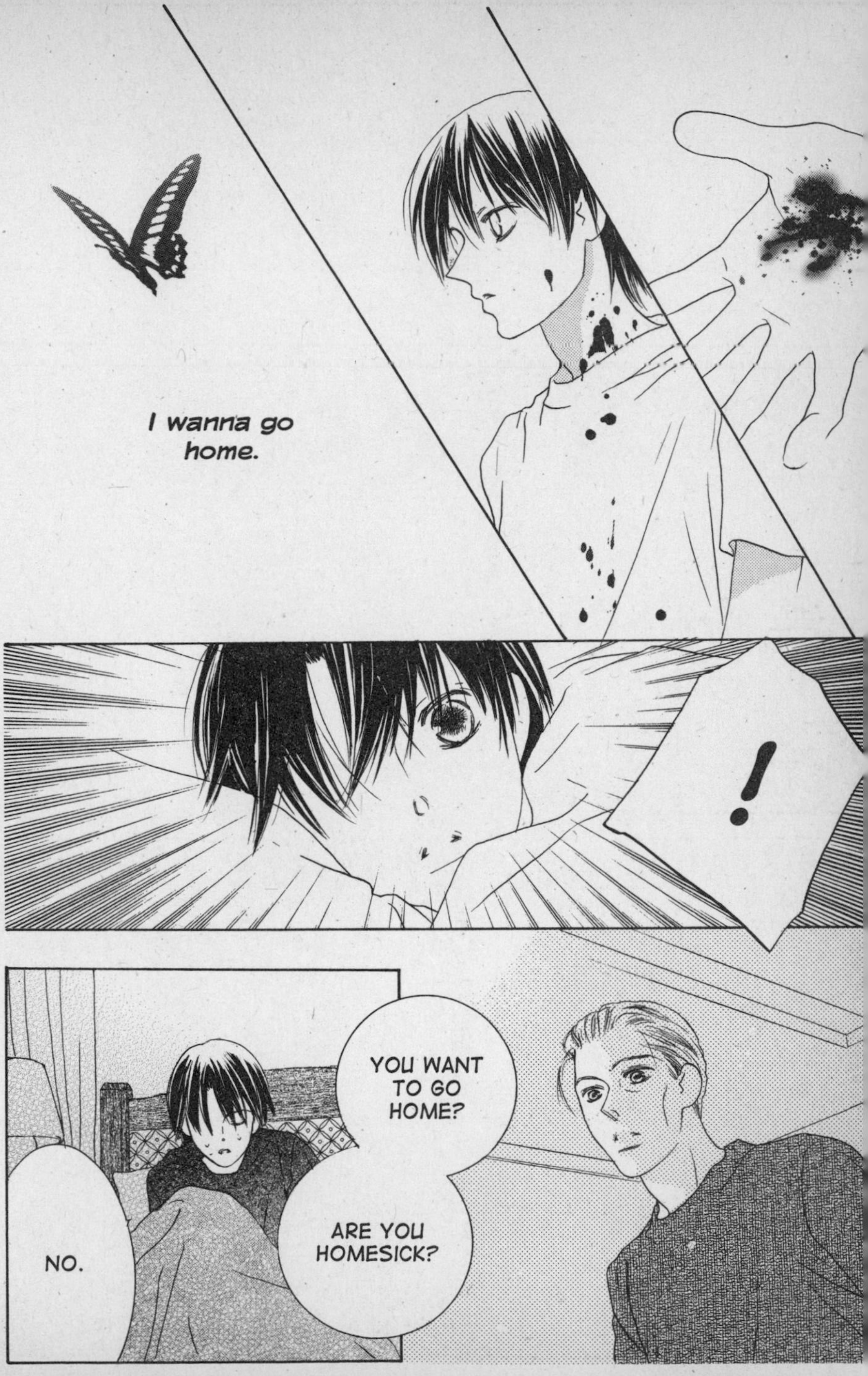
I wanna go home.
!
YOU WANT TO GO HOME?
ARE YOU HOMESICK?
NO.

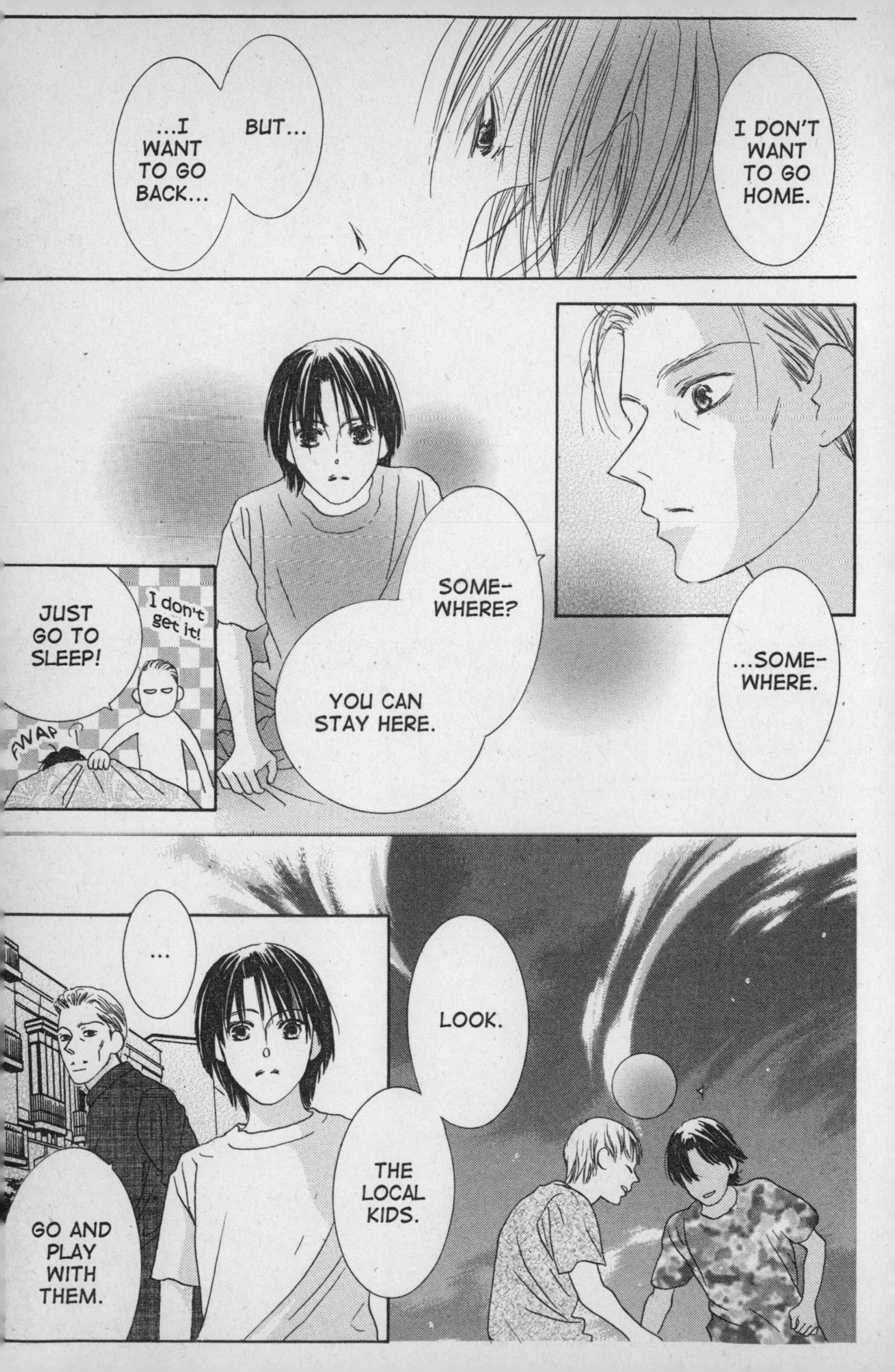
I DON'T WANT TO GO HOME.
BUT...
...I WANT TO GO BACK...
...SOMEWHERE.
SOMEWHERE?
YOU CAN STAY HERE.
I don't get it!
JUST GO TO SLEEP!
FWAP
LOOK.
THE LOCAL KIDS.
...
GO AND PLAY WITH THEM.

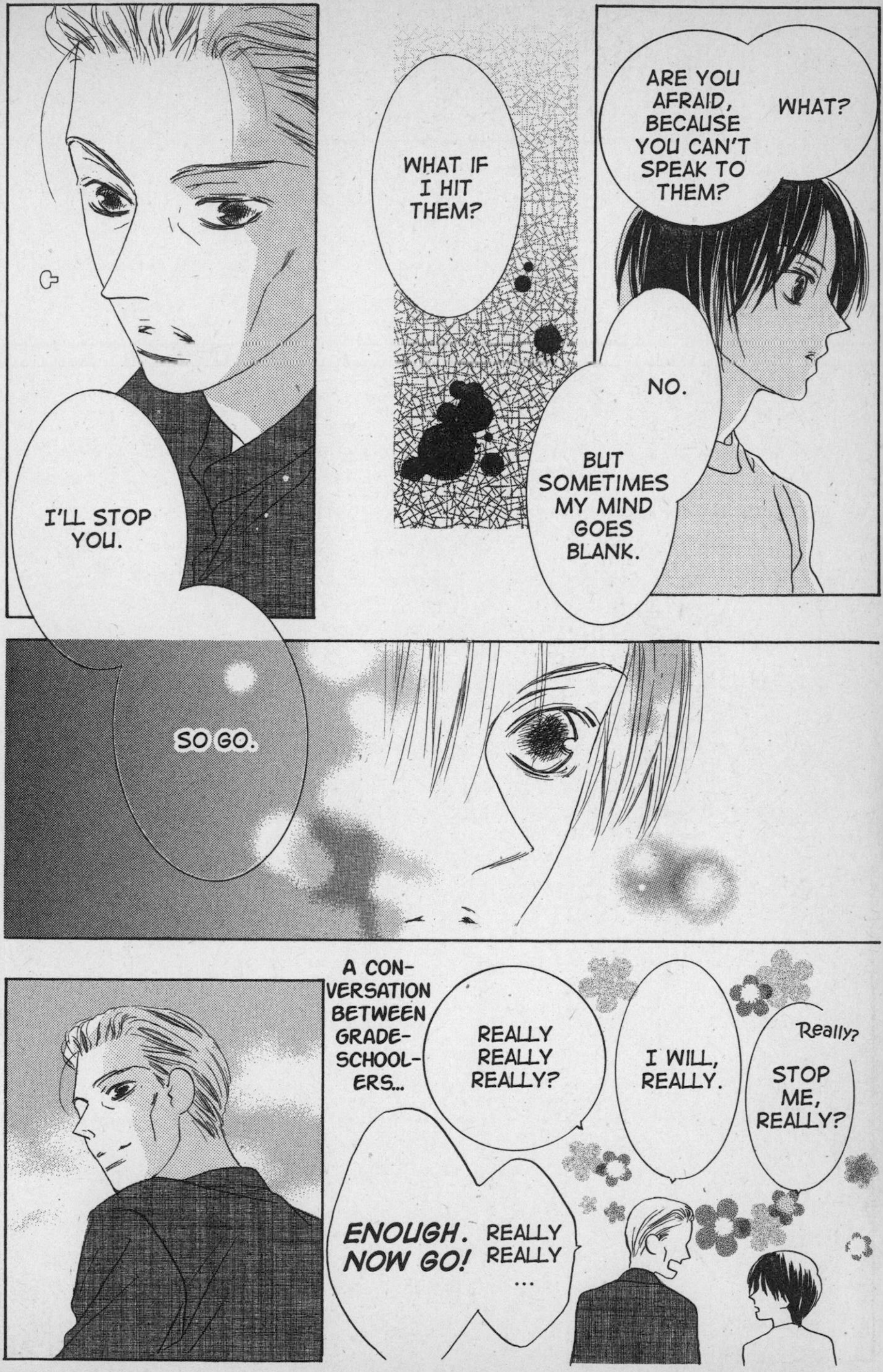
WHAT?
ARE YOU AFRAID, BECAUSE YOU CAN'T SPEAK TO THEM?
NO.
BUT SOMETIMES MY MIND GOES BLANK.
WHAT IF I HIT THEM?
I'LL STOP YOU.
SO GO.
Really?
STOP ME, REALLY?
I WILL, REALLY.
REALLY REALLY REALLY?
A CON-VERSATION BETWEEN GRADE-SCHOOL-ERS...
REALLY REALLY ...
ENOUGH. NOW GO!

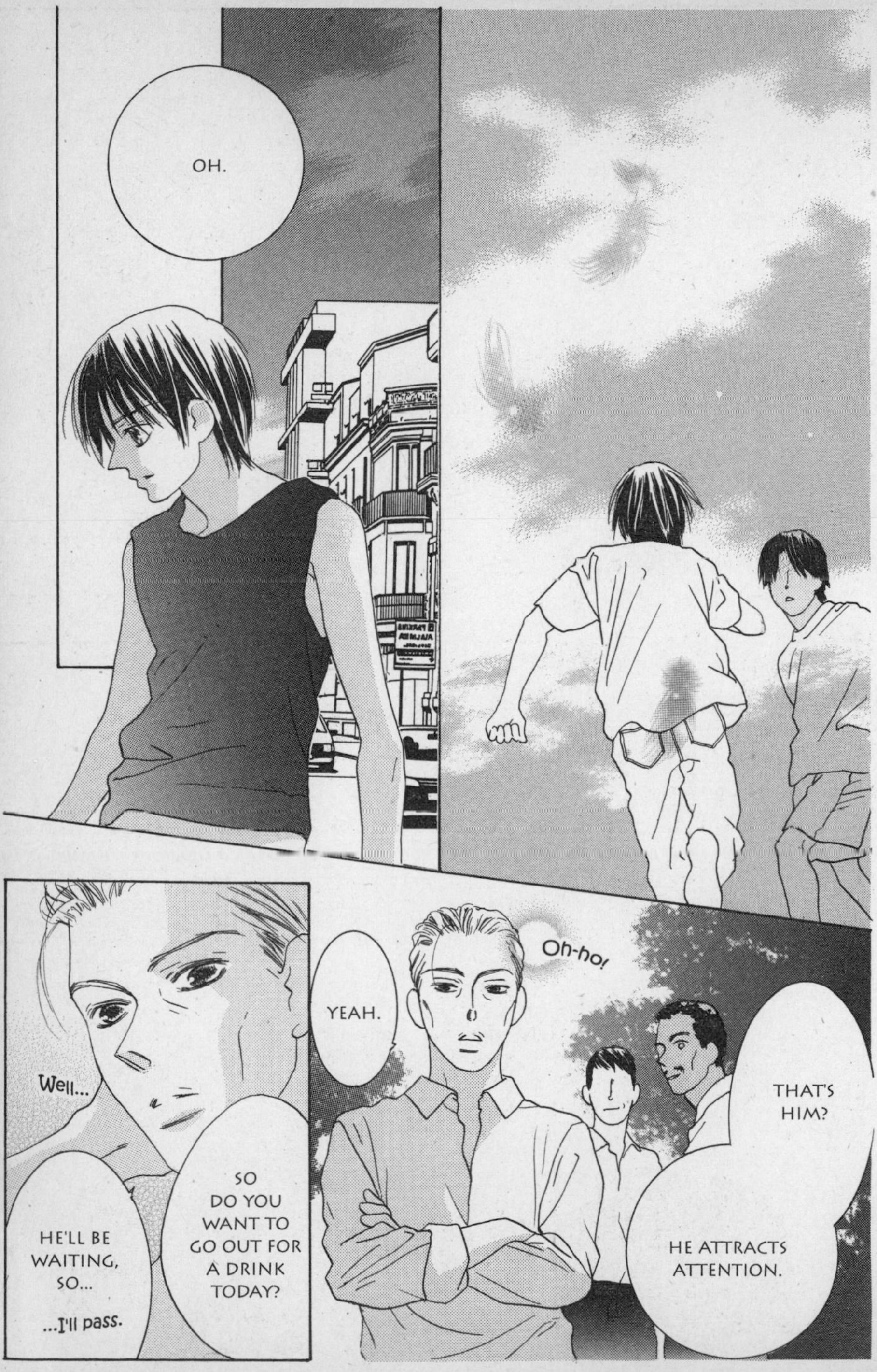
OH.
Oh-ho!
THAT'S HIM?
HE ATTRACTS ATTENTION.
YEAH.
SO DO YOU WANT TO GO OUT FOR A DRINK TODAY?
Well...
HE'LL BE WAITING, SO...
...I'll pass.

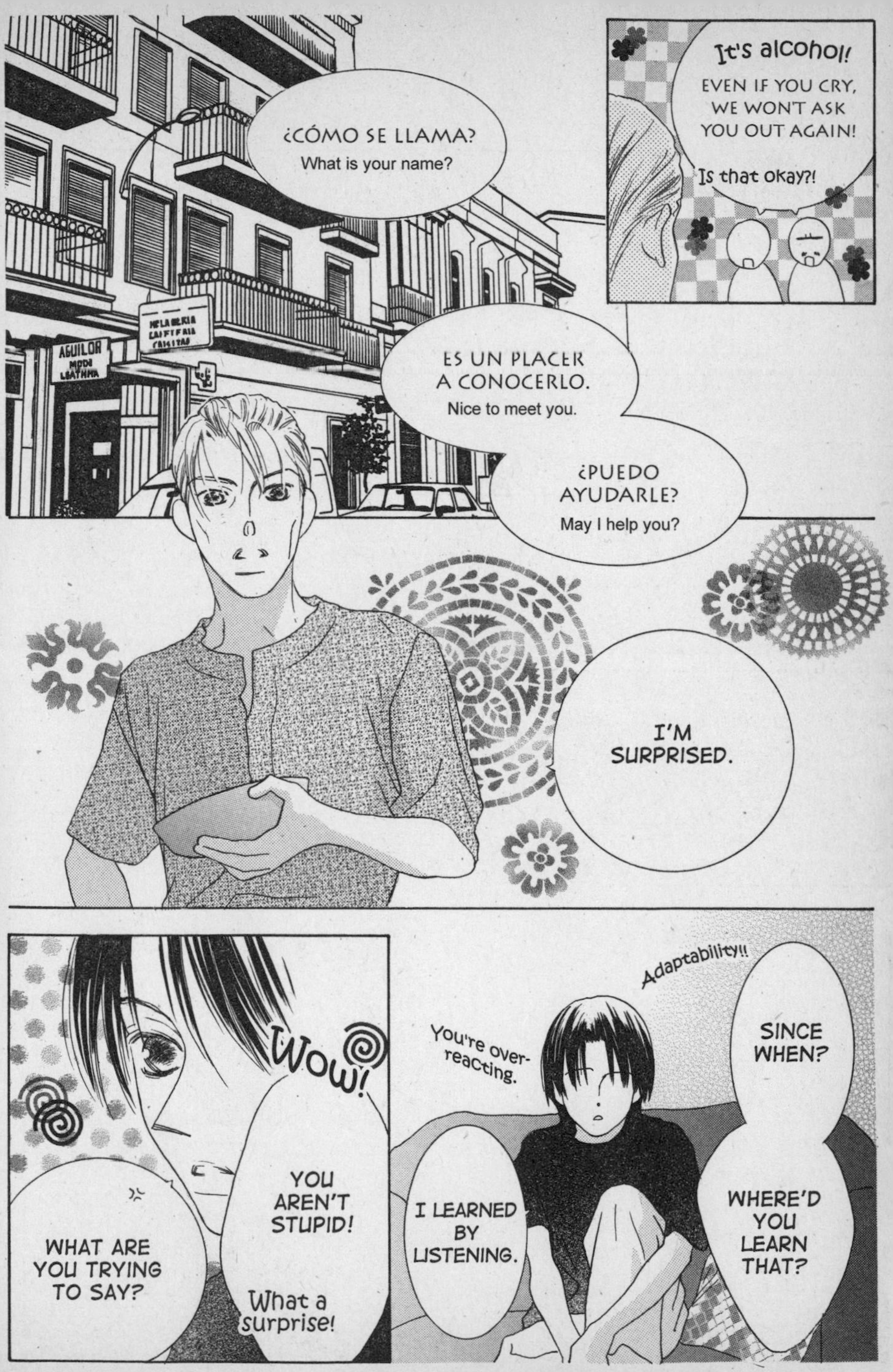
It's alcohol!
EVEN IF YOU CRY, WE WON'T ASK YOU OUT AGAIN!
Is that okay?!
¿CÓMO SE LLAMA? What is your name?
ES UN PLACER A CONOCERLO. Nice to meet you.
¿PUEDO AYUDARLE? May I help you?
I'M SURPRISED.
Adaptability!!
SINCE WHEN?
WHERE'D YOU LEARN THAT?
You're over-reacting.
I LEARNED BY LISTENING.
WOW!
YOU AREN'T STUPID!
What a surprise!
WHAT ARE YOU TRYING TO SAY?

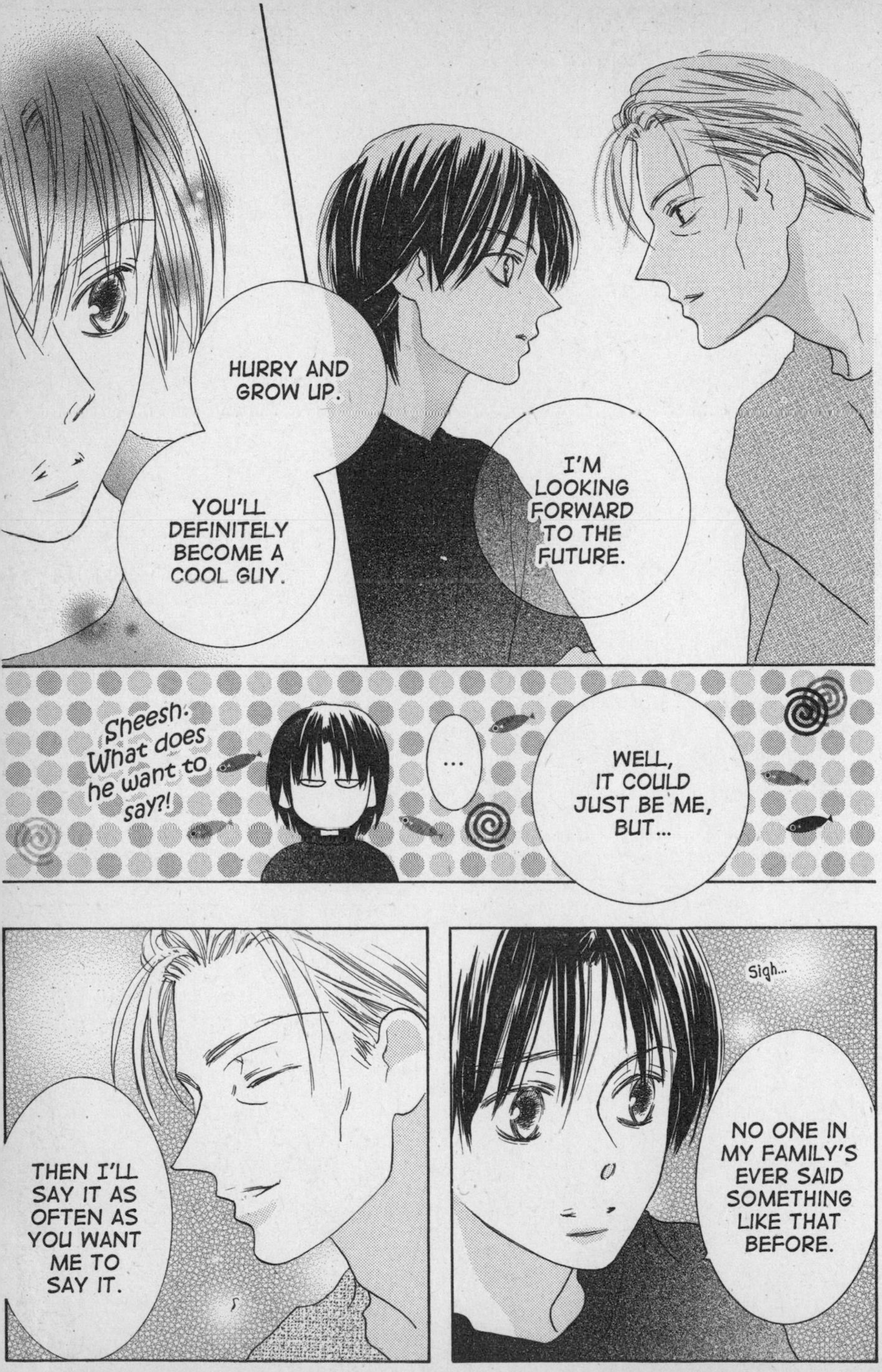

HURRY AND GROW UP.
YOU'LL DEFINITELY BECOME A COOL GUY.
I'M LOOKING FORWARD TO THE FUTURE.
WELL, IT COULD JUST BE ME, BUT...
...
Sheesh. What does he want to say?!
Sigh...
NO ONE IN MY FAMILY'S EVER SAID SOMETHING LIKE THAT BEFORE.
THEN I'LL SAY IT AS OFTEN AS YOU WANT ME TO SAY IT.

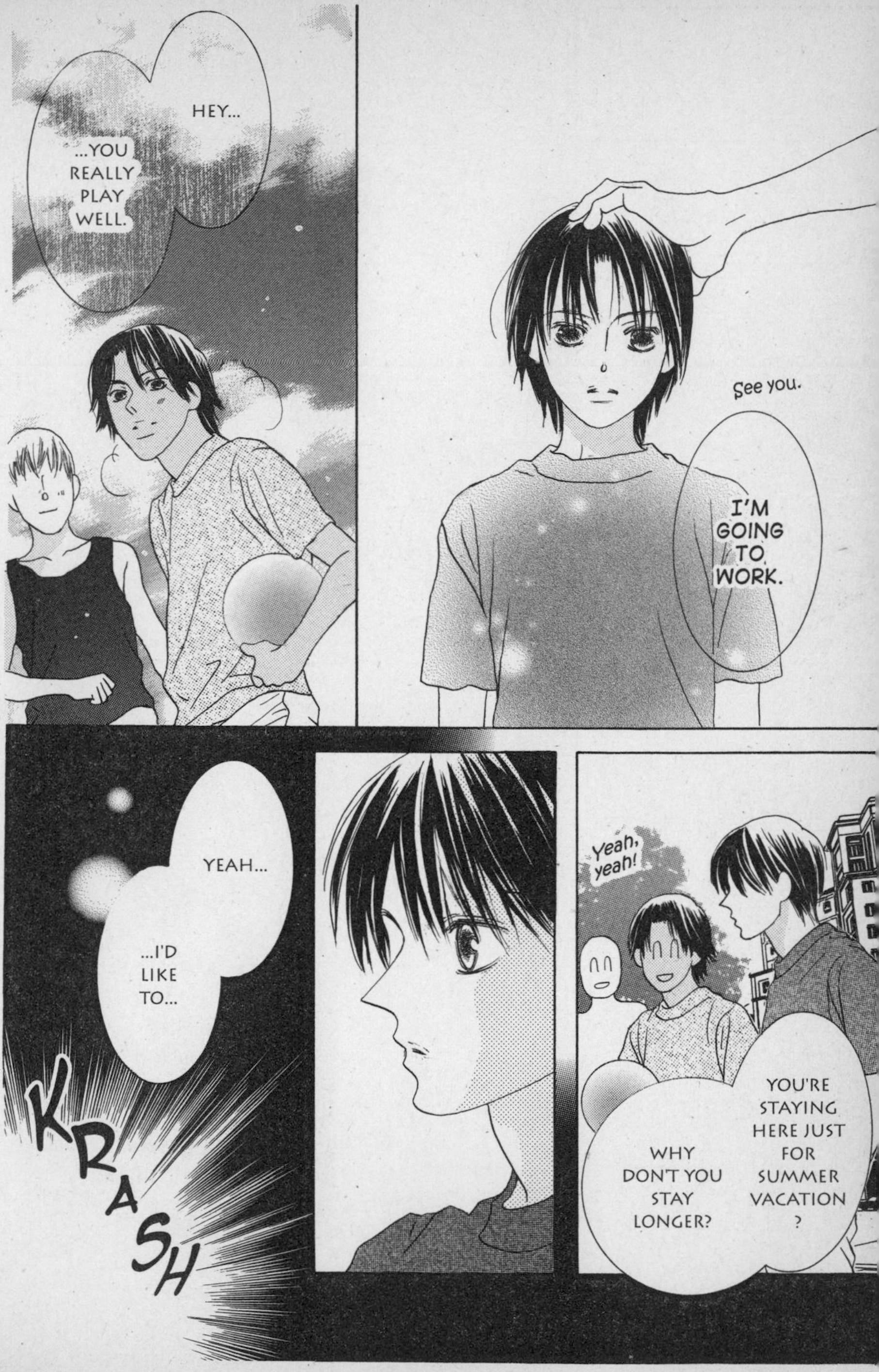
I'M GOING TO WORK.
See you.
HEY...
...YOU REALLY PLAY WELL.
Yeah, yeah!
YOU'RE STAYING HERE JUST FOR SUMMER VACATION?
WHY DON'T YOU STAY LONGER?
YEAH...
...I'D LIKE TO...
KRASH

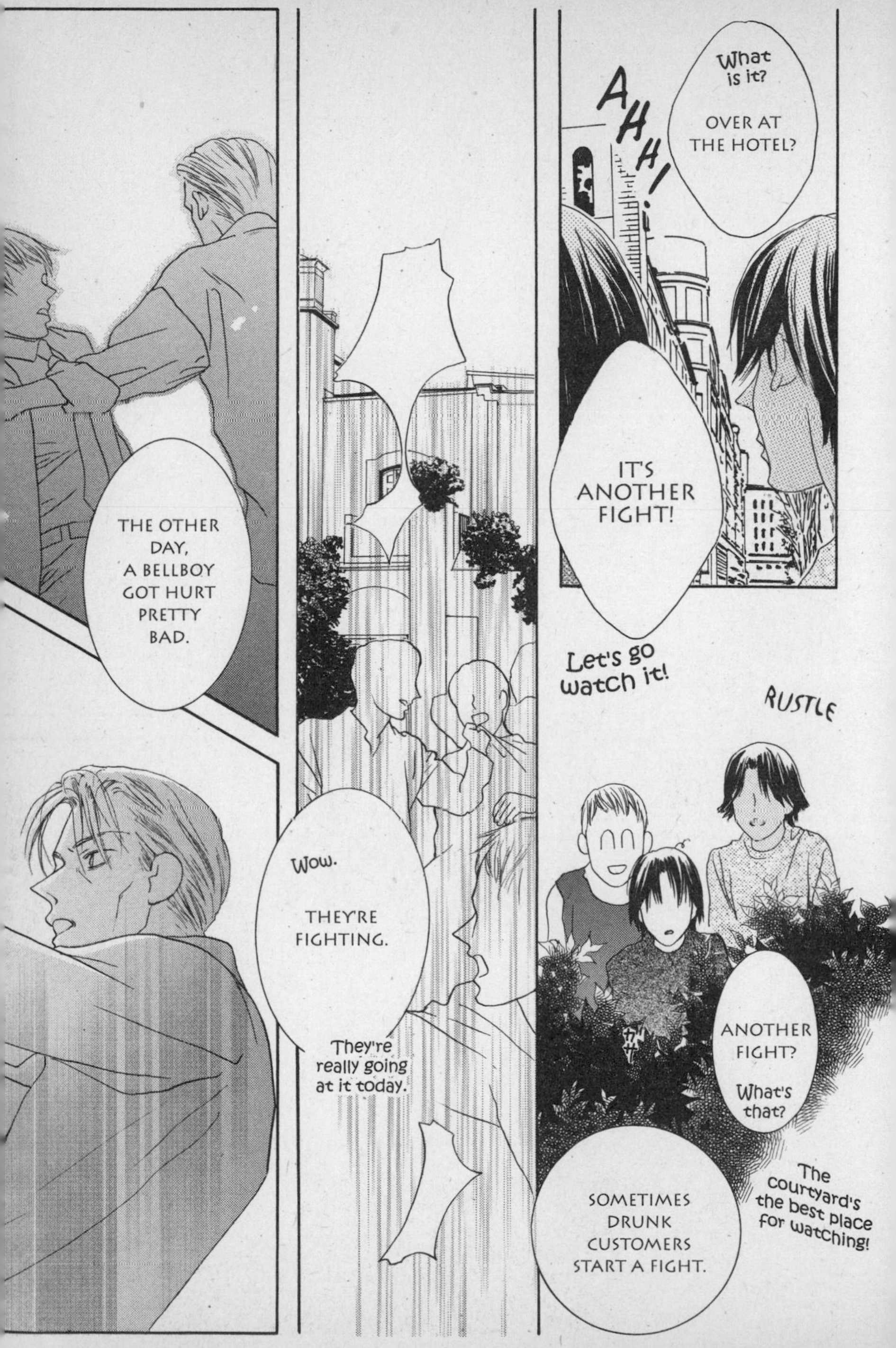
AHH!
What is it?
OVER AT THE HOTEL?
IT'S ANOTHER FIGHT!
Let's go watch it!
RUSTLE
ANOTHER FIGHT?
What's that?
The courtyard's the best place for watching!
SOMETIMES DRUNK CUSTOMERS START A FIGHT.
Wow.
THEY'RE FIGHTING.
They're really going at it today.
THE OTHER DAY, A BELLBOY GOT HURT PRETTY BAD.

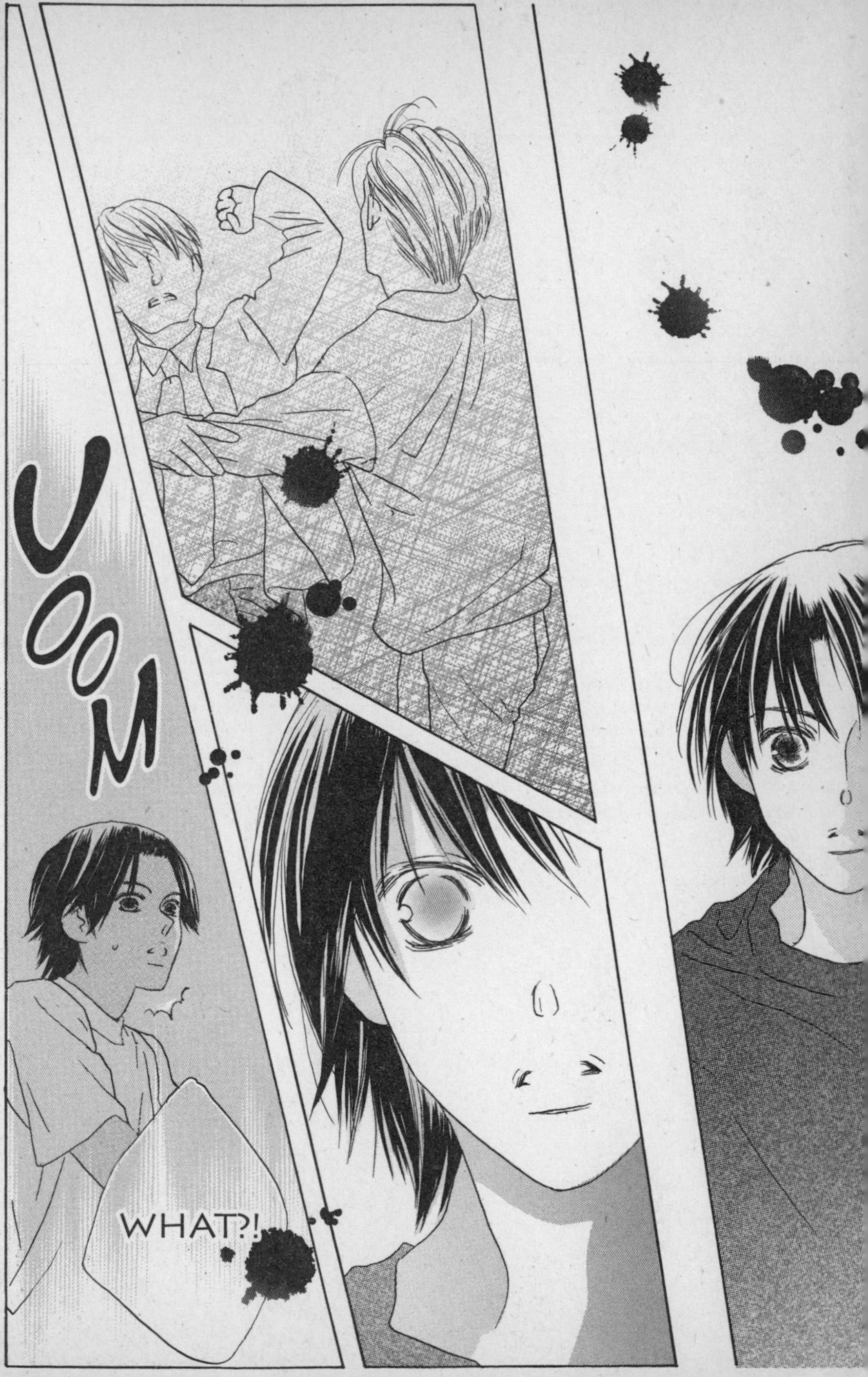
VOOM
WHAT?!

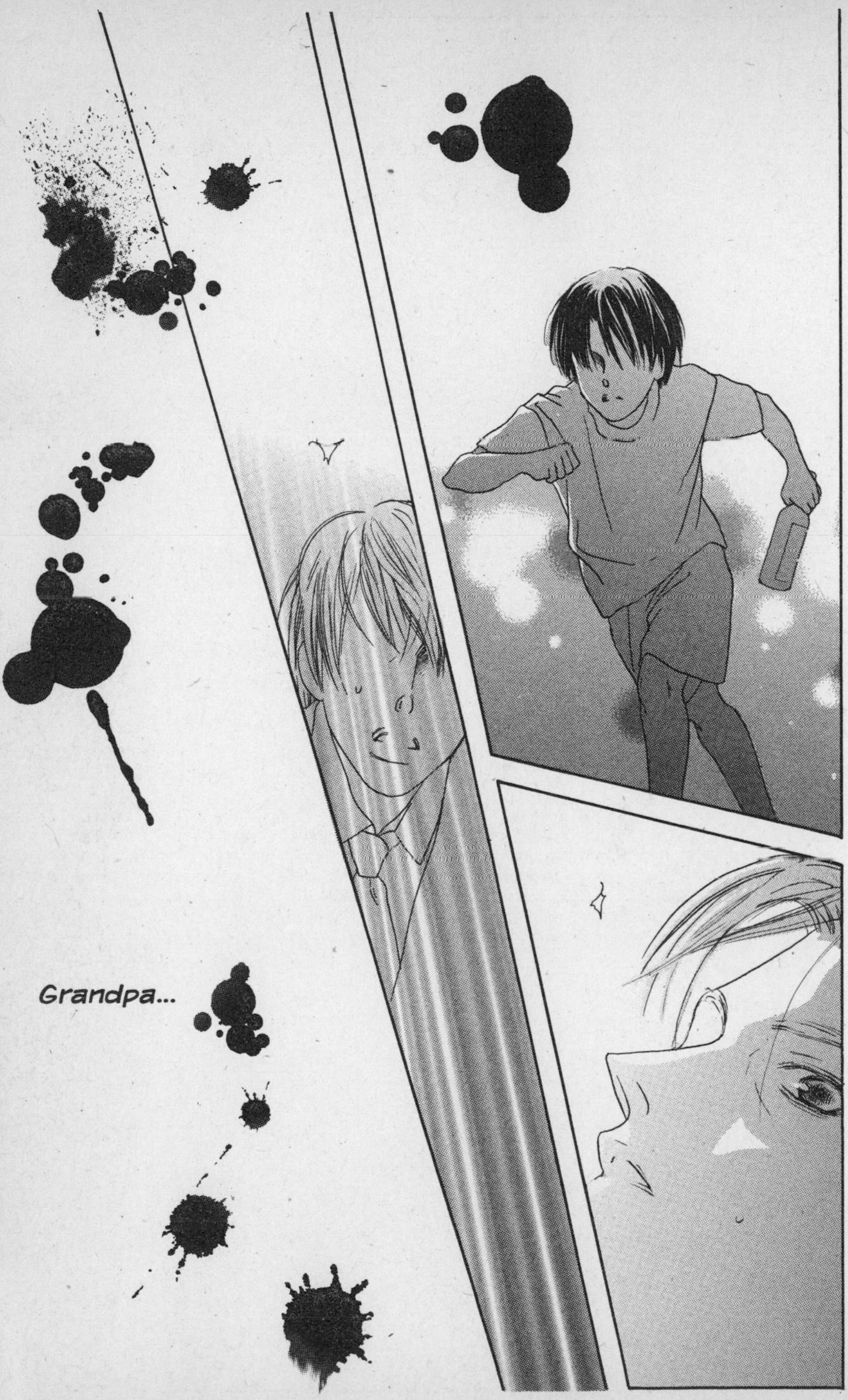
Grandpa...

When I grow up...

...will I be able to live...

...without knowing what to do with myself...

...without regretting anything...

...without making any mistakes?

If that is so...

...I want...

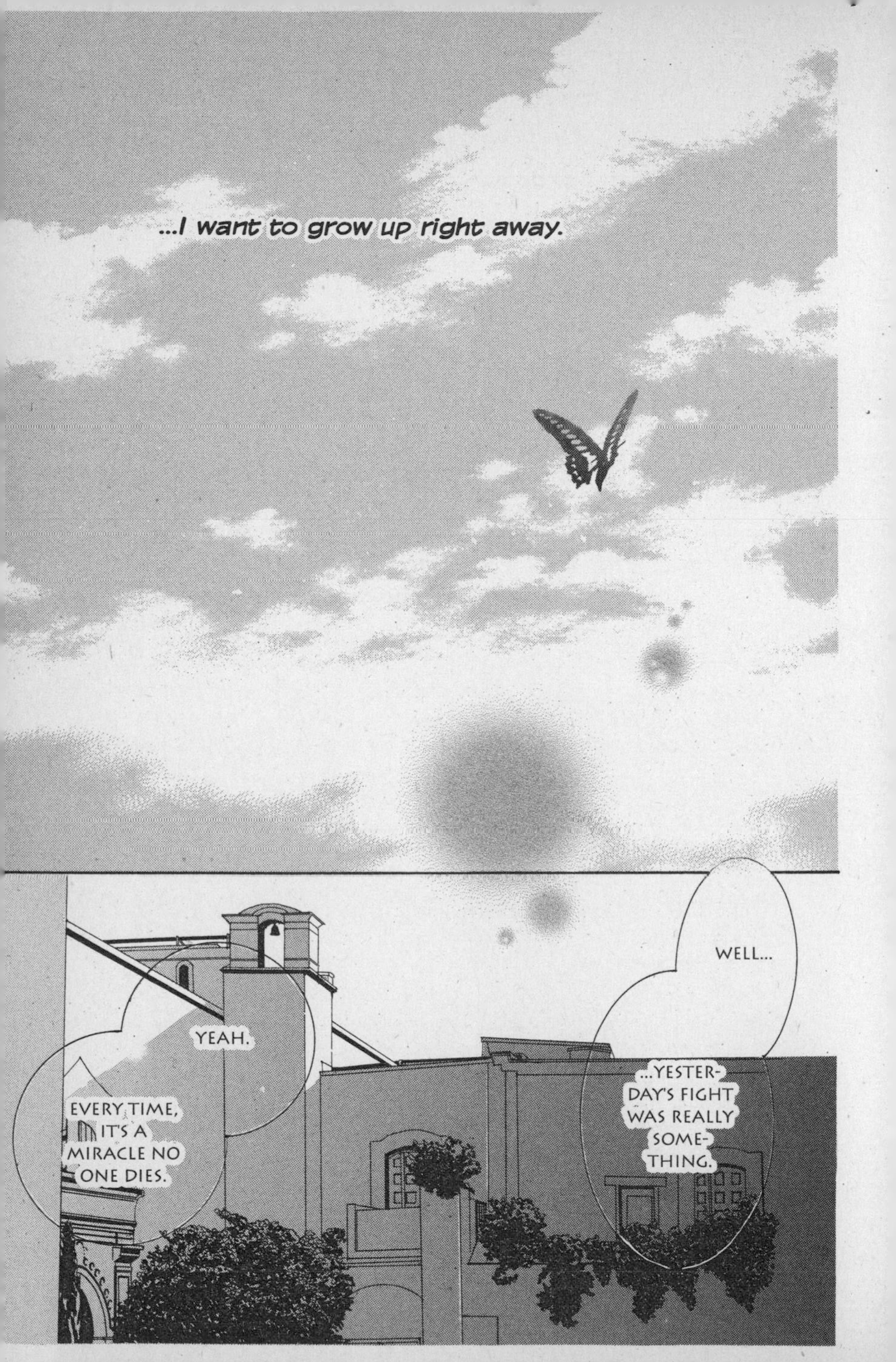
...I want to grow up right away.
WELL...
...YESTER-DAY'S FIGHT WAS REALLY SOME-THING.
YEAH.
EVERY TIME, IT'S A MIRACLE NO ONE DIES.

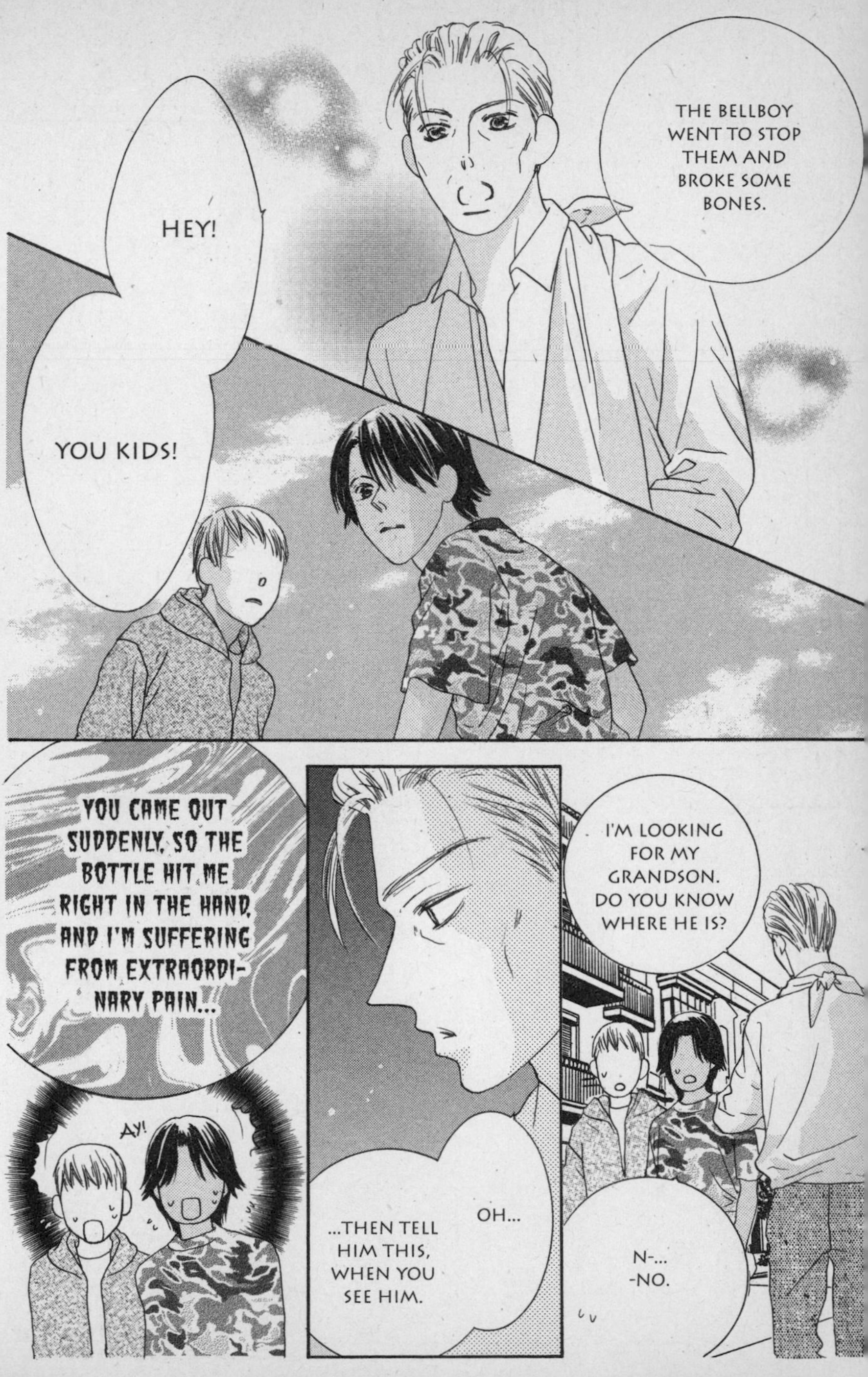
THE BELLBOY WENT TO STOP THEM AND BROKE SOME BONES.
HEY!
YOU KIDS!
I'M LOOKING FOR MY GRANDSON. DO YOU KNOW WHERE HE IS?
N-... -NO.
OH...
...THEN TELL HIM THIS, WHEN YOU SEE HIM.
YOU CAME OUT SUDDENLY, SO THE BOTTLE HIT ME RIGHT IN THE HAND, AND I'M SUFFERING FROM EXTRAORDI-NARY PAIN...
AY!

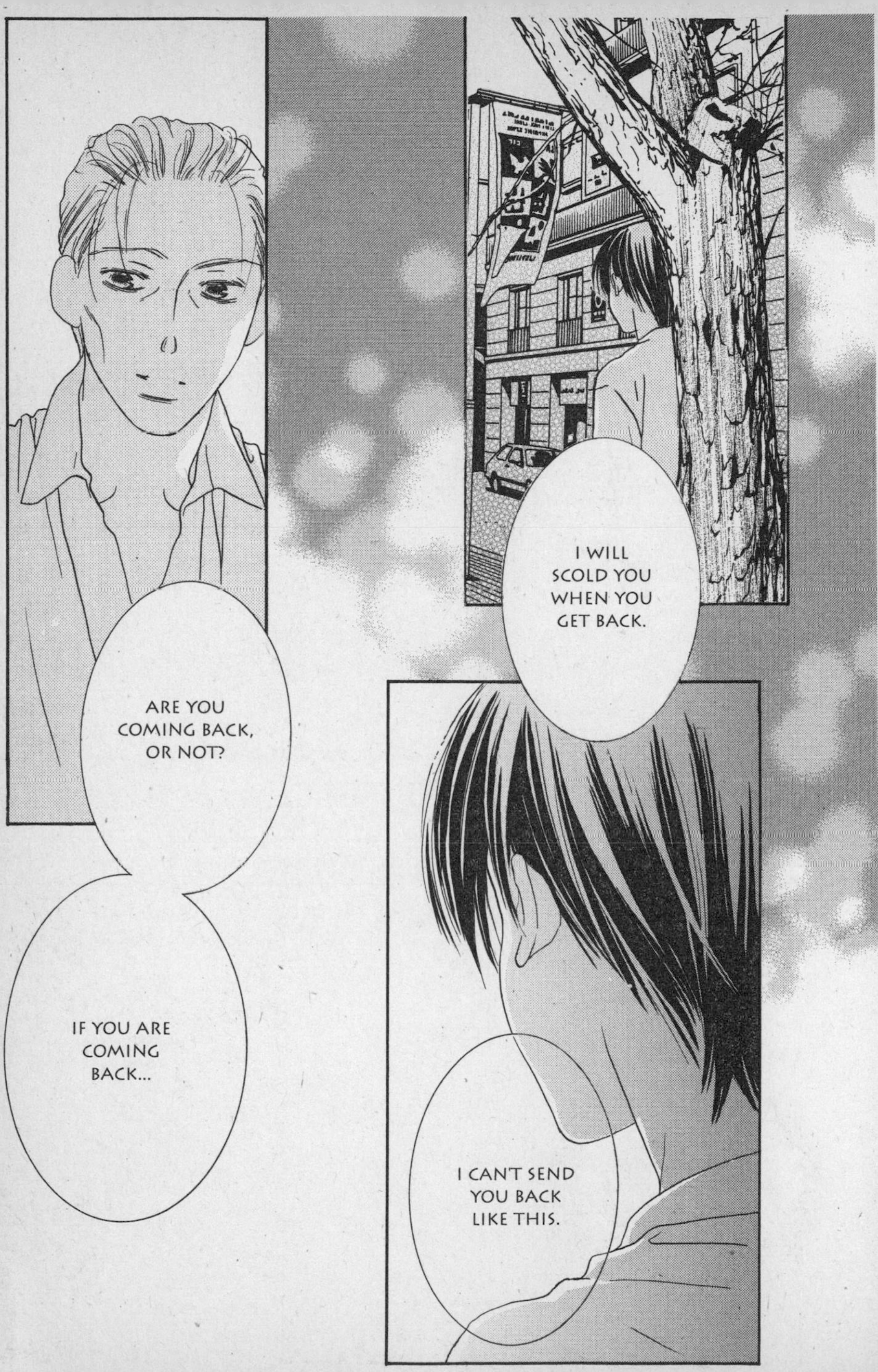
ARE YOU COMING BACK, OR NOT?
IF YOU ARE COMING BACK...
I WILL SCOLD YOU WHEN YOU GET BACK.
I CAN'T SEND YOU BACK LIKE THIS.

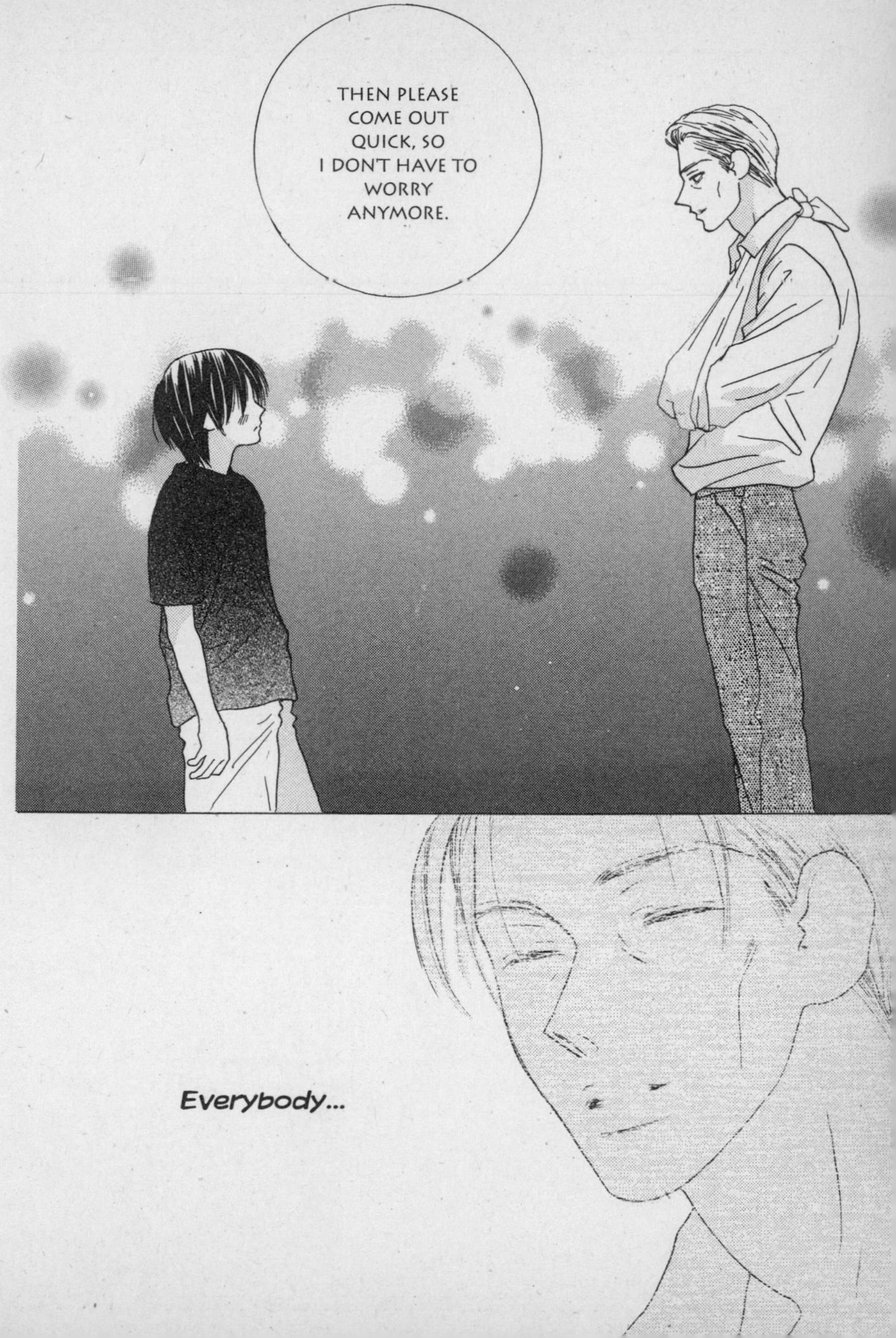
THEN PLEASE COME OUT QUICK, SO I DON'T HAVE TO WORRY ANYMORE.
Everybody...

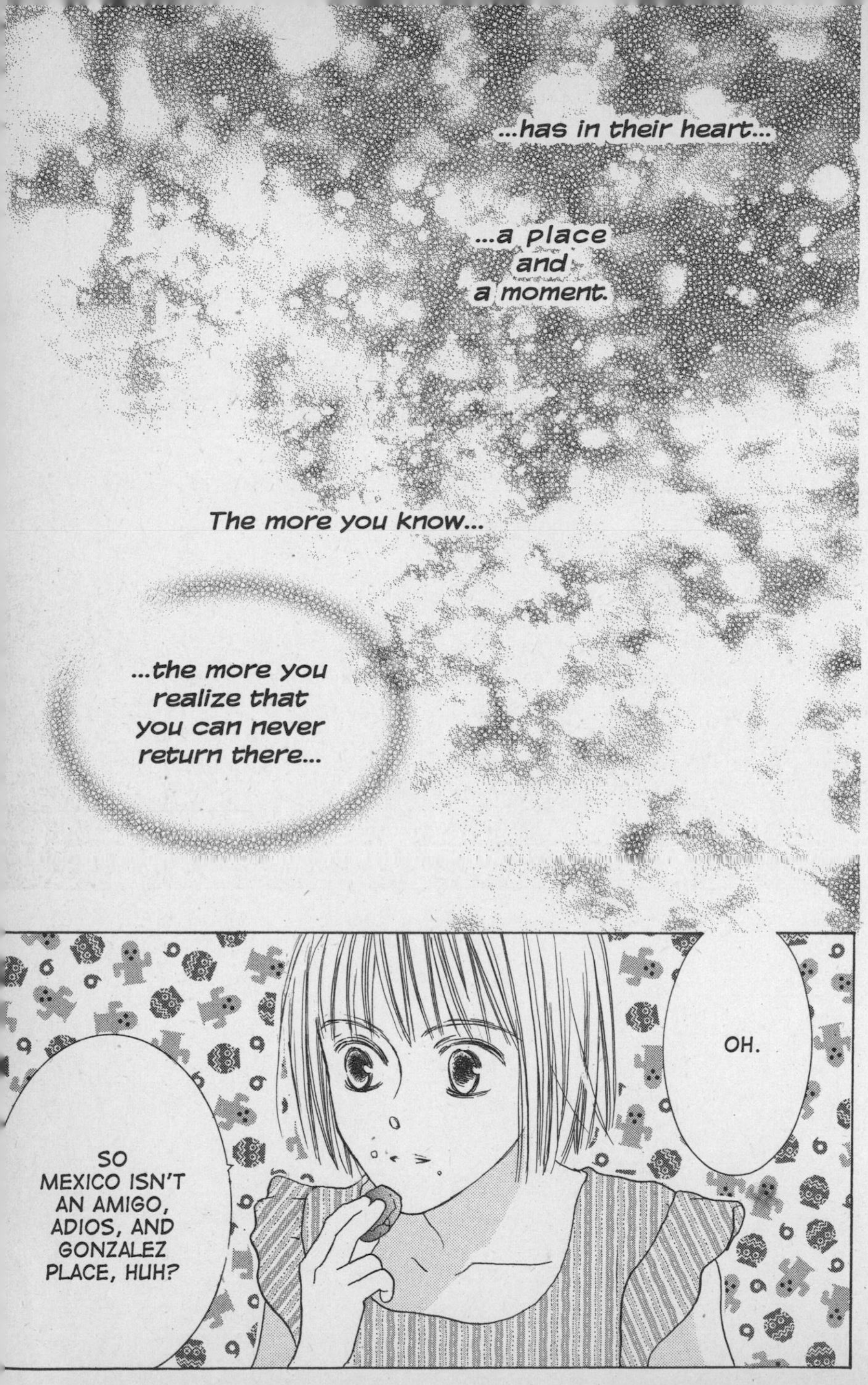
...has in their heart...
...a place and a moment.
The more you know...
...the more you realize that you can never return there...
OH.
SO MEXICO ISN'T AN AMIGO, ADIOS, AND GONZALEZ PLACE, HUH?

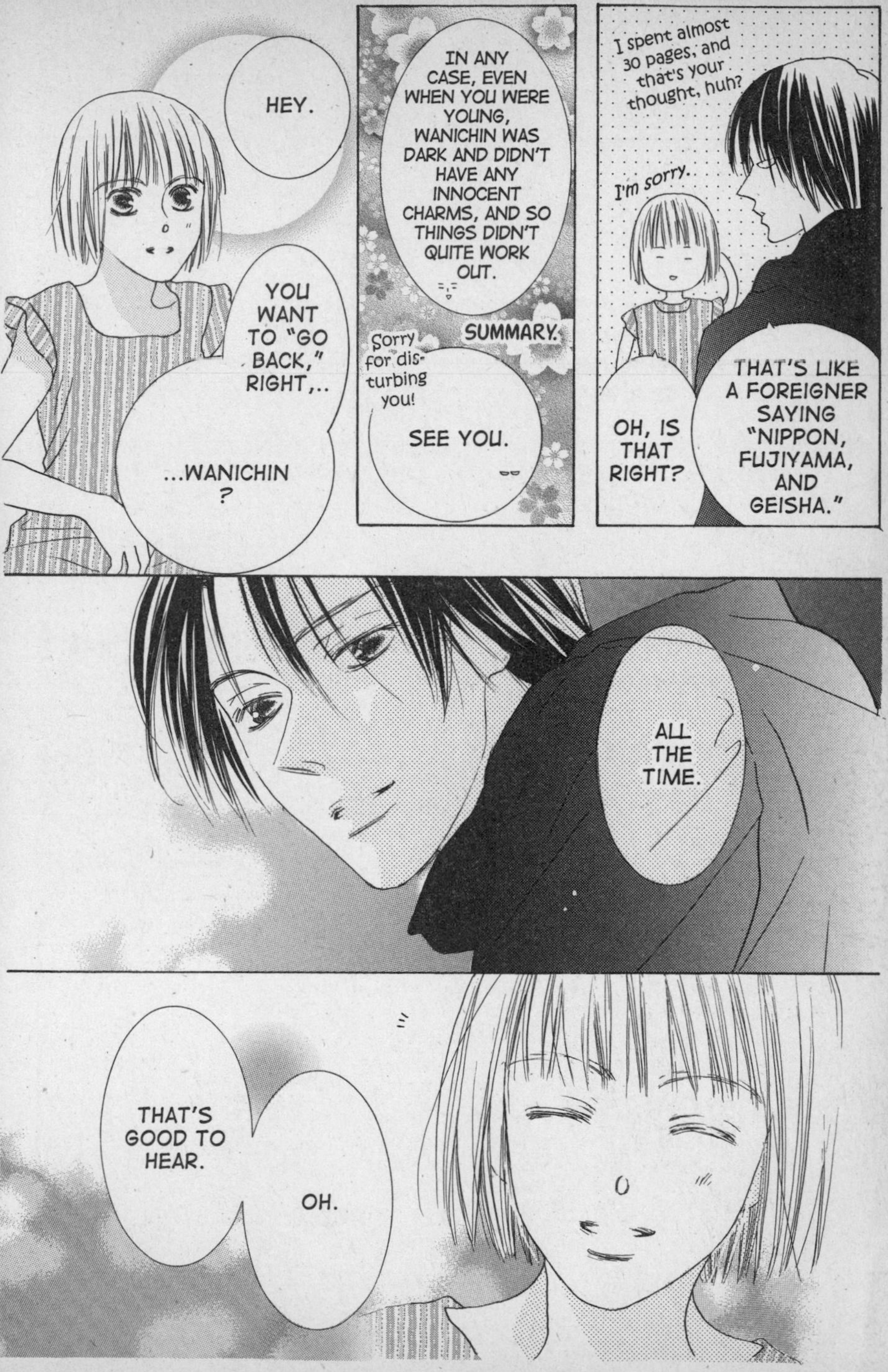
I spent almost 30 pages, and that's your thought, huh?
I'm sorry.
THAT'S LIKE A FOREIGNER SAYING "NIPPON, FUJIYAMA, AND GEISHA."
OH, IS THAT RIGHT?
IN ANY CASE, EVEN WHEN YOU WERE YOUNG, WANICHIN WAS DARK AND DIDN'T HAVE ANY INNOCENT CHARMS, AND SO THINGS DIDN'T QUITE WORK OUT.
SUMMARY.
Sorry for disturbing you!
SEE YOU.
HEY.
YOU WANT TO "GO BACK," RIGHT,..
...WANICHIN ?
ALL THE TIME.
OH.
THAT'S GOOD TO HEAR.

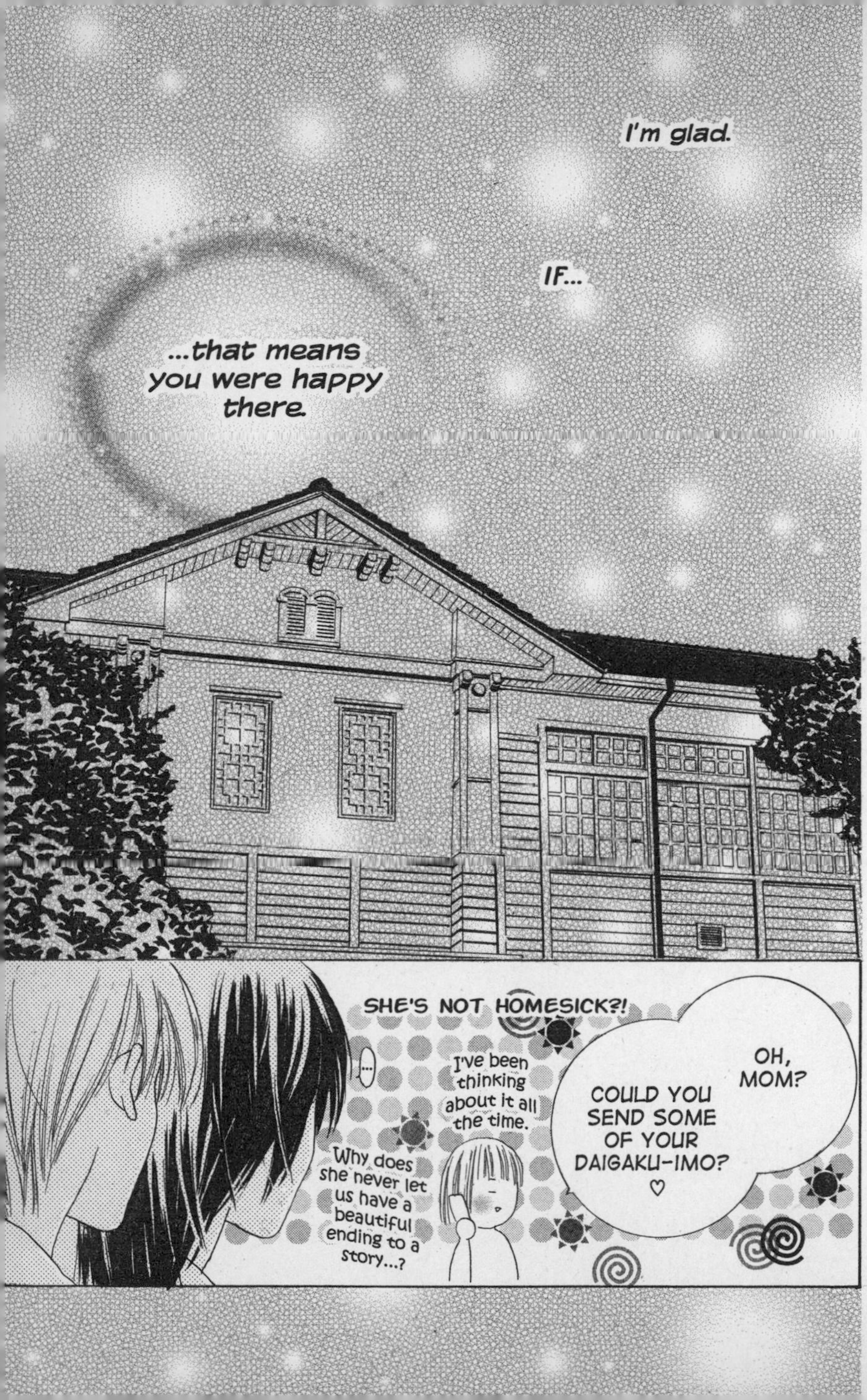
I'm glad.
IF...
...that means you were happy there.
OH, MOM?
COULD YOU SEND SOME OF YOUR DAIGAKU-IMO? ♡
SHE'S NOT HOMESICK?!
I've been thinking about it all the time.
Why does she never let us have a beautiful ending to a story...?
...

BEAUTY
IS THE
BEAST

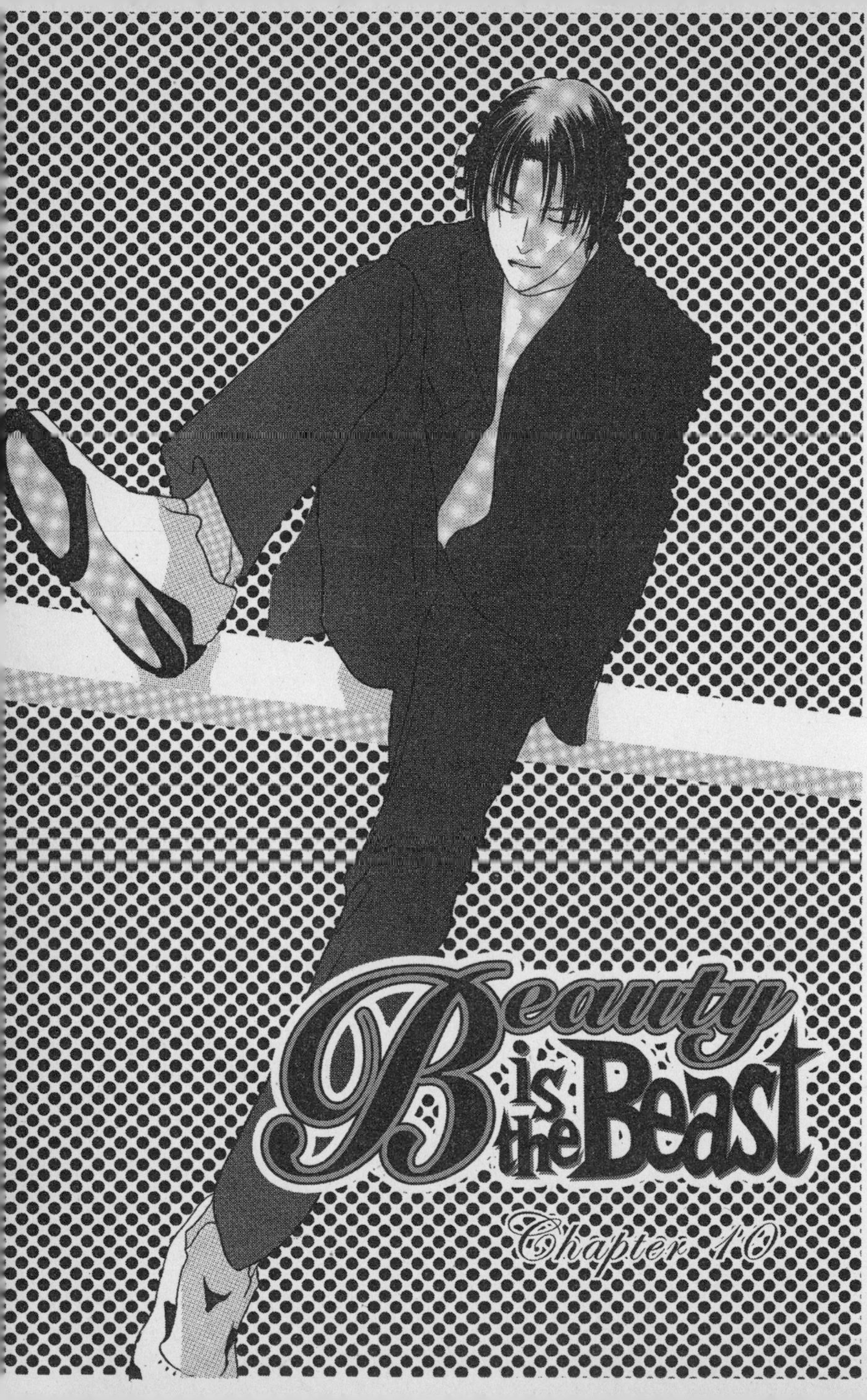
Beauty is the Beast
Chapter 10

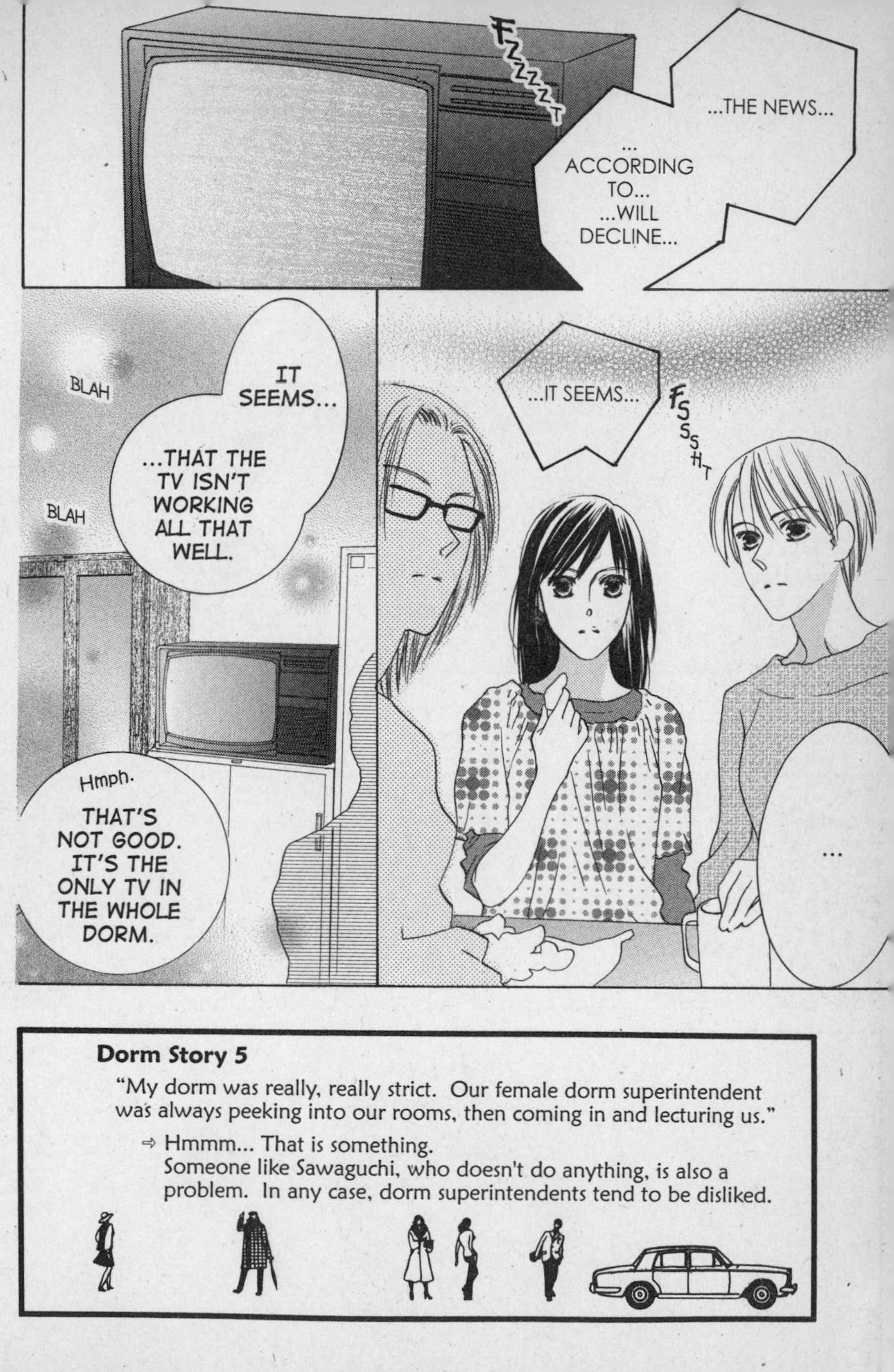
FZZZZT
...THE NEWS...
... ACCORDING TO... ...WILL DECLINE...
...IT SEEMS...
FSSSHT
...
IT SEEMS...
...THAT THE TV ISN'T WORKING ALL THAT WELL.
BLAH
BLAH
Hmph.
THAT'S NOT GOOD. IT'S THE ONLY TV IN THE WHOLE DORM.

Dorm Story 5

"My dorm was really, really strict. Our female dorm superintendent was always peeking into our rooms, then coming in and lecturing us."

⇨ Hmmm... That is something.
Someone like Sawaguchi, who doesn't do anything, is also a problem. In any case, dorm superintendents tend to be disliked.

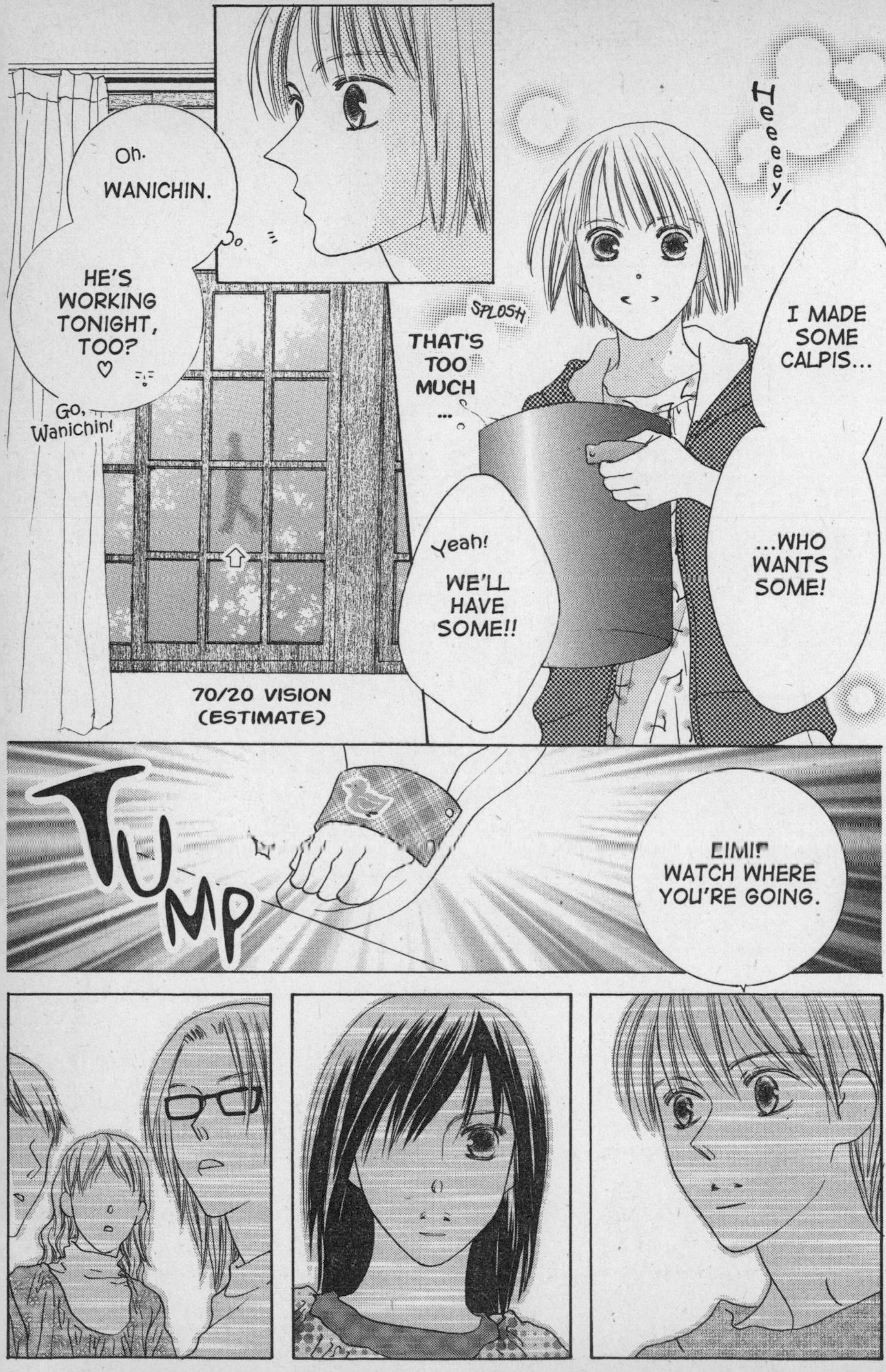
Heeeeey!
I MADE SOME CALPIS...
...WHO WANTS SOME!
SPLOSH
THAT'S TOO MUCH ...
Yeah! WE'LL HAVE SOME!!
Oh. WANICHIN.
HE'S WORKING TONIGHT, TOO? ♡
Go, Wanichin!
70/20 VISION (ESTIMATE)
EIMI!? WATCH WHERE YOU'RE GOING.
TUMP

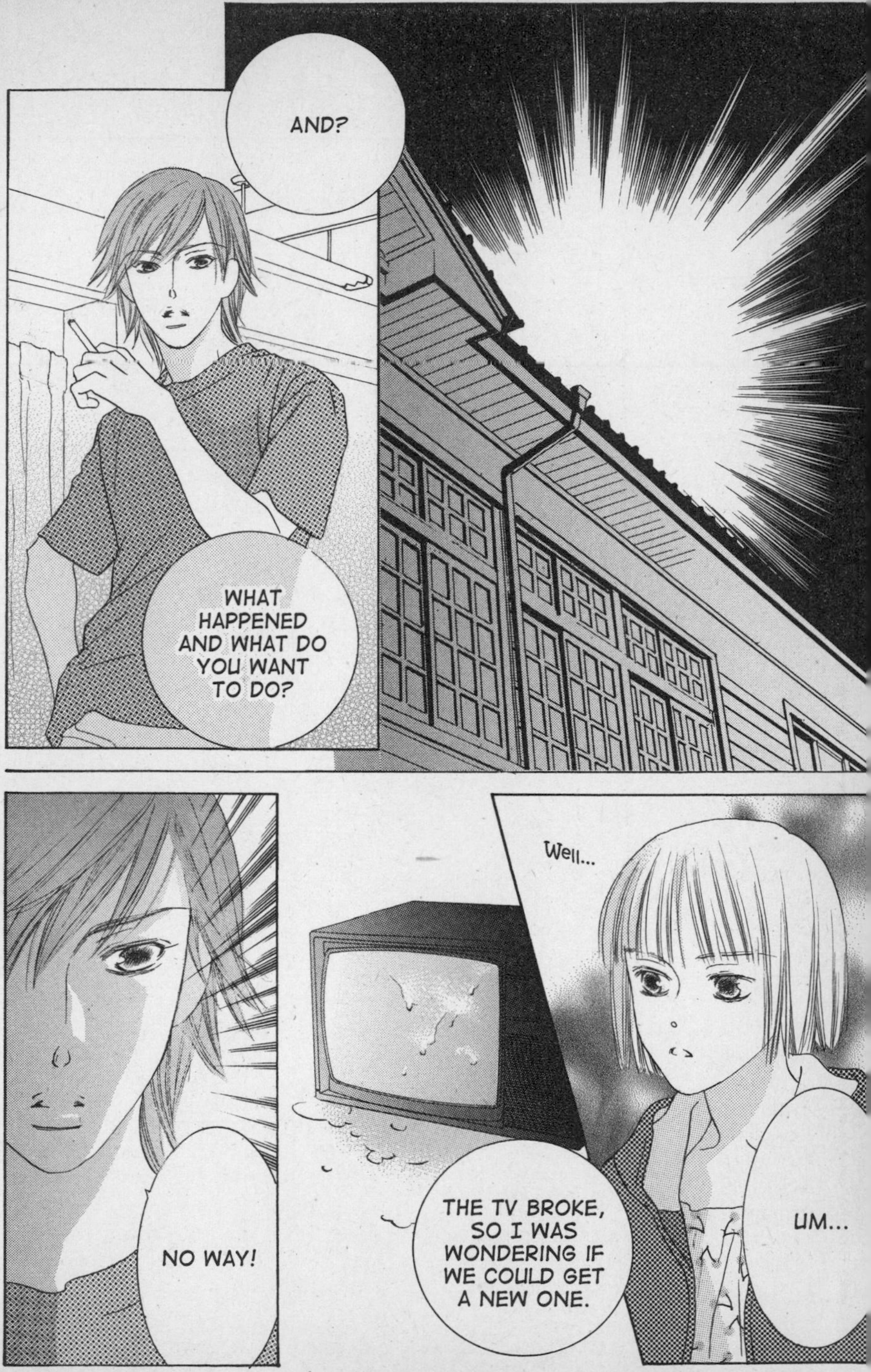
AND?
WHAT HAPPENED AND WHAT DO YOU WANT TO DO?
Well...
UM...
THE TV BROKE, SO I WAS WONDERING IF WE COULD GET A NEW ONE.
NO WAY!

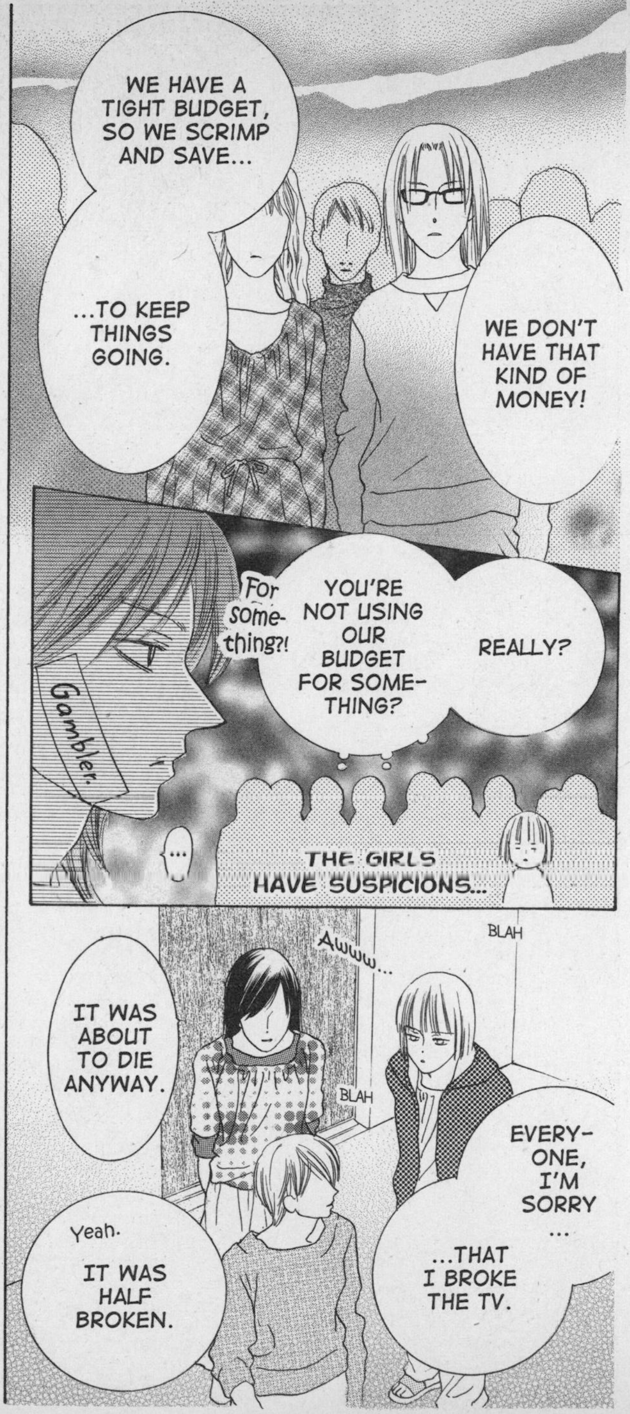
WE HAVE A TIGHT BUDGET, SO WE SCRIMP AND SAVE...
...TO KEEP THINGS GOING.
WE DON'T HAVE THAT KIND OF MONEY!
REALLY?
YOU'RE NOT USING OUR BUDGET FOR SOMETHING?
For some-thing?!
Gambler.
...
THE GIRLS HAVE SUSPICIONS...
BLAH
EVERY-ONE, I'M SORRY ...
...THAT I BROKE THE TV.
Awww...
BLAH
IT WAS ABOUT TO DIE ANYWAY.
Yeah.
IT WAS HALF BROKEN.

⑤ I Paint and Paste

I use khaki and gray color tones. With this manga, I use edgy colors too. I feel they match Eimi and the other characters' personalities. I use Pantone, IC, Deleter and Maxon...I use all sorts of stuff.

I use color markers for hair colors, for example. I mainly use Deleter and Staedtler's gray. Copic is difficult for me, so I only use them when coloring sections of my drawings.

There's a chemistry between an artist and art materials, so I have to buy them to see how they work out. It is a gamble. Really.

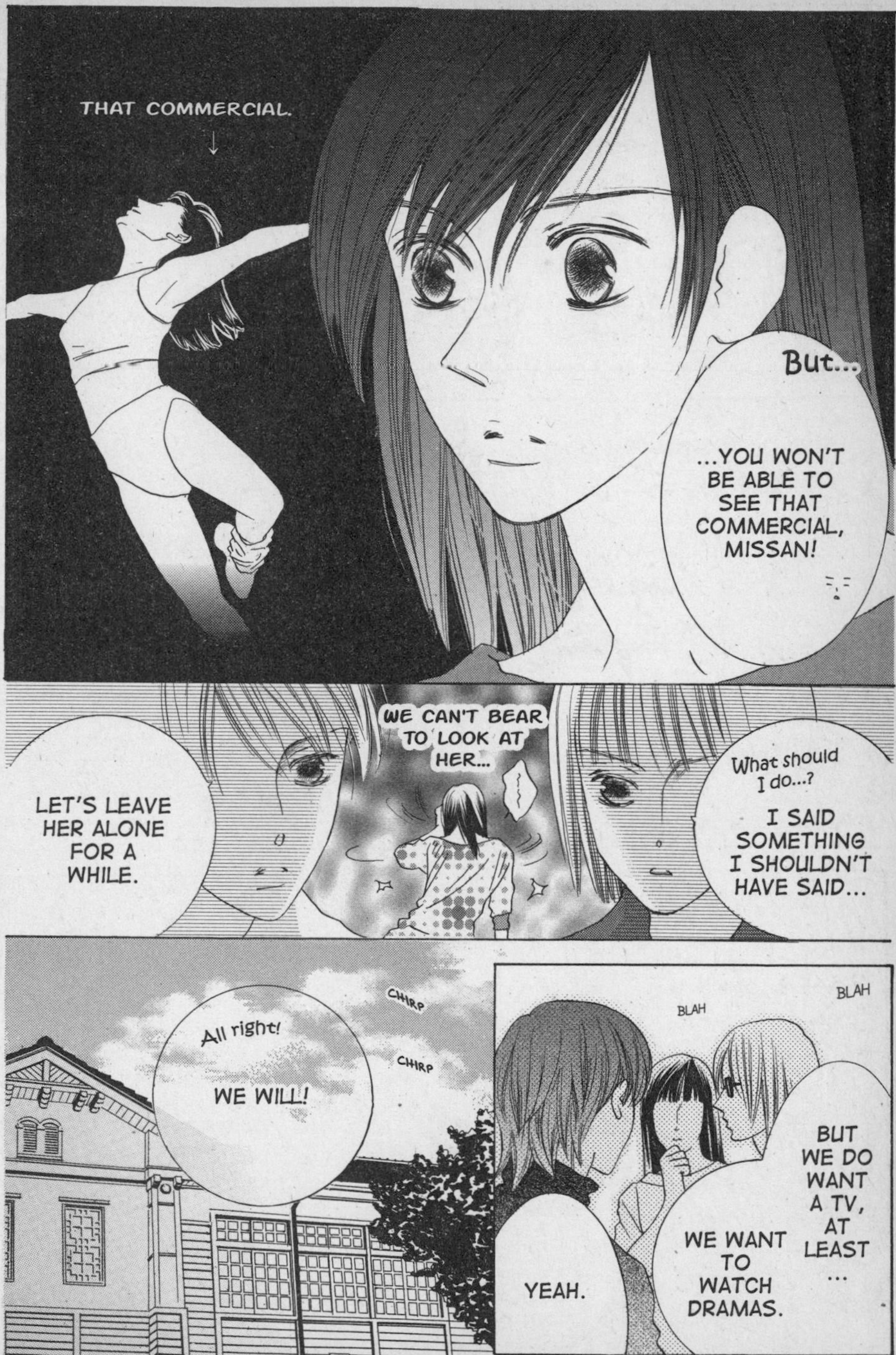
But...
...YOU WON'T BE ABLE TO SEE THAT COMMERCIAL, MISSAN!
THAT COMMERCIAL.
What should I do...?
I SAID SOMETHING I SHOULDN'T HAVE SAID...
WE CAN'T BEAR TO LOOK AT HER...
LET'S LEAVE HER ALONE FOR A WHILE.
BLAH
BLAH
BUT WE DO WANT A TV, AT LEAST ...
WE WANT TO WATCH DRAMAS.
YEAH.
CHIRP
CHIRP
All right!
WE WILL!

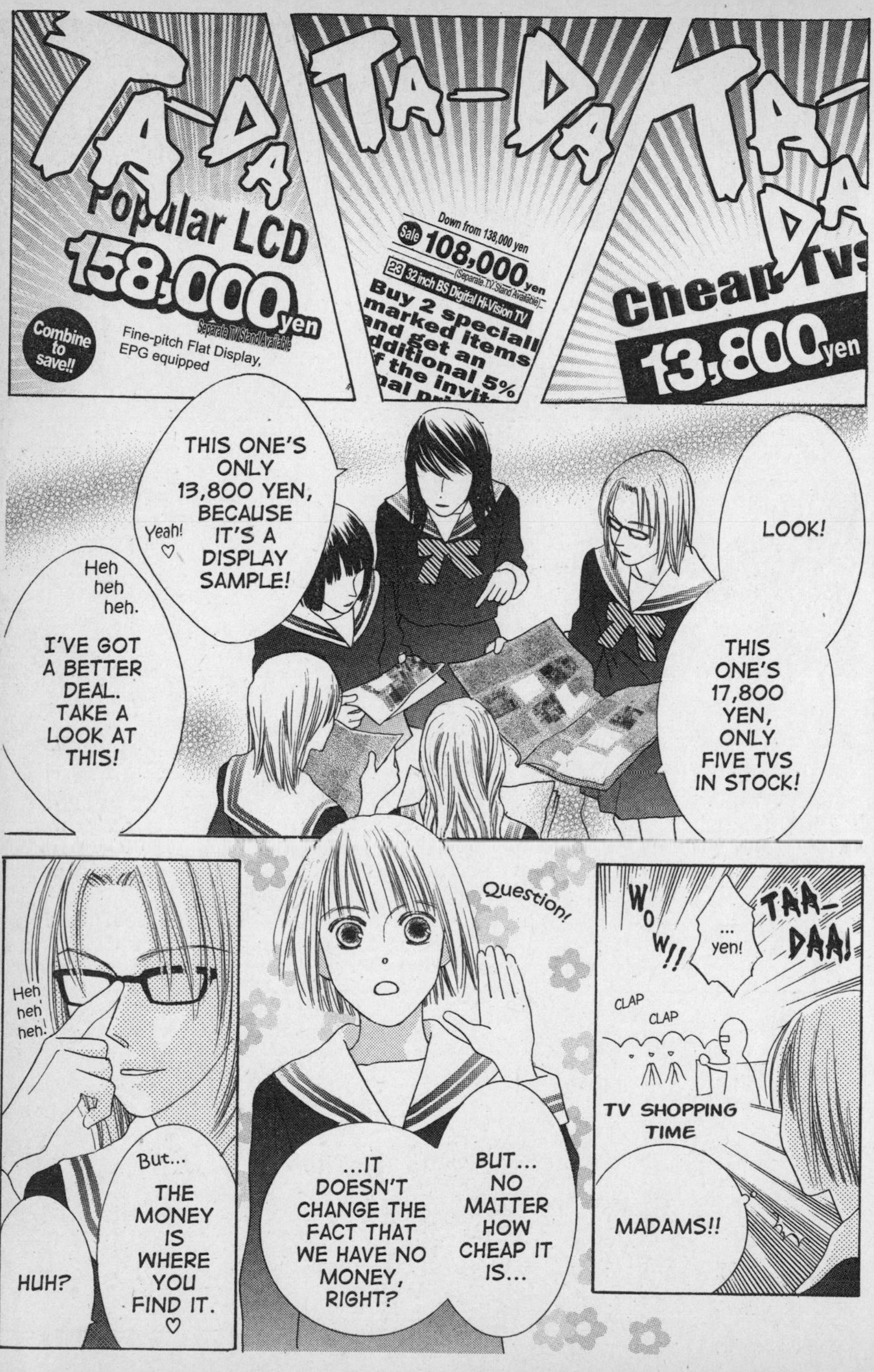
TA-DA
Cheap TVs
13,800 yen
TA-DA
Down from 138,000 yen
Sale 108,000 yen
(Separate TV Stand Available)
23 32 inch BS Digital Hi-Vision TV
Buy 2 special
marked items
and get an
TA-DA
Popular LCD
158,000 yen
Separate TV Stand Available
Fine-pitch Flat Display, EPG equipped
Combine to save!!
LOOK!
THIS ONE'S 17,800 YEN, ONLY FIVE TVS IN STOCK!
THIS ONE'S ONLY 13,800 YEN, BECAUSE IT'S A DISPLAY SAMPLE!
Yeah! ♡
Heh heh heh.
I'VE GOT A BETTER DEAL. TAKE A LOOK AT THIS!
WOW!!
... yen!
TAR-DAA!
CLAP
CLAP
TV SHOPPING TIME
MADAMS!!
Question!
BUT... NO MATTER HOW CHEAP IT IS...
...IT DOESN'T CHANGE THE FACT THAT WE HAVE NO MONEY, RIGHT?
Heh heh heh.
But...
THE MONEY IS WHERE YOU FIND IT. ♡
HUH?

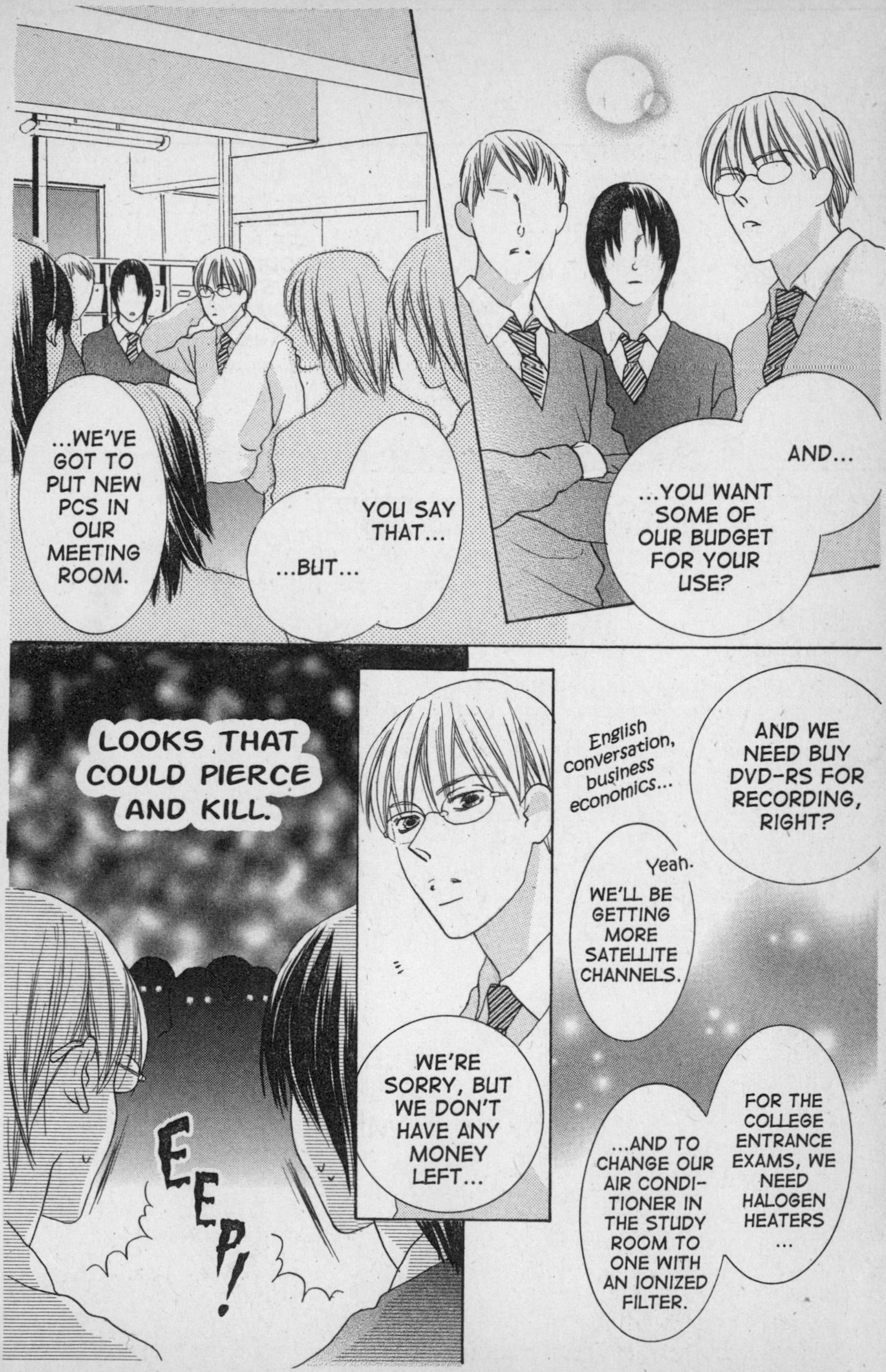
AND...
...YOU WANT SOME OF OUR BUDGET FOR YOUR USE?
YOU SAY THAT...
...BUT...
...WE'VE GOT TO PUT NEW PCS IN OUR MEETING ROOM.
AND WE NEED BUY DVD-RS FOR RECORDING, RIGHT?
English conversation, business economics...
Yeah.
WE'LL BE GETTING MORE SATELLITE CHANNELS.
FOR THE COLLEGE ENTRANCE EXAMS, WE NEED HALOGEN HEATERS ...
...AND TO CHANGE OUR AIR CONDITIONER IN THE STUDY ROOM TO ONE WITH AN IONIZED FILTER.
WE'RE SORRY, BUT WE DON'T HAVE ANY MONEY LEFT...
LOOKS THAT COULD PIERCE AND KILL.
EEP!

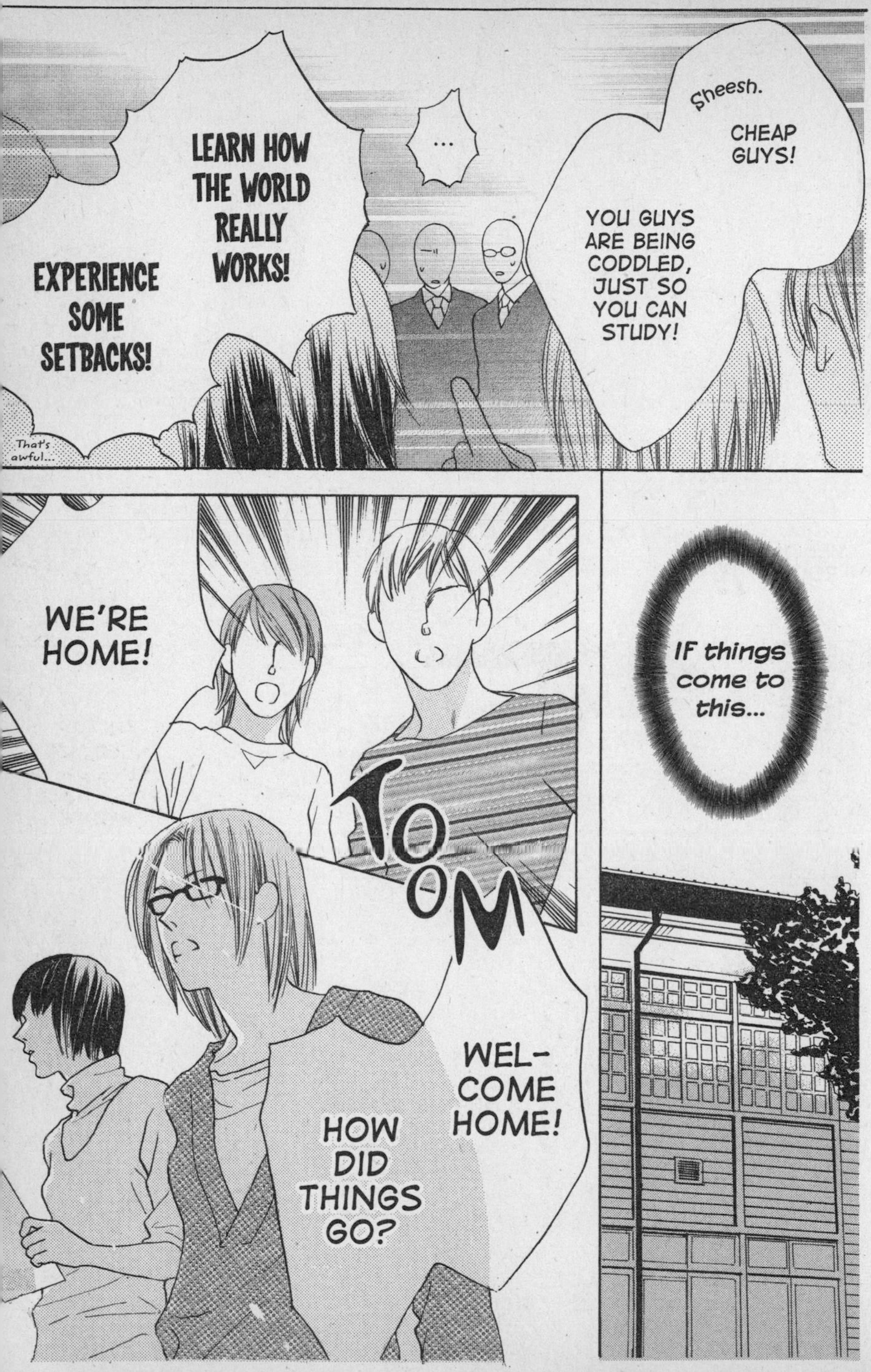
Sheesh.
CHEAP GUYS!
YOU GUYS ARE BEING CODDLED, JUST SO YOU CAN STUDY!
...
LEARN HOW THE WORLD REALLY WORKS!
EXPERIENCE SOME SETBACKS!
That's awful...
IF things come to this...
WE'RE HOME!
TOOM
WEL-COME HOME!
HOW DID THINGS GO?

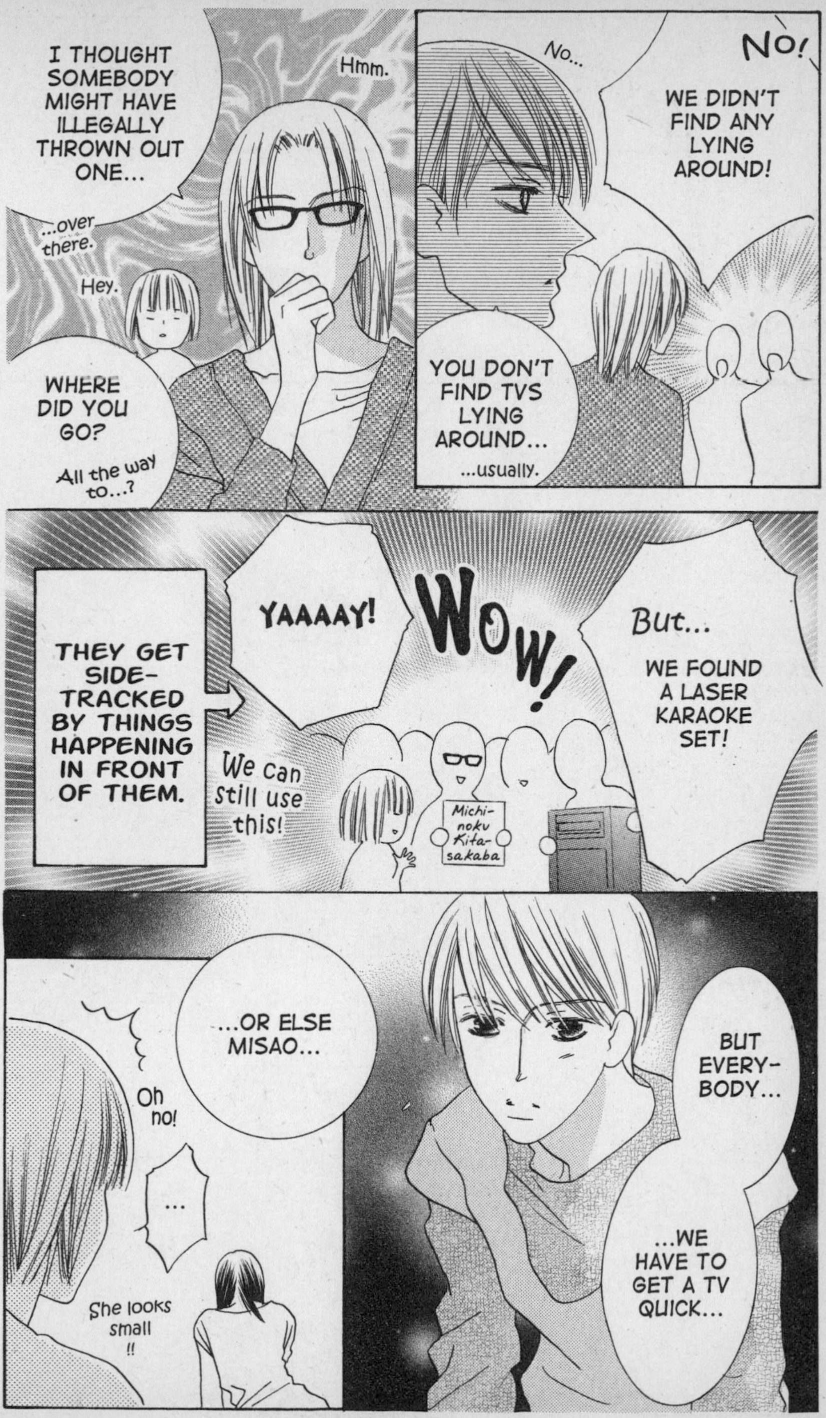
No...
NO!
WE DIDN'T FIND ANY LYING AROUND!
YOU DON'T FIND TVS LYING AROUND...
...usually.
Hmm.
I THOUGHT SOMEBODY MIGHT HAVE ILLEGALLY THROWN OUT ONE...
...over there.
Hey.
WHERE DID YOU GO?
All the way to...?
But...
WE FOUND A LASER KARAOKE SET!
WOW!
YAAAAY!
Michi-noku Kita-sakaba
We can still use this!
THEY GET SIDE-TRACKED BY THINGS HAPPENING IN FRONT OF THEM.
BUT EVERYBODY...
...WE HAVE TO GET A TV QUICK...
...OR ELSE MISAO...
Oh no!
...
She looks small !!

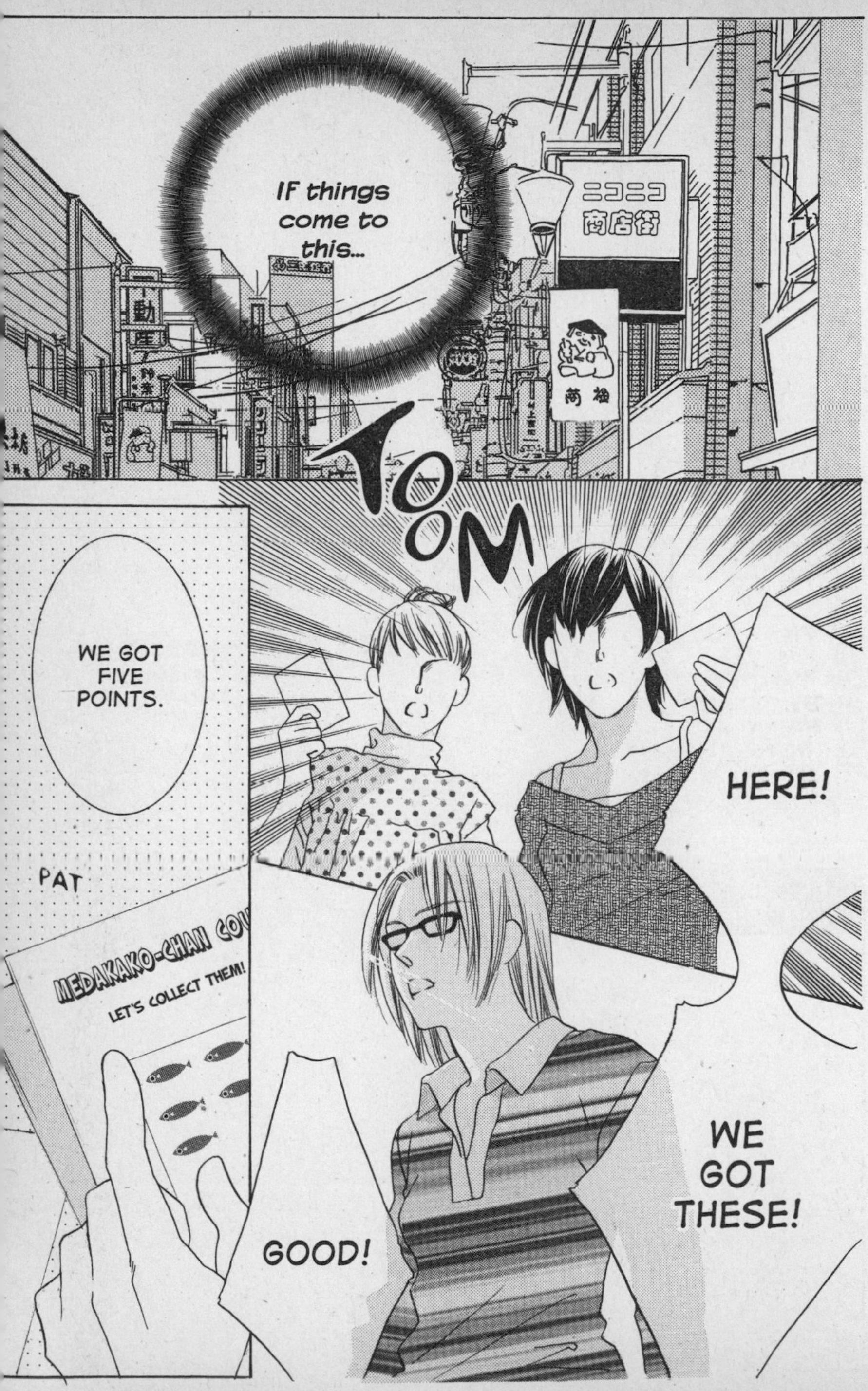
IF things come to this...
ニコニコ
商店街
TOOM
HERE!
WE GOT THESE!
GOOD!
WE GOT FIVE POINTS.
PAT
MEDAKAKO-CHAN COU
LET'S COLLECT THEM!

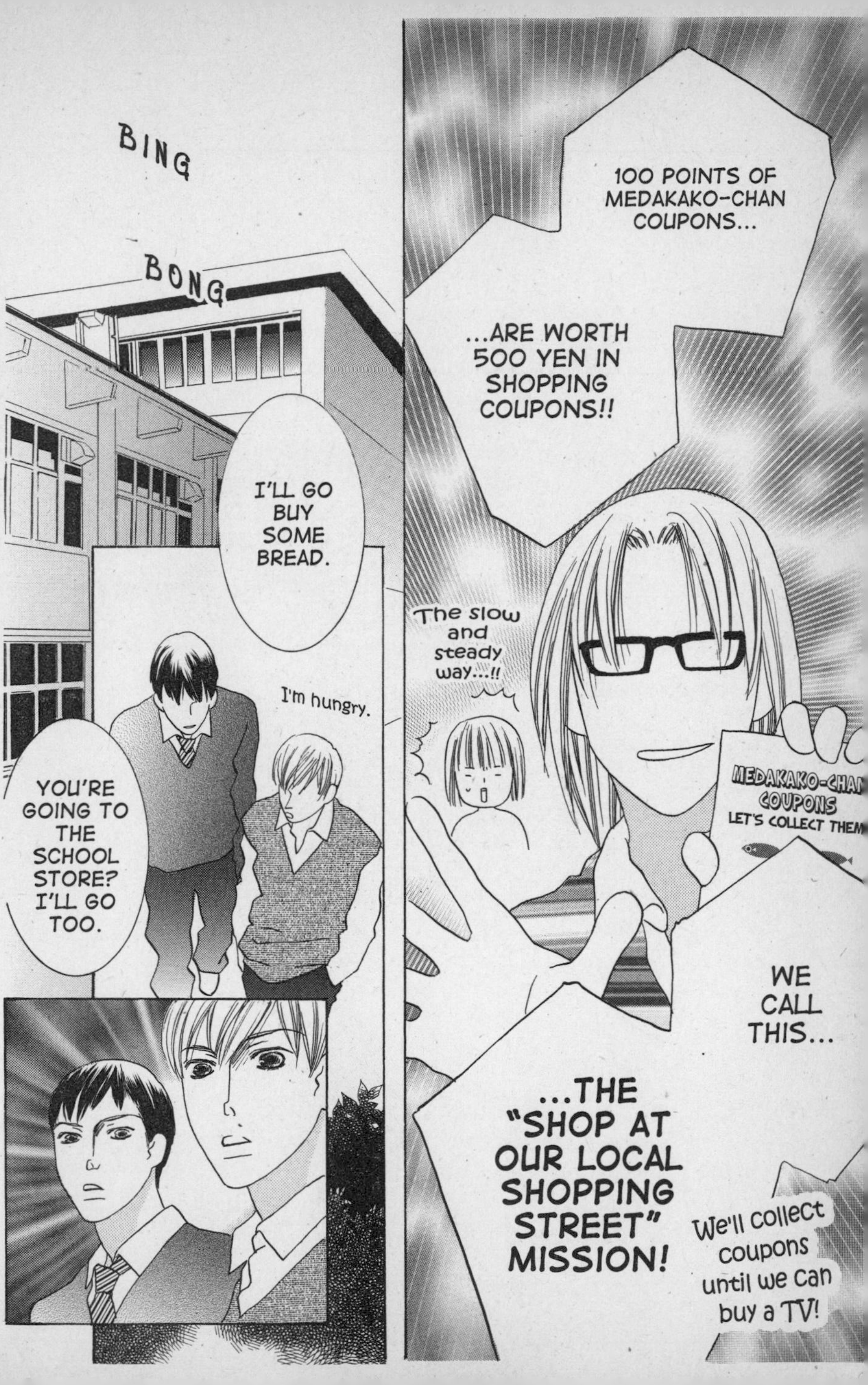
100 POINTS OF MEDAKAKO-CHAN COUPONS...
...ARE WORTH 500 YEN IN SHOPPING COUPONS!!
The slow and steady way...!!
MEDAKAKO-CHAN COUPONS
LET'S COLLECT THEM
WE CALL THIS...
...THE "SHOP AT OUR LOCAL SHOPPING STREET" MISSION!
We'll collect coupons until we can buy a TV!
BING
BONG
I'LL GO BUY SOME BREAD.
I'm hungry.
YOU'RE GOING TO THE SCHOOL STORE? I'LL GO TOO.

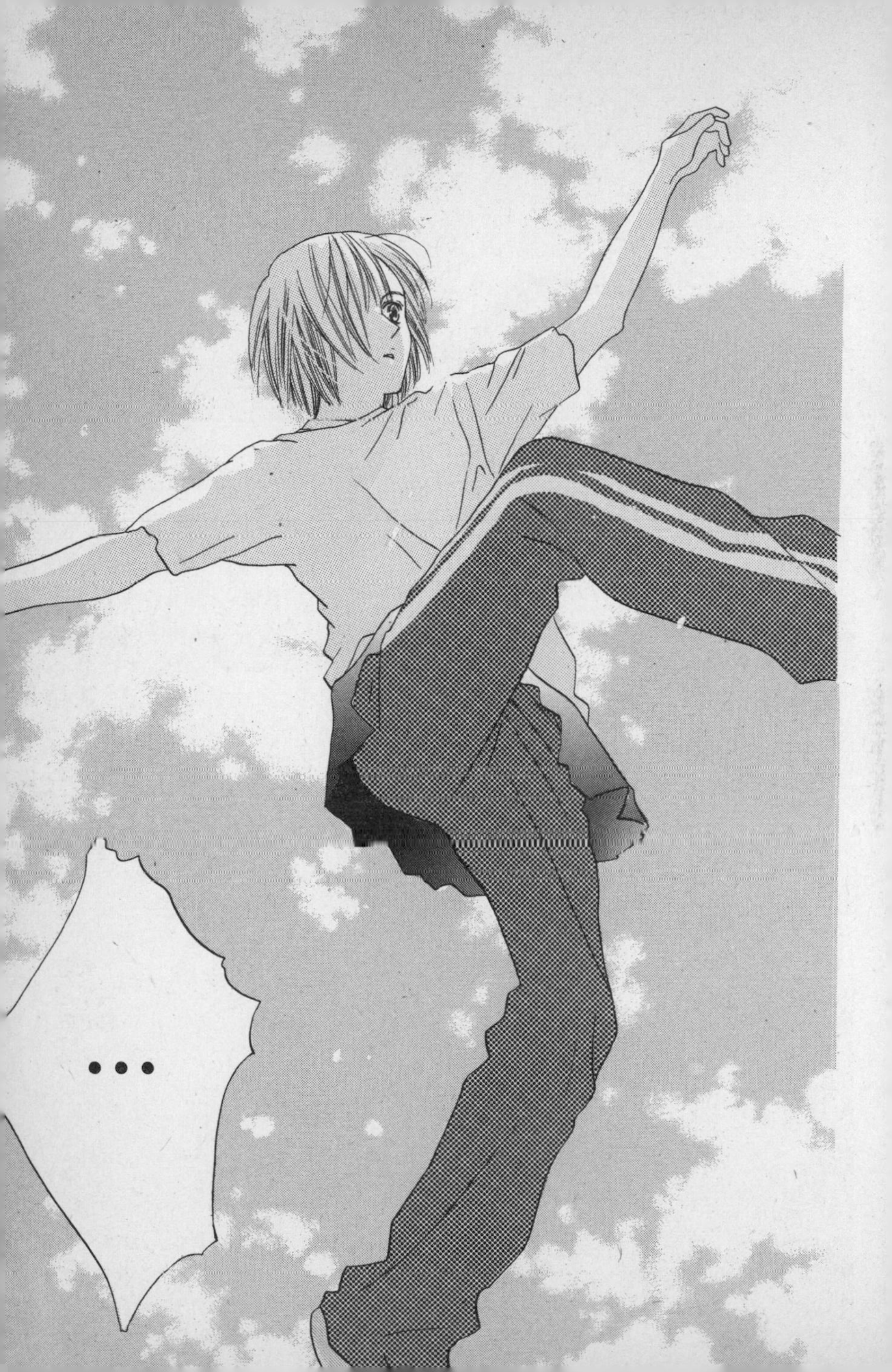
...

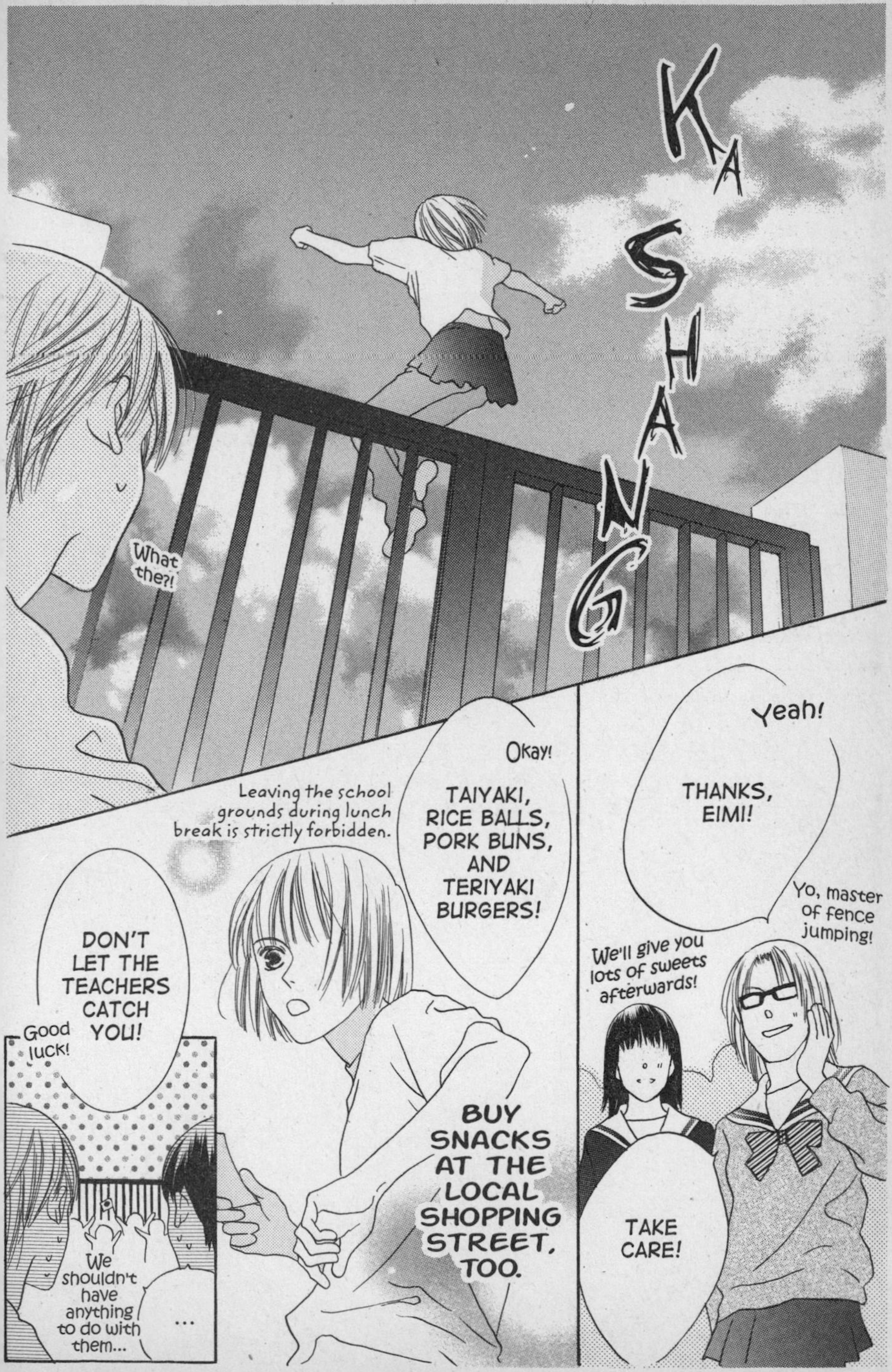
KASHANG
What the?!
Yeah!
THANKS, EIMI!
Yo, master of fence jumping!
We'll give you lots of sweets afterwards!
TAKE CARE!
Okay!
TAIYAKI, RICE BALLS, PORK BUNS, AND TERIYAKI BURGERS!
Leaving the school grounds during lunch break is strictly forbidden.
DON'T LET THE TEACHERS CATCH YOU!
BUY SNACKS AT THE LOCAL SHOPPING STREET, TOO.
Good luck!
We shouldn't have anything to do with them...
...

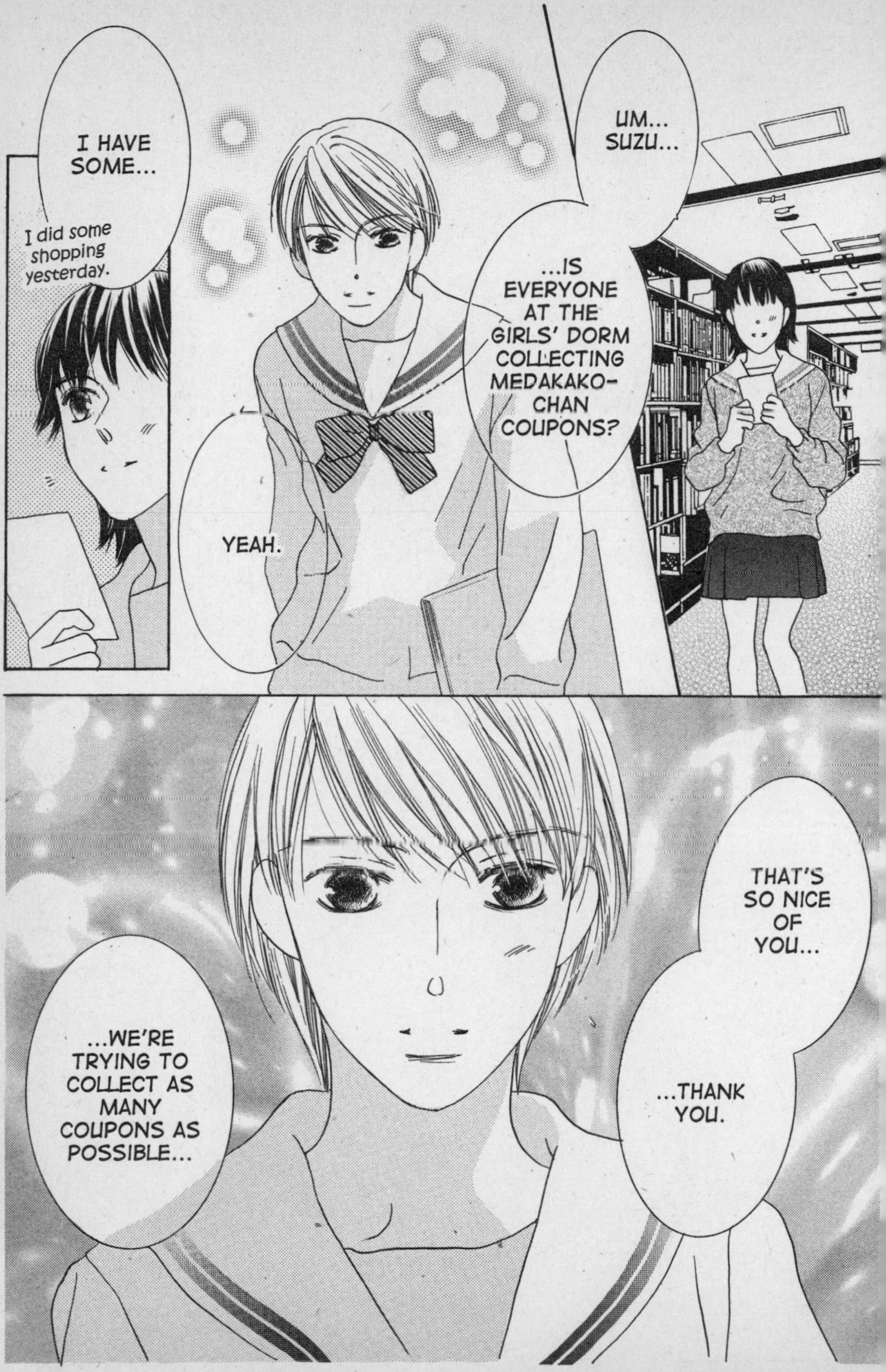
UM... SUZU...
...IS EVERYONE AT THE GIRLS' DORM COLLECTING MEDAKAKO-CHAN COUPONS?
YEAH.
I HAVE SOME...
I did some shopping yesterday.
THAT'S SO NICE OF YOU...
...THANK YOU.
...WE'RE TRYING TO COLLECT AS MANY COUPONS AS POSSIBLE...

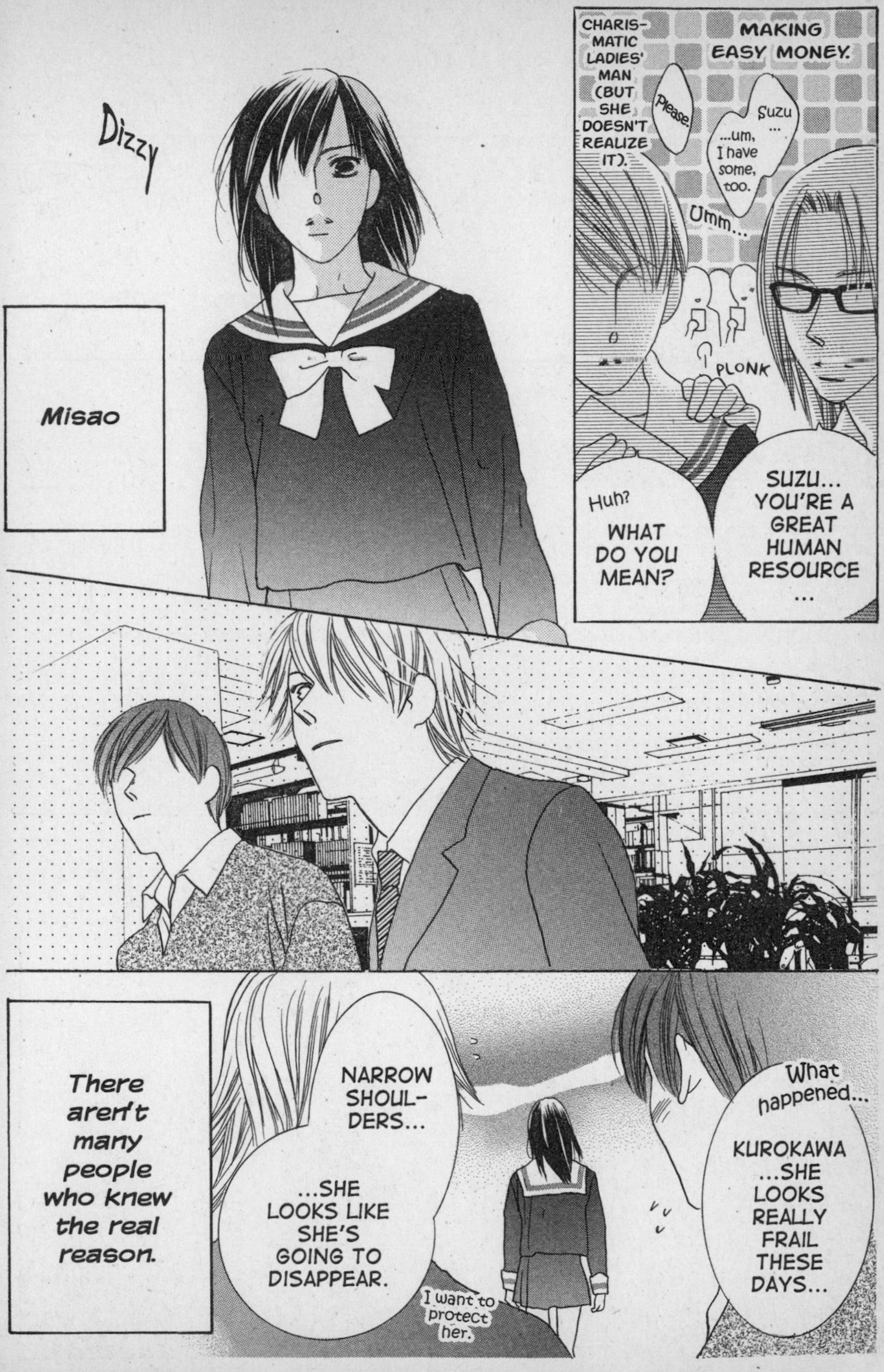
MAKING EASY MONEY.
Suzu... ...um, I have some, too.
Please.
CHARISMATIC LADIES' MAN (BUT SHE DOESN'T REALIZE IT).
Umm...
PLONK
SUZU... YOU'RE A GREAT HUMAN RESOURCE...
Huh? WHAT DO YOU MEAN?
Dizzy
Misao
What happened...
KUROKAWA ...SHE LOOKS REALLY FRAIL THESE DAYS...
I want to protect her.
NARROW SHOULDERS...
...SHE LOOKS LIKE SHE'S GOING TO DISAPPEAR.
There aren't many people who knew the real reason.

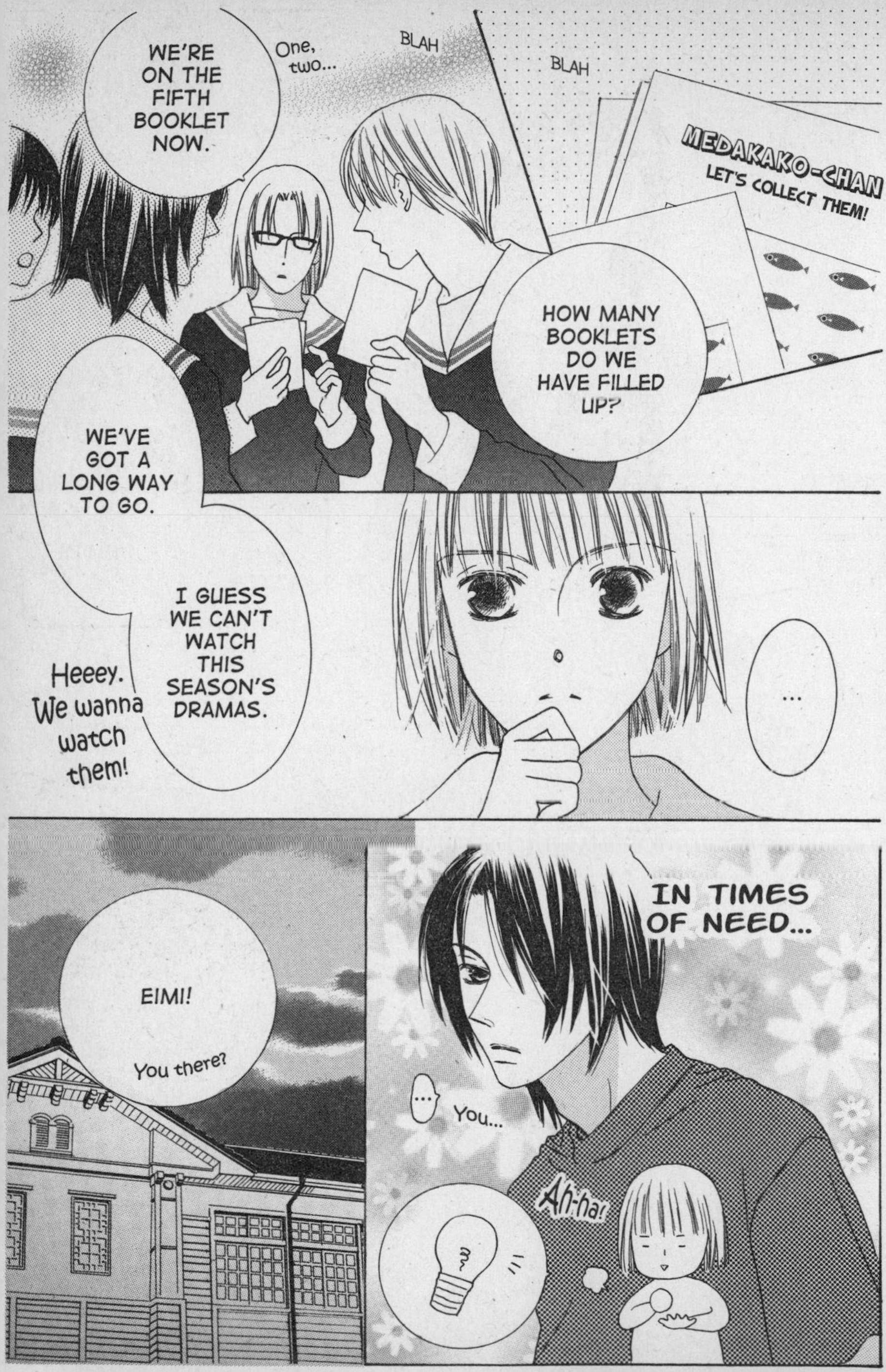
BLAH
MEDAKAKO-CHAN
LET'S COLLECT THEM!
HOW MANY BOOKLETS DO WE HAVE FILLED UP?
BLAH
One, two...
WE'RE ON THE FIFTH BOOKLET NOW.
WE'VE GOT A LONG WAY TO GO.
...
I GUESS WE CAN'T WATCH THIS SEASON'S DRAMAS.
Heeey. We wanna watch them!
IN TIMES OF NEED...
...
You...
Ah-ha!
EIMI!
You there?

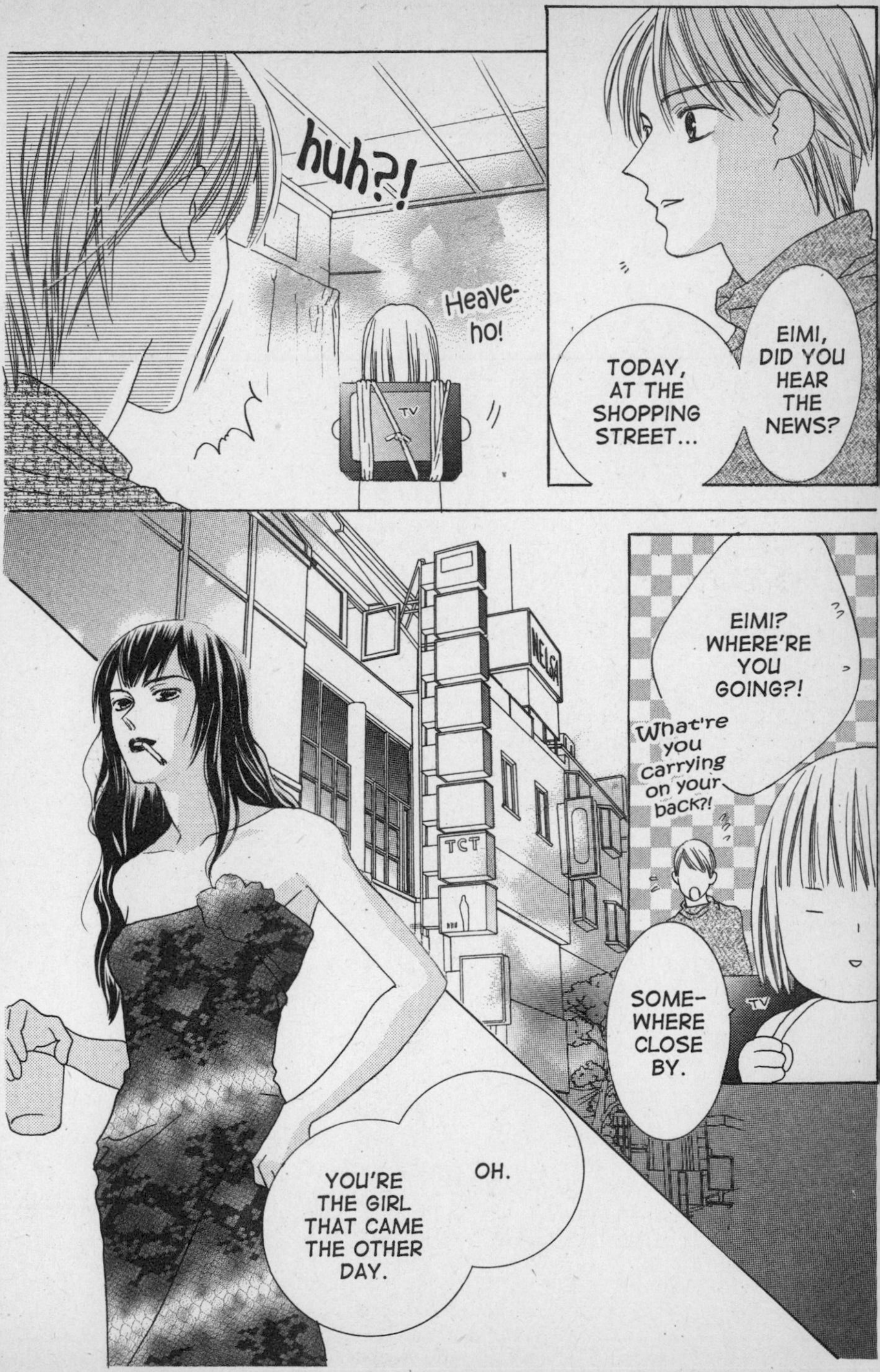
EIMI, DID YOU HEAR THE NEWS?
TODAY, AT THE SHOPPING STREET...
huh?!
Heave-ho!
EIMI? WHERE'RE YOU GOING?!
What're you carrying on your back?!
SOME-WHERE CLOSE BY.
OH.
YOU'RE THE GIRL THAT CAME THE OTHER DAY.

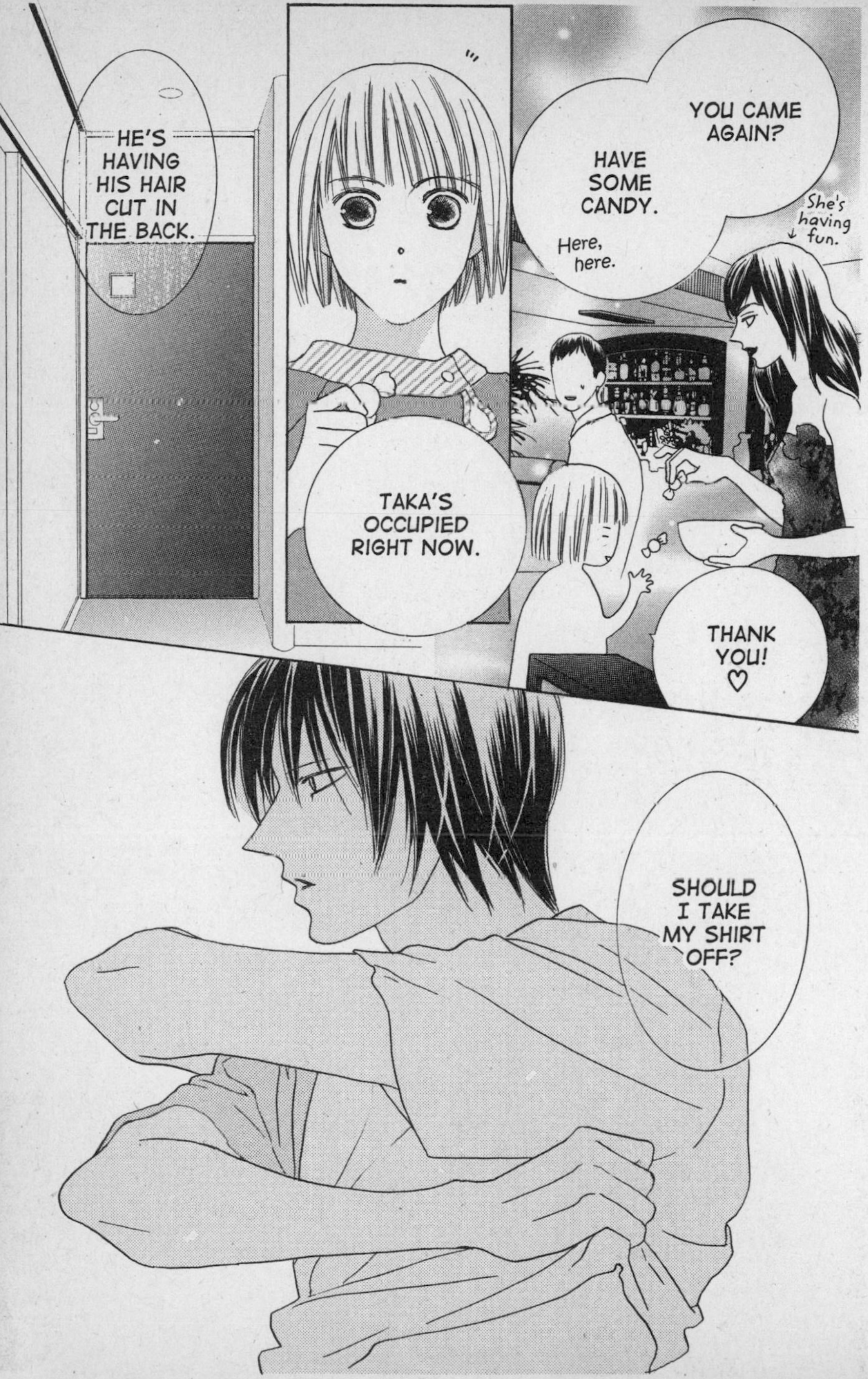
YOU CAME AGAIN?
HAVE SOME CANDY.
Here, here.
She's having fun.
THANK YOU! ♡
TAKA'S OCCUPIED RIGHT NOW.
HE'S HAVING HIS HAIR CUT IN THE BACK.
SHOULD I TAKE MY SHIRT OFF?

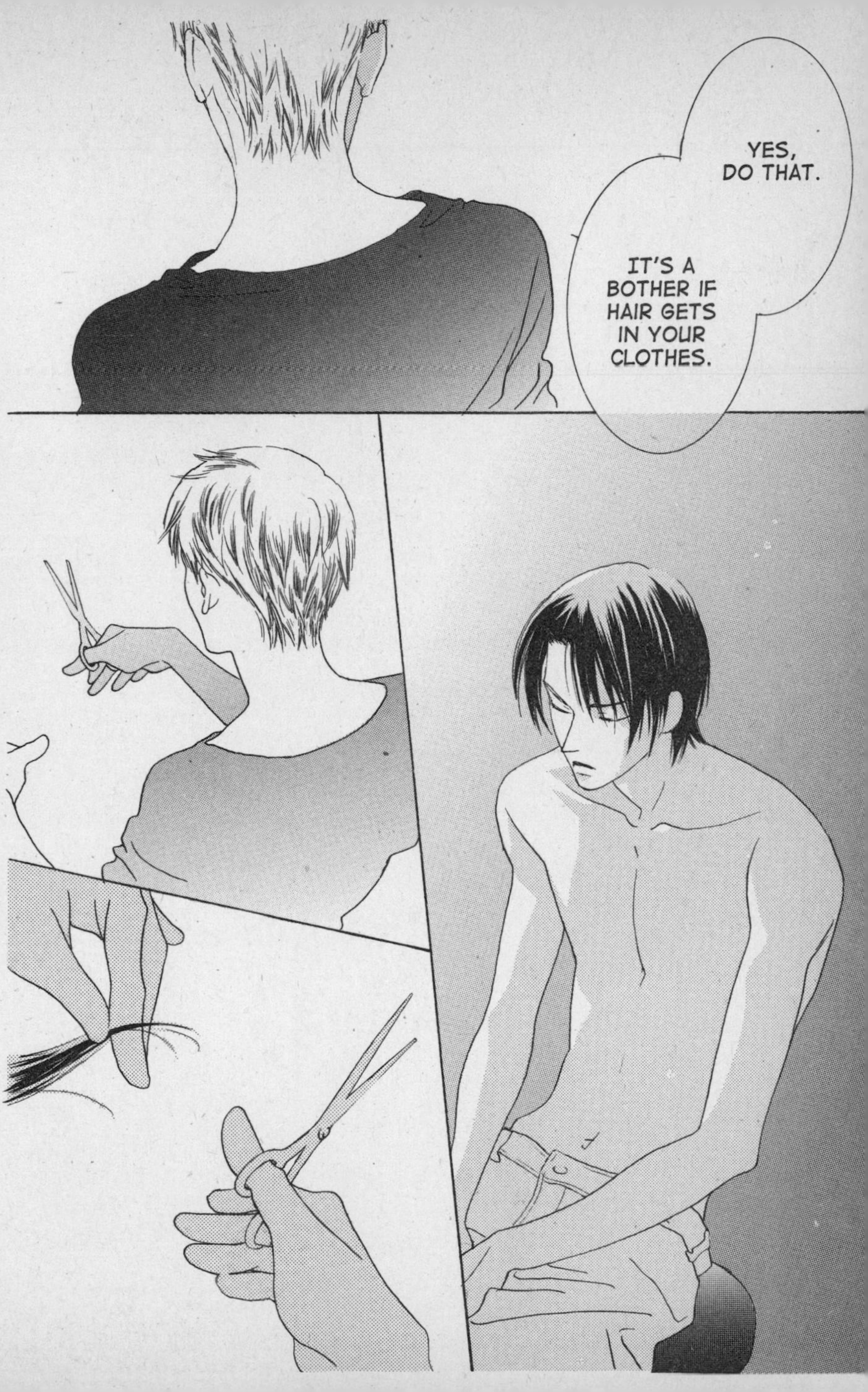
YES, DO THAT.
IT'S A BOTHER IF HAIR GETS IN YOUR CLOTHES.

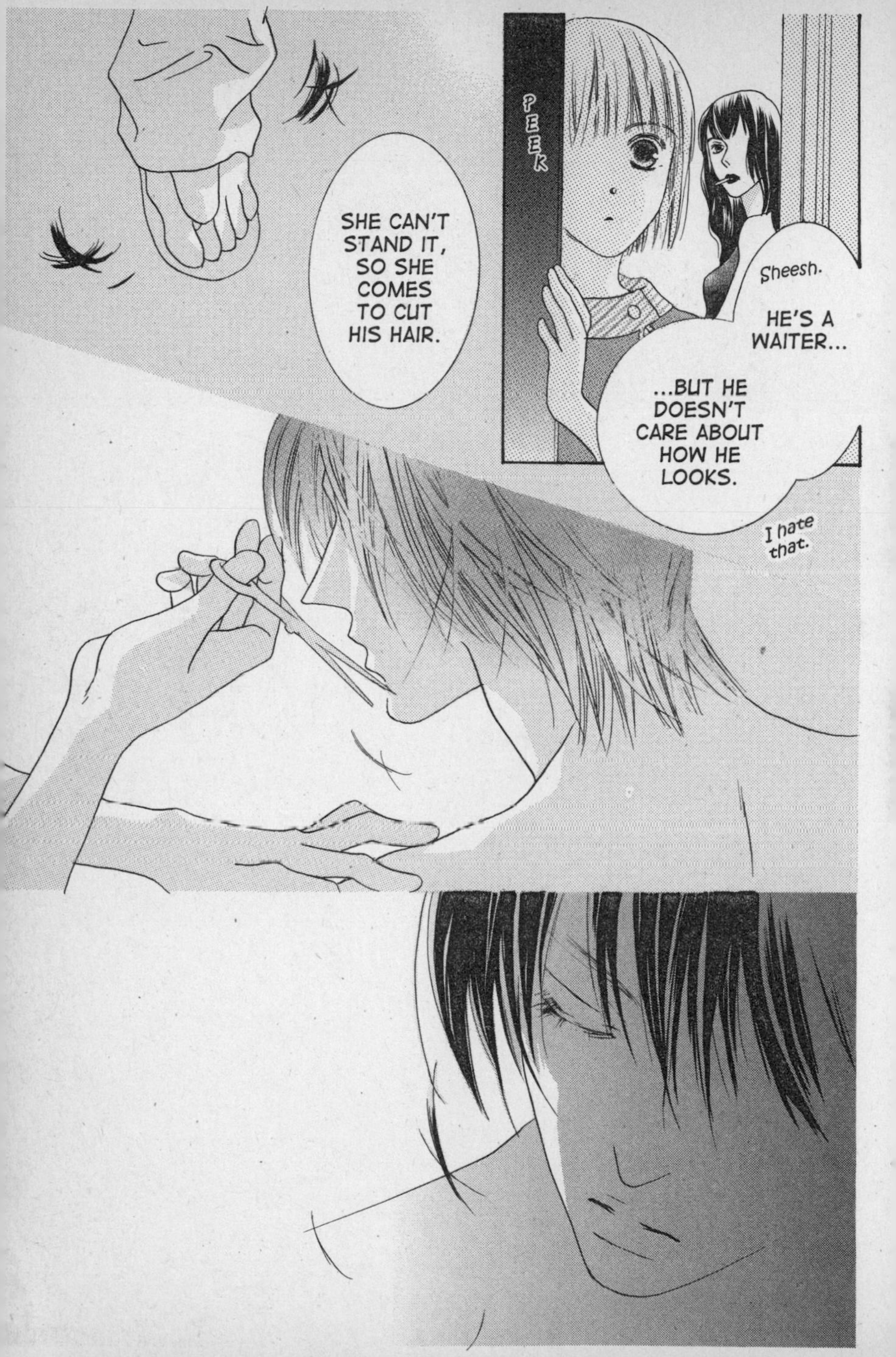
PEEK
Sheesh.
HE'S A WAITER...
...BUT HE DOESN'T CARE ABOUT HOW HE LOOKS.
I hate that.
SHE CAN'T STAND IT, SO SHE COMES TO CUT HIS HAIR.

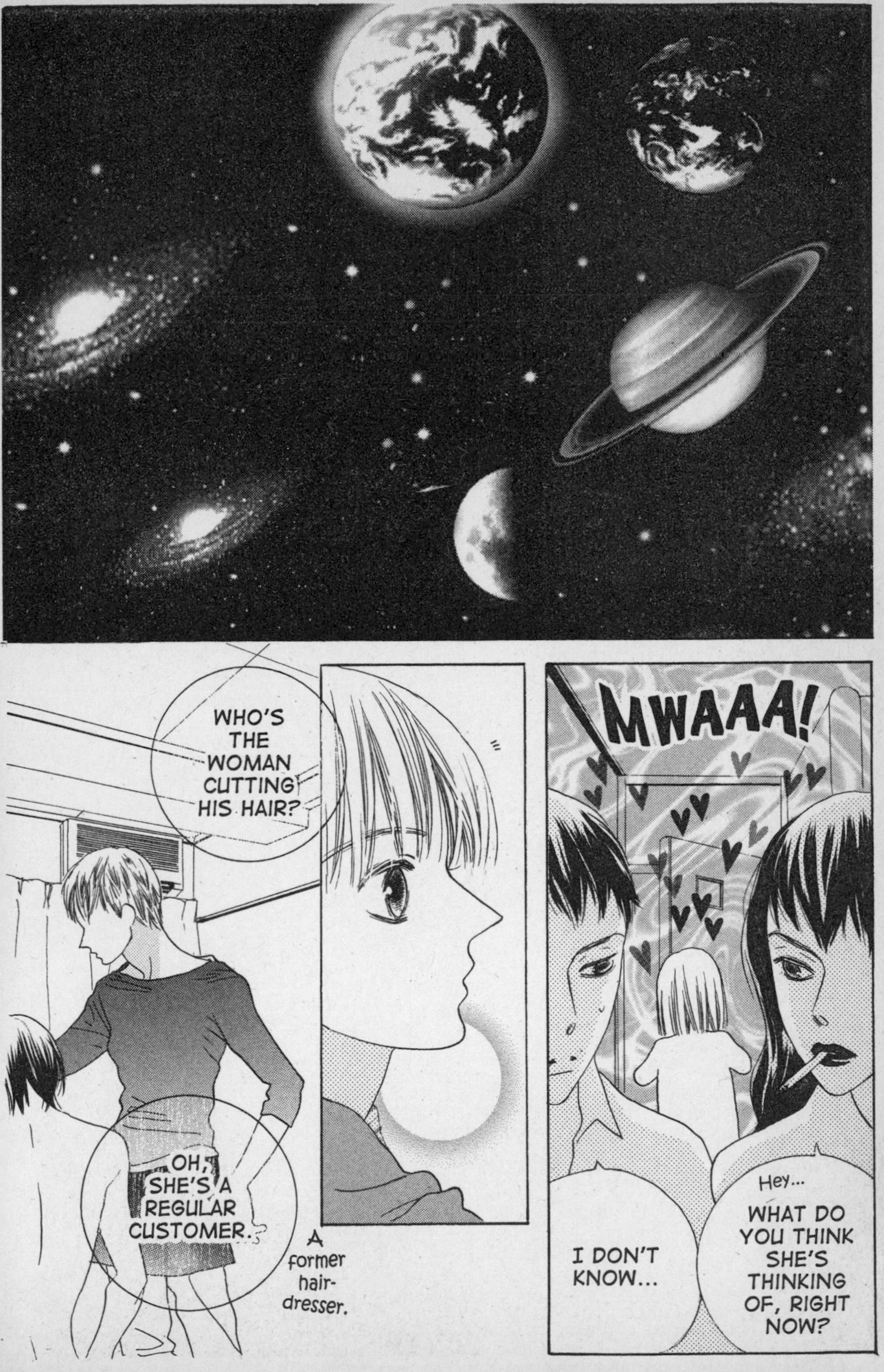

MWAAA!
Hey...
WHAT DO YOU THINK SHE'S THINKING OF, RIGHT NOW?
I DON'T KNOW...
WHO'S THE WOMAN CUTTING HIS HAIR?
OH, SHE'S A REGULAR CUSTOMER.
A former hair-dresser.

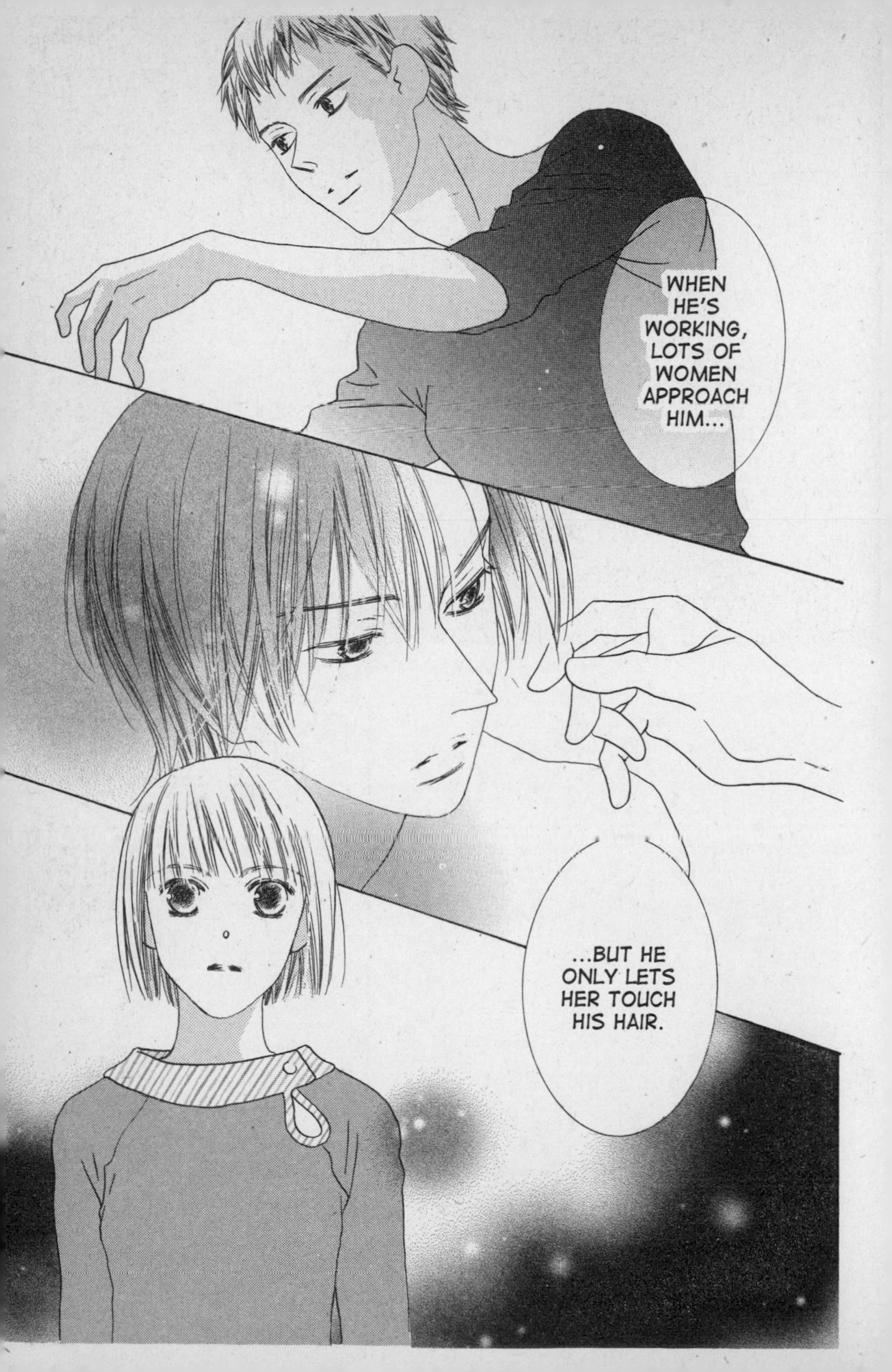
WHEN HE'S WORKING, LOTS OF WOMEN APPROACH HIM...
...BUT HE ONLY LETS HER TOUCH HIS HAIR.

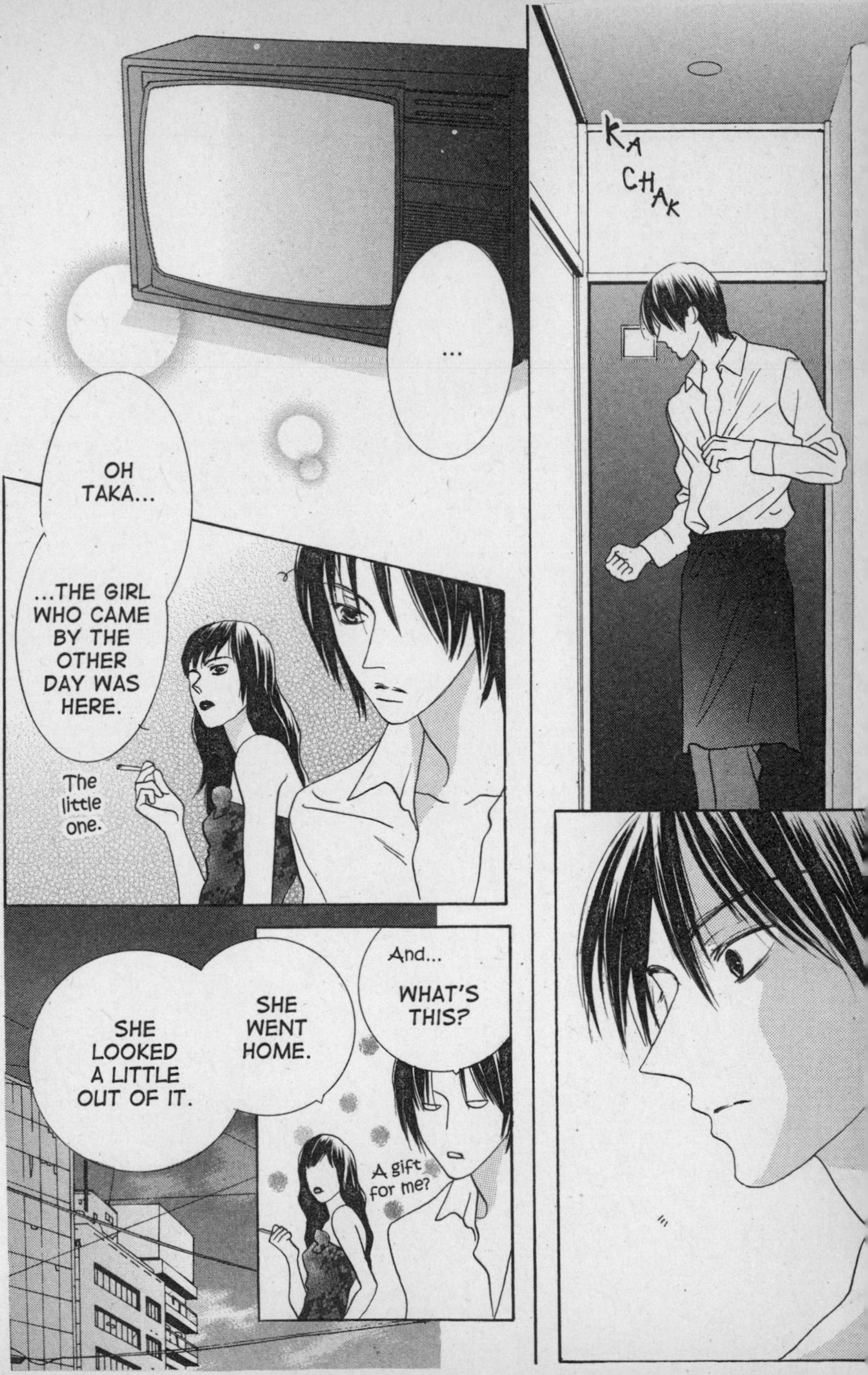
KA CHAK
...
OH TAKA...
...THE GIRL WHO CAME BY THE OTHER DAY WAS HERE.
The little one.
And...
WHAT'S THIS?
SHE WENT HOME.
SHE LOOKED A LITTLE OUT OF IT.
A gift for me?

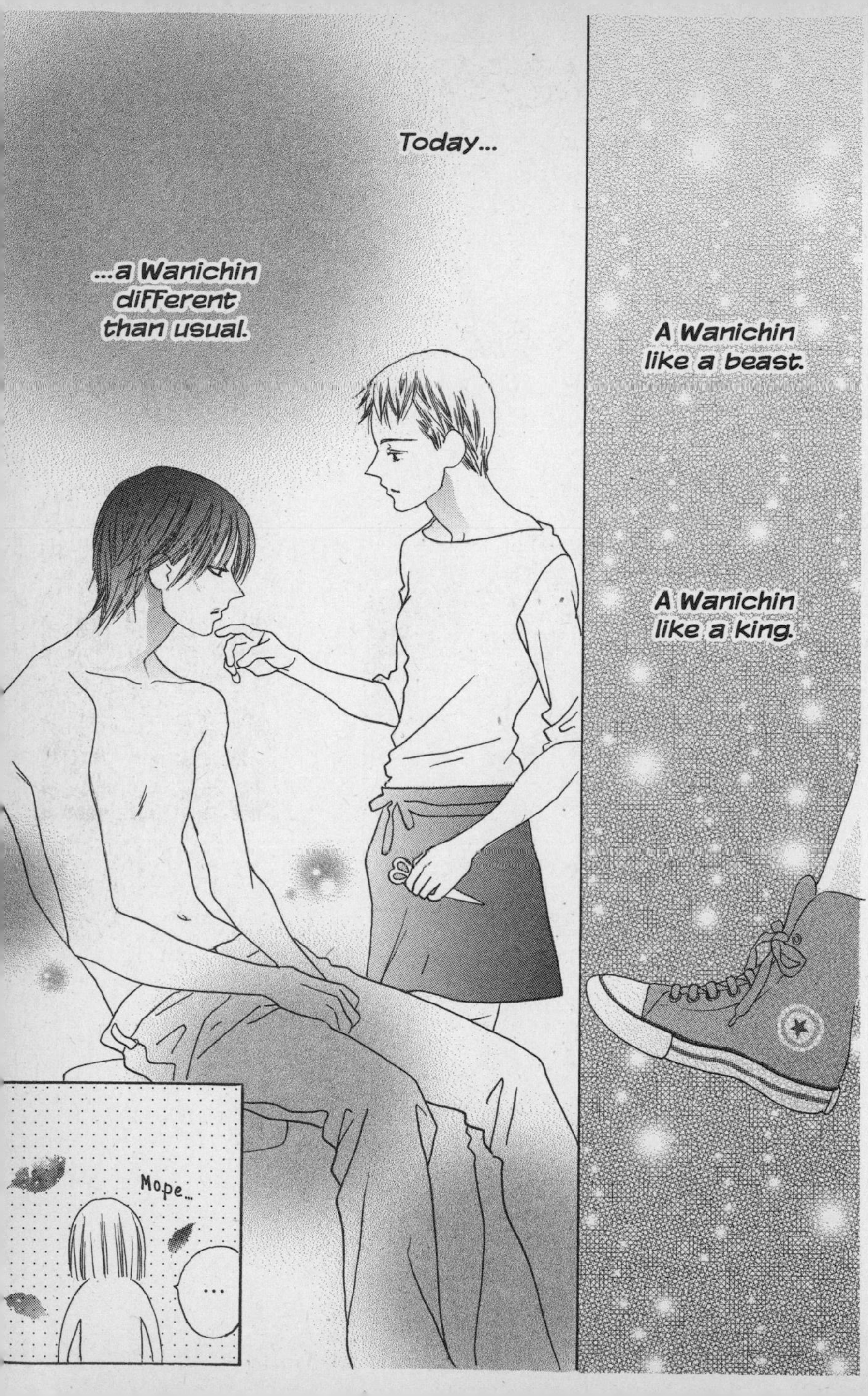
A Wanichin like a beast.
A Wanichin like a king.
Today...
...a Wanichin different than usual.
Mope...
...

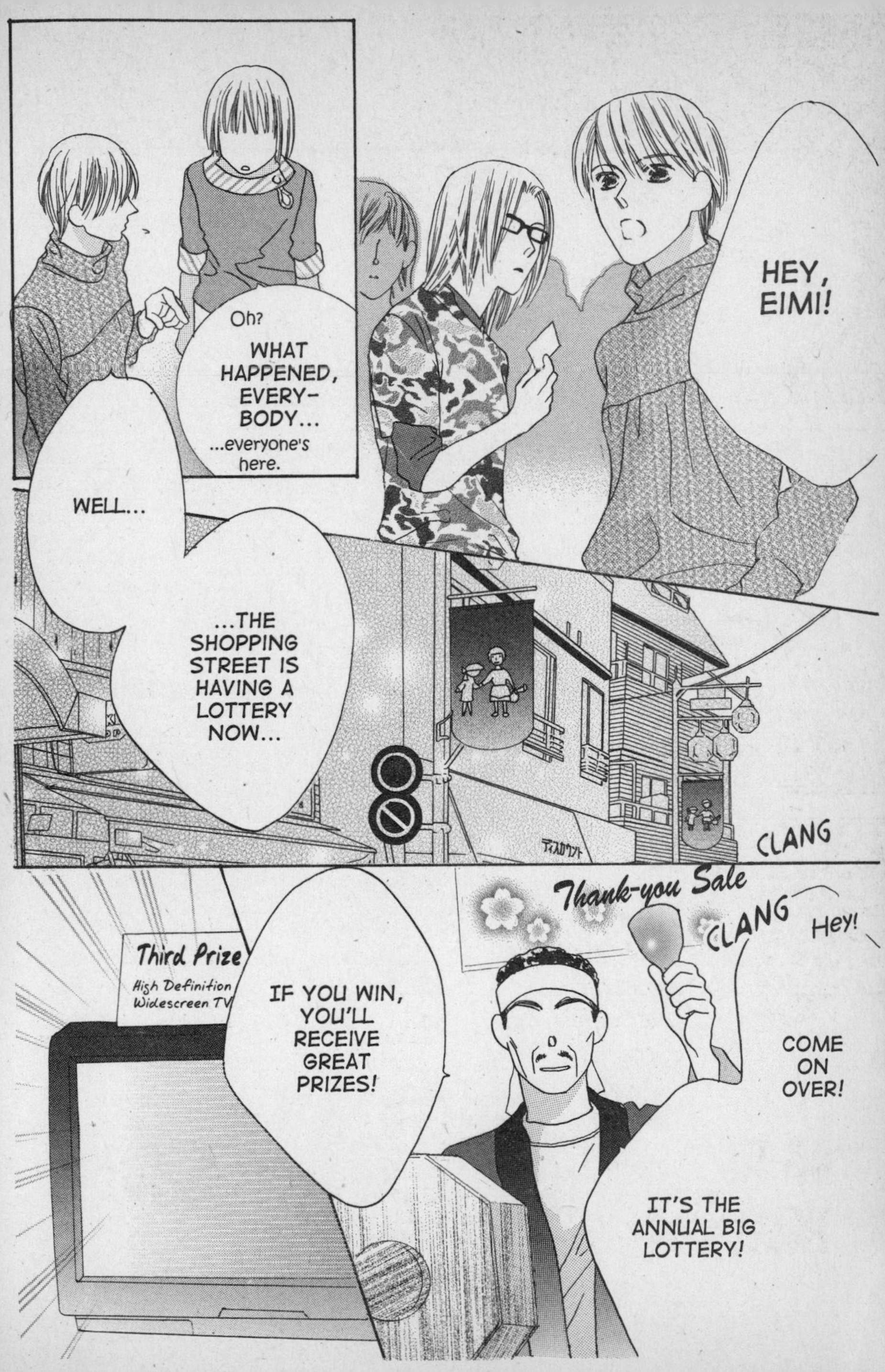
HEY, EIMI!
Oh? WHAT HAPPENED, EVERY-BODY... ...everyone's here.
WELL...
...THE SHOPPING STREET IS HAVING A LOTTERY NOW...
CLANG
Thank-you Sale
CLANG
Hey!
COME ON OVER!
IT'S THE ANNUAL BIG LOTTERY!
IF YOU WIN, YOU'LL RECEIVE GREAT PRIZES!
Third Prize
High Definition Widescreen TV

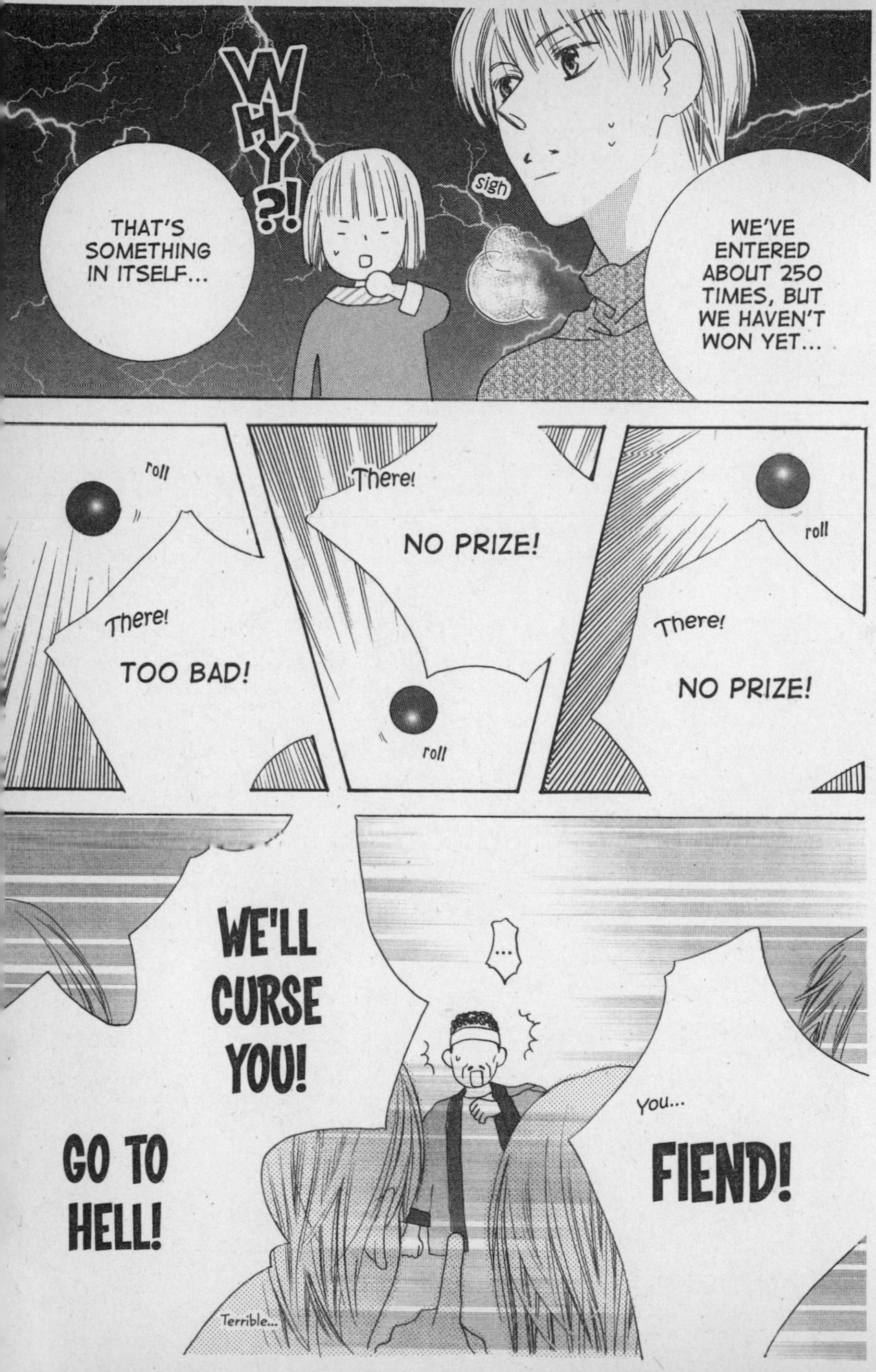
WE'VE ENTERED ABOUT 250 TIMES, BUT WE HAVEN'T WON YET...
sigh
WHY?!
THAT'S SOMETHING IN ITSELF...
roll
There!
NO PRIZE!
There!
NO PRIZE!
roll
roll
There!
TOO BAD!
You...
FIEND!
...
WE'LL CURSE YOU!
GO TO HELL!
Terrible...

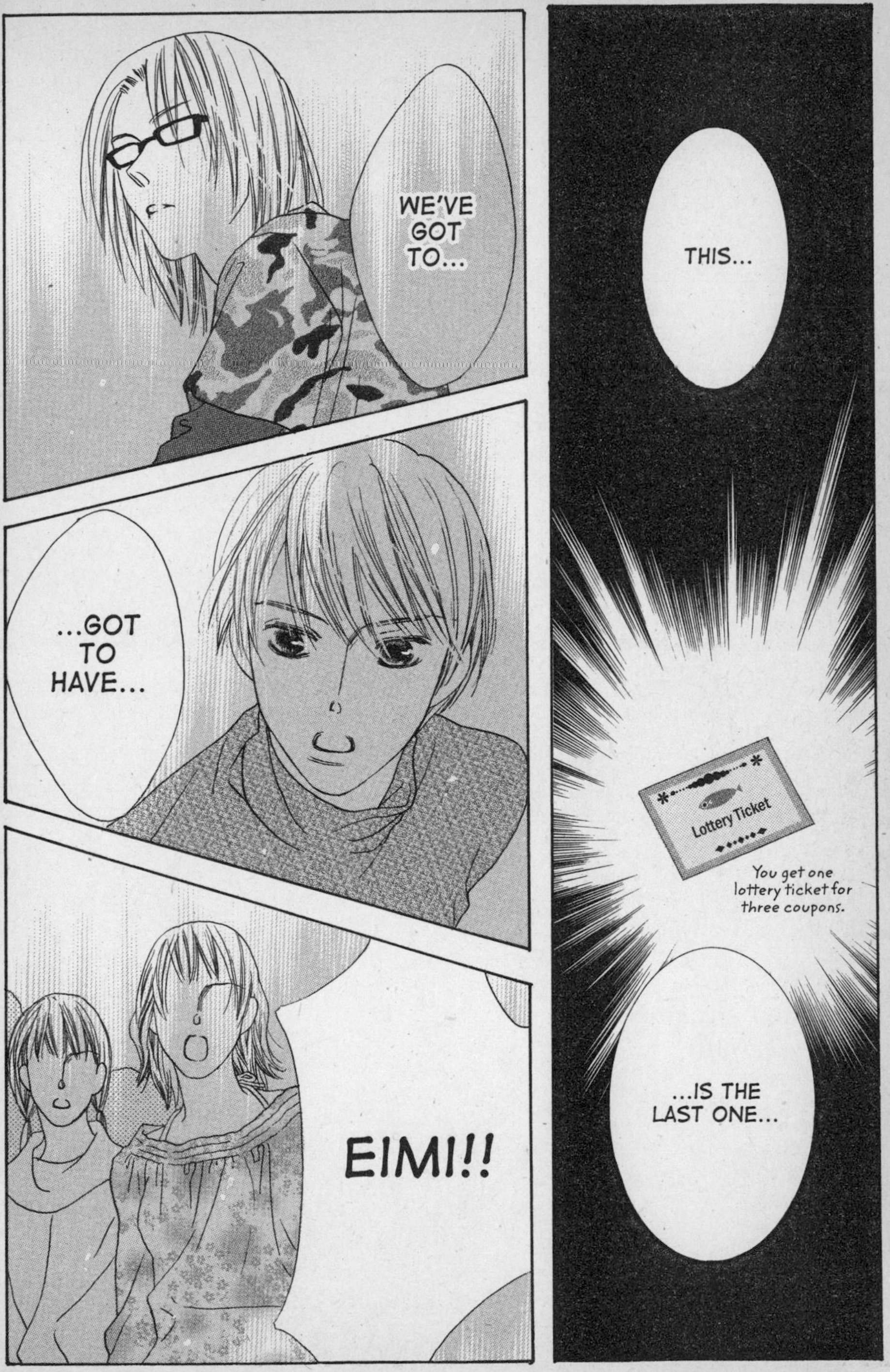
THIS...
Lottery Ticket
You get one lottery ticket for three coupons.
...IS THE LAST ONE...
WE'VE GOT TO...
...GOT TO HAVE...
EIMI!!

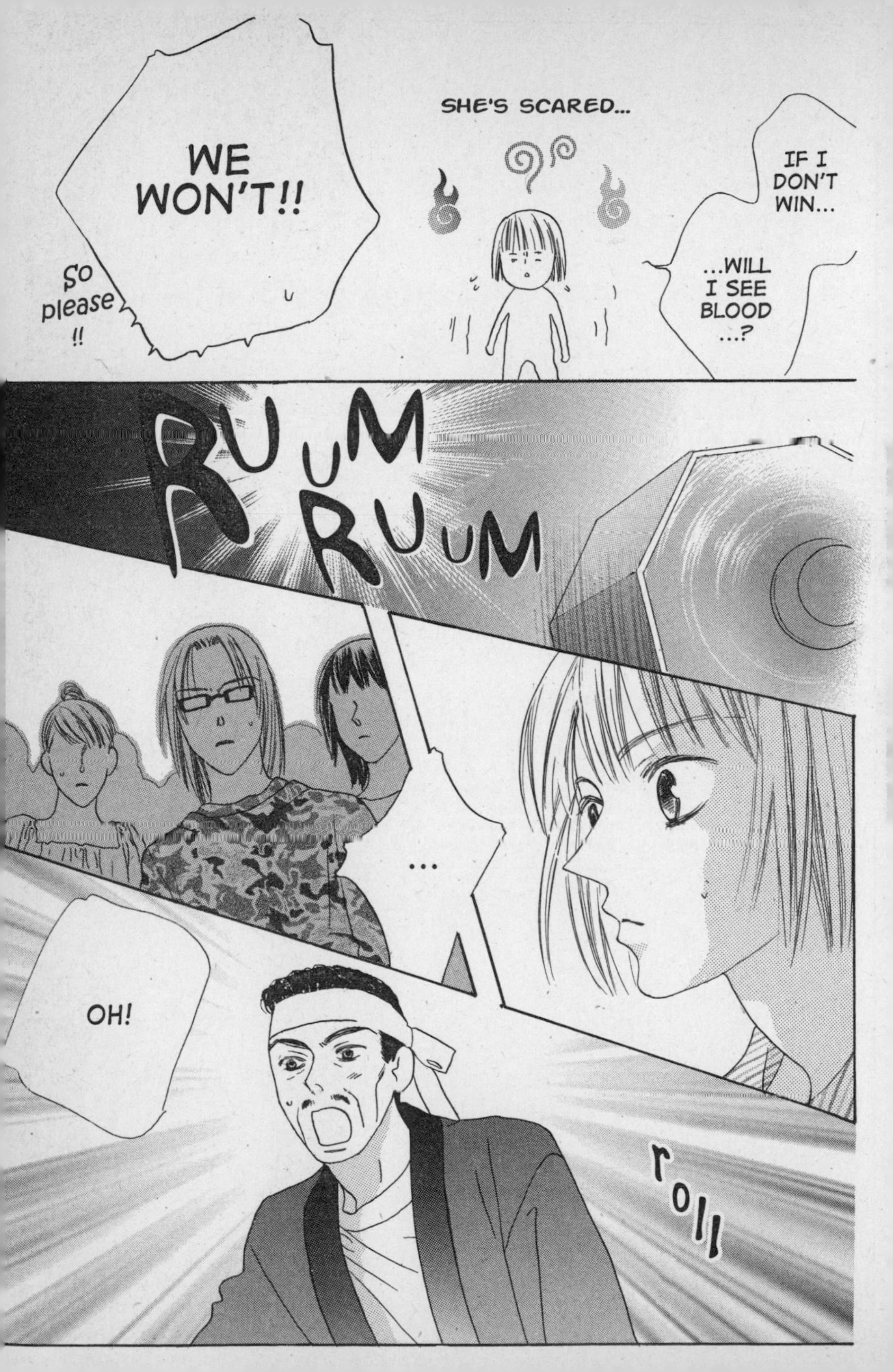
IF I DON'T WIN...
...WILL I SEE BLOOD ...?
SHE'S SCARED...
WE WON'T!!
So please !!
RUUM RUUM
...
roll
OH!

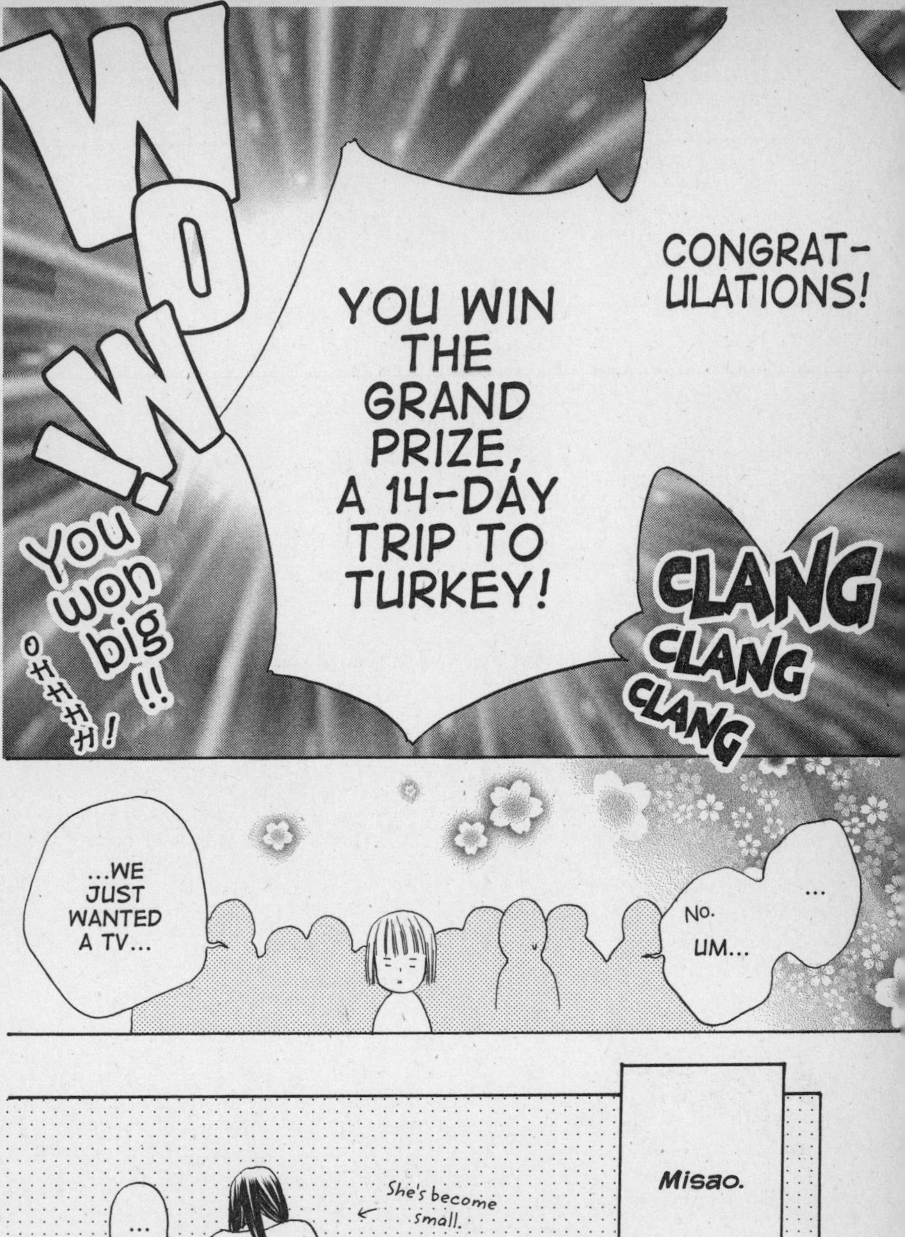
CONGRAT-ULATIONS!
YOU WIN THE GRAND PRIZE, A 14-DAY TRIP TO TURKEY!
CLANG CLANG CLANG CLANG
WOW!!
You won big!!
OHHHHH!
...
No. UM...
...WE JUST WANTED A TV...
Misao.
...
She's become small.

BEAUTY
IS THE
BEAST

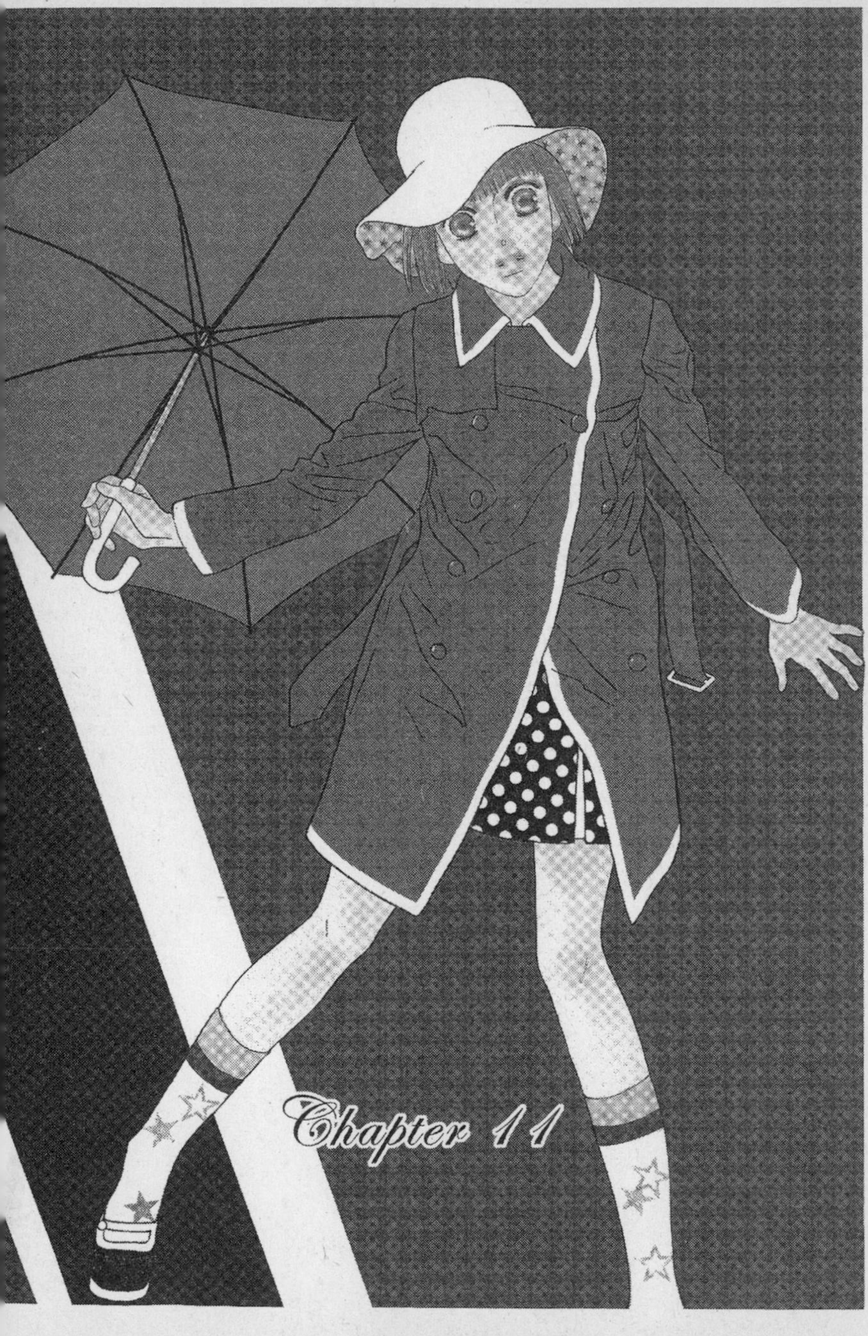
Chapter 11

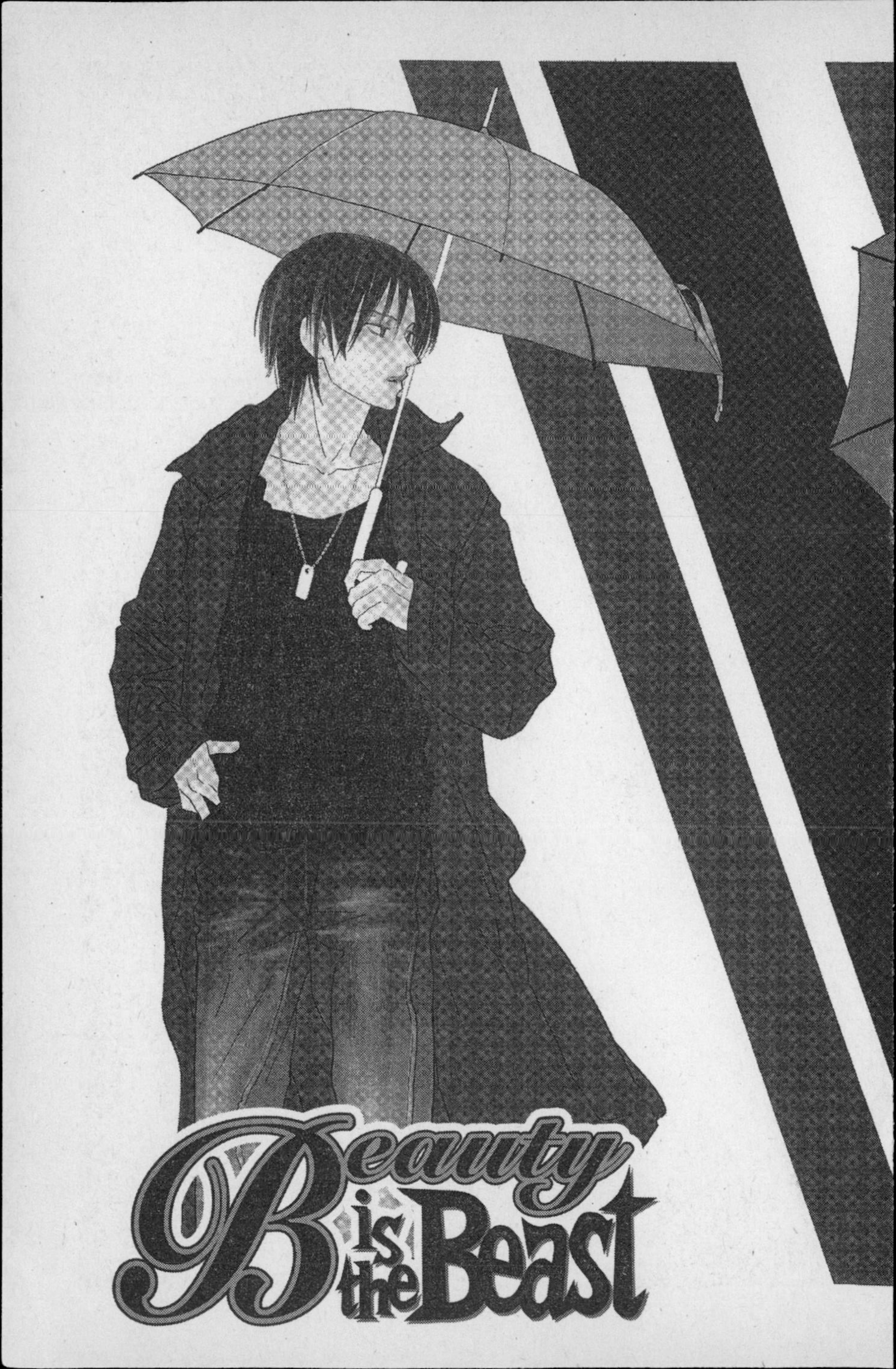
Beauty is the Beast

BEAUTY
IS THE
BEAST

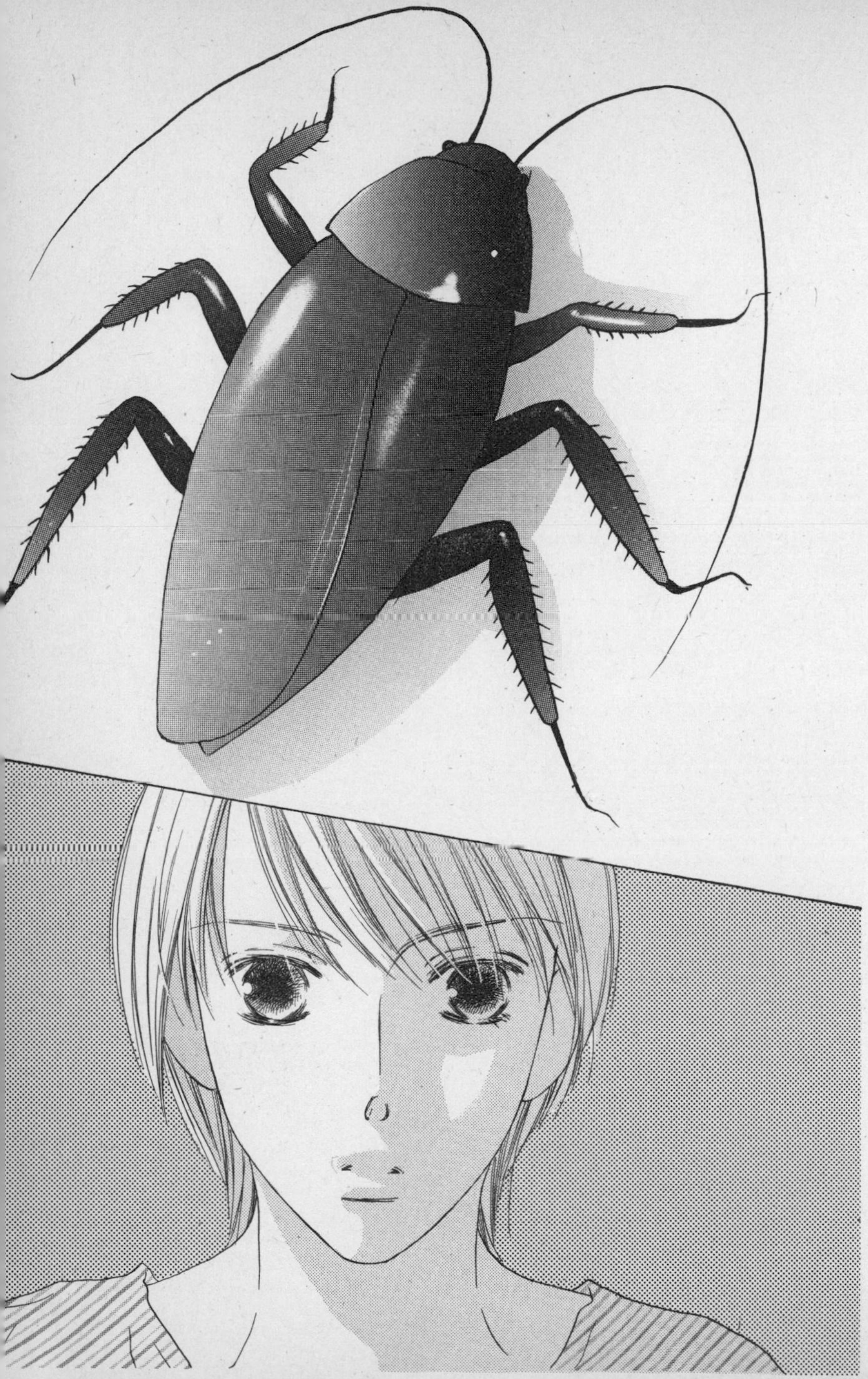

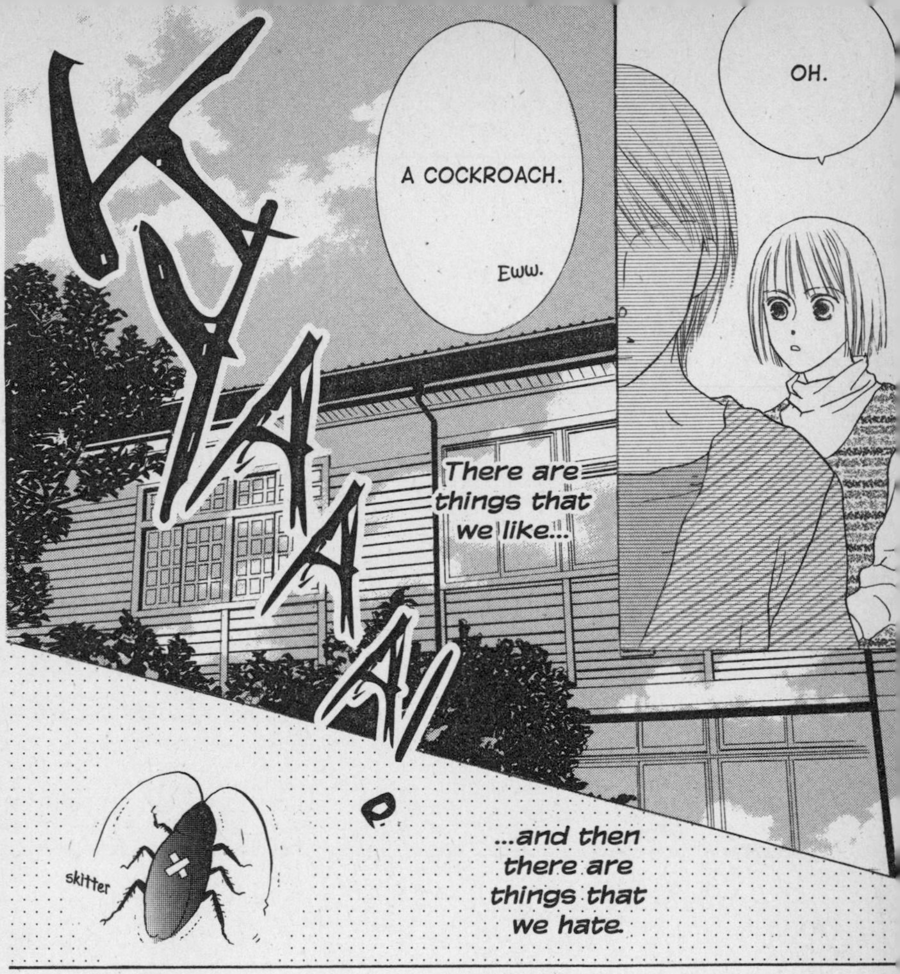
OH.
A COCKROACH.
Eww.
There are things that we like...
...and then there are things that we hate.
skitter

Dorm Story 6

"The dorm put air conditioners in the year I entered.
I would have almost died of heat and cold otherwise. (☺)"

⇨ Oops. It saved your life. (☺)

By the way, thanks to everyone who read volume 1 and wrote in saying that they "want a washbowl!" I was tempted to hand the washbowls out...!! (tears)

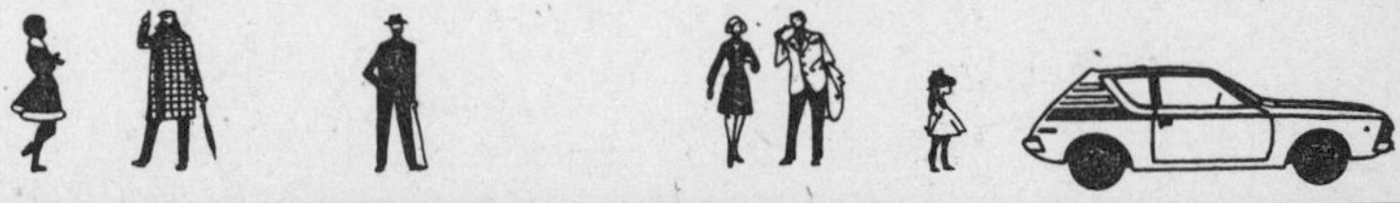

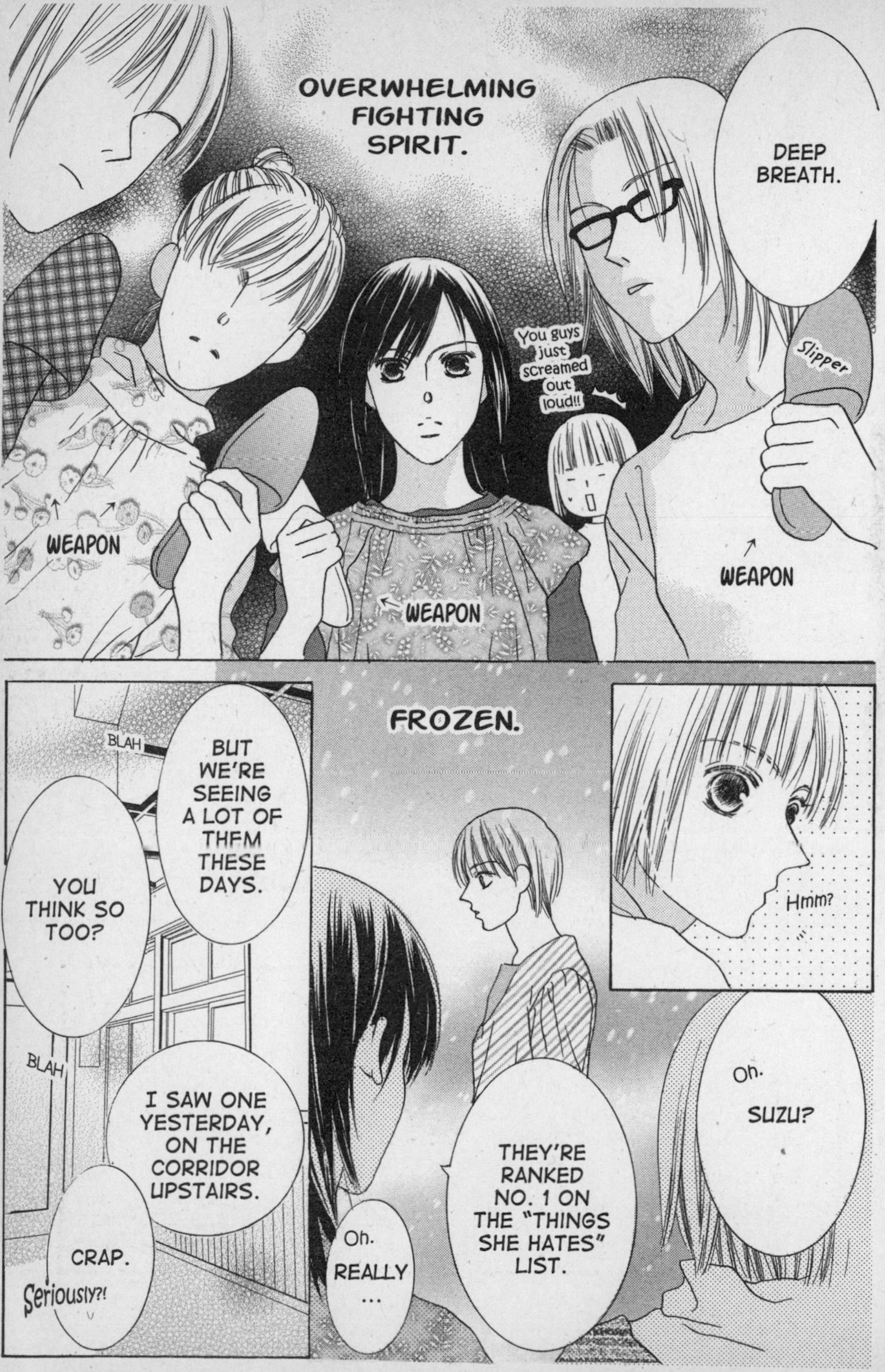
DEEP BREATH.
Slipper
WEAPON
You guys just screamed out loud!!
OVERWHELMING FIGHTING SPIRIT.
WEAPON
WEAPON
Hmm?
FROZEN.
Oh.
SUZU?
THEY'RE RANKED NO. 1 ON THE "THINGS SHE HATES" LIST.
Oh.
REALLY ...
BLAH
BUT WE'RE SEEING A LOT OF THEM THESE DAYS.
YOU THINK SO TOO?
BLAH
I SAW ONE YESTERDAY, ON THE CORRIDOR UPSTAIRS.
CRAP.
Seriously?!

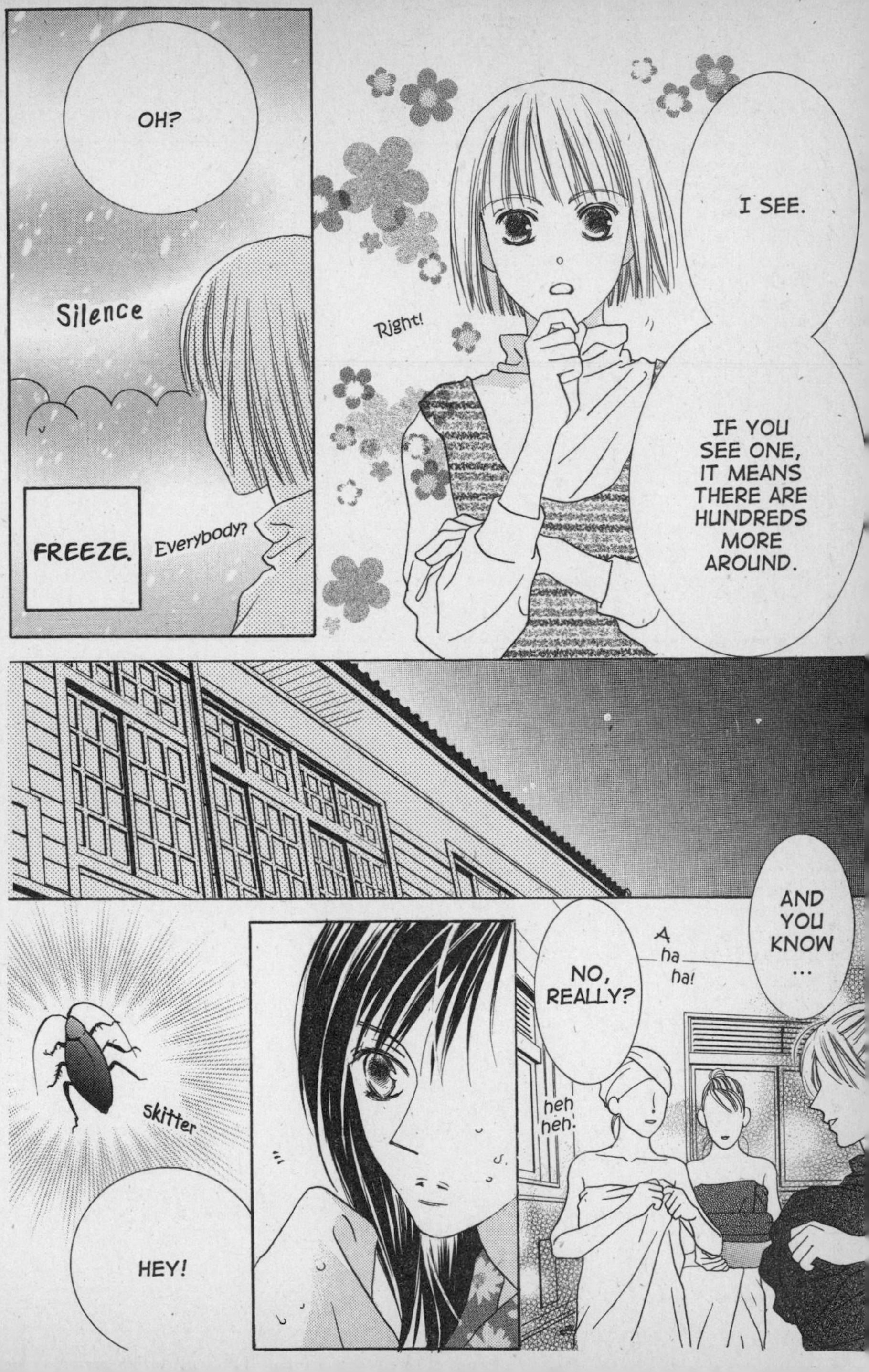
I SEE.
Right!
IF YOU SEE ONE, IT MEANS THERE ARE HUNDREDS MORE AROUND.
OH?
Silence
Everybody?
FREEZE.
AND YOU KNOW ...
A ha ha!
NO, REALLY?
heh heh!
skitter
HEY!

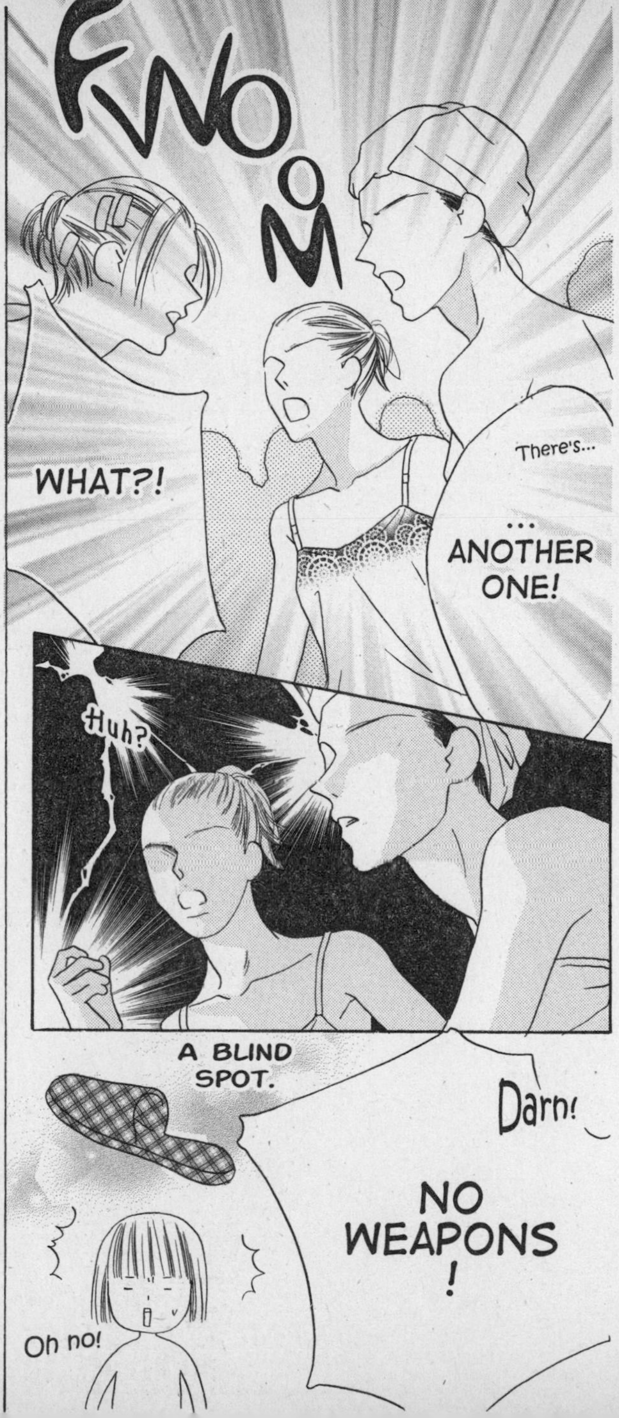
FWOOM
There's...
... ANOTHER ONE!
WHAT?!
Huh?
Darn!
A BLIND SPOT.
NO WEAPONS !
Oh no!

Hmm... Now that I've written out how I do my work, it's really ordinary. I'm not doing anything that would be of use to other people. Ha ha. (↑) Oh dear.

The art materials I use are ones that are sold at art supplies stores.

I haven't used any computer graphics in my work yet. I'd like to use them someday, but I'll hold off until I can use ordinary art materials well.

With this volume, I couldn't put any extra manga at the end of the volume, because of the number of pages in the volume. I'm sorry... I hope I'll be able to see you again. Thank you for reading this far. See you then!

From,
Tomo Matsumoto.

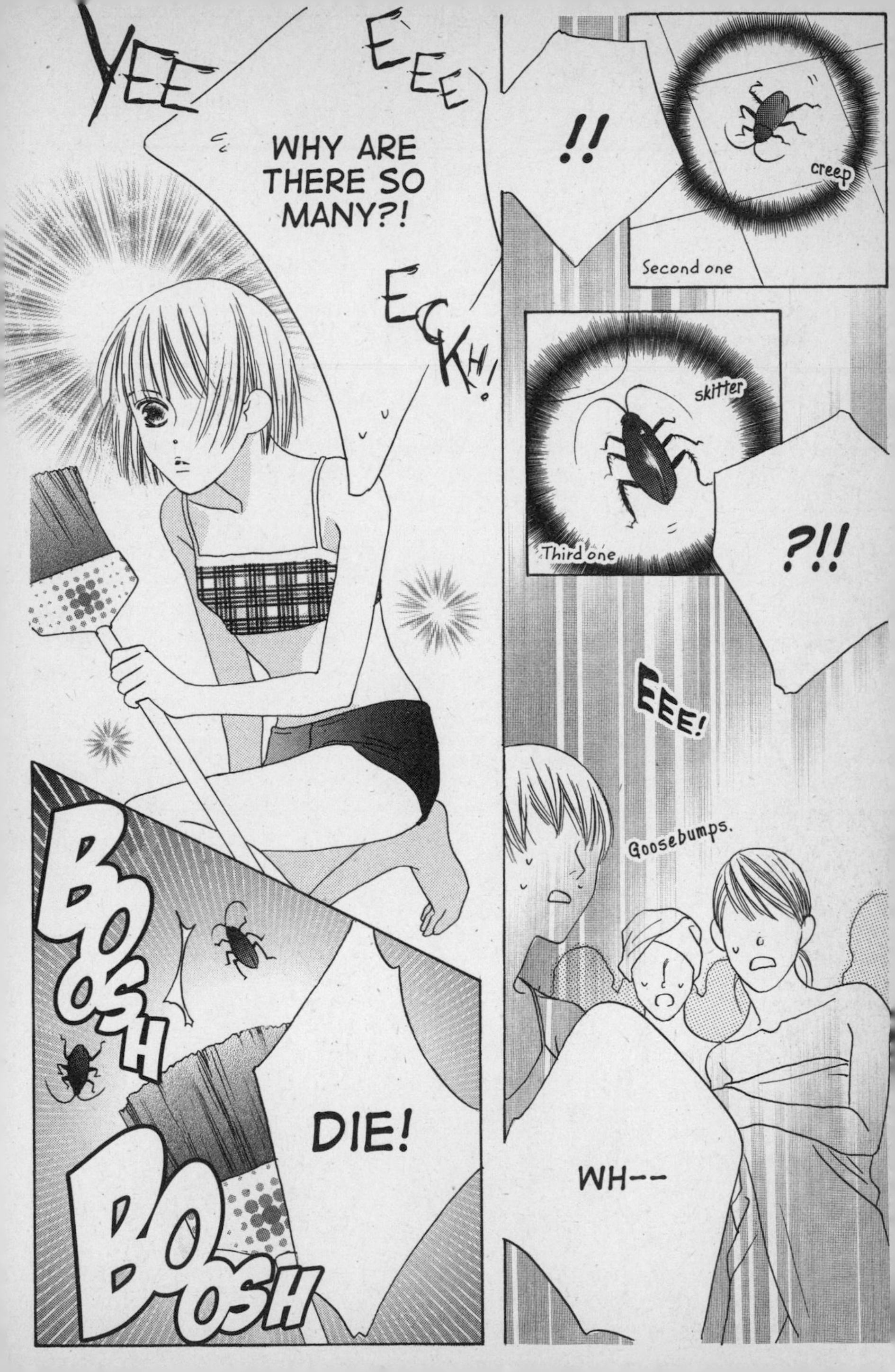
creep
Second one
!!
skitter
Third one
?!!
EEE!
Goosebumps.
WH--
YEEEEE
WHY ARE THERE SO MANY?!
ECKH!
DIE!
BOSH
BOSH

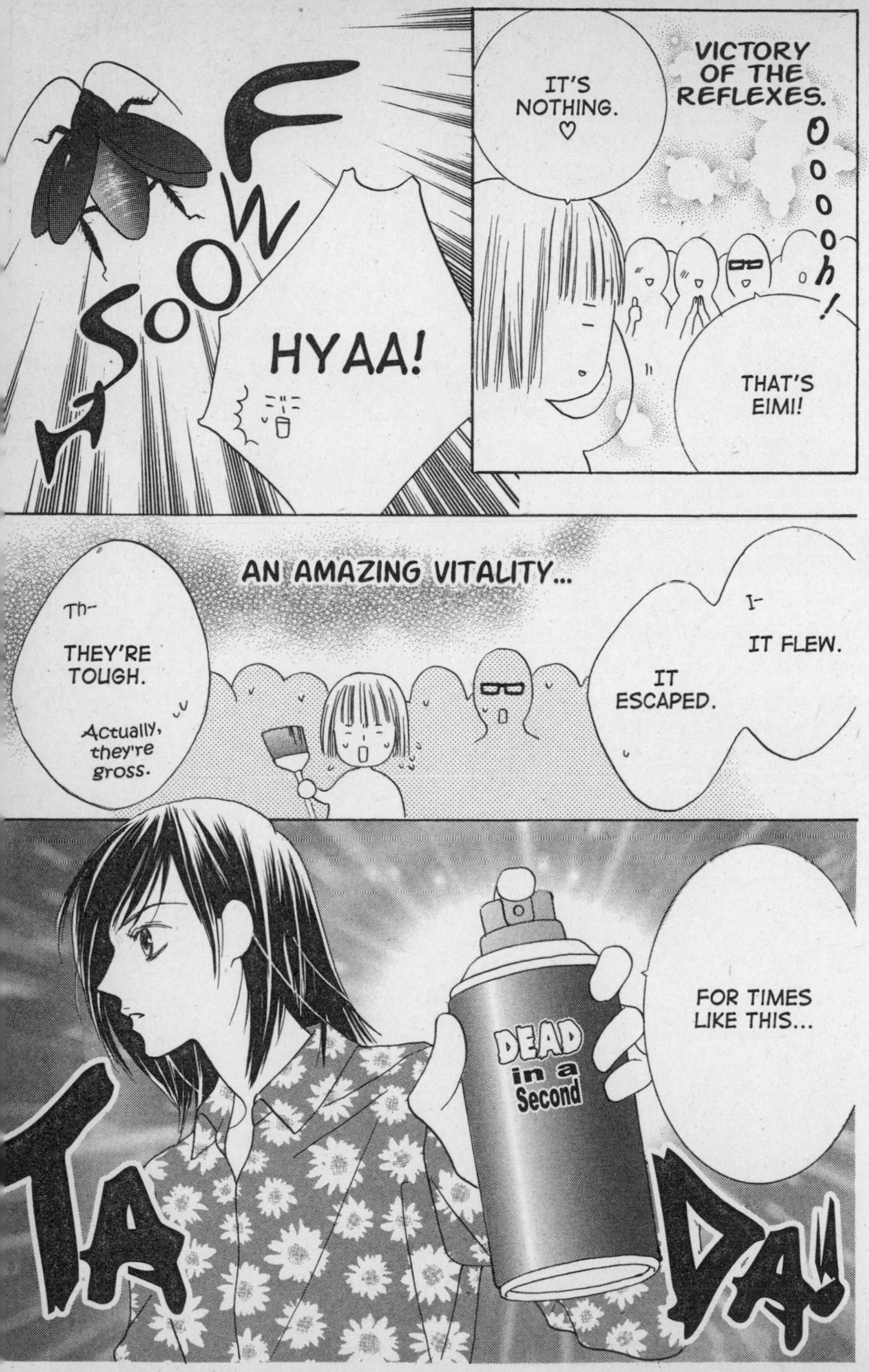
VICTORY OF THE REFLEXES.
IT'S NOTHING. ♡
Ooooh!
THAT'S EIMI!
SOOWF
HYAA!
AN AMAZING VITALITY...
I- IT FLEW.
IT ESCAPED.
Th- THEY'RE TOUGH.
Actually, they're gross.
FOR TIMES LIKE THIS...
DEAD in a Second
TA DA!

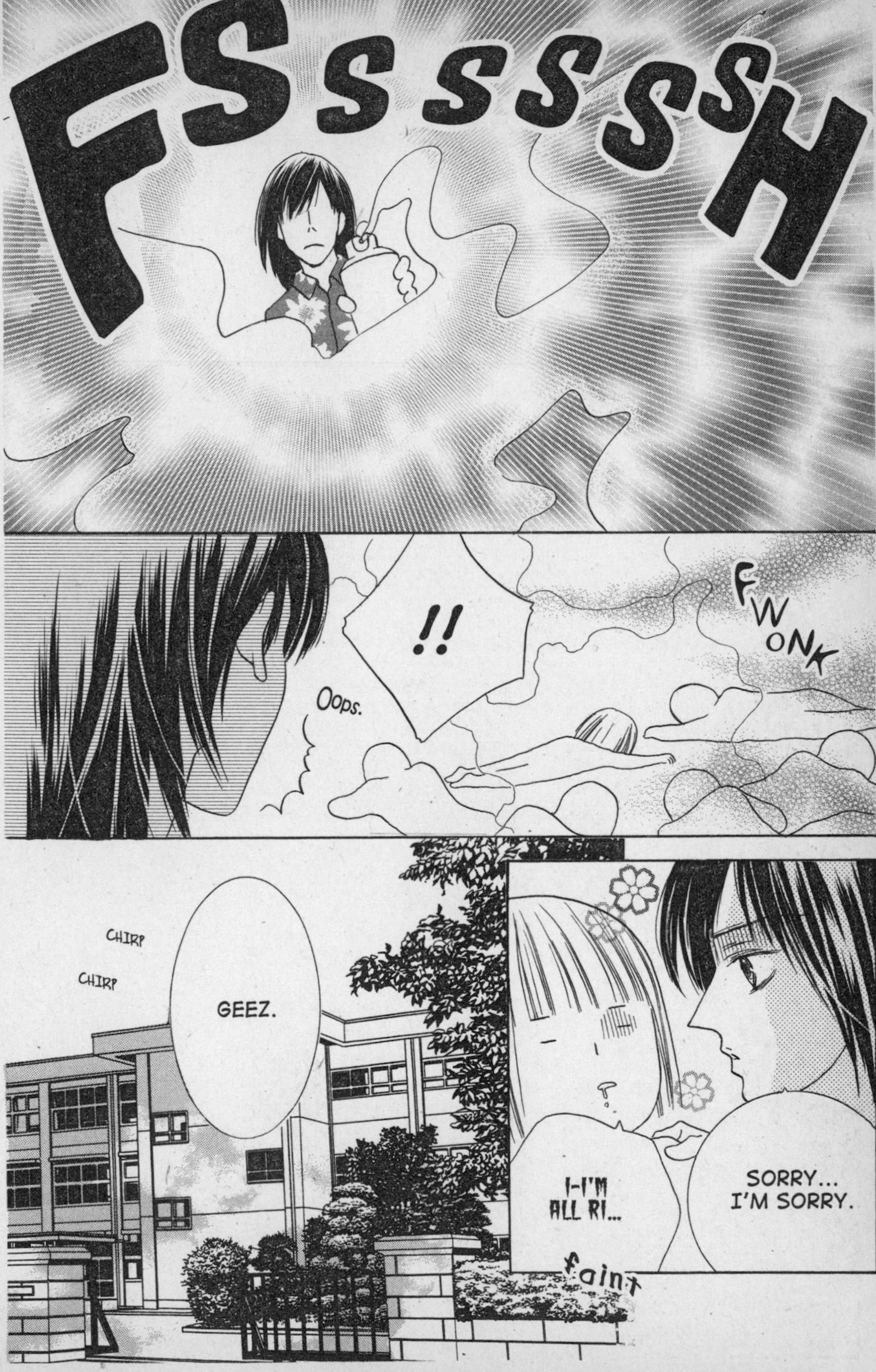
FSSSSSH
FWONK
!!
Oops.
SORRY... I'M SORRY.
I-I'M ALL RI...
faint
CHIRP
CHIRP
GEEZ.

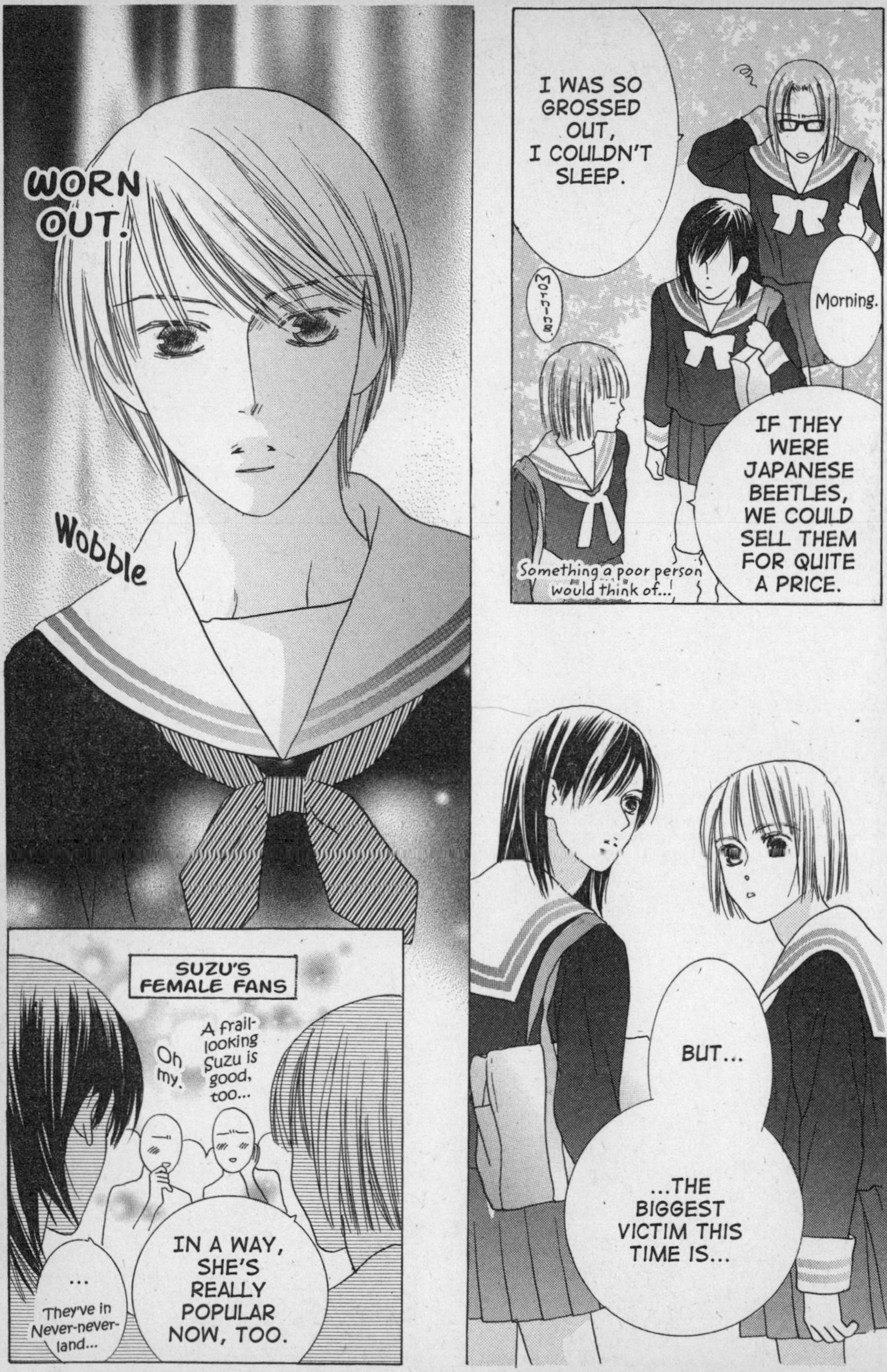
I WAS SO GROSSED OUT, I COULDN'T SLEEP.
Morning.
Morning.
IF THEY WERE JAPANESE BEETLES, WE COULD SELL THEM FOR QUITE A PRICE.
Something a poor person would think of...!
BUT...
...THE BIGGEST VICTIM THIS TIME IS...
WORN OUT.
Wobble
SUZU'S FEMALE FANS
A frail-looking Suzu is good, too...
Oh my.
IN A WAY, SHE'S REALLY POPULAR NOW, TOO.
...
They've in Never-never-land...

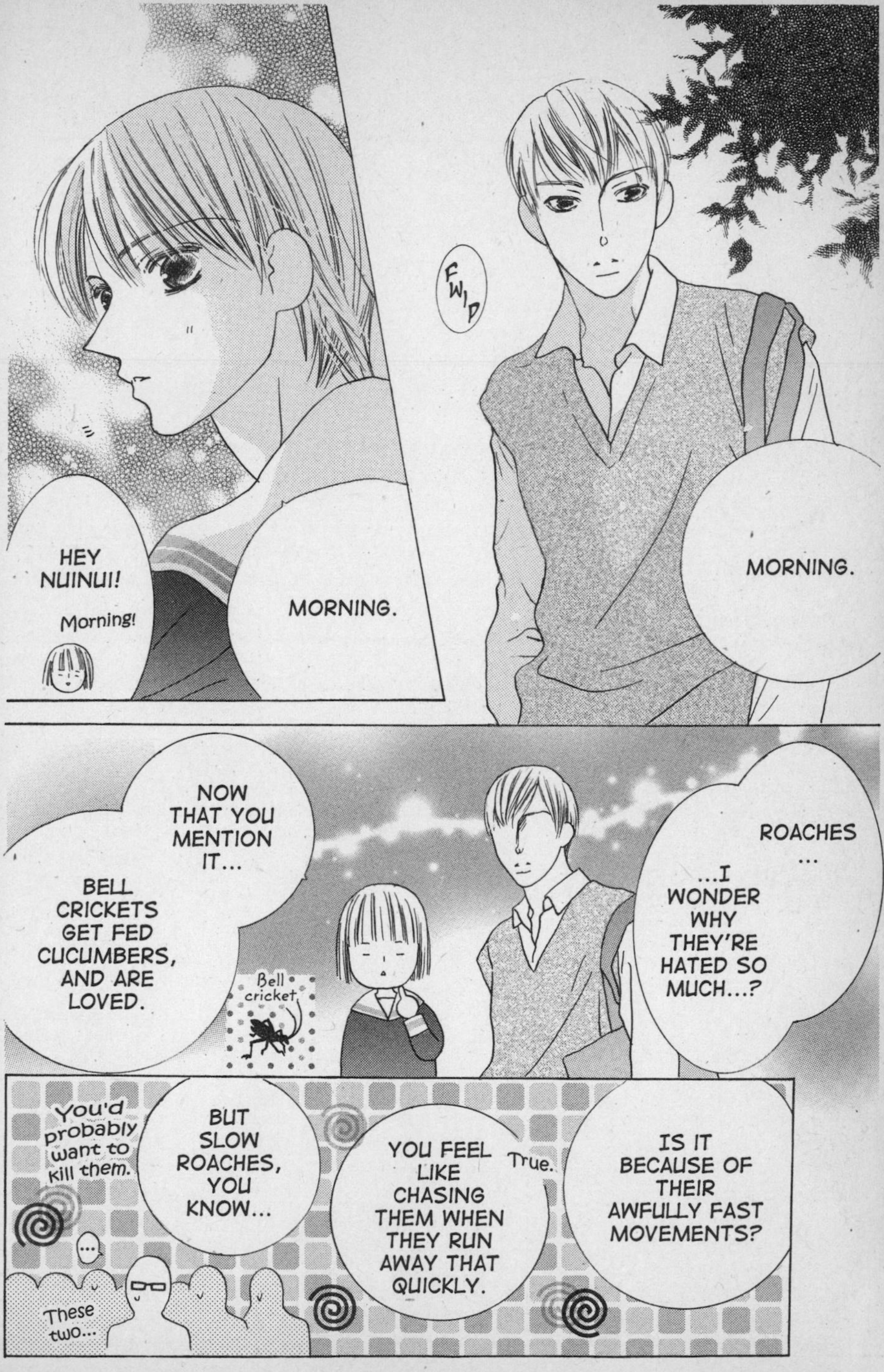
FWIP
MORNING.
MORNING.
HEY NUINUI!
Morning!
ROACHES...
...I WONDER WHY THEY'RE HATED SO MUCH...?
NOW THAT YOU MENTION IT...
BELL CRICKETS GET FED CUCUMBERS, AND ARE LOVED.
Bell cricket
IS IT BECAUSE OF THEIR AWFULLY FAST MOVEMENTS?
True.
YOU FEEL LIKE CHASING THEM WHEN THEY RUN AWAY THAT QUICKLY.
BUT SLOW ROACHES, YOU KNOW...
You'd probably want to kill them.
...
These two...

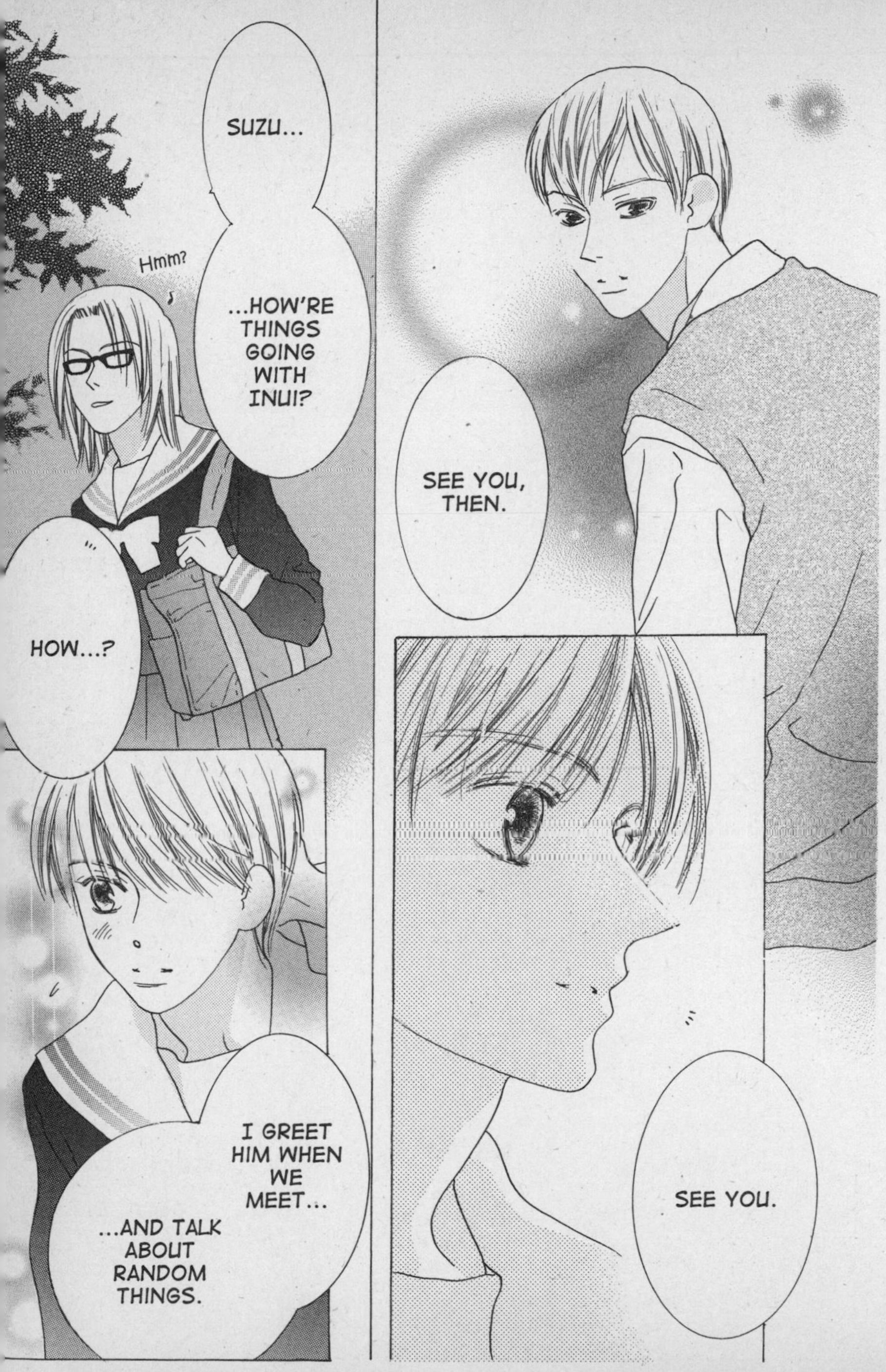
SEE YOU, THEN.
SEE YOU.
SUZU...
...HOW'RE THINGS GOING WITH INUI?
Hmm?
HOW...?
I GREET HIM WHEN WE MEET...
...AND TALK ABOUT RANDOM THINGS.

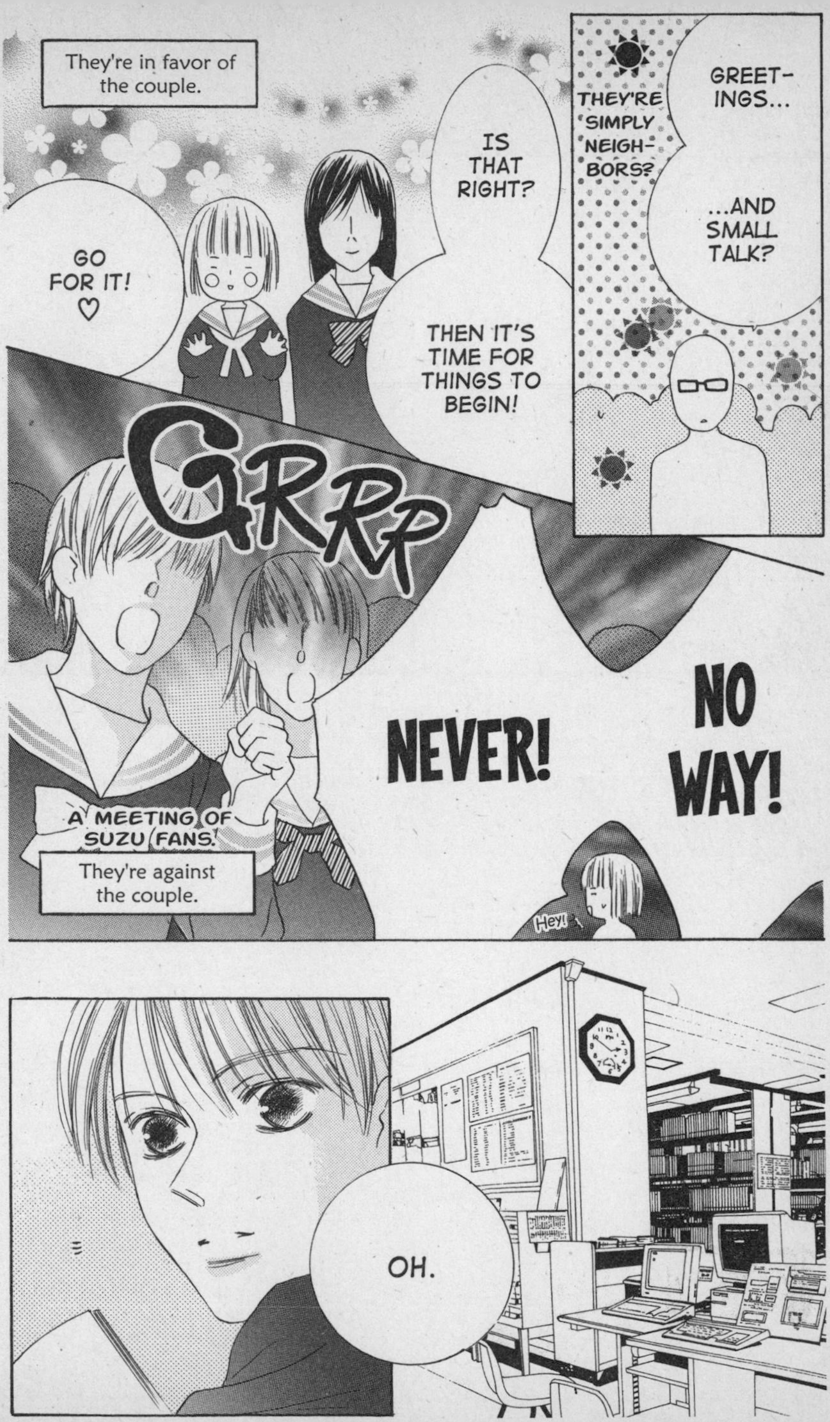
GREET-INGS...
THEY'RE SIMPLY NEIGH-BORS?
...AND SMALL TALK?
IS THAT RIGHT?
They're in favor of the couple.
THEN IT'S TIME FOR THINGS TO BEGIN!
GO FOR IT! ♡
NO WAY!
NEVER!
GRRR
A MEETING OF SUZU FANS.
They're against the couple.
Hey!
OH.

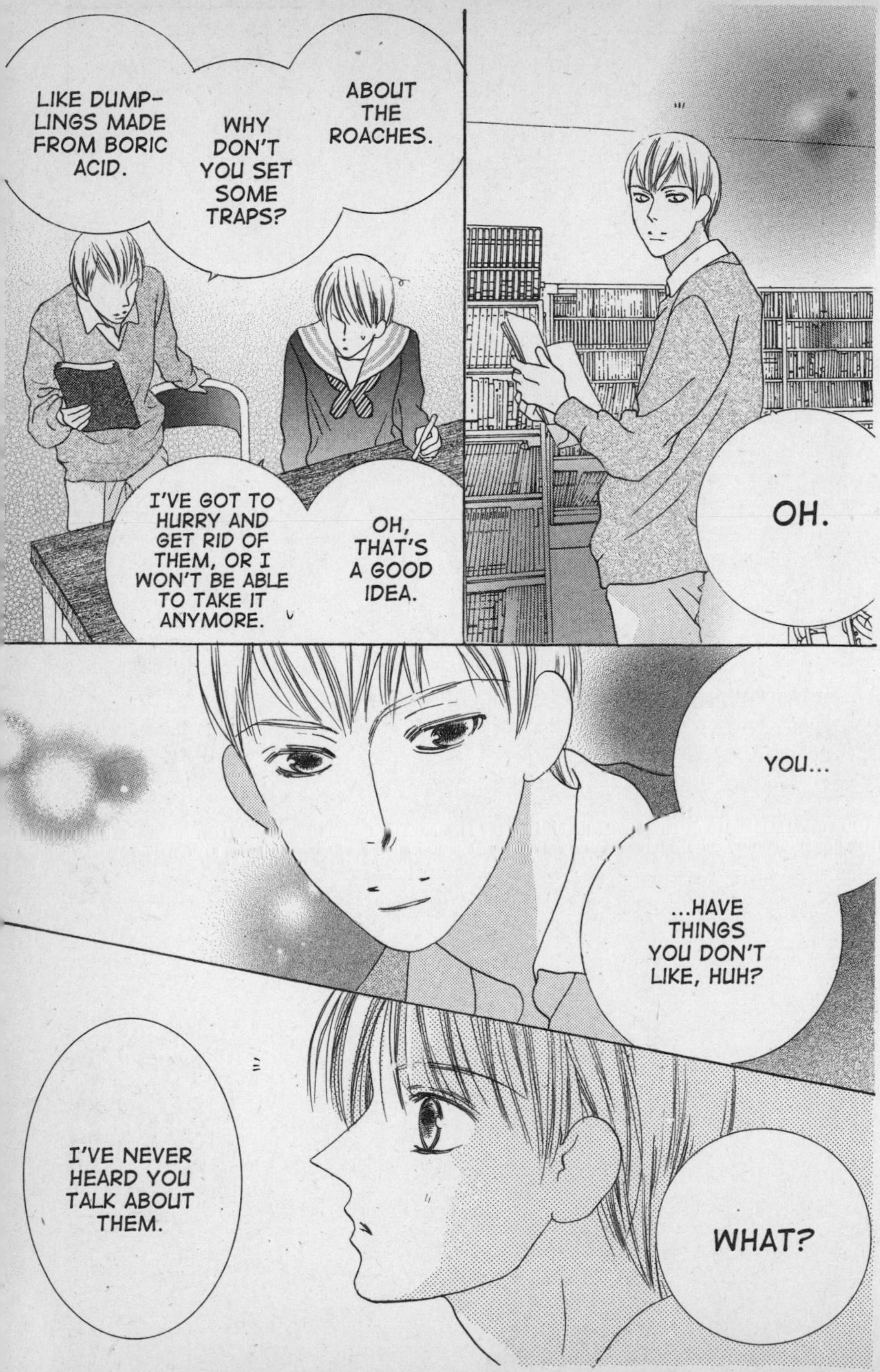
OH.
ABOUT THE ROACHES.
WHY DON'T YOU SET SOME TRAPS?
LIKE DUMPLINGS MADE FROM BORIC ACID.
OH, THAT'S A GOOD IDEA.
I'VE GOT TO HURRY AND GET RID OF THEM, OR I WON'T BE ABLE TO TAKE IT ANYMORE.
YOU...
...HAVE THINGS YOU DON'T LIKE, HUH?
WHAT?
I'VE NEVER HEARD YOU TALK ABOUT THEM.

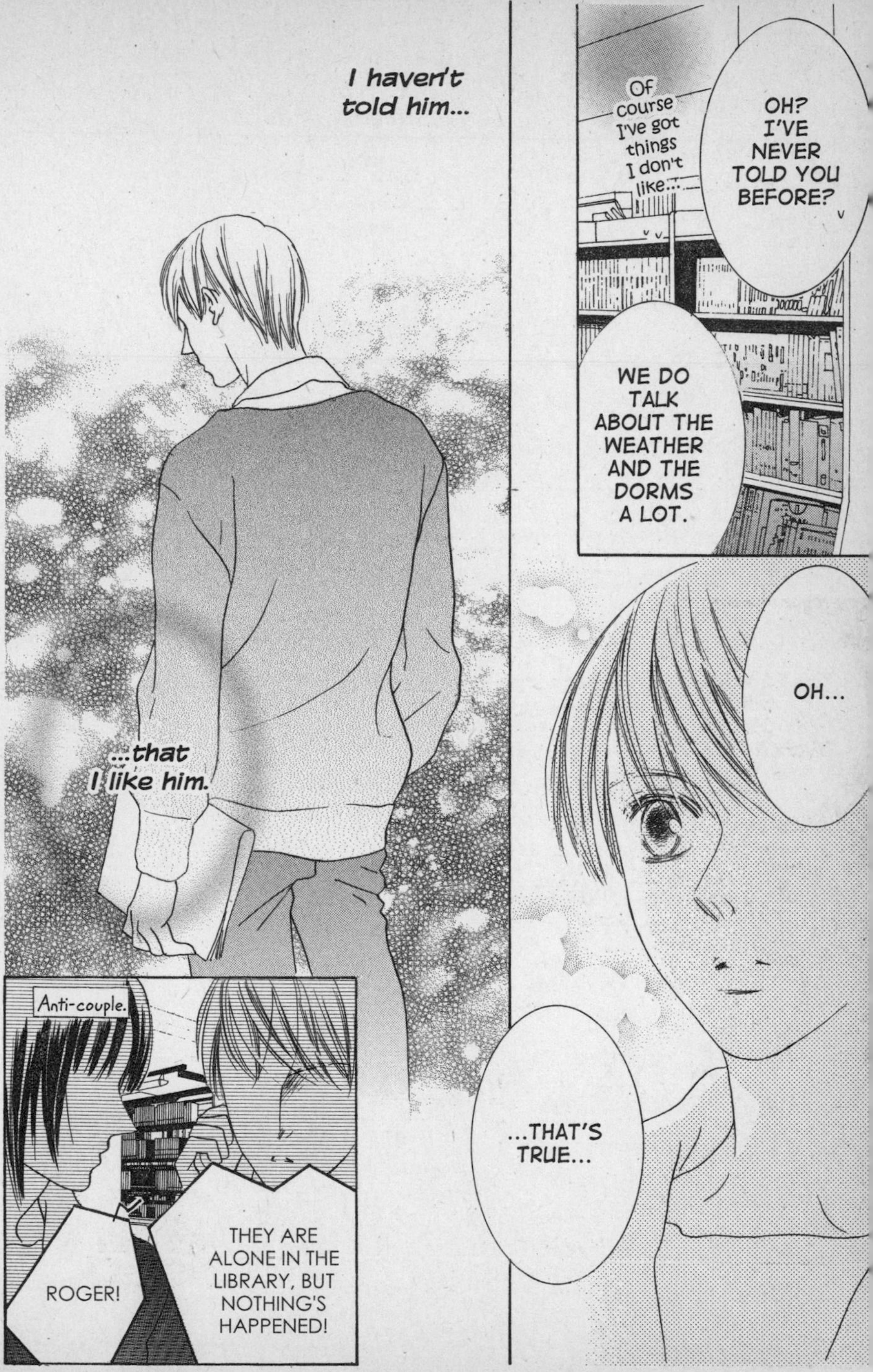

OH? I'VE NEVER TOLD YOU BEFORE?
Of course I've got things I don't like...
WE DO TALK ABOUT THE WEATHER AND THE DORMS A LOT.
OH...
...THAT'S TRUE...
I haven't told him...
...that I like him.
Anti-couple.
THEY ARE ALONE IN THE LIBRARY, BUT NOTHING'S HAPPENED!
ROGER!

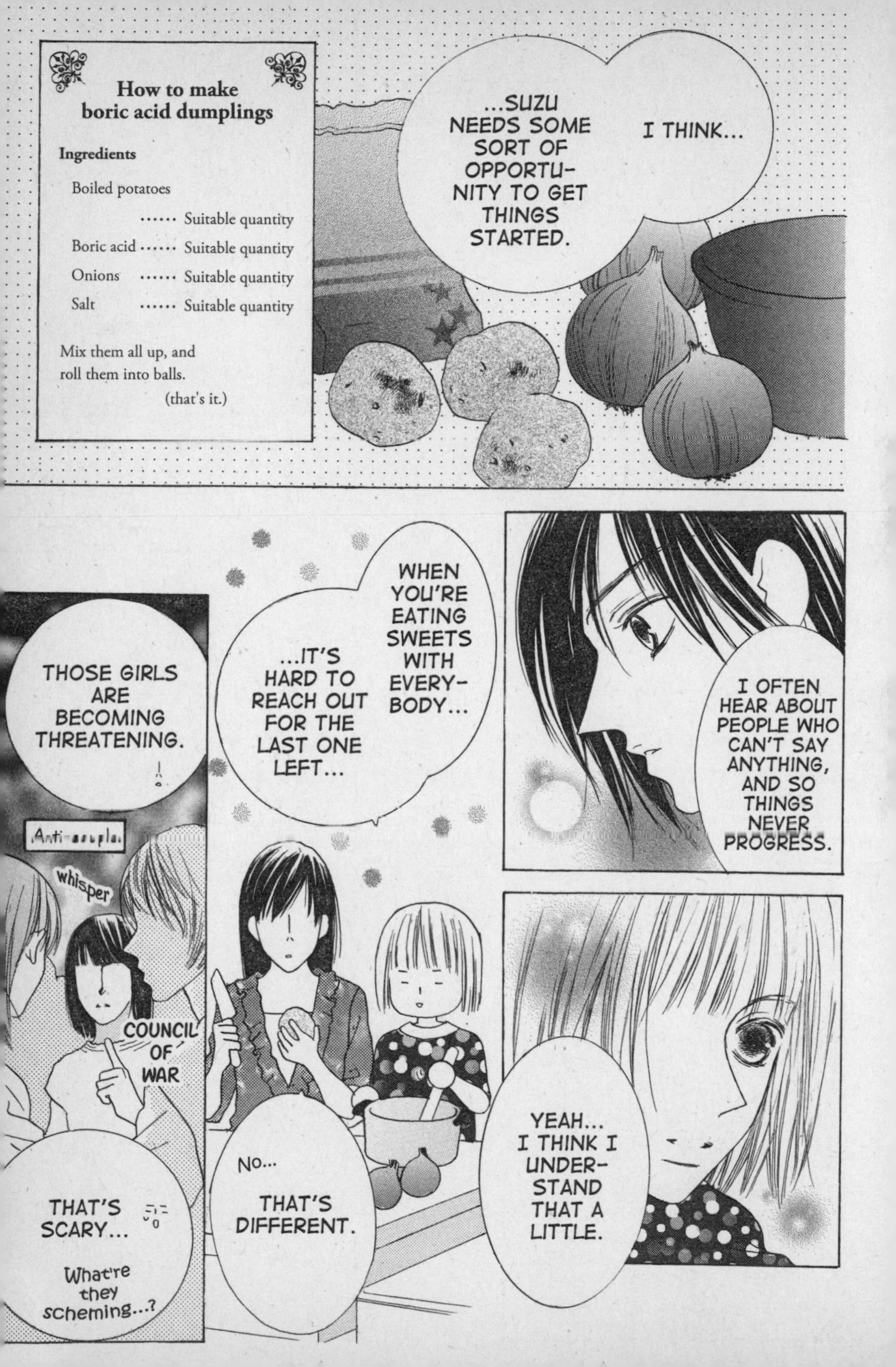
I THINK...
...SUZU NEEDS SOME SORT OF OPPORTUNITY TO GET THINGS STARTED.
How to make boric acid dumplings
Ingredients
Boiled potatoes ...... Suitable quantity
Boric acid ...... Suitable quantity
Onions ...... Suitable quantity
Salt ...... Suitable quantity
Mix them all up, and roll them into balls.
(that's it.)
I OFTEN HEAR ABOUT PEOPLE WHO CAN'T SAY ANYTHING, AND SO THINGS NEVER PROGRESS.
YEAH... I THINK I UNDERSTAND THAT A LITTLE.
WHEN YOU'RE EATING SWEETS WITH EVERYBODY...
...IT'S HARD TO REACH OUT FOR THE LAST ONE LEFT...
No...
THAT'S DIFFERENT.
THOSE GIRLS ARE BECOMING THREATENING.
whisper
COUNCIL OF WAR
THAT'S SCARY...
What're they scheming...?

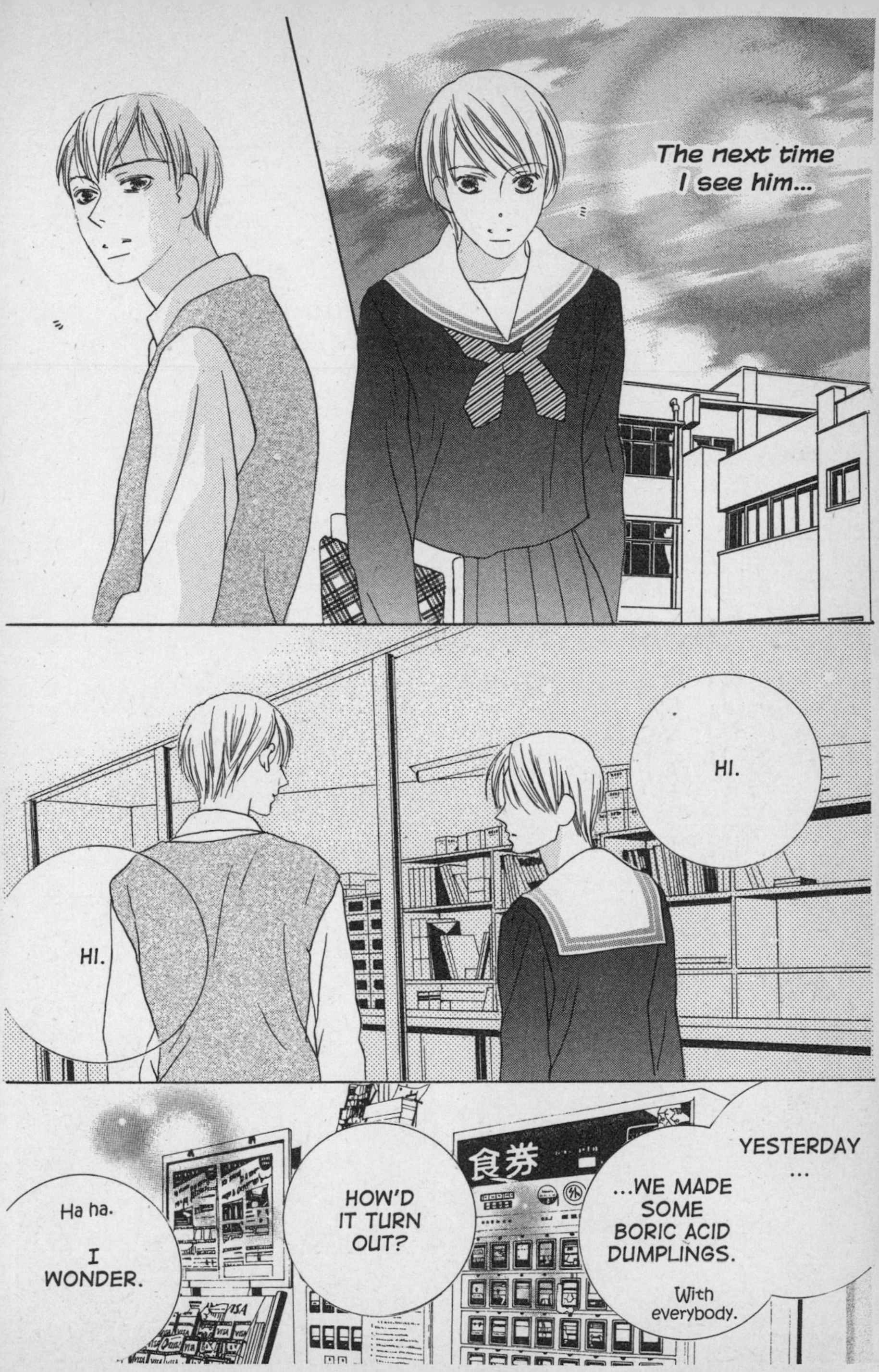
The next time I see him...
HI.
HI.
YESTERDAY ...
...WE MADE SOME BORIC ACID DUMPLINGS.
With everybody.
食券
HOW'D IT TURN OUT?
Ha ha.
I WONDER.

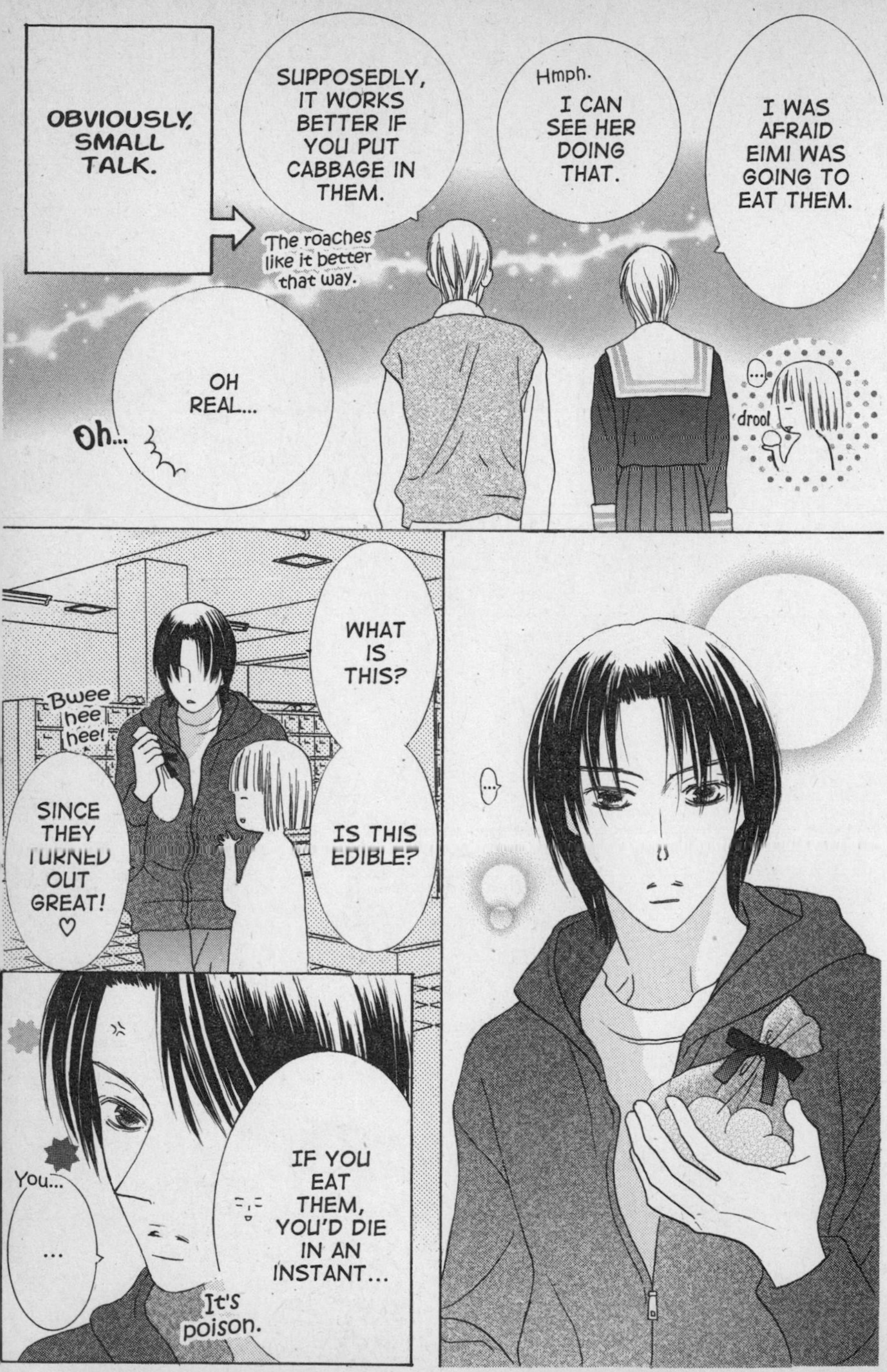
I WAS AFRAID EIMI WAS GOING TO EAT THEM.
...
drool
Hmph.
I CAN SEE HER DOING THAT.
SUPPOSEDLY, IT WORKS BETTER IF YOU PUT CABBAGE IN THEM.
The roaches like it better that way.
OBVIOUSLY, SMALL TALK.
OH REAL...
Oh...
...
WHAT IS THIS?
IS THIS EDIBLE?
Bwee hee hee!
SINCE THEY TURNED OUT GREAT! ♡
IF YOU EAT THEM, YOU'D DIE IN AN INSTANT...
It's poison.
You...
...

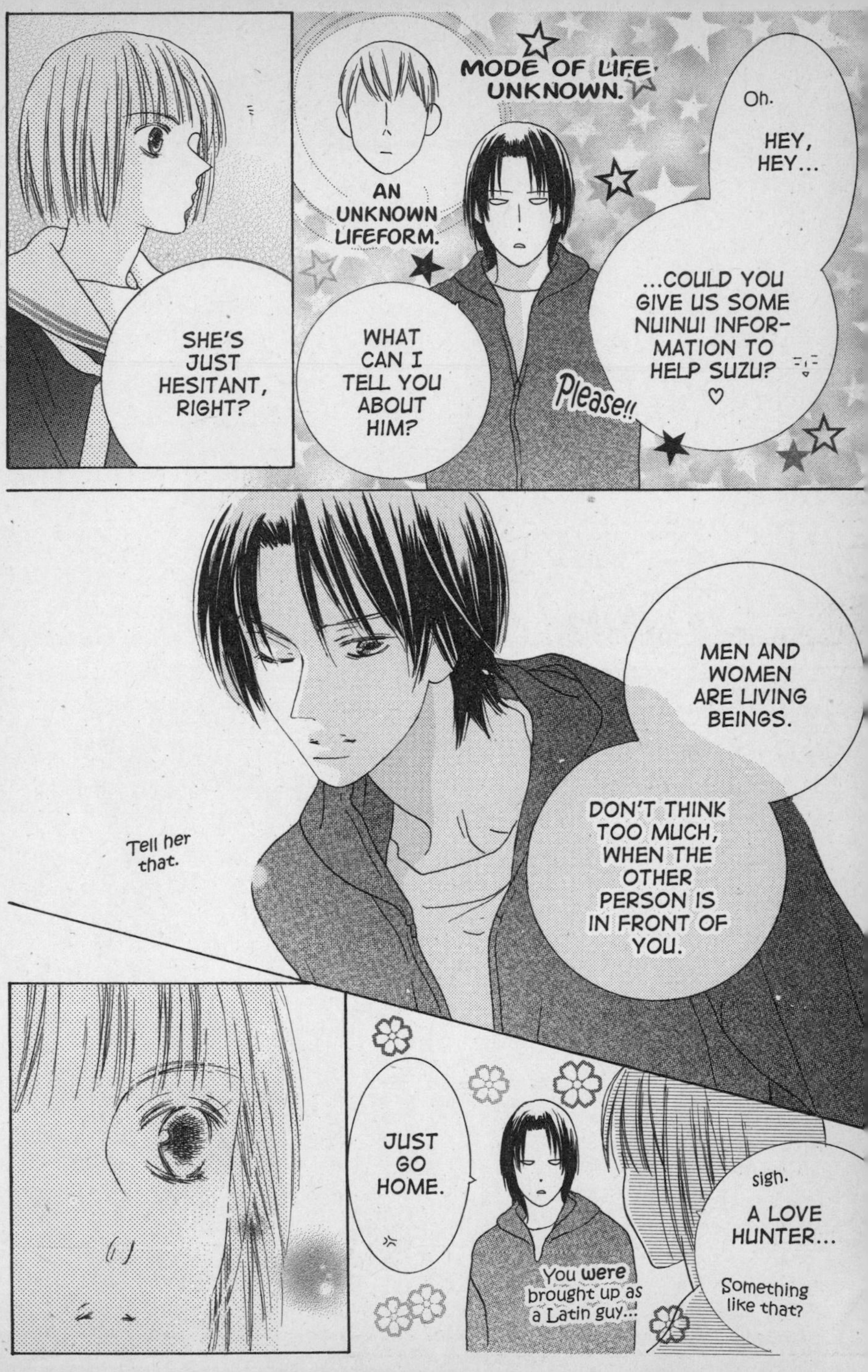
Oh.
HEY, HEY...
...COULD YOU GIVE US SOME NUINUI INFORMATION TO HELP SUZU? ♡
Please!!
MODE OF LIFE UNKNOWN.
AN UNKNOWN LIFEFORM.
WHAT CAN I TELL YOU ABOUT HIM?
SHE'S JUST HESITANT, RIGHT?
MEN AND WOMEN ARE LIVING BEINGS.
DON'T THINK TOO MUCH, WHEN THE OTHER PERSON IS IN FRONT OF YOU.
Tell her that.
sigh.
A LOVE HUNTER...
Something like that?
You were brought up as a Latin guy...
JUST GO HOME.

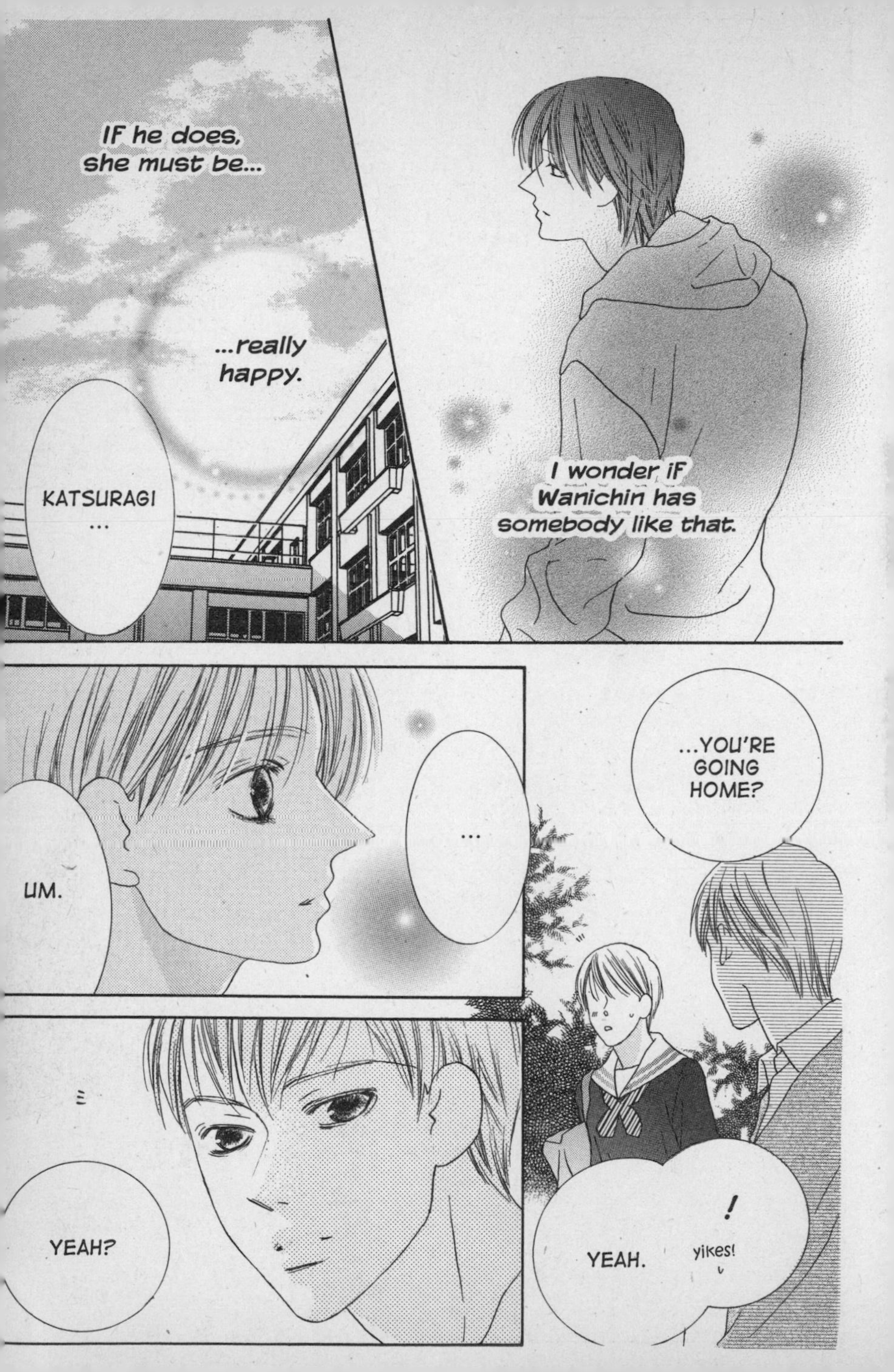
I wonder if Wanichin has somebody like that.
If he does, she must be...
...really happy.
KATSURAGI ...
...YOU'RE GOING HOME?
!
YEAH.
yikes!
...
UM.
YEAH?

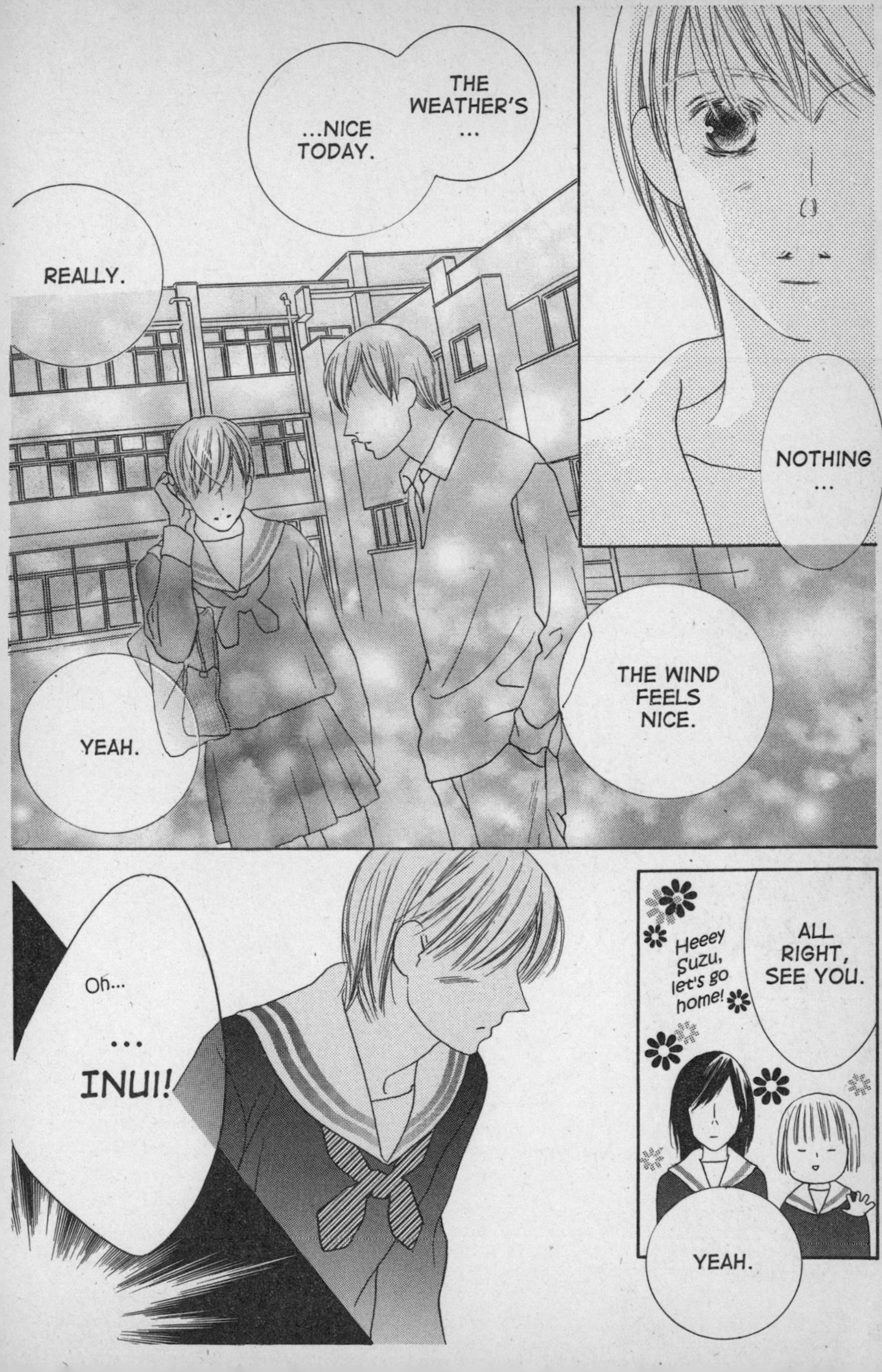
NOTHING ...
THE WEATHER'S ...
...NICE TODAY.
REALLY.
THE WIND FEELS NICE.
YEAH.
ALL RIGHT, SEE YOU.
Heeey Suzu, let's go home!
YEAH.
Oh...
... INUI!

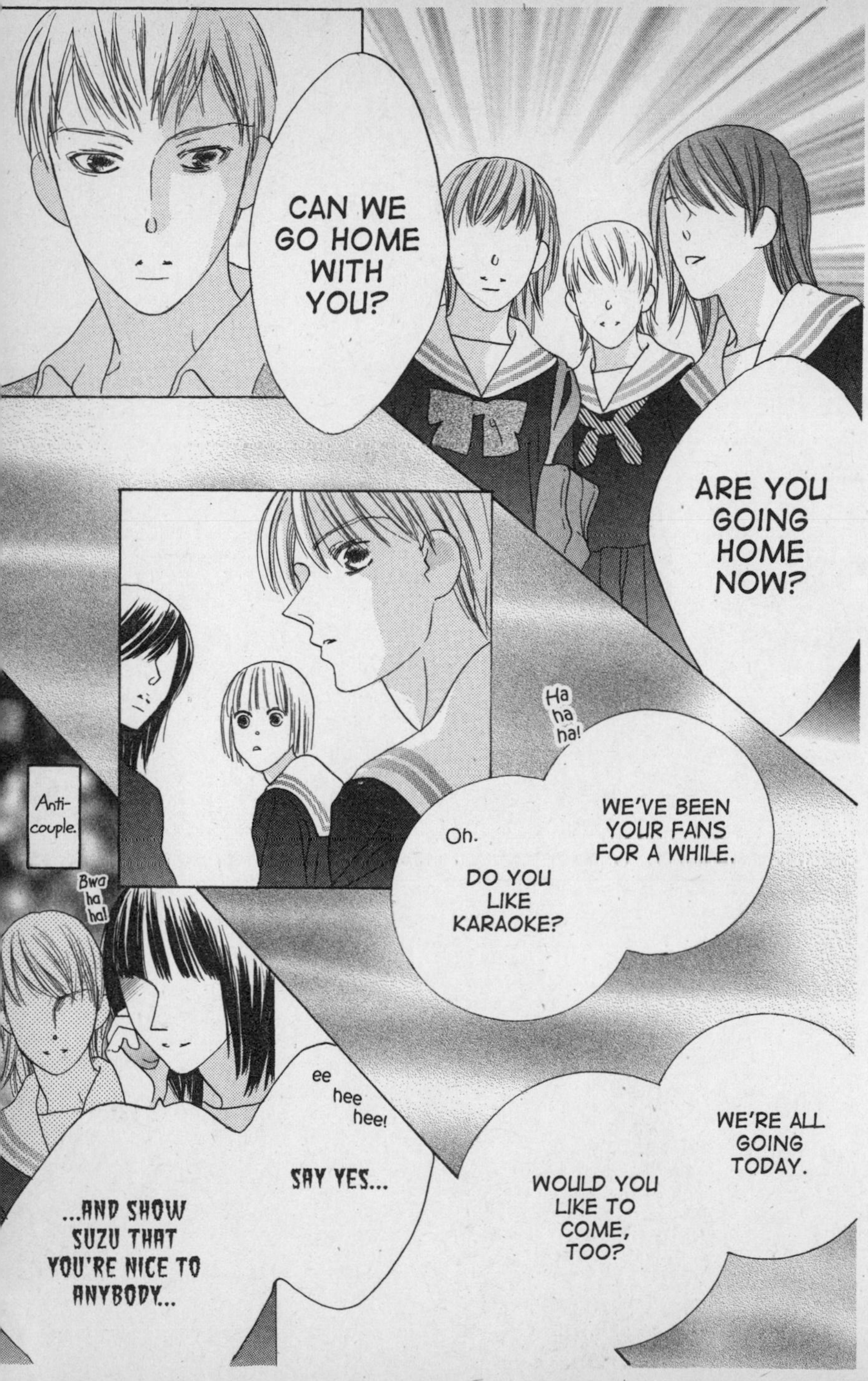
ARE YOU GOING HOME NOW?
CAN WE GO HOME WITH YOU?
Ha ha ha!
WE'VE BEEN YOUR FANS FOR A WHILE.
Oh.
DO YOU LIKE KARAOKE?
Anti-couple.
Bwa ha ha!
WE'RE ALL GOING TODAY.
WOULD YOU LIKE TO COME, TOO?
ee hee hee!
SAY YES...
...AND SHOW SUZU THAT YOU'RE NICE TO ANYBODY...

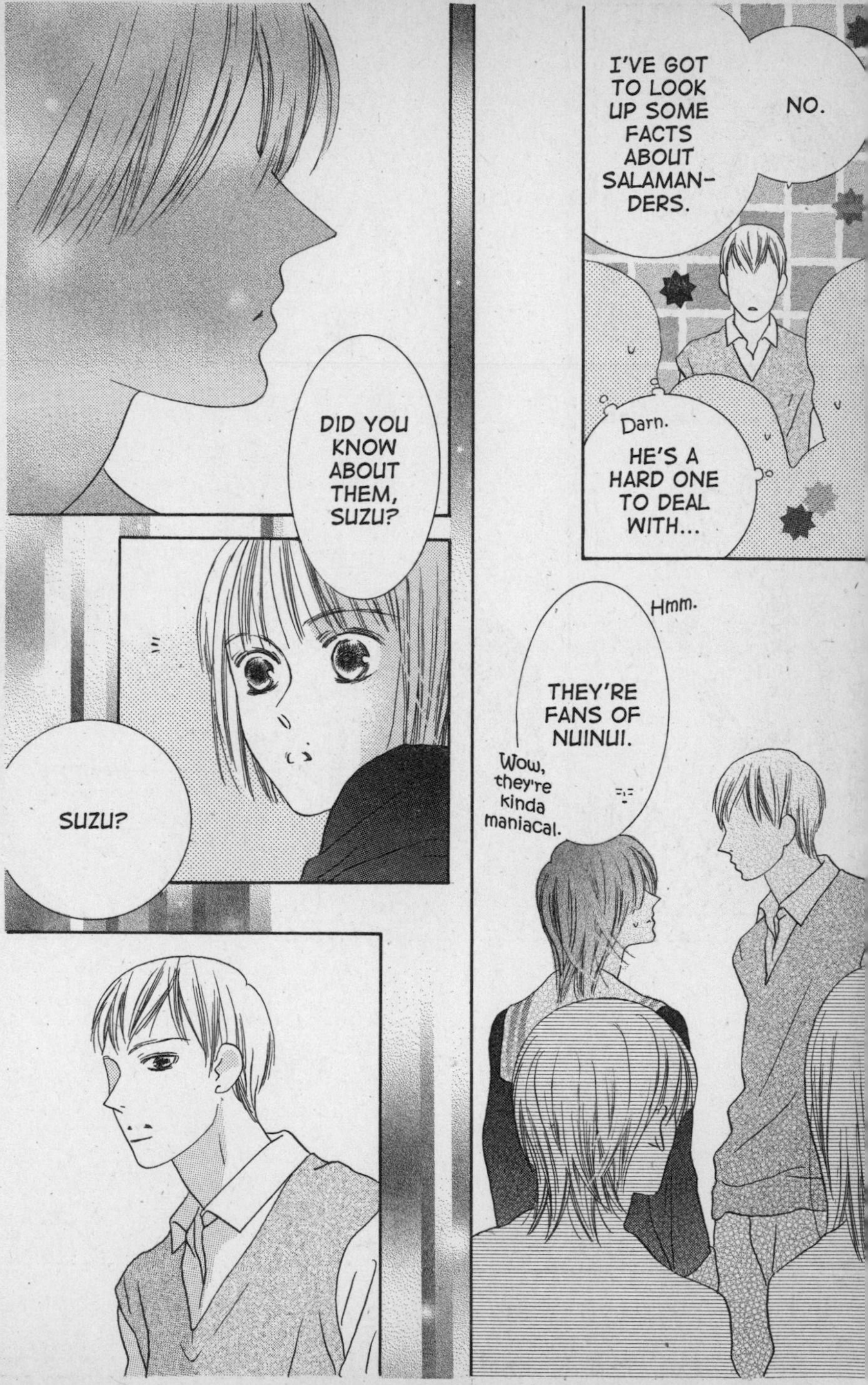
NO.
I'VE GOT TO LOOK UP SOME FACTS ABOUT SALAMANDERS.
Darn.
HE'S A HARD ONE TO DEAL WITH...
Hmm.
THEY'RE FANS OF NUINUI.
Wow, they're kinda maniacal.
DID YOU KNOW ABOUT THEM, SUZU?
SUZU?

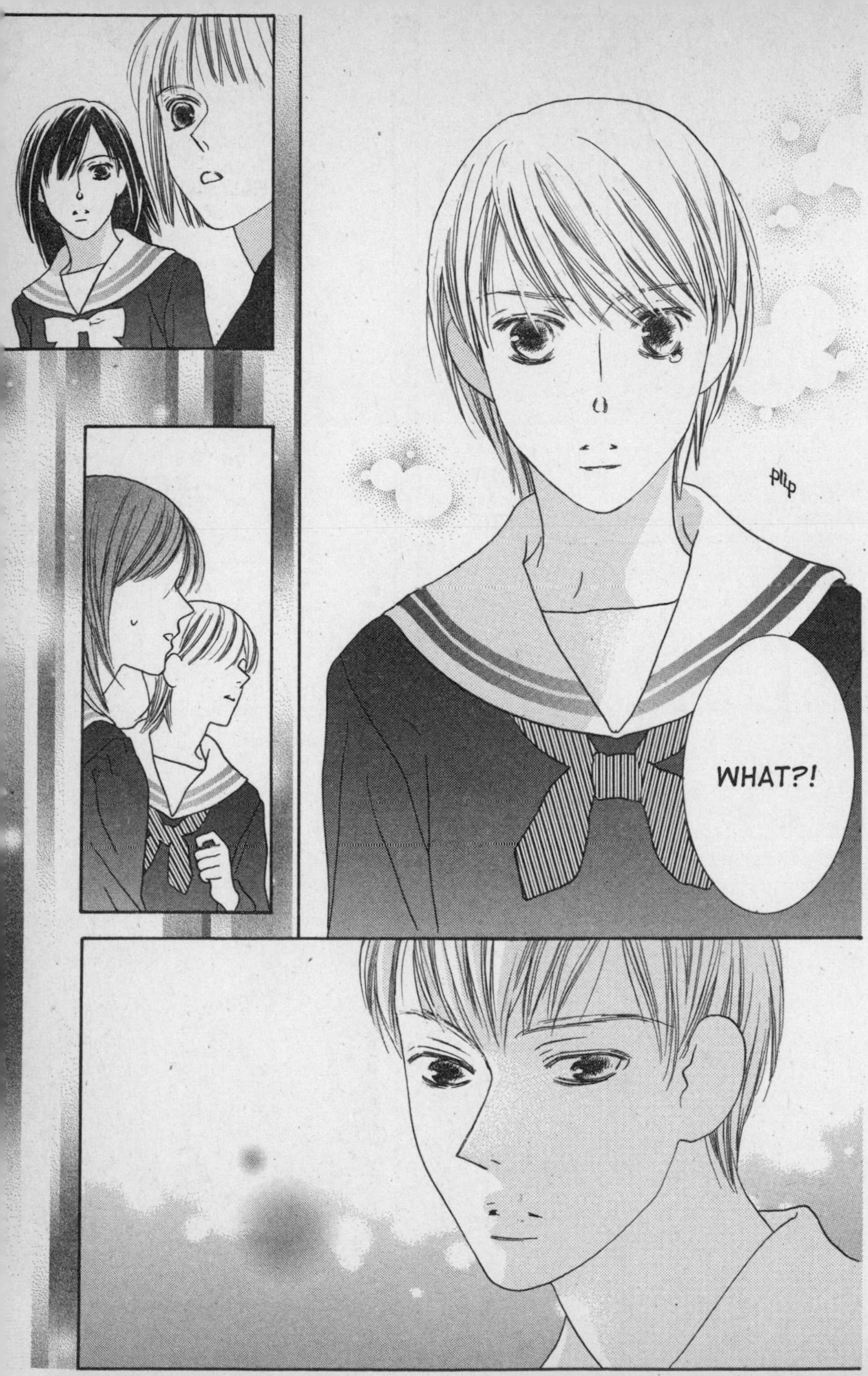
plip
WHAT?!

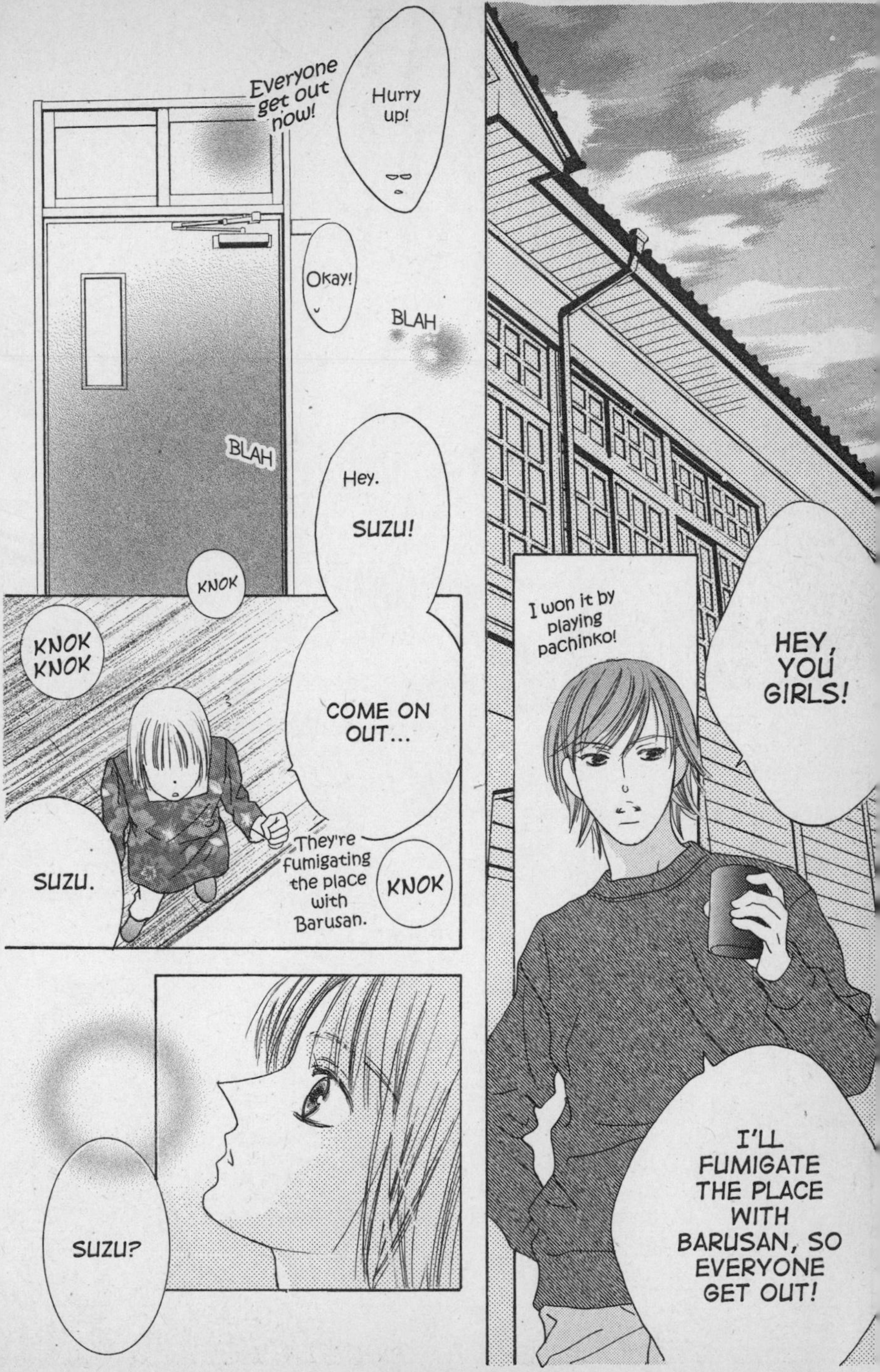
HEY, YOU GIRLS!
I won it by playing pachinko!
I'LL FUMIGATE THE PLACE WITH BARUSAN, SO EVERYONE GET OUT!
Hurry up!
Everyone get out now!
Okay!
BLAH
BLAH
Hey.
SUZU!
COME ON OUT...
KNOK
KNOK KNOK
They're fumigating the place with Barusan.
KNOK
SUZU.
SUZU?

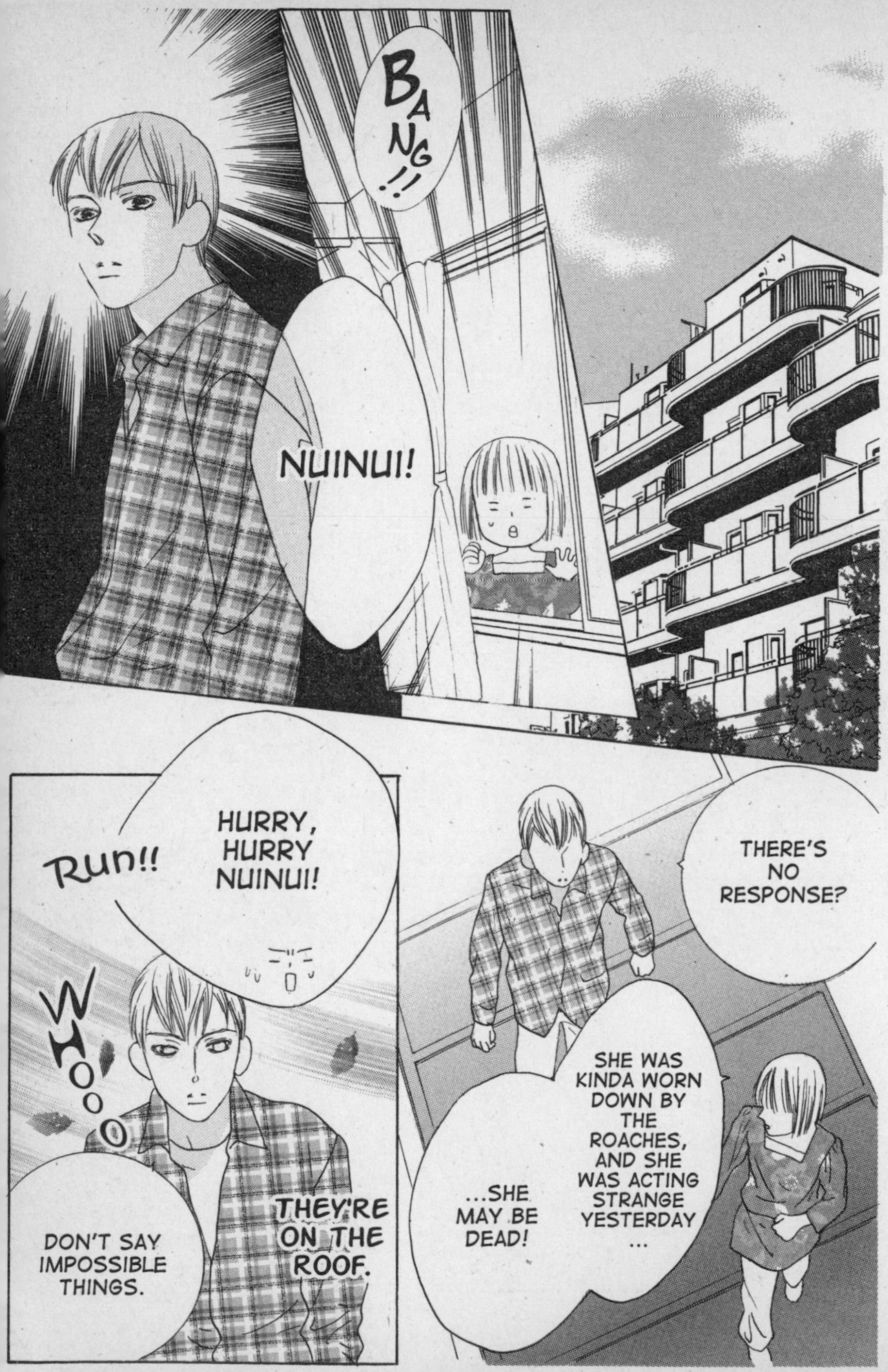
BANG!!
NUINUI!
THERE'S NO RESPONSE?
SHE WAS KINDA WORN DOWN BY THE ROACHES, AND SHE WAS ACTING STRANGE YESTERDAY ...
...SHE MAY BE DEAD!
HURRY, HURRY NUINUI!
RUN!!
WHOOO
THEY'RE ON THE ROOF.
DON'T SAY IMPOSSIBLE THINGS.

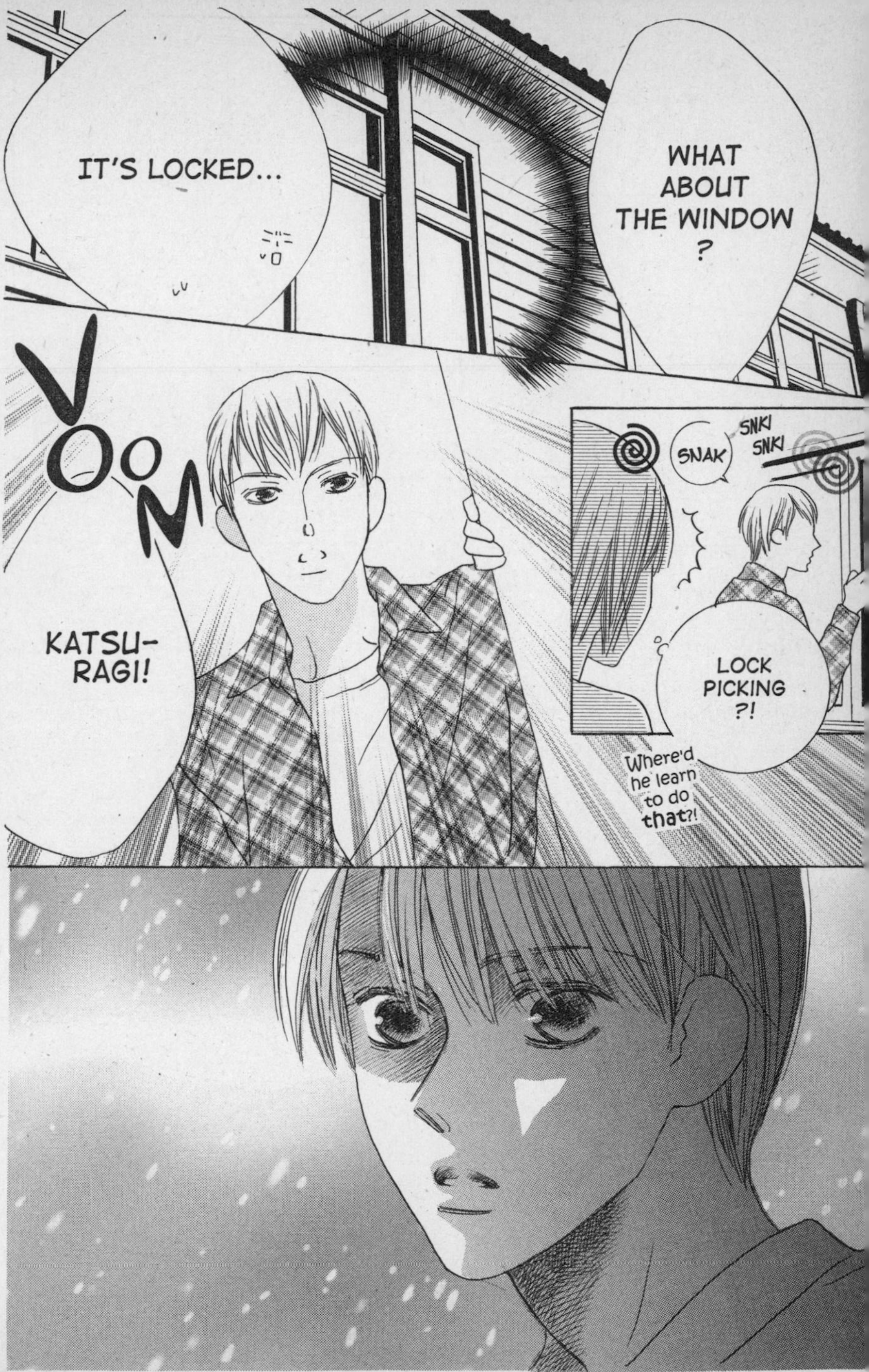
WHAT ABOUT THE WINDOW ?
IT'S LOCKED...
SNAK
SNKI SNKI
LOCK PICKING ?!
Where'd he learn to do that?!
VOOM
KATSU-RAGI!

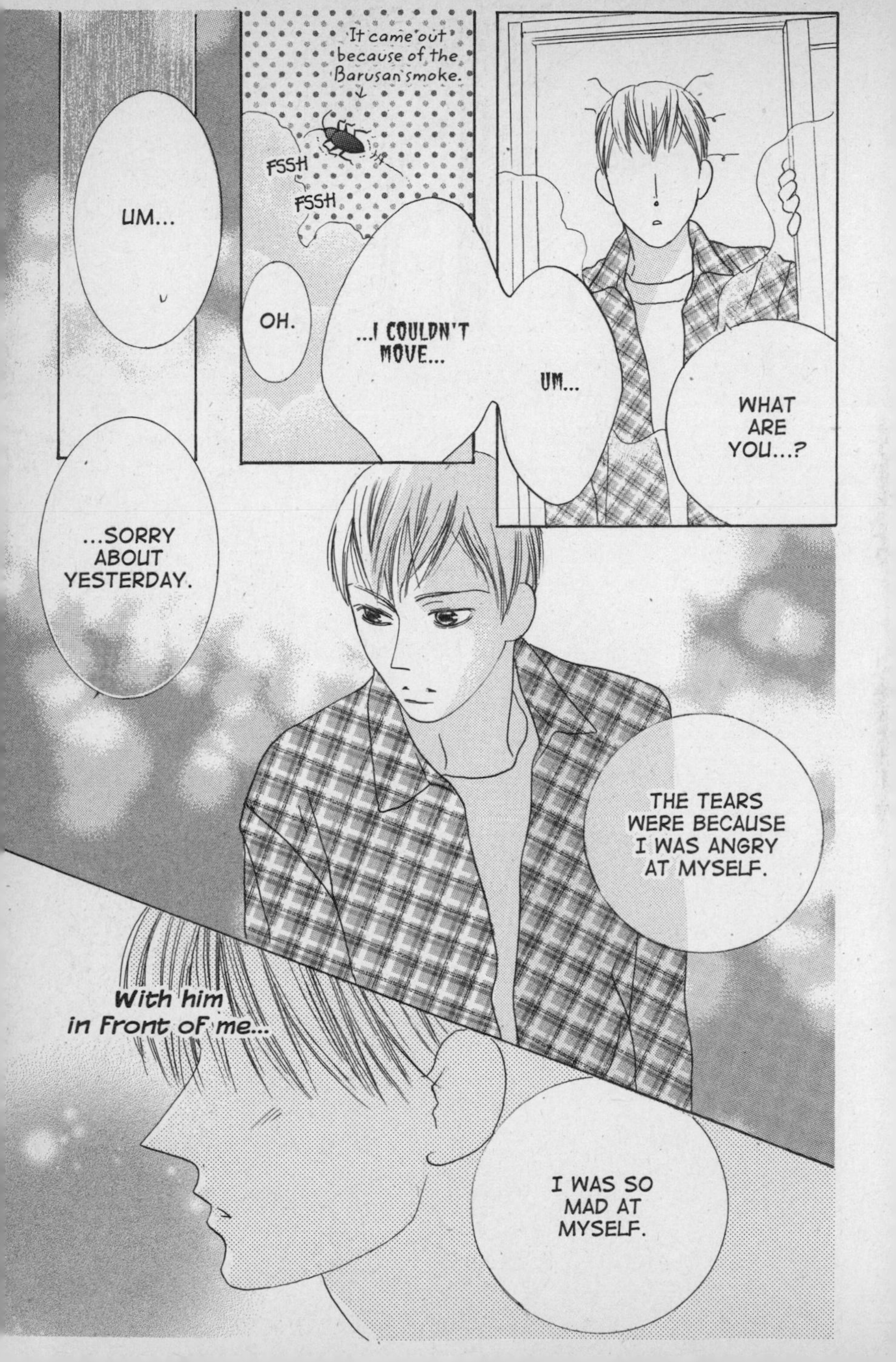
WHAT ARE YOU...?
UM...
...I COULDN'T MOVE...
It came out because of the Barusan smoke.
FSSH
FSSH
OH.
UM...
...SORRY ABOUT YESTERDAY.
THE TEARS WERE BECAUSE I WAS ANGRY AT MYSELF.
I WAS SO MAD AT MYSELF.
With him in Front of me...

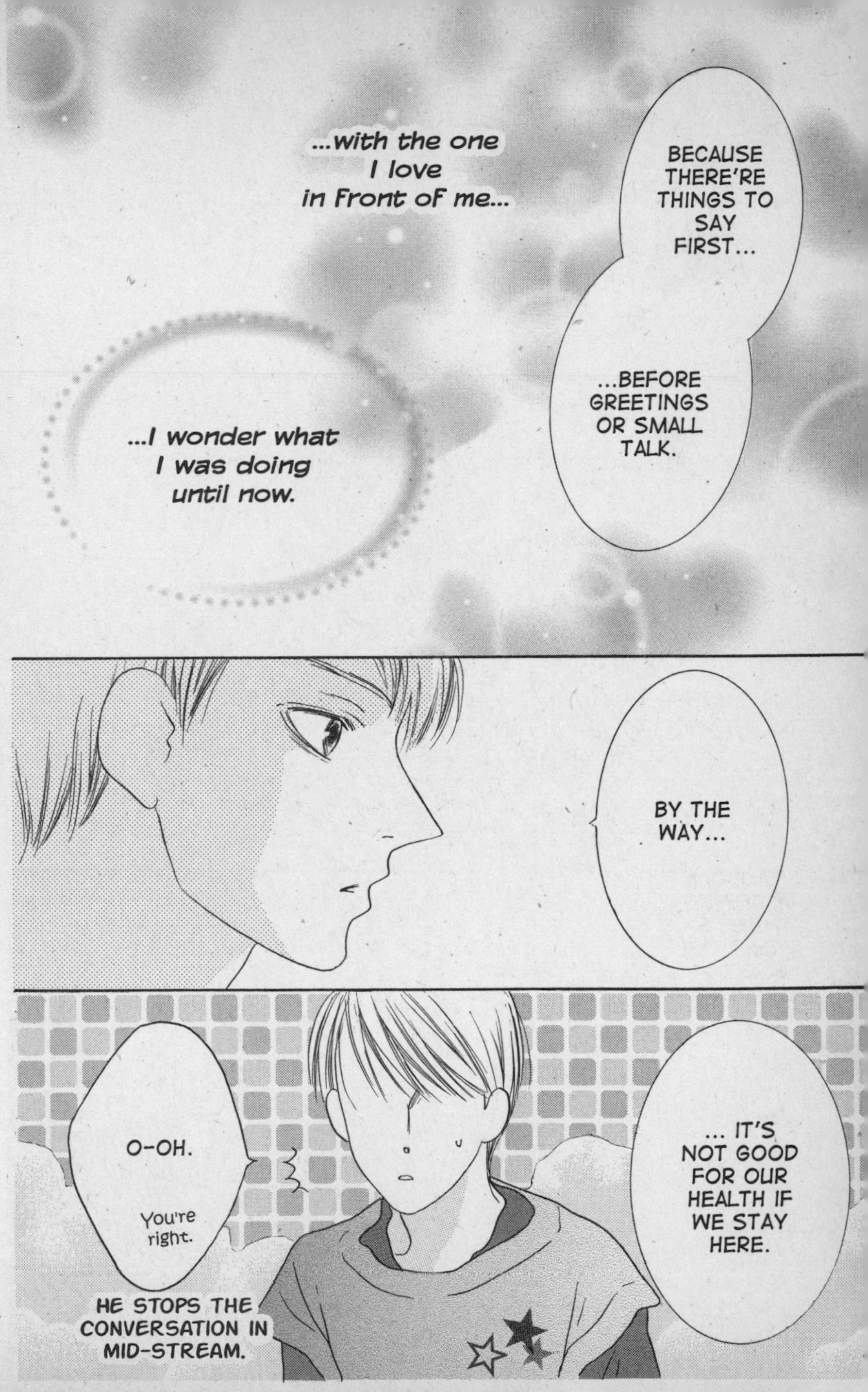
BECAUSE THERE'RE THINGS TO SAY FIRST...
...BEFORE GREETINGS OR SMALL TALK.
...with the one I love in Front of me...
...I wonder what I was doing until now.
BY THE WAY...
... IT'S NOT GOOD FOR OUR HEALTH IF WE STAY HERE.
O-OH.
You're right.
HE STOPS THE CONVERSATION IN MID-STREAM.

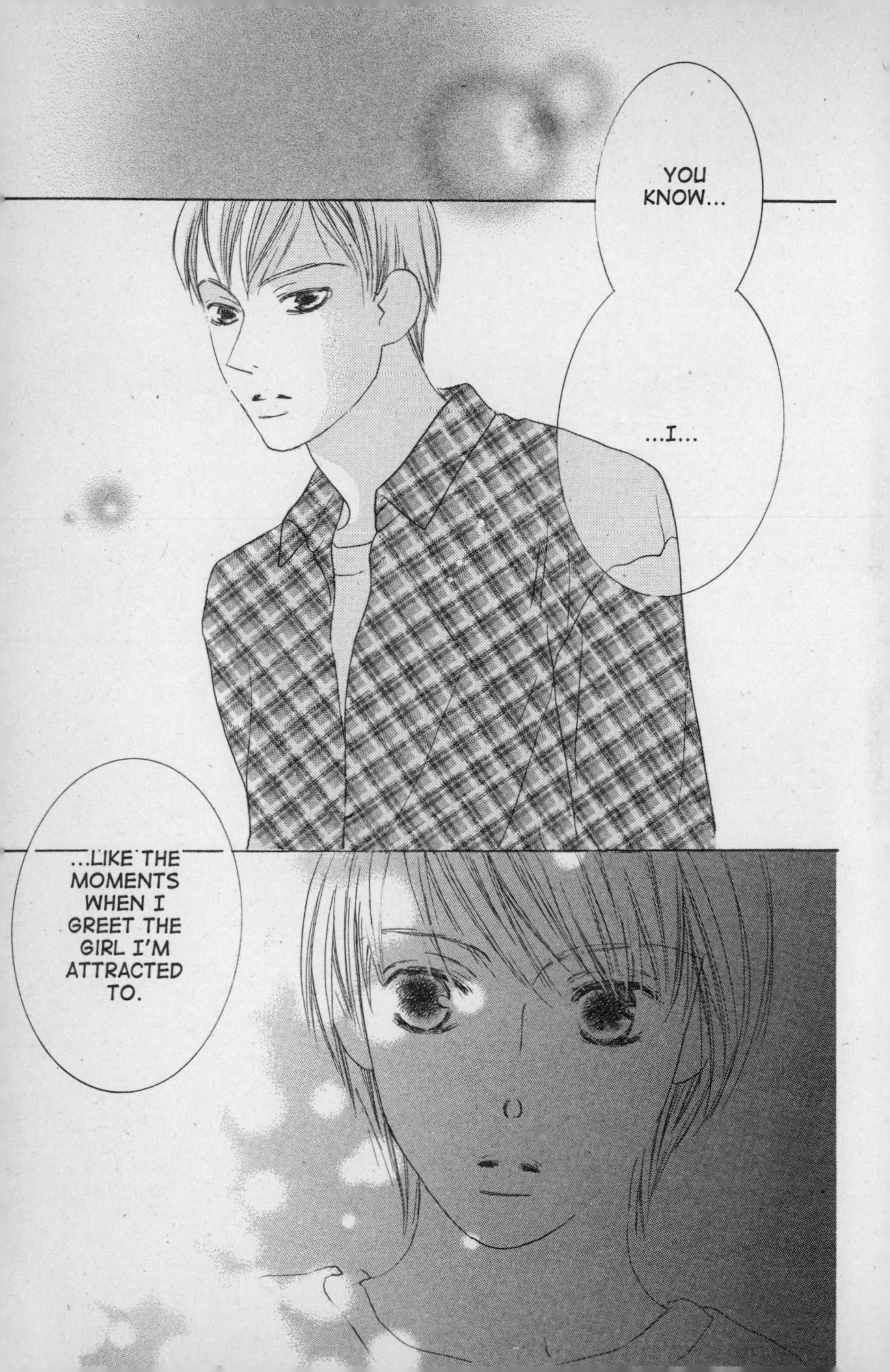
YOU KNOW...
...I...
...LIKE THE MOMENTS WHEN I GREET THE GIRL I'M ATTRACTED TO.

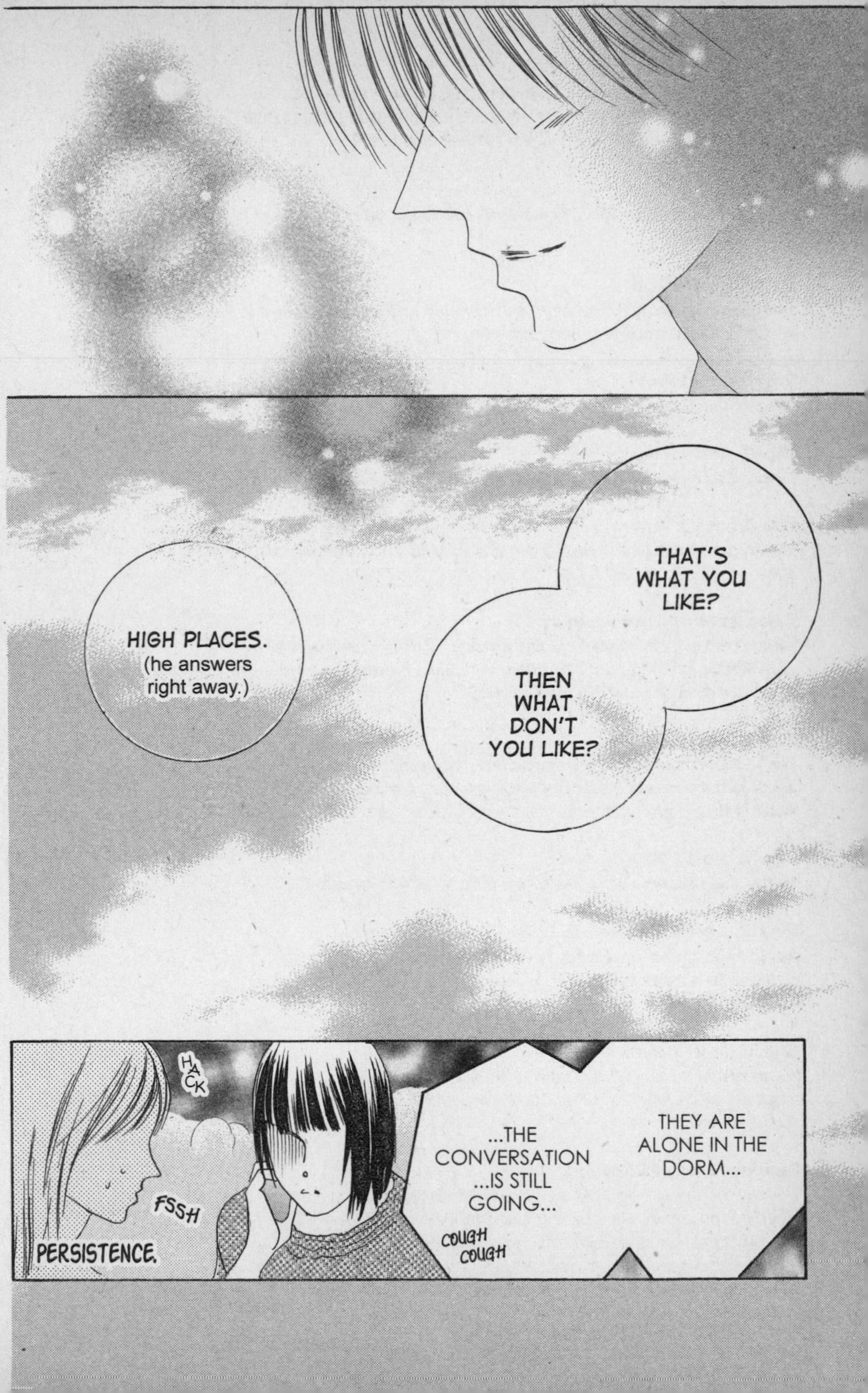
THAT'S WHAT YOU LIKE?
THEN WHAT DON'T YOU LIKE?
HIGH PLACES.
(he answers right away.)
THEY ARE ALONE IN THE DORM...
...THE CONVERSATION ...IS STILL GOING...
COUGH COUGH
HACK
FSSH
PERSISTENCE.

Glossary

Some high school experiences are universal. Others need a little more explanation. In these notes you will find interesting information to enhance your *Beauty Is the Beast* reading enjoyment.

Page 7, panel 1: Ryosai
Dorm festival. Among other things, these festivals help classes, clubs, or in this case dorms, earn money.

Page 8, panel 1: Sozai
Fresh ready-made food from department stores, cafes, and specialty stores. Somewhat like the food available in fancier grocery store delis.

Page 8, panel 1: Pon
Mahjong term. A series of three identical tiles.

Page 8, panel 2: Chii
Mahjong term. A series of three tiles in ascending order.

Page 8, panel 3: Tsumo
Mahjong term. Drawing a tile yourself, rather than accepting a discard or being dealt a tile.

Page 8, panel 4: Sumire Dormitory
Sumire means violet, which is a flower that represents faithfulness, modesty, and virtue. A fitting name for a dormitory with the motto "To be courteous and uphold principles, and always act in the name of tradition."

Page 13, panel 2: Dim Sum
This Cantonese phrase means "to touch your heart," and refers to the buns, dumplings, and other tasty goodies served á la carte from actual carts wheeled around by the waitstaff.

Page 14, panel 2: Nippori
An area in the Arakawa ward of Tokyo with a wholesale fabric district.

Page 27, panel 3: Red bean jelly
A sweet made from red beans, called "yokan" in Japanese. Some yokan come in candy-bar size, while the mini-yokan Eimi prefers are cut into bite-sized pieces and individually wrapped.

Page 36, panel 3: Yankii
A slang term for teen gangs of delinquents, bikers, and dropouts. The word probably originates from the American "Yankee" GIs, who brought their love of rock 'n' roll and rebellion to Japan.

Page 56, panel 1: Shichigosan
A non-national holiday in November that celebrates children. It literally means "seven-five-three," and commemorates rites of passage for children aged 3, 5, and 7. In medieval times, children were allowed to grow their hair out at age 3, boys began to wear hakama (a type of pants) in public at age 5, and girls began to tie their kimono with sashes instead of cords at age 7. These days, children dress up and go to a Shinto shrine with their families and receive candy sticks in bags decorated with turtles and cranes, all of which symbolize a long life.

Page 65, panel 7: Bancho Sarayashiki
A kwaidan, or ghost story about the maid Okiku who either breaks her master's precious Dutch plates, or is accused of breaking them. She either throws herself down a well or is murdered and thrown in the well. However she becomes a ghost, all the stories agree that she comes out of the well at night, sobbing and counting to nine.

Page 80, panel 6: Pachislot
A pachinko parlor. Pachinko is a mix between pinball and slot machines, where the player tries to collect little steel balls. The balls can be redeemed for prizes, like game tickets in arcades. But most parlors also have small shops around the corner where the balls can be exchanged for cash.

Page 83, panel 3: Manbaken
A bet of 100 yen that wins at least 10,000 yen.

Page 103, panel 1: Milk Bread
A type of rich bread made with milk rather than water. It often has custard like cream in the middle.

Page 107, panel 2: Yakult
A fermented milk drink, somewhat like drinkable yogurt, with a sweet citrus flavor.

Page 133, panel 2: Daigaku-imo
Candied sweet potatoes flavored with sesame seeds and sometimes soy sauce.

Page 137, panel 1: Calpis
A very sweet yogurt-flavored soft drink that comes in carbonated and concentrated, non-carbonated form.

Page 146, panel 1: Shopping Coupons
Handed out by the Japanese government in 1999 as an attempt to improve the economy, the shopping coupons were good for six months and had to be used at local merchants.

Page 148, panel 3: Taiyaki
Fish-shaped cake, usually filled with sweet black bean paste.

Page 181, panel 2: Boric Acid
A natural insecticide mined from the Mojave Desert in California. It's toxicity for humans is comparable to table salt, and it is also used in eyewashes and ointments for diaper rash.

Page 192, panel 2: Barusan
A chemical pesticide that reacts with water to release smoke.

Tomo Matsumoto was born on January 8th in Osaka and made the switch from nurse to mangaka with her debut story "Nemuru Hime" (Sleeping Princess) in *Lunatic LaLa* magazine in 1995. Her other works include *Kiss*, a series about piano lessons and love, *23:00*, a book about street dancing, and *Eikaiwa School Wars* (English School Wars), which is currently serialized in *Monthly LaLa* magazine. Ms. Matsumoto loves dancing and taking English lessons.

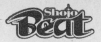

BEAUTY IS THE BEAST
Vol. 2
The Shojo Beat Manga Edition

STORY & ART BY
TOMO MATSUMOTO

English Translation & Adaptation/Tomo Kimura
Touch-up & Lettering/Inori Fukuda Trant
Graphics & Cover Design/Yukiko Whitley
Editor/Pancha Diaz

Managing Editor/Megan Bates
Director of Production/Noboru Watanabe
Vice President of Publishing/Alvin Lu
Vice President & Editor in Chief/Yumi Hoashi
Sr. Director of Acquisitions/Rika Inouye
Vice President of Sales & Marketing/Liza Coppola
Publisher/Hyoe Narita

Printed in Canada

Published by VIZ Media, LLC
P.O. Box 77010
San Francisco, CA 94107

Shojo Beat Manga Edition
10 9 8 7 6 5 4 3 2 1
First printing, January 2006

store.viz.com

PARENTAL ADVISORY
BEAUTY IS THE BEAST is rated T for Teen and is recommended for ages 13 and up. It contains mature situations.

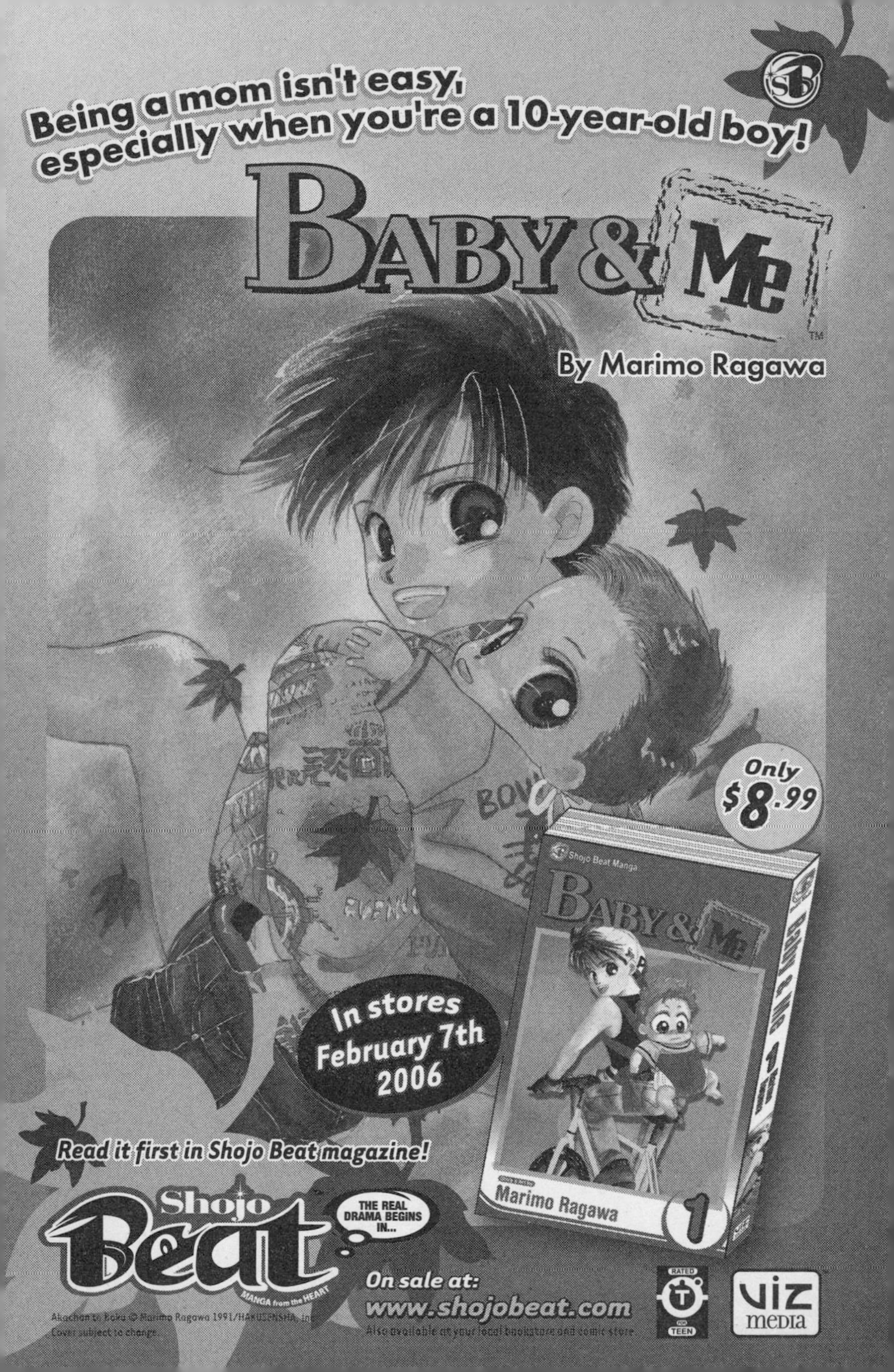
Being a mom isn't easy,
especially when you're a 10-year-old boy!
BABY & Me
By Marimo Ragawa
Only $8.99
In stores February 7th 2006
Shojo Beat Manga
BABY & Me
Marimo Ragawa
1
Read it first in Shojo Beat magazine!
Shojo Beat
MANGA from the HEART
THE REAL DRAMA BEGINS IN...
On sale at:
www.shojobeat.com
Also available at your local bookstore and comic store
Akachan to Boku © Marimo Ragawa 1991/HAKUSENSHA, Inc.
Cover subject to change.
RATED T FOR TEEN
VIZ media

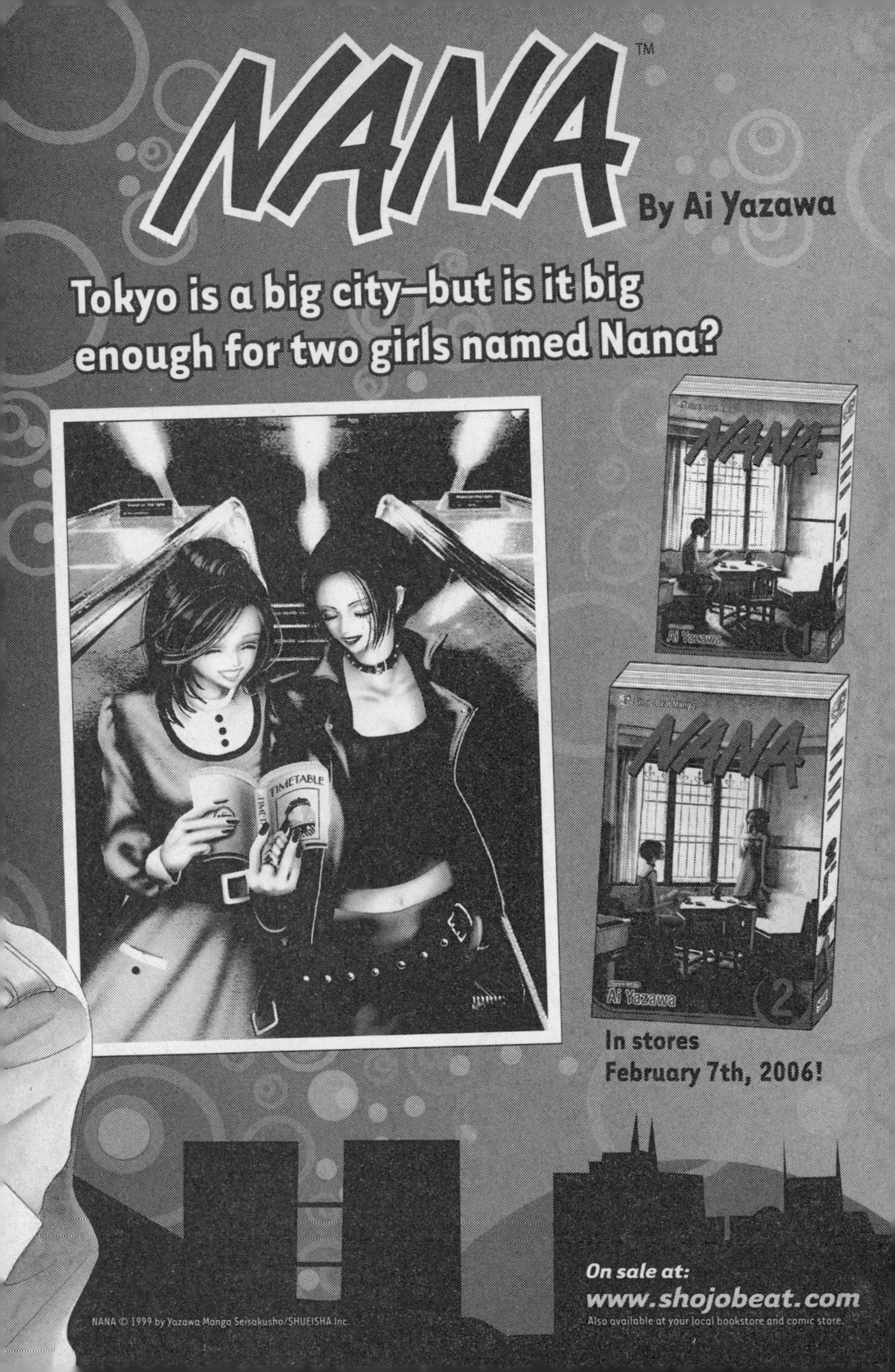
NANA™
By Ai Yazawa
Tokyo is a big city—but is it big enough for two girls named Nana?
TIMETABLE
NANA
Ai Yazawa
NANA
Ai Yazawa
2
In stores February 7th, 2006!
On sale at:
www.shojobeat.com
Also available at your local bookstore and comic store.
NANA © 1999 by Yazawa Manga Seisakusho/SHUEISHA Inc.

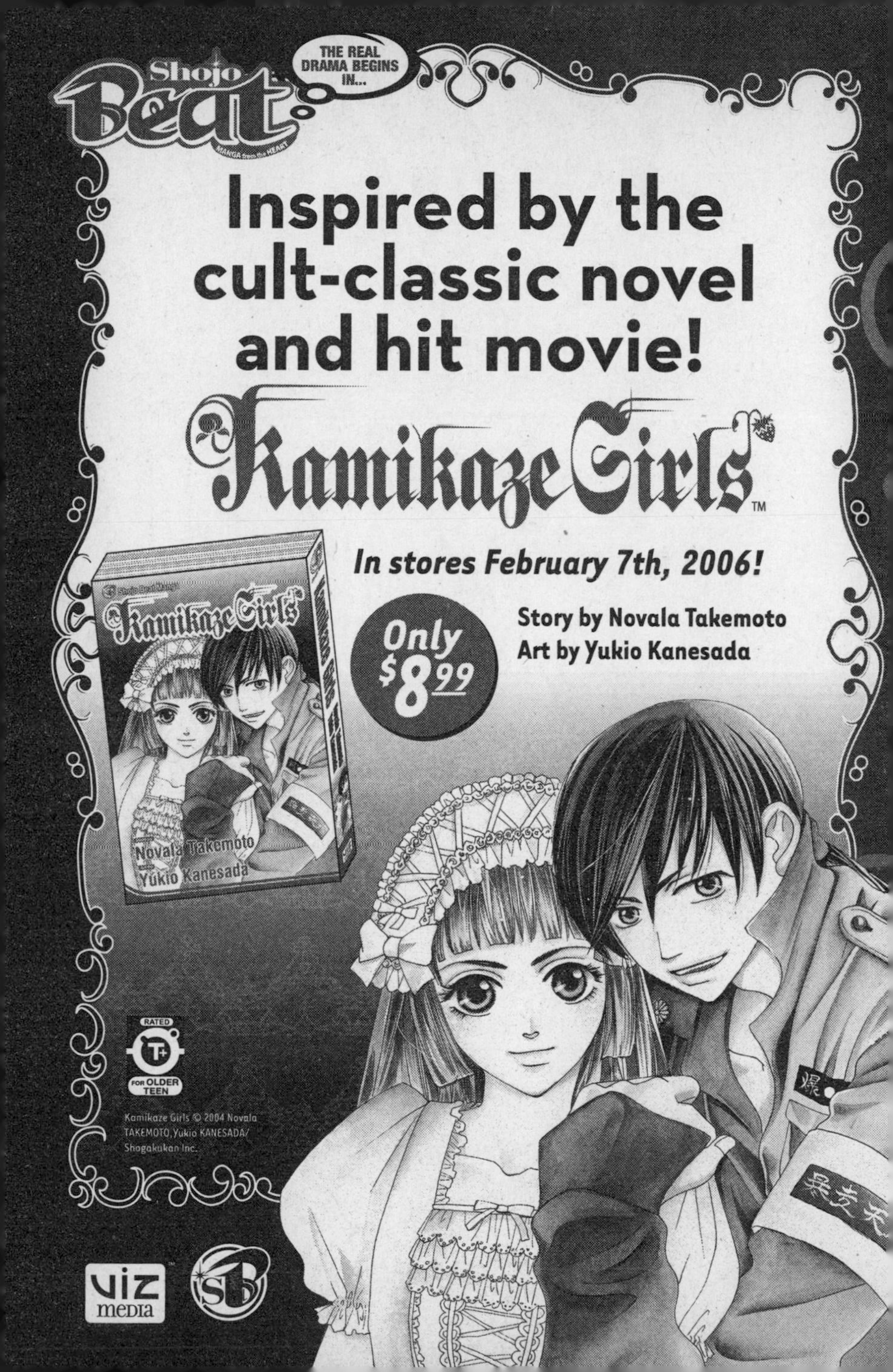
Shojo Beat
MANGA from the HEART
THE REAL DRAMA BEGINS IN...
Inspired by the cult-classic novel and hit movie!
Kamikaze Girls™
In stores February 7th, 2006!
Only $8.99
Story by Novala Takemoto
Art by Yukio Kanesada
Kamikaze Girls
Novala Takemoto
Yukio Kanesada
RATED T+ FOR OLDER TEEN
Kamikaze Girls © 2004 Novala TAKEMOTO, Yukio KANESADA/ Shogakukan Inc.
viz media

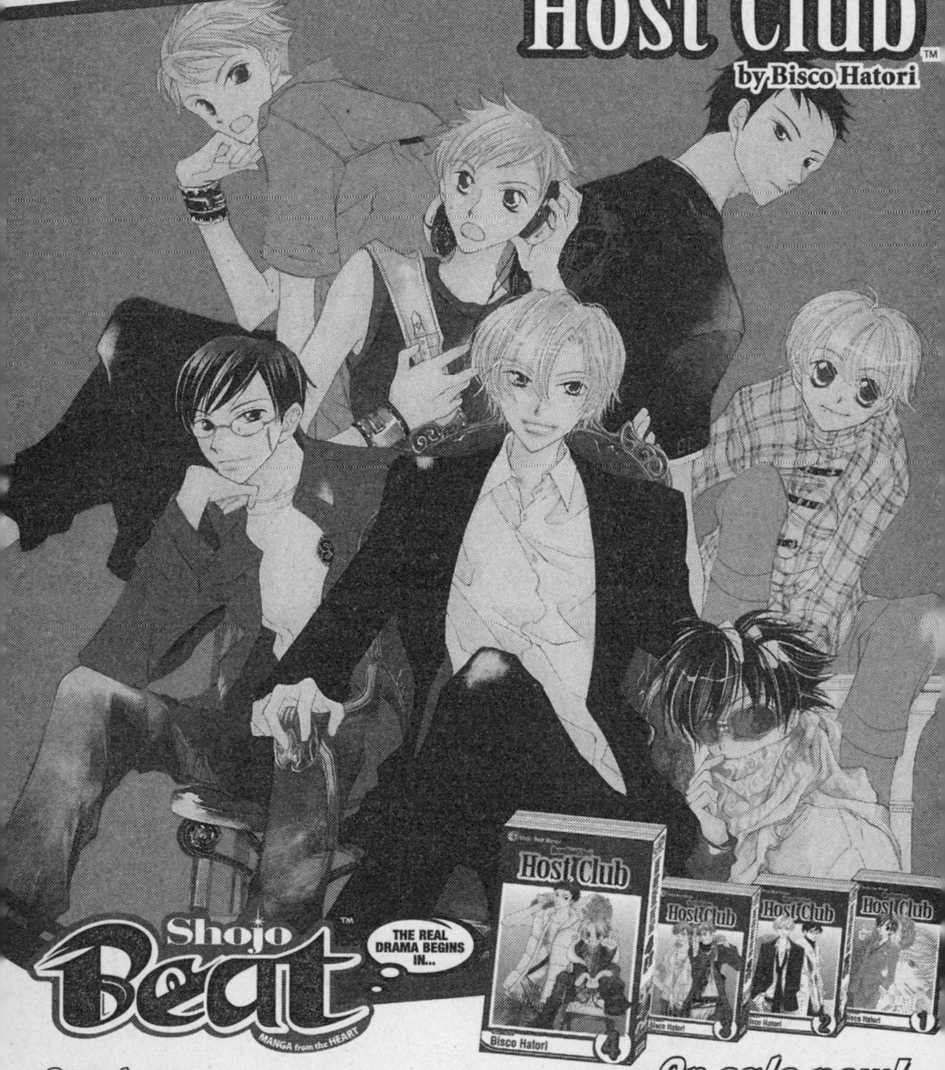
Host Club
Bisco Hatori
4
Host Club
3
Host Club
2
Host Club
1

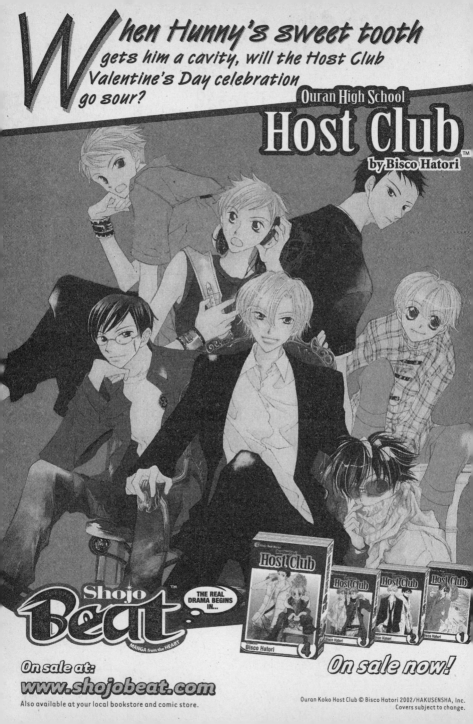

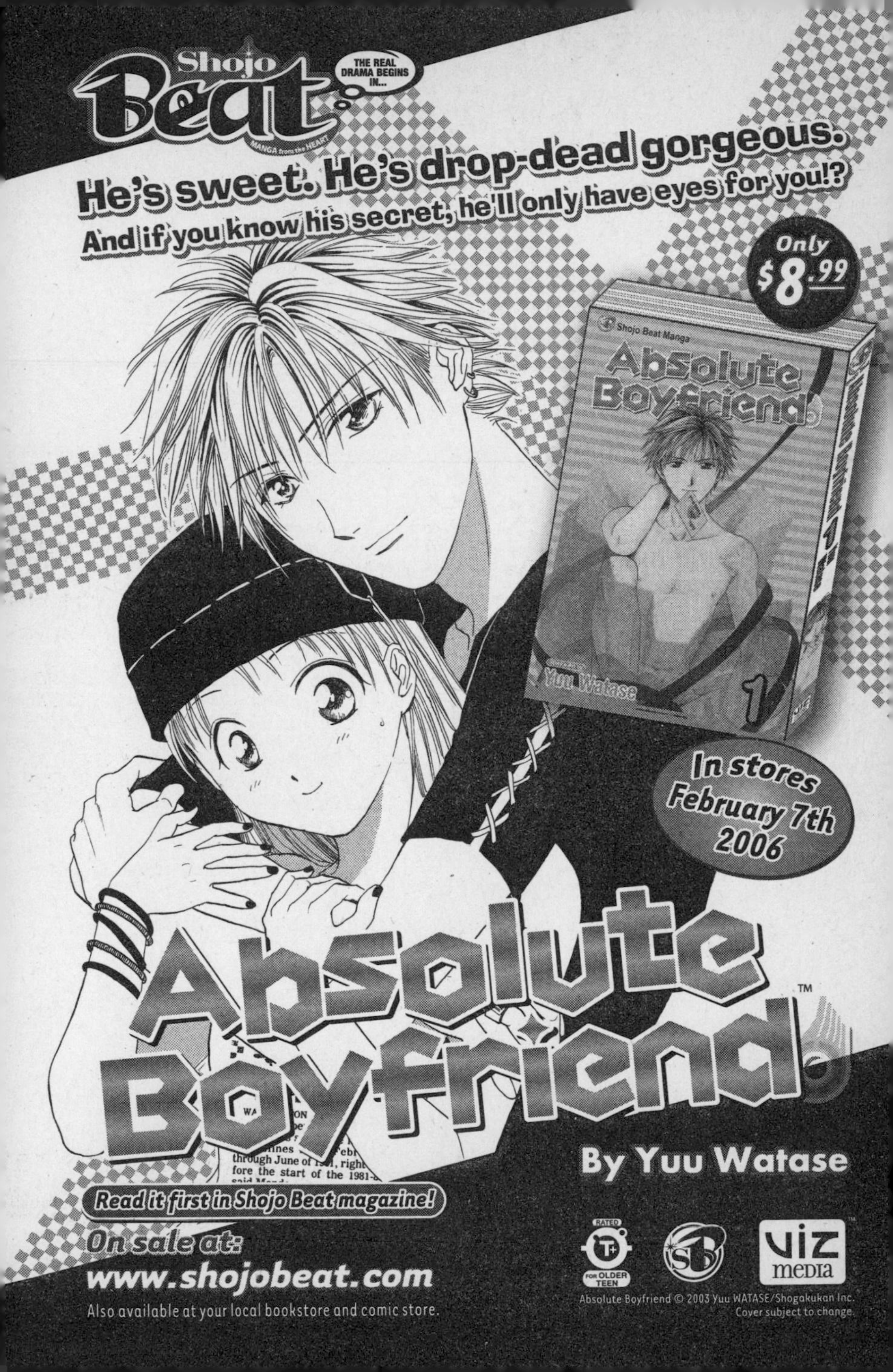
Shojo Beat
THE REAL DRAMA BEGINS IN...
MANGA from the HEART
He's sweet. He's drop-dead gorgeous.
He'll only have eyes for you!?
And if you know his secret,
Only $8.99
Shojo Beat Manga
Absolute Boyfriend
Yuu Watase
1
In stores February 7th 2006
Absolute Boyfriend™
By Yuu Watase
Read it first in Shojo Beat magazine!
On sale at:
www.shojobeat.com
Also available at your local bookstore and comic store.
RATED T+ FOR OLDER TEEN
VIZ media
Absolute Boyfriend © 2003 Yuu WATASE/Shogakukan Inc.
Cover subject to change.

Get the Beat online!
Check us out at

www.shojobeat.com!

4 Do you plan to purchase Shojo Beat Manga volumes of titles serialized in SB magazine?

☐ Yes ☐ No

If **YES**, which one(s) do you plan to purchase? (check all that apply)

☐ Absolute Boyfriend ☐ Baby & Me ☐ Crimson Hero
☐ Godchild ☐ Kaze Hikaru ☐ Nana

If **YES**, what are your reasons for purchasing? (please pick up to 3)

☐ Favorite title ☐ Favorite creator/artist
☐ I want to read the full volume(s) all at once ☐ I want to read it over and over again
☐ There are extras that aren't in the magazine ☐ Recommendation
☐ The quality of printing is better than the magazine
☐ Other ______________________

If **NO**, why would you not purchase it?

☐ I'm happy just reading it in the magazine ☐ It's not worth buying the graphic novel
☐ All the manga pages are in black and white ☐ There are other graphic novels that I prefer
☐ There are too many to collect for each title ☐ It's too small
☐ Other ______________________

5 Of the titles NOT serialized in the magazine, which ones have you purchased? (check all that apply)

☐ Beauty Is The Beast ☐ Full Moon ☐ Fushigi Yûgi: Genbu Kaiden
☐ MeruPuri ☐ Ouran High School Host Club ☐ Socrates In Love
☐ Tokyo Boys & Girls ☐ Ultra Maniac ☐ Other ______

If you did purchase any of the above, what were your reasons for purchase?

☐ Advertisement ☐ Article ☐ Favorite creator/artist
☐ Favorite title ☐ Gift ☐ Recommendation
☐ Read a preview online and wanted to read the rest of the story
☐ Read introduction in *Shojo Beat* magazine ☐ Special offer
☐ Website ☐ Other ______________________

Will you purchase subsequent volumes?

☐ Yes ☐ No ☐ Not Applicable

6 What race/ethnicity do you consider yourself? (please check one)

☐ Asian/Pacific Islander ☐ Black/African American ☐ Hispanic/Latino
☐ Native American/Alaskan Native ☐ White/Caucasian ☐ Other

THANK YOU! Please send the completed form to: **Shojo Survey**
42 Catharine St.
Poughkeepsie, NY 12601

All information provided will be used fo
divulge your information.

NO PURCHASE NECESSARY. Requests not in complia
missions are subject to verification and become th
addresses or P.O. boxes to obtain additional VIZ Me
right to withdraw or modify any terms of this form.
for lost, misdirected, mutilated, illegible, incomplet
LLC, property titles, characters, names and plots th

Shojo Beat
MANGA FROM THE HEART

COMPLETE OUR SURVEY AND LET US KNOW WHAT YOU THINK!

☐ Please do NOT send me information about VIZ Media and Shojo Beat products, news and events, special offers, or other information.

☐ Please do NOT send me information from VIZ Media's trusted business partners.

Name: _____

Address: _____

City:_____ State:_____ Zip: _____

E-mail: _____

☐ Male ☐ Female   Date of Birth (mm/dd/yyyy): ___/___/___   (Under 13? Parental consent required)

① Do you purchase *Shojo Beat* magazine?

☐ Yes   ☐ No (if no, skip the next two questions)

If **YES**, do you subscribe?

☐ Yes   ☐ No

If you do **NOT** subscribe, why? (please check one)

☐ I prefer to buy each issue at the store.   ☐ I prefer to buy the manga volumes instead.

☐ I share a copy with my friends/family.   ☐ It's too expensive.

☐ My parents/guardians won't let me.   ☐ Other

② Which particular Shojo Beat Manga did you purchase? (please check one)

☐ Beauty Is The Beast   ☐ Full Moon   ☐ Fushigi Yûgi: Genbu Kaiden

☐ MeruPuri   ☐ Ouran High School Host Club   ☐ Socrates In Love

☐ Tokyo Boys & Girls   ☐ Ultra Maniac   ☐ Other _____

Will you purchase subsequent volumes?

☐ Yes   ☐ No   ☐ Not Applicable

③ How did you learn about this title? (check all that apply)

☐ Advertisement   ☐ Article   ☐ Favorite creator/artist

☐ Favorite title   ☐ Gift   ☐ Recommendation

☐ Read a preview online and wanted to read the rest of the story

☐ Read introduction in *Shojo Beat* magazine   ☐ Special offer

☐ Website   ☐ Other _____